COMMENTARY

2023–2024

VOLUME 116

These commentaries are based on the International Sunday School Lessons and International Bible Lessons for Christian Teaching, copyrighted by the International Council of Religious Education, and is used by permission.

Entered according to Act of Congress in the Office of Librarian of Congress in the year 1903 at Washington, DC, by R. H. Boyd, D.D., LL.D.

R. H. Boyd, D.D., LL.D., Founder (1896–1922)

H. A. Boyd, D.D. (1922–1959) • T. B. Boyd Jr., D.D. (1959–1979) • T. B. Boyd III, D.D. (1979–2017)

LaDonna Boyd, Ed.D.
President/CEO (2017–Present)

LaDonna Boyd, Ed.D.
President/CEO

David Groves, D.Min., Ph.D.
Director of Publications

EDITORIAL STAFF
Olivia M. Cloud, M.R.E.
Associate Editor

Monique Gooch, B.A.; Brittany Batson, B.A.; Carla Davis, B.A.

Dr. Barry Johnson • Rev. Nikki L. Harris Tolliver
Ms. Antoinette Mosley • Dr. Bernard Williams
Writers

Jasmine Cole
Cover Design

For Customer Service and Toll–Free Ordering, Call
1–877–4RHBOYD (474–2693)
Monday–Friday
8 a.m.–5 p.m. Central Time or
Fax Toll–Free (800) 615–1815

www.rhboyd.com
R.H. Boyd Publishing Corporation
6717 Centennial Blvd.• Nashville, Tennessee 37209–1017

A WORD FROM THE PUBLISHER

To Our Readers,

As always, thank you for your patronage to our resources. What a blessing that you have chosen to share in the Gospel ministry of this commentary! For over a century, *Boyd's Commentary for the Sunday School* has been a mainstay in the ministry of Christian education. This commentary has been prepared and informed by prayerful and Spirit-led scholarship, so you can rest assured it can be trusted to edify and encourage students and instructors alike.

Our hope is that you will encounter the Spirit as you work through this year's lessons. As you read, may these lessons give you new vitality as a leader, minister, and as a member of the community of faith. As we've seen even more uncertainty in the past year, and the world is seemingly more lost than ever before, it is imperative to stand firm on the Word of God. Our goal is to equip readers with a solid foundation for the unpredictable world in which we live today. May this commentary be a blessing to those you teach, and also to you as you utilize its godly instruction.

Once again, thank you for your support. As you enjoy this resource, please visit our website, *www.rhboyd.com*, and follow us on social media @rhboydco to stay abreast of all the latest resources offered by R.H. Boyd.

Onward.

LaDonna Boyd
Fifth–generation President/CEO

A WORD FROM THE DIRECTOR

Greetings!

For well over a century, *Boyd's Commentary* has been an expositional resource for those who have a passion to study God's Word with depth and clarity. Therefore, you can fully trust that this commentary has been developed by people of faith who serve in all manner of leadership capacities within the Church. From the youngest child to the oldest congregant, we believe that everyone needs sound biblical teaching to stand on, especially during these unprecedented times.

At R.H. Boyd, our goal is to provide you with a commentary that will meet your needs as you apply biblical messages to guide, enlighten, and give voice to your students. We pray that the carefully selected Scriptures will address your contemporary issues and needs in a way that brings you closer to God and allows your individual walk with Him to deepen. Our goal, hope, and prayer is that *Boyd's Commentary for the Sunday School* will serve your biblical and theological training needs. Thank you for your continued support of our products. May you be blessed during this next year of teaching and learning.

Rev. David Groves, D.Min., Ph.D.

NOTES FROM THE EDITOR

The layout of the *2023–2024 Boyd's Commentary* has been formatted for easy use in the classroom. In keeping with our rich history of publishing quality Christian literature, we have added the Unifying Principle as a feature that will enhance our commentary. Listed below is an explanation of each feature and the intended use of each.

Lesson Setting: Gives the basic timeline and place for the events in the lesson.

Lesson Outline: Provides the topics used in the exposition of the lesson.

Unifying Principle: States the main idea for the lesson across age groups. This feature allows the teacher to understand exactly what each lesson is about.

Introduction: Gives the thesis and any background information that will be useful in the study of the lesson.

Exposition: Provides the exegetical study done by the writer, breaking down the text for discussion.

The Lesson Applied: Provides possible life applications of the biblical text for today's learners.

Let's Talk About It: Highlights ideas from the text in a question-and-answer format.

Home Daily Devotional Readings: Located at the end of each lesson, the topics are designed to lead into the following lesson.

KNOW YOUR WRITERS

Dr. Barry Johnson

Dr. Barry C. Johnson, a native of Louisville, serves as the Pastor of the Southern Star Baptist Church of Louisville, Kentucky. Dr. Johnson holds bachelor's (BM) and master's degrees (MM) in music composition from the University of Louisville, a Doctor of Musical Arts (DMA) degree in music composition from the University of Kentucky, and Master of Theology (M.Div) and Doctor of Ministry (D.Min) degrees in Black Church Studies from the Southern Baptist Theological Seminary. Additionally, he has done post-doctoral studies at Berklee College of Music. His previous teaching assignments were at Savannah State University, Western Kentucky University, and Kentucky State University, where he retired as a full professor of music. An avid musician, scholar, and composer, Dr. Johnson is owner of TNT Productions and Recording Studios and teaches part-time at the University of Louisville in the School of Music.

Rev. Nikki L. Harris Tolliver

Rev. Nikki L. Harris Tolliver is a sought-after, aspiring scholar, second-generation preacher, and innovator who seeks to share the Gospel of Jesus Christ. Nikki is a proud alumnus of historic Fisk University and a recent graduate of Vanderbilt Divinity School. Nikki aims to make every effort to put her training to use for the advancement of the Kingdom. She currently serves as an associate minister at First Baptist South Inglewood, Nashville, TN. She is also a co-host of *The Wolves Podcast*, a conversation of explicitly honest speaking and progressive-minded faith leaders discussing a wide range of topics. Nikki is the proud daughter of Pastor and Mrs. Napoleon Harris IV of Cleveland, Ohio. She is grateful to have married her best friend, Rev. Kevin E. Tolliver, and together they parent their twin sons.

Ms. Antoinette H. Mosely

Ms. Antoinette H. Mosely received a B.A. in English Education from McNeese State University and a M.Ed. from Southern University. She has a Master of Divinity degree in Christian Education and Youth Ministry from the Southern Baptist Theological Seminary and is youth minister at Centennial Olivet Baptist Church in Louisville, Kentucky. She has done mission work in several states and has taught public school. She is passionate about helping each youth to find his or her place in God's plan. She enjoys writing, traveling, and spending time with family. She has been inspired by her parents' and grandmother's commitment to teaching Sunday School.

Dr. Bernard Williams

Dr. Bernard Williams is a native of Nashville, Tennessee. He has pastored churches in Tennessee and Florida. He is a graduate of the University of Tennessee, Knoxville and the Southern Baptist Theological Seminary in Louisville, Kentucky. He also holds a Ph.D. in homiletics and church and society. Dr. Williams is a great proponent of small-group Bible study and serves as a teacher in Christian education. He holds numerous revivals, conferences, workshops, and seminars each year. He is a member of the American Academy of Religion and the Academy of Homiletics.

2023–2024 LESSON OVERVIEW

The Fall Quarter considers the role of God's Law as it relates to faith in Christ. Unit I, "Love Completes, Law Falls Short," draws on the Gospels of Luke and John. Unit II, "Faith Triumphs, Law Fails," draws from Paul's epistles to both the Romans and the Galatians to contrast the inability of the Law to provide justification with the promise of justification by faith. The four lessons of Unit III, "Christ Frees, Law Enslaves," highlight the ways in which Jewish and Gentile Christians wrestled with Mosaic Law in light of Christ's teaching.

The Winter Quarter explores faith that pleases God. Unit I, "Profiles in Faith," has five lessons in which we begin to see faith in action. Unit II, "Learning about Faith," has four lessons that allow us to learn more about faith, its description, its importance and its transformation. Unit III, "The Righteous Live by Faith," has four lessons that allow us to see how the righteous live by faith.

In the Spring Quarter, we explore the fullness of faith as a response to God's desire to be in relationship with us. Unit I, "Faith-FULL Versus Faith-LESS," has five lessons that invite learners to turn the challenges of life into opportunities for nurturing a vibrant faith instead of rejecting faith. Unit II, "The Measure of Faith," has four lessons drawn from Luke and Matthew to discuss the range of Christian faith. Unit III, "Standing in the Faith," has four lessons drawn from Romans that encourage believers to continue standing in the faith.

The Summer Quarter looks at expressions of Christian hope both in this present age and in the glorious future God is preparing for us. The five lessons of Unit I, "Experiencing Hope," consider Christian hope through the lens of those whose faith in Christ gave shape to the early church. Unit II, "Expressing Hope," turns attention to the prayers of ancient Israel as a model for offering to God our praise and petitions. The four lessons of Unit III, "Eternal Hope," consider facets of the promised future God is preparing for those who call on the name of Jesus.

• •

Boyd's Commentary for the Sunday School (2023–2024)

Copyright © 2023 by R.H. Boyd Publishing Corporation
6717 Centennial Blvd., Nashville, TN 37209–1017

Printed in the United States of America.

PREFACE

The *2023–2024 Boyd's Commentary* has been formatted and written with you in mind. This format is to help you further your preparation and study of the Sunday school lessons.

We have presented a parallel Scripture lesson passage with the *New Revised Standard Version* alongside the *King James Version*. This allows you to have a clearer and more contemporary approach to the Scripture passages each week. This version is reliable and reputable. It will bless you as you rightly divide the word of truth (2 Tim. 2:15, KJV).

These lessons have a new look, but they still have the same accurate interpretation, concise Christian doctrine, and competent, skilled scholarship.

The abbreviations used throughout the commentary are as follows:

KJV — King James Version
NIV — New International Version
NKJV — New King James Version
NLT — New Living Translation
NRSV — New Revised Standard Version
RSV — Revised Standard Version
TLB — The Living Bible
NEB — New English Bible
JB — Jerusalem Bible
ESV — English Standard Version

To the pastor: Our hope is that this commentary will provide context and insight for your sermons. Also, we hope this commentary will serve as a preparatory aid for the message of God.

To the Bible teacher: This commentary also has you in mind. You can use it as a ready reference to the background of the text and difficult terms that are used in the Bible. To be sure, this commentary will provide your lesson study with the historical context that will enable you to interpret the text for your students more effectively.

This text is for anyone who wants to get a glimpse at the glory of God. This commentary seeks to highlight and lift the workings of God with His people and to make God's history with humanity ever present.

We hope and pray God will bless you and keep you as you diligently study His mighty and majestic Word. Remain ever steadfast to our one eternal God. Keep the faith, and pray always.

CONTENTS

1ST QUARTER

CONTENTS

2ND QUARTER

CONTENTS

3RD QUARTER

CONTENTS

4TH QUARTER

FIRST QUARTER

September

October

November

JESUS EATS WITH A PHARISEE

ADULT TOPIC:	BACKGROUND SCRIPTURE: LUKE 11:37–44
ATTITUDES AND ACTIONS	LESSON PASSAGE: LUKE 11:37–44

LUKE 11:37—44

King James Version

AND as he spake, a certain Pharisee besought him to dine with him: and he went in, and sat down to meat.

38 And when the Pharisee saw it, he marvelled that he had not first washed before dinner.

39 And the Lord said unto him, Now do ye Pharisees make clean the outside of the cup and the platter; but your inward part is full of ravening and wickedness.

40 Ye fools, did not he that made that which is without make that which is within also?

41 But rather give alms of such things as ye have; and, behold, all things are clean unto you.

42But woe unto you, Pharisees! for ye tithe mint and rue and all manner of herbs, and pass over judgment and the love of God: these ought ye to have done, and not to leave the other undone.

43 Woe unto you, Pharisees! for ye love the uppermost seats in the synagogues, and greetings in the markets.

44 Woe unto you, scribes and Pharisees, hypocrites! for ye are as graves which appear not, and the men that walk over them are not aware of them.

New Revised Standard Version

WHILE he was speaking, a Pharisee invited him to dine with him; so he went in and took his place at the table.

38 The Pharisee was amazed to see that he did not first wash before dinner.

39 Then the Lord said to him, "Now you Pharisees clean the outside of the cup and of the dish, but inside you are full of greed and wickedness.

40 You fools! Did not the one who made the outside make the inside also?

41 So give for alms those things that are within; and see, everything will be clean for you.

42"But woe to you Pharisees! For you tithe mint and rue and herbs of all kinds, and neglect justice and the love of God; it is these you ought to have practiced, without neglecting the others.

43 Woe to you Pharisees! For you love to have the seat of honor in the synagogues and to be greeted with respect in the marketplaces.

44 Woe to you! For you are like unmarked graves, and people walk over them without realizing it."

LESSON SETTING
Circa AD 28
Place: Bethany-Judea

LESSON OUTLINE
I. The Question of
Ceremonial Washing
(Luke 11:37–38)

II. A Clean Exterior,
a Dirty Interior
(Luke 11:39–41)

III. Jesus Pronounces Three
Woes on the Pharisees
(Luke 11:42–44)

MAIN THOUGHT: And the Lord said unto him, Now do ye Pharisees make clean the outside of the cup and the platter; but your inward part is full of ravening and wickedness. (Luke 11:39, KJV)

UNIFYING PRINCIPLE

Rules and ceremony provide necessary parameters for everyone. How do we avoid the hollow legalism that sometimes results? Jesus demands heartfelt commitment to justice and love as demonstrations of true faith rather than mere outward adherence to the Law.

INTRODUCTION

Prior to the events in our lesson, Jesus had visited the home of Martha and Mary, who were the sisters of Lazarus (Luke 10:38–44), although he is not mentioned. While in Bethany, Jesus provided instruction to the people, and after finding a certain place to pray, Jesus provided His disciples with the Lord's Prayer (Matthew 6:9–13). Away from His base in Galilee, Luke does not indicate that Jesus has visited Jerusalem during this trek or His purpose for being in the area. His presence in Bethany could have been as simple as Jesus being with friends. However, following His teaching to the people, Jesus was invited to have lunch in the home of an unnamed Pharisee where He would challenge the sect on their principles and values.

EXPOSITION

I. THE QUESTION OF CEREMONIAL WASHING (LUKE 11:37–38)

We will assume that Jesus was invited to lunch because He had been teaching among the people and His disciples. Actually, the word used here for lunch is ἀριστάω (aristao), which means to eat breakfast, or to take any meal before the principle one or supper (deípnon). At this point, Jesus could have been tired and ready to rest from the crowds, coupled with His desire to use this opportunity to have a dialogue with the Pharisee, who probably invited some of his Pharisee friends to join them. As they prepared to dine, Jesus is described as reclining at a table or on cushions, which was the custom of their culture. Christ often used dinner invitations as opportunities to reach people, such as was offered by Levi (Luke 5:29) and another group of Pharisees (Luke 7:36).

Obviously, the contents of the meal were unimportant because the host noticed something that caused some irritation and distress. Jesus had not washed His hands before He sat for the meal. According to the custom of the period, the servants of the house would offer water to wash the feet, head, and hands of the guests who entered the house. Although it seems as if these rituals were observed, Jesus broke with the tradition, not engaging with the normal ritual washings before taking His place at the table. The Pharisees were a group who held fast to the traditions of the nation, and aside from the hygienic purposes of washing, their belief in ceremonial washing was spiritual.

II. A CLEAN EXTERIOR, A DIRTY INTERIOR (LUKE 11:39–41)

The host Pharisee was astonished and alarmed that Jesus skirted this ritual. Mark reported that there was another instance where Jesus was confronted by a group of Pharisees because His disciples were observed eating bread with unwashed hands (Mark 7:1–5ff.). In this case, washing before the meal was essential, both hygienically and ceremoniously, so, why did Jesus purposely skip the ritual? The focus for Jesus went beyond the contents and conversation of the meal, as He pointed out that the Pharisees' ritualistic commitment had serious issues. First, Jesus noted that the Pharisees were obsessed with cleaning the utensils and vessels. However, what Jesus observed was that the cleaning of the cups was relegated to the outside, which metaphorically indicated that only the surface area could be seen. This is where Jesus noted the problem. The outside of the "clean" cups represented the dress and mannerisms of the Pharisees, which presented a false front to the people who could only understand these men by what they saw and heard from an external point of view. In this case, their obsession with the exterior of the clean and shiny cup was a hindrance to the truth, actually masking their real identity and dedication to the Lord. Jesus saw through the exterior of the Pharisees by pointing out that their interior (the inside of the cup) was dirty because it was filled with greed. Jesus declared that they were occupied with robbery and wickedness, which altered their spiritual compasses, allowing the group to commit subtle, covert acts of theft against their fellow countrymen. Jesus' accusation of greed against the Pharisees was based on their becoming rich while ignoring the plight of their not-so-fortunate countrymen.

Jesus reveals the foolishness and stupidity of the Pharisees, noting that in their various degrees of self-exaltation, they have omitted the supposed Source of their reason for existence, who is the Lord! These Pharisees were obviously living in a situation where their happiness was based on an unreal existence. Here, Jesus referred to the One who created humanity by indicating that the "He" who made the outside of the cup also made the inside. Therefore, if the Pharisees were concerned with the cleanliness of the outside of the cup, they should have the same concern for the inside.

III. JESUS PRONOUNCES THREE WOES ON THE PHARISEES (LUKE 11:42–44)

Continuing with His chastisement of the Pharisees, Jesus projects a series of three woes, which are designed to predict punishment and sorrow on the accused. Pronouncements of woe have been brought from the time of Moses toward the Moabites (Numbers 21:29) until the present condemnations from Jesus. Here, Jesus indicts them for paying tithes of mint (an aromatic plant) and rue (also called a common rue, which is used as a medicinal herb). In an Old Testament system of tithing, one-tenth of the increase of the land, trees, herds, and flocks had to be given to the Lord as His tithe. The tithing of various herbs was based on Leviticus 27:30. Though tithing of grain, fruit, wine, and oil was demanded (see also Numbers 18:12; Deuteronomy 14:22–23), the scribes had expanded the items required to be tithed to include even the smallest of herbs.

Jesus does not condemn these men for tithing, but rather, compares their strict detail of giving the exact tithe to God while at the same time, not reflecting justice and the love of God toward their fellow countrymen. In this case, these Pharisees are adhering to the letter of the Law but are guilty of ignoring the spirit of the Law, which included many items centered around compassion for the poor and things such as being the keeper of one's brother. For Jesus, the Pharisees could not have obtained their wealth and status without marginalizing the group of people at the bottom of the social strata, the poor and forgotten. Jesus excoriates these men by referring to them as hypocrites, saying that they could have done both—tithed to God and uplifted the unfortunate. They could have had the best of both worlds and been blessed by the Lord interminably; yet, they had taken their chosen path of greed and avarice.

Jesus' second woe of condemnation toward the Pharisees is due to their personal sense of entitlement and their craving for power through their status in the Sanhedrin, the supreme council or court of the Jewish nation. The Sanhedrin consisted of seventy-one members, all of whom were required to be over thirty years of age and married. They must also have been of good reputation and well-instructed in the Law. During this period, Caiaphas (18–36 CE) was the Chief Priest and leader of the Sanhedrin. Although he had succeeded to the position from his father-in-law, Annas, competition for that seat (and its riches) was constantly in the background. Additionally, the chief positions were usually reserved for the more important members of the council, although the at-large seats were considered equal. These were the voices and personalities that defined what Jesus referred to as the "chief seats." Moreover, because of their sense of entitlement, these Pharisees demanded to be accorded the best seats in the synagogue and the theater, and would not have to wait in line at the marketplaces. The Pharisees were to be given the utmost of respect in their religious and social positions in the community. However, a warning from Psalm 49:12, KJV, "But man in his pomp will not endure, he is like the beasts that perish" is fitting here as a poignant example of the downfall of those who promote themselves unduly.

Jesus' third and final woe contains an ominously sinister series of overtones with deadly consequences. In this pronouncement, Jesus aligns the plight of the Pharisees with death as He compares their nature to places of interment. Saying, "You are like concealed tombs," Jesus indicates that the graves in this example are unlike the ones we observe in a contemporary cemetery, where they are marked with headstones and floral arrangements. One must remember that the sepulchers of the Jews were often caverns (Genesis 23:9ff.; 35:20; 49:30) or were hewn artistically out of rocks or in the sides of hills in various forms and sizes, sometimes with several compartments. They were closed by doors or layers of stone, and the entrances were often whitewashed and decorated with ornaments. Whitewash was a form of white paint made of a solution of lime and water. Additionally, a whitewashed tomb was visible and its location, noticeable. However, Jesus notes that the tombs in this example are hidden from sight, which causes people to sin by being unaware that they are walking on and over them. Contact with graves brought impurity on a person, as declared in Numbers 19:16, that "anyone who in the open field touches one who has been slain with a sword or who has died naturally, or a human bone or a grave, shall be unclean for seven days." Referring back to the cup that is washed on the outside but dirty on the inside, the tombs are whitewashed on the outside but are filled with decay on the inside. No matter how the whitewashed tombs are "dressed up" on the outside for a favorable appearance, nothing will change the fact that they house perishable bodies that are mortal and, according to Paul (1 Corinthians 15:42), corrupt. Jesus says that the Pharisees cause men to break the Law and defile themselves. Rather than guiding the people rightly, they caused people who followed them to be contaminated, just as unmarked graves, when walked upon, would defile a Jew without his knowing it. The Pharisees feared contamination from ritual uncleanness, but Jesus pointed out that their greed, pride, and wickedness contaminated the entire nation.

The Lesson Applied

Jesus' criticism of the Pharisees, especially that of His host, must not be viewed as Jesus being a hostile or ungrateful guest. As previously mentioned, Jesus often accepted dinner, or in this case, lunch invitations in the homes of people who were insincere in their reasons for hosting Him. In these cases, the hosts and their friends used Jesus' presence as an opportunity to challenge or trap Him. Luke will later provide an example where Jesus is invited to the home of another Pharisaic leader, during which they watched Him closely (Luke 14:1). In this lesson, Jesus reveals the hypocrisy of people who create a false image of themselves.

Let's Talk About It

Can you be a Christian and still participate in mainstream activities?

Adults gain an ability to choose Christlike actions instead of what is popular and expected. There was maybe a time when we "lived for the city." This meant that the clothing we wore, the cars we drove, and the crowd we hung with was based on approval from our peers, which could be a factor of self-satisfaction and self-esteem. Christians may continue to dress, drive, and live in a manner that is popular; however, because of a Christlike attitude and outlook, our secular mannerisms will not drive our Christian attributes.

Home Daily Devotional Readings
September 4–10, 2023

Monday	Tuesday	Wednesday	Thursday	Friday	Saturday	Sunday
Bless the Lord Who Heals	Bless the Lord of Compassion	Remember the Sabbath Day	Rest for God's People	Enter God's Rest	God's People Must Care for Others	The Sabbath Is for Doing Good
Psalm 103:1–12	Psalm 103:13–22	Exodus 20:8–11	Hebrews 4:1–10	Hebrews 4:11–16	Deuteronomy 22:1–4	Luke 14:1–6

IS IT LAWFUL TO HEAL ON THE SABBATH?

ADULT TOPIC: DOING GOOD DEEDS AT THE WRONG TIME	BACKGROUND SCRIPTURE: LUKE 14:1–6 LESSON PASSAGE: LUKE 14:1–6

LUKE 14:1–6

King James Version

AND it came to pass, as he went into the house of one of the chief Pharisees to eat bread on the sabbath day, that they watched him.

2 And, behold, there was a certain man before him which had the dropsy.

3 And Jesus answering spake unto the lawyers and Pharisees, saying, Is it lawful to heal on the sabbath day?

4 And they held their peace. And he took him, and healed him, and let him go;

5 And answered them, saying, Which of you shall have an ass or an ox fallen into a pit, and will not straightway pull him out on the sabbath day?

6 And they could not answer him again to these things.

New Revised Standard Version

ON one occasion when Jesus was going to the house of a leader of the Pharisees to eat a meal on the sabbath, they were watching him closely.

2 Just then, in front of him, there was a man who had dropsy.

3 And Jesus asked the lawyers and Pharisees, "Is it lawful to cure people on the sabbath, or not?"

4 But they were silent. So Jesus took him and healed him, and sent him away.

5 Then he said to them, "If one of you has a child or an ox that has fallen into a well, will you not immediately pull it out on a sabbath day?"

6 And they could not reply to this.

LESSON SETTING
Time: Circa AD 28
Place: On the Way to
        Jerusalem

LESSON OUTLINE
I. An Unclean Man is Presented
   to Jesus
   (Luke 14:1–3)
II. The Sacredness of the
    Sabbath
    (Luke 14:3–4)
III. Jesus Challenges the
     Pharisees' Humanity
     (Luke 14:5–6)

UNIFYING PRINCIPLE
There's a time and place for everything. Is it right to do a good deed at the wrong time? Jesus demonstrates compassion for a sick man when He heals him at a Sabbath meal despite the critical eyes of the Pharisees.

INTRODUCTION
Jesus had previously been invited to lunch in the home of a prominent Pharisee, during which He chastised the group about their greed and lack of concern for the poor and unfortunate. Jesus had accused them of parading a holy outward appearance

MAIN THOUGHT: And Jesus answering spake unto the lawyers and Pharisees, saying, Is it lawful to heal on the sabbath day? And they held their peace. And he took him, and healed him, and let him go. (Luke 14:3–4, KJV)

while being unclean on the inside. He pronounced three woes upon these men (Luke 11:42–44). More than likely, word spread about the attitude Jesus had presented toward His host by ignoring the customary pre-meal washing. Nonetheless, although this news had become known among the Pharisees, here, we find Jesus being invited to another meal in the home of another Pharisee where (while others had failed) there would be another entrapment attempt. The setting is on the Sabbath, which could mean that this was a dinner meal following sundown on Friday. Present were Pharisees, lawyers (scribes), and an ill man, who is used as a pawn in their scheme to trick Jesus.

EXPOSITION

I. AN UNCLEAN MAN IS PRESENTED TO JESUS
(LUKE 14:1–3)

In attendance at the house was a man who was suffering from an illness known at the time as dropsy. Jesus had previously healed a woman who had suffered from a constant blood flow for twelve years (Matthew 9:20); however, unlike the account of the woman, Luke does not detail the length of time the man had suffered from his illness. What is important is that he was suffering at all, while he was in the home of the host Pharisee. With all of the eyes of the Pharisees fixed on Him, Luke records that the man was placed directly in front of Jesus, meaning that the seating of the guests was purposefully arranged.

As aforementioned, the unnamed man was suffering from a condition known as dropsy, which refers to the swelling of a body cavity or extremity due to internal fluid buildup and is commonly seen with inflammation of an artery or major organ such as the kidneys, liver, or heart. Dropsy is evident at the end of a long day, as the majority of the excess fluid collects in the feet and lower legs. It can cause several pounds of visible weight gain, and the skin can appear shiny and stretched. This condition can also cause painful aching in the local muscles. Moreover, dropsy is a sign of congestive heart failure, liver kidney, and vein damage. This man's body, especially his feet, ankles, and legs, would have been severely swollen, and he would have had difficulty breathing. This was an illness that would have been quite visible to all who were around the man, which would have subjected him to stares and whispers. Of all of the guests that had gathered, the spotlight was on a sick man, who seemingly is not there for dinner. Suffering from a very painful condition, the man would have been uncomfortable in this formal setting.

II. THE SACREDNESS OF THE SABBATH
(LUKE 14:3–4)

Here, it is important to examine the importance of the Sabbath and how Jesus controlled the narrative of this situation. In verse 3, Jesus answers a question; however, the question is not recorded nor is the person who asked identified. What is important here is the nature of the question or statement that was presented to Jesus. The question could have been as obvious as saying to Jesus, "Here before You is a sick man. We have heard that You have healing powers; so, what are You going to do about this?" Jesus realized that this situation was designed to trap Him;

therefore, the verse starts with Jesus' response, which included reversing the narrative and asking the Pharisees a question: "Is it lawful to heal on the Sabbath or not?"

The Sabbath is a very sacred day, and it is to be honored. The first command concerning the observance of the Sabbath is found in Exodus 16:22–30, where God provides Israel manna. As part of Mosaic Law, the requirement of the Law forbids any work to be done on the Sabbath, which is in accordance with God's resting on the seventh day of creation. Additionally, the conviction of breaking the Sabbath laws could result in the death penalty. The Pharisees had this component of the Law in their arsenal and would not hesitate to use it against Jesus. There are six recorded confrontations between Jesus and Jewish religious leaders over Sabbath observance. Five involve healing on the Sabbath, and the remaining incident involves picking corn on the Sabbath (Mark 2:23–26ff.).

In all six Sabbath confrontations, Jesus did not question the principle of a day of rest. Rather, the right use of the day is at the heart of these controversies. In some cases, such as in the picking of grain on the Sabbath, human need overrides the ritual Law. In other cases, Jesus is challenging the kind of regulations that go against the purpose of the Law, which is to bring healing and wholeness. Although Jesus broke with rabbinic traditions about the Sabbath, He did not seek to annul the observance of the Sabbath day. In Mark's account of the disciples' plucking grain, Jesus answered His critics by stating that "the Sabbath was made for man not man for the Sabbath" (Mark 2:27). In this instance, the Sabbath

was made (*ginomai*) or was brought into existence by the Creator of all things, both natural and spiritual, to serve both mankind and its connection to heaven. Even though it was considered a day of rest, God never rests in His quest to supply the needs of His people. It seems as if the Pharisees had never considered their need to call on the Lord if a tragedy occurred on the Sabbath, or to pray for protection from an invader if such might happen on the Sabbath. In their misinterpretation of the Sabbath, the Pharisees appropriated the Sabbath for their own selfish purposes, while relegating the compassion of the Lord to specific days. God is holy every day; therefore, every day is also holy, prompting Jesus to define the Sabbath as a day of service.

Stumped, they kept silent. The Pharisees did not know what to say because they did not have any answers. In all of their plotting and scheming, their objective had been to embarrass Jesus and discredit His ministry and teachings. Because Jesus was a threat and a challenge to their authority, their purpose was to label Jesus an imposter, but when this did not work, they would later conspire to kill Him. Jesus knew what was in the hearts and minds of the Pharisees; yet, here, the immediate need was to have compassion on this sick man who had been manipulated in a plot to reduce Jesus to the role of a false teacher. What is interesting is that the Pharisees do not doubt that Jesus can heal the man, which makes them either believe He is sent from God or that His work is from Satan. It is possible that they could have believed that Jesus was of God; however, because their hearts were hardened and their livelihoods depended upon their status as the nation's holy men, they had to maintain their belief system and their social and religious order. In the face of such pretense, Jesus did not acquiesce to the plot by the Pharisees; He simply straightforwardly and compassionately healed the man and sent him away.

III. JESUS CHALLENGES THE PHARISEES' HUMANITY (LUKE 14:5–6)

Continuing, Jesus presents a scenario that would be easily understood within the scope of human reality. Jesus poses a question, asking which one of them that had a child or an animal fall into a well or even a river would not jump in and rescue them, even if it occurred on the Sabbath? Jesus had previously asked a sect of the group about the morality of observing Sabbath laws when He healed the man with the withered hand, asking, "Is it lawful on the Sabbath to do good or to do evil, to save life or to destroy it?" (Luke 6:9). With this question, He proved that refusing to do good on the Sabbath is tantamount to doing evil.

If suffering is not alleviated, then one is doing evil to the sufferer. In all of the aforementioned cases, when He is accused of disrespecting the Sabbath, Jesus consistently uses the same logic that the Sabbath is not just a day of rest or even worship, but the Sabbath is primarily a day of compassion. Additionally, Jesus notes the hypocrisy of the Pharisees, i.e., their agreeing that rescuing a child or an animal on the Sabbath is acceptable, while rescuing (and healing) a person in the deluge of hunger, deformity, or sickness is breaking the Law, was absurd. By grouping the Pharisees and the sick man together, Jesus reveals that they both are equally yoked and in need of spiritual healing. Although this encounter does not have Jesus declaring that the man's sins are forgiven, Jesus was always concerned with the effects of sin, which is defined as people being separated from God.

Additionally, recall Jesus saying that it is not the healthy who need a physician but those who are sick (Matthew 9:12), which confirms Jesus' need to heal. Thus, these Pharisees and their accompanying scribes needed Jesus for themselves because they were deeply sick in their hearts, minds, and souls. Yet, their greatest sin was not recognizing Jesus and accepting Him for who He truly was.

The Pharisees had no reply for the actions or the questions that Jesus presented to them in the home of the host Pharisee. They were perplexed and confounded with what was another attempt at entrapment. One of their greatest failures to respond was in their understanding of the person of Jesus; however, where they fell woefully short was in their lack of commitment to the Lord and their communication with Him. These notable men of the Law were so transfixed on what they had conceived as the static nature of right and wrong, while refusing to understand the flexibility that served the needs of the people. Moreover, the Pharisees refused to acknowledge that Jesus, as the Son of Man, is also the Lord of the Sabbath.

THE LESSON APPLIED

Maybe the man who had dropsy was a simple pawn in a game played by the Pharisees; however, after his encounter with Jesus and his healing, he should have never been the same, having experienced an increase in his faith. We do not know what happened to the man, but an encounter of this magnitude should have produced the desired results of gratitude from one who had been transformed by Jesus. The Pharisees invited a man to a meal, knowing that he was sick and possibly unclean, yet, they did not have any type of resolution for restoring the man to his health or restoring his commitment to the faith. Luke does not indicate whether Jesus had encountered the man on a previous occasion, but Jesus loved the man because he was one of God's creations. In this case, love and compassion trumped the supposed interpretation of the Sabbath laws. Luke's account of this meeting reveals the cruel manner of the Pharisees, in that they would use the Law to harm Jesus and deny the restoration of the sick man. As Christians, we must not become entrapped by the rigidity of man-made traditions and customs that circumvent the spirit of the natural laws and processes of the Lord.

LET'S TALK ABOUT IT

In what ways do you honor the Sabbath in our modern society?

Adults act without thinking when life and livelihood are threatened. Although contemporary Christians are not tethered to the customs of the Pharisees during the time of Jesus, we can become traditionalists to such an extent that it sometimes hampers common sense and decency. If one witnesses a vehicular crash, decent people will attempt to assist in any manner possible. News accounts recall people who risk their lives in apartment and house fires to help those who are in danger to safety. The majority of people of goodwill are at the ready to serve people they do not know who are faced with a possible tragedy if they do not react. Medical emergencies are not relegated to Monday through Saturday. Childbirth on the Sabbath involves a woman giving birth (work) and doctors and nurses assisting in the delivery (work). The gift of a child is considered a component of God's blessings; therefore, if the Lord blesses on the Sabbath, He is not breaking Sabbath laws.

HOME DAILY DEVOTIONAL READINGS
SEPTEMBER 11–17, 2023

MONDAY	TUESDAY	WEDNESDAY	THURSDAY	FRIDAY	SATURDAY	SUNDAY
God Demands Justice and Promises Healing	Do You Want to Be Well?	God's Work Faces Resistance	The Father Works on the Sabbath	Obedience Shows Wisdom and Discernment	God, Teach Us Your Statutes	Jesus Speaks to Glorify the Father
Isaiah 58:6–14	John 5:1–9	John 5:10–16	John 5:17–21	Deuteronomy 4:1–14	Psalm 119:113–128	John 7:14–24

JESUS GIVES GOD GLORY

ADULT TOPIC:	BACKGROUND SCRIPTURE: JOHN 7:14–24
WHO IS TRUSTWORTHY?	LESSON PASSAGE: JOHN 7:14–24

JOHN 7:14—24

King James Version

NOW about the midst of the feast Jesus went up into the temple, and taught.

15 And the Jews marvelled, saying, How knoweth this man letters, having never learned?

16 Jesus answered them, and said, My doctrine is not mine, but his that sent me.

17 If any man will do his will, he shall know of the doctrine, whether it be of God, or whether I speak of myself.

18 He that speaketh of himself seeketh his own glory: but he that seeketh his glory that sent him, the same is true, and no unrighteousness is in him.

19 Did not Moses give you the law, and yet none of you keepeth the law? Why go ye about to kill me?

20 The people answered and said, Thou hast a devil: who goeth about to kill thee?

21 Jesus answered and said unto them, I have done one work, and ye all marvel.

22 Moses therefore gave unto you circumcision; (not because it is of Moses, but of the fathers;) and ye on the sabbath day circumcise a man.

23 If a man on the sabbath day receive circumcision, that the law of Moses should not be broken; are ye angry at me, because I have made a man every whit whole on the sabbath day?

24 Judge not according to the appearance, but judge righteous judgment.

New Revised Standard Version

ABOUT the middle of the festival Jesus went up into the temple and began to teach.

15 The Jews were astonished at it, saying, "How does this man have such learning, when he has never been taught?"

16 Then Jesus answered them, "My teaching is not mine but his who sent me.

17 Anyone who resolves to do the will of God will know whether the teaching is from God or whether I am speaking on my own.

18 Those who speak on their own seek their own glory; but the one who seeks the glory of him who sent him is true, and there is nothing false in him.

19 "Did not Moses give you the law? Yet none of you keeps the law. Why are you looking for an opportunity to kill me?"

20 The crowd answered, "You have a demon! Who is trying to kill you?"

21 Jesus answered them, "I performed one work, and all of you are astonished.

22 Moses gave you circumcision (it is, of course, not from Moses, but from the patriarchs), and you circumcise a man on the sabbath.

23 If a man receives circumcision on the sabbath in order that the law of Moses may not be broken, are you angry with me because I healed a man's whole body on the sabbath?

24 Do not judge by appearances, but judge with right judgment."

MAIN THOUGHT: He that speaketh of himself seeketh his own glory: but he that seeketh his glory that sent him, the same is true, and no unrighteousness is in him. (John 7:18, KJV)

UNIFYING PRINCIPLE

We expect our leaders to tell the truth, but sometimes they distort the facts. How can we decide who is trustworthy? Jesus told the crowds to judge the truth of His words by the fact that His teaching was not self-serving, but instead, directed all glory to God.

INTRODUCTION

The Feast of Booths was occurring in Jerusalem, and Jesus initially decided not to attend. This was an important festival, yet, Jesus remained in Galilee because the Jewish religious leaders and authorities were seeking ways to discredit Him and subsequently, kill Him. Incredibly, His brothers (who were unbelievers at the time) chided Jesus to go to the festival, resplendent with massive crowds, where He could "show off" His powers, which had a smaller platform in Galilee. In Jerusalem, Jesus could settle the question as to whether He was truly the Messiah. It did not seem rational to Jesus' brothers for Him not to show off His glory. If He really was what He claimed to be, they reasoned, He should publicly demonstrate it. In Jerusalem, Jesus would spar with the religious leaders over the correct interpretation of Sabbath laws.

EXPOSITION

I. JESUS' AUTHORITY AND TEACHING IS QUESTIONED (JOHN 7:14–18)

At the midpoint of the festival, Jesus goes into the Temple and begins to teach. The occasion is the Feast of Booths, which was one of the three pilgrimage festivals of the Jewish year, occurring in the autumn after the harvest. In reenacting the celebration, the Jews lived in booths made of the boughs of trees for the seven days of the festival. Recall that during the days of Ezra, the Feast of Booths were restored (Nehemiah 8:14). The festival was celebrated during Tishri (September/October) 15–22. The title "Booths" was also known as *Succoth*, commemorating God's sustenance during the difficult and threatening journey from Egypt to the "land flowing with milk and honey." These festivals were filled with the voices of celebration, complete with music, dancing, and abundant food for the masses. It was not simply a large party but a celebration of God's goodness toward His people. Moreover, the fellowship and gathering of the people served as a sign of God's future blessings! Jesus did not attend the feast until the midpoint or possible midweek of the celebration, and when He arrived, He went up (*anabaínō*) to the Temple. Remember that the language here is important, as Jerusalem was located on the heights of Mount Moriah, and in honor of Yahweh, the Temple was the highest place in the land.

At some point after entering the Temple with the gathered assembly, Jesus began to teach. John does not provide any background to detail whether or not Jesus was invited, as was customary; however, it seemed that the Jewish leaders were interested in what He had to say, rather than (at the time) plotting to discredit Him. As Jesus taught, the Jewish leaders were astonished! Obviously, Jesus' words and instructional skills had amazed these leaders because they knew that He had not been trained or schooled in the art of rabbinical methodology. Yet, Jesus' teaching was learned and spiritually penetrating, causing the leaders to wonder, "How could this be possible?" Still, this was not the first time that Jesus had astonished people gathered in the Temple. Recall that at the age of twelve, the Holy Family and friends had attended Passover in Jerusalem when they discovered that Jesus was not with the party on the return trip to Galilee. When His parents returned to the city, they found Him in the Temple, dialoguing with the teachers and elders and (because of his youth and maturity) baffling them with His questions and answers (Luke 2:41–46ff.) Jesus was most comfortable teaching, especially in the Temple, which He would later refer to as "My House" and call it a "House of Prayer" (Matthew 21:13).

As the crowds marveled at His instruction and perception, it would have been easy for Jesus to bask in their adulation. When He was asked the source of His knowledge and wisdom, Jesus gave the credit to His Father who had sent Him into the world. His stating, "My teaching is not Mine," not only credits Yahweh, but urges the audience to change their focus from Jesus to the Father. Although the Jewish leaders were interested in His intellect, Jesus revealed the importance of knowing the Father, stating that "if anyone is willing to do His will, he will know of the [Source of My] teaching." However, there seemed to be another perspective circulating in the assembly, which was whether Jesus was espousing His personal philosophy or even being influenced by another source. At this point, John does not mention the possibility of Jesus' teachings being of Satan, although Jesus would later be accused of collusion with him (see Matthew 12:26–27). Here, Jesus turns the questions back to the critics, saying that they would be able to properly judge whether His knowledge came from God or was self-determined.

II. ACKNOWLEDGING, BUT NOT KEEPING THE LAW (JOHN 7:19–21)

In the pantheon of the Jewish culture, Moses is indeed a hero. Throughout the history of Judaism, one consistent and common denominator that served to bind the nation was the Law of Moses. Additionally, Moses' role in leading Israel from Egyptian captivity (and his close relationship with Yahweh) continued to be a source of pride, even when Israel disobeyed the laws. Nevertheless, many Jews would point to the Law of Moses as commandments or a contract for governing their lives, but there was a clear difference between those who were practitioners of the Law and those who simply espoused its contents when convenient. Here, Jesus acknowledges Moses' contributions, yet, declares that for all of their identification with Moses, the people disregard the very Law they embrace as their national identity (v. 19). Israel had been guilty of acknowledging the Law yet breaking the same commandments, which had contributed to the nation's troubles. Then again, in His remonstration against these supposedly righteous Jews, Jesus asks why they seek to kill Him? Jesus knew that their stance on their religious principles would lead to their hatred of Him, which would allow evil to overcome their senses in a healthy religious debate. Since the leaders could not convince the people to ignore Jesus, the next step would be to eliminate Him.

In response to Jesus' realization that these men wanted His death, the crowd faked disbelief and incredulity, asking, "Who seeks to kill You?" Jesus had exposed the malice that was guiding these Jews to actually plot to commit murder. Here, John does not describe the details of the plotters; however, Jesus is able to see into the hearts and minds of these men, knowing that their rationale to eliminate Him will serve as a precursor of thoughts and events yet to come. Nevertheless, even though their inner thoughts were now exposed, the Jews attempted to deflect Jesus' accusation by alleging that He is demon-possessed. In their feeble and far-fetched retort, to now place Jesus in the grip of a demon was a sign of desperation. Previously, the religious leaders and crowds had marveled at Jesus' wisdom and knowledge and now, their attitudes had disintegrated toward Him being demon–possessed. In general, many of the Jewish leaders would fear being in the presence of a demon because they did not have the power or spiritual acumen to battle the unclean spirit. Someone suffering from a condition such as epilepsy that affected the person's mentality and reasoning was (out of convenience and a possible lack of concern) labeled "demon-possessed." And now, to declare that Jesus was demon-possessed meant that He was a fallen angel or that He was spiritually compromised. Nonetheless, this attempt at sidetracking does not alter the reality that thoughts of murdering Jesus were actually planted in their hearts.

In His answer to their accusations that He was demon-possessed, Jesus declared that their current issue with Him was due to the fact that He performed one compassionate deed, which was healing the paralytic man on the Sabbath. Although John uses the term *thaumázō*, meaning to marvel or to be astonished, many of the authorities and leaders that were present were not amazed in a positive way. For some of Jesus' detractors, the healing of the paralytic was not perceived in amazement but could have been thought of as a cheap magician's trick. What John is conveying is that Jesus' enemies marveled in a negative manner, seeing His power as something coming from Satan and not of God. What these religious detractors failed to see was that Jesus' healing was a true gift from God that the Pharisees could also have possibly obtained; yet, their lack of faith would remain an obstacle to the benefits of serving the Lord.

III. UNDERSTANDING THE LAW OF CIRCUMCISION (JOHN 7:22–24)

To amplify the importance and reality of the Sabbath serving mankind, Jesus offers the example of circumcision. During Old Testament times, circumcision was practiced by most of the other nations near Israel, including the Egyptians, so that in and of itself, it was not a distinguishing mark. However, the significance attached to it by Israel was unique. Only in Israel did it have a clearly defined theological significance that extended beyond the individual who received it to his family and wider community. When Jesus said that Moses has given [you] circumcision, He does not mean that circumcision began with the Law. Actually, this tradition of circumcision began with the patriarchs, long before the Law of Moses. These are the "fathers" that Jesus is speaking of, as Abraham was the first of the patriarchs to be circumcised. Remember, circumcision functioned as a symbolic act of a covenant between God and man (Israel). Following Abraham's circumcision, Yahweh declared, "This is My covenant, which you shall keep, between Me and you and your descendants after you: every male among you shall be circumcised" (Genesis 17:10). Moses, however, made circumcision a part of the Law, writing that every male among you who is eight days old shall be circumcised throughout [your] generations, a servant who is born in the house or who is bought with money from any foreigner, who is not of [your] descendants (Genesis 17:12). Jesus knew this commandment well because He was circumcised on the eighth day according to the Law of Moses (Luke 2:21–23). Moreover, the religious leaders understood that they did not have control over what would be the eight days after childbirth or upon which day they would fall during the week. Therefore, in their reasoning, circumcision on the Sabbath was exempt and was not to be condemned because it could only be controlled by God.

For Jesus, healing a man on the Sabbath was equal to circumcising a male child on the eighth day, regardless of which day it fell on. Therefore, it is logical that the law of Moses would not be broken. In verse 23, John uses the term *lambánō*, meaning to receive, but it also may be translated as to accept under the conditions of a favorable reception. In this perspective, the parents of the child accept the circumcision as part of the Law of Moses with a favorable and joyous attitude; and because the circumcision of their son represents the continuation of the covenant with Yahweh, it is a unique time for celebration. In verses 22–23, Jesus speaks of the circumcision of a man rather than that of a man-child. In this comparison, adult males (for example, proselytes) were circumcised but probably not on the Sabbath because their circumcision was not connected to the birth of a son. Therefore, adult males who underwent circumcision could schedule their appointment at any time, but it would not mean that their rite of passage was diminished in their connection to God. When Jesus asks the Jewish leaders if they were angry with Him because He supposedly broke Sabbath laws or misinterpreted how circumcision could be ordered on the Sabbath, it creates a conundrum for them. The religious leaders acknowledged that circumcision could override the Sabbath laws, yet, Jesus declared that mercy must also triumph Sabbath laws. In His reasoning with these leaders, they may have accepted that if a man's life was in danger, performing a rescue would have priority over the Sabbath laws. However, in Jesus' healing of the paralytic, the man's life was not in immediate danger because he had been lame for thirty eight years. From the Jewish perspective, Jesus could have waited one more day to heal him, so as not to break the law of the Sabbath day.

Yet, in reality, the restoration could not have waited for another day because the situation and circumstances represented an act of faith, which in this case, honored the Sabbath.

Restoring the man to God served as a blessing, even on the day of rest. Therefore, Jesus admonishes these religious leaders to realize the entirety of the Law, not just selective components that "fit" their agenda when needed. Moreover, they were ordered to move beyond superficial thoughts.

THE LESSON APPLIED

In the ongoing debate with the religious leaders, Jesus proved that compassion and the restoration of the entire body was akin to a life-saving measure. Circumcision and healing were simply tools or aspects granted by God to redeem those who would follow Jesus and be committed to Him. In our present society, EMTs, doctors, and hospitals operate on Sundays, and in most cases, we are glad that they do. Simultaneously, on Sundays, pastors continue to preach, and churches continue to praise God in worship services across the world. Although we do not have Sabbath conflicts, we must not fail to realize that compassion and love dominate any rules that may regulate the Sabbath.

LET'S TALK ABOUT IT

Should we still honor old traditions in the church?

In many cases, adults get into arguments over the meaning of laws and traditions. There has always existed a chasm over the boundaries of tradition versus the scriptural laws that guide the contemporary church. In the world we serve, the traditions of the church are important. However, in many cases, adherents to tradition will often merge Scripture and tradition into church policy. Moreover, many aspects of church traditions are unique to certain churches, and the supporters may not know how the traditions started. Nevertheless, in our contemporary society that seems to devalue the Church, we must not misunderstand the difference between church traditions and the traditions of the Church.

GET SOCIAL

Share your views and tag us @rhboydco and use #mercy.

Twitter
@rhboydco (#rhboydco)

Instagram
@rhboydco (#rhboydco)

Facebook
@rhboydco (#rhboydco)

www.rhboyd.com

HOME DAILY DEVOTIONAL READINGS
SEPTEMBER 18–24, 2023

MONDAY	TUESDAY	WEDNESDAY	THURSDAY	FRIDAY	SATURDAY	SUNDAY
Forgive as God in Christ Has Forgiven You	God Forgives	Adultery in the Heart	You Get the Judgment You Give	Rejoice in God's Forgiveness	Let the Wicked Forsake Their Way	Neither Do I Condemn You
Ephesians 4:17–32	Psalm 130	Matthew 5:27–32	Matthew 7:1–5	Psalm 32	Isaiah 55:6–13	John 8:1–11

JESUS EXTENDS FORGIVENESS

ADULT TOPIC: BACKGROUND SCRIPTURE: JOHN 8:1–11, 39–59
JUDGE NOT   LESSON PASSAGE: JOHN 8:1–11, 56–59

JOHN 8:1–11, 56–59

King James Version	*New Revised Standard Version*
JESUS went unto the mount of Olives.	WHILE Jesus went to the Mount of Olives.
2 And early in the morning he came again into the temple, and all the people came unto him; and he sat down, and taught them.	2 Early in the morning he came again to the temple. All the people came to him and he sat down and began to teach them.
3 And the scribes and Pharisees brought unto him a woman taken in adultery; and when they had set her in the midst,	3 The scribes and the Pharisees brought a woman who had been caught in adultery; and making her stand before all of them,
4 They say unto him, Master, this woman was taken in adultery, in the very act.	4 they said to him, "Teacher, this woman was caught in the very act of committing adultery.
5 Now Moses in the law commanded us, that such should be stoned: but what sayest thou?	5 Now in the law Moses commanded us to stone such women. Now what do you say?"
6 This they said, tempting him, that they might have to accuse him. But Jesus stooped down, and with his finger wrote on the ground, as though he heard them not.	6 They said this to test him, so that they might have some charge to bring against him. Jesus bent down and wrote with his finger on the ground.
7 So when they continued asking him, he lifted up himself, and said unto them, He that is without sin among you, let him first cast a stone at her.	7 When they kept on questioning him, he straightened up and said to them, "Let anyone among you who is without sin be the first to throw a stone at her."
8 And again he stooped down, and wrote on the ground.	8 And once again he bent down and wrote on the ground.
9 And they which heard it, being convicted by their own conscience, went out one by one, beginning at the eldest, even unto the last: and Jesus was left alone, and the woman standing in the midst.	9 When they heard it, they went away, one by one, beginning with the elders; and Jesus was left alone with the woman standing before him.
10 When Jesus had lifted up himself, and saw none but the woman, he said unto her, Woman, where are those thine accusers? hath no man condemned thee?	10 Jesus straightened up and said to her, "Woman, where are they? Has no one condemned you?"
11 She said, No man, Lord. And Jesus said unto her, Neither do I condemn thee: go, and sin no more.	11 She said, "No one, sir." And Jesus said, "Neither do I condemn you. Go your way, and from now on do not sin again."
• • • • • •	• • • • • •

MAIN THOUGHT: She said, No man, Lord. And Jesus said unto her, Neither do I condemn thee: go, and sin no more. (John 8:11, KJV)

JOHN 8:1–11, 56–59

King James Version	*New Revised Standard Version*
56 Your father Abraham rejoiced to see my day: and he saw it, and was glad.	56 Your ancestor Abraham rejoiced that he would see my day; he saw it and was glad."
57 Then said the Jews unto him, Thou art not yet fifty years old, and hast thou seen Abraham?	57 Then the Jews said to him, "You are not yet fifty years old, and have you seen Abraham?"
58 Jesus said unto them, Verily, verily, I say unto you, Before Abraham was, I am.	58 Jesus said to them, "Very truly, I tell you, before Abraham was, I am."
59 Then took they up stones to cast at him: but Jesus hid himself, and went out of the temple, going through the midst of them, and so passed by.	59 So they picked up stones to throw at him, but Jesus hid himself and went out of the temple.

LESSON SETTING
   Time: Circa AD 28
   Place: Jerusalem

LESSON OUTLINE
   I. The Adulterous Woman
   (John 8:1–6)
   II. Who Will Throw the First Stone?
   (John 8:7–11)
   III. Jesus' Relationship to Abraham
   (John 8:56–59)

UNIFYING PRINCIPLE

Others may be quick to judge someone who breaks the Law—whether moral, ethical, or civil. Who has authority to enact judgment on another person's wrongdoing? After confronting her accusers with their own sinfulness, Jesus forgives the woman caught in adultery, saying, "Go your way, and from now on do not sin again."

INTRODUCTION

In this account, we find Jesus in Jerusalem, as the Feast of Booths had come to a close. During the Feast, Jesus presented several declarations that had created a series of debates between Himself and the religious authorities. One such proclamation was that "if anyone thirsts, let him come to me and let him drink" (John 7:37). His words created two camps—one that supported Him and believed that He was the Messiah, and the another that resented Him and thought He was an impostor. The Pharisees wanted to arrest Jesus, ensuring that "no prophet arises out of Galilee" (John 7:52), but they could not find Him, and everyone went home, whereas, Jesus went to the Mount of Olives. However, Jesus returned to the Temple where He was asked to judge a woman caught in an adulterous act. Although this story is probably authentic, it is omitted in many manuscripts and may not have originally been a part of this Gospel.

EXPOSITION
I. THE ADULTEROUS WOMAN (JOHN 8:1–6)

As Jesus escapes the crowds and the Pharisees by going to the Mount of Olives, He is able to remain in Jerusalem. The Mount of Olives is directly across the deep Kidron Valley from the Temple and will play a prominent role in the narrative of Jesus' withdrawal following the Last Supper and His timely arrest by the Temple guards. The Mount of Olives houses an olive press (called Gethsemane), and in that area was located a garden where Jesus went to pray on the night of His arrest. John does not mention if Jesus was accompanied by His disciples; however, we may assume that they were present, which would give the Judas account a clearer sense of understanding.

Early the next morning, Jesus left the security of the Mount of Olives and returned to the city and the Temple. This must have stressed and perplexed the disciples because they would have known of Jesus' enemies wishes to eliminate Him. Remember, the disciples were not simply His traveling companions but were also His friends, and as friends, they—especially the impetuous Cephas (Peter)—would be concerned about Jesus' security and protection. To return to the Temple after the threat of the previous week would have seemed reckless, yet, it was Jesus' desire to return to the people. The Temple would contain the regular crowds, as people sought the presence and closeness of Yahweh who they believed lived in "His house." These people were firm believers in the prophecy and promise of God, who were eagerly looking for the Messiah. Unfortunately, many of the Gospel accounts seem to focus on the scribes, Pharisees, and anyone else who is constantly trying to condemn Jesus, but the light that Jesus shines illuminates these people, who in many cases, are the poor, marginalized, and victimized of society. They are consistent in their love and desire to be comforted by Jesus, regardless of the arena, whether in the Temple, on the hillsides, or by the sea. They came to Him as devout Jews who believed in and needed the Savior, listened to Him, and were comforted by Him.

He began to teach, and although John does not record His discourse, Jesus was soon interrupted. First, it may seem incredible that His enemies actually found Him, although Jesus was not hiding. Second, the Pharisees and scribes wished to eliminate Jesus, yet, had settled on another method to discredit Him. Third, it would have taken some time to catch the woman, seize her, alert the authorities, and then, decide on taking her to where Jesus was teaching, rather than impose sentence on her at the place and the moment. Nonetheless, the authorities, who were men, brought a woman caught in adultery to the center of the court near where Jesus was teaching.

For most traditionalists, the act of adultery is simple: if one has intercourse, or in contemporary thought, any type of sexual act (even though it may not include penetration), it is considered adultery. The Law of Moses did not anticipate or describe any other forms of sexual pursuit and therefore, seems to only examine one aspect of the sex act. However, a closer examination of the Law reveals some interesting details surrounding the infidelity directives. First, in the ancient Near East (and the Old Testament), adultery meant consensual sexual intercourse by a married woman with a man other than her husband. However, intercourse between a married man and another woman was not considered adultery, again, unless she was married. The betrothed woman was also bound to fidelity, but leniency is shown to a married or betrothed man (Exodus 22:16–17 [MT 15–16]; Deuteronomy 22:28–29; Proverbs

5:15–20; Malachi 2:14–15). Some scholars distinguish between the ancient Near Eastern laws, (1) where adultery was a private wrong against the husband who could prosecute an offender, and (2) the biblical laws where adultery was an offense against God, with mandatory prosecution and a sentence of death, or in some cases, atonement through a sin offering (Leviticus 19:20–21).

Ironically, instead of persecuting her at the place where the event occurred (or in the halls of the Sanhedrin), the religious authorities brought her before Jesus and asked Him to judge what should be done with her. Although Jesus was not a witness to her act and only had the word of the accusers, He knew that these Pharisees were creating a scenario where He would be trapped into either accepting the Law or defending the plight of the embarrassed woman. If He recommended leniency, He would alienate the legalists. If He supported the death penalty, He would alienate the many who opposed it, even in those days. In either scenario, the authorities were attempting to have Jesus declare the Law invalid, thereby placing Himself above the person of Moses. Thy were not actually concerned with the adultery of the woman; they were obsessed with condemning Jesus. John uses the term *katēgoréō*, which is derived from the words *katá*, meaning "against," and *agoreúō*, "to speak." This indicated that the Pharisees were determined to openly speak against Jesus and to condemn Him in the Temple before the assembled people. Jesus, however, did not react to their ruse. Rather that succumbing to their deception, Jesus stooped to the ground and wrote something only known to Him in the dust.

II. WHO WILL THROW THE FIRST STONE? (JOHN 8:7–11)

Here, the Pharisees and scribes continued to press Jesus for a response and after a period during which He ignored them, He stood and declared, "He who is without sin among you, let him be the first to throw a stone at her" (John 8:7). The analysis of the Jerusalem Bible is more direct; Jesus places the crowd on trial by giving them a chance to reveal their own purity, asking, "If there is one of you who has not sinned," lead the execution by striking the first blow. Verse 7 reveals several observations. First, Jesus uses the personal pronoun "he" because the accusers were all men, as women were not to participate in acts such as stoning. Second, Jesus invited the lead accuser to be the first to throw the stone, which would have revealed the person who brought the charges against the hapless woman. In this rush to judgment, it seems that there was no eyewitness testimony, just an unruly mob of accusers. The sin Jesus speaks of here is not simply the act of something such as adultery or drunkenness; it stems from the depths of an unholy place where man finds himself separated from God.

There was silence among the Pharisees, scribes, and "hangers-on," as Jesus returned to writing in the dust. The accusers were left astonished, speechless, and angry, yet, they did not have any type of rebuttal for the defense that Jesus had displayed. In their defeat, they began to leave the area. John delights in describing their departure, (i.e., "one by one"), and notes that the older ones (men) led the retreat. Finally, the only persons left were probably those of the group that Jesus had ministered to, His disciples, and the rescued woman. Although verse 9 mentions that "He" (meaning Jesus) was left alone, it should be understood as His antagonists had left Him alone, i.e., the antagonism had ended, when they fled from the area. The woman remained standing in the center of the court where her nightmare had begun; however, Jesus had removed the veil of humiliation and the threat of a possible execution in this place, which was now filled with hope and promise.

As Jesus stood to speak, He calls her "woman." This is not a term of disrespect, but rather, could be thought of as a term of endearment in the language of their culture. For example, Jesus referred to His mother as "woman" when He was asked to change the water into wine (John 2:1–4). Nonetheless, Jesus asks, "Where are your accusers," and, "Did any one condemn you?" Relieved, she replied, "No one." In the presence of Jesus, the authoritarian bullies did not have a case and rather than admit defeat or agree with Jesus, they merely slithered away. These Pharisees knew in the beginning that they did not have a case; yet, as it is with the actions of rogue lawyers who are only interested in settlements, their sole purpose was to discredit Jesus, at the expense of the injured female. Jesus refused to condemn the woman; however, He issued a compassionate warning for her to "sin no more" (v. 11). Some translators take the command "do not sin again" as a specific reference to the sin of adultery and so, render "avoid this sin" (*New American Bible*). Nonetheless, the command is clear, as

Jesus is giving this woman an opportunity to take advantage of a "fresh" start and a new life.

III. JESUS' RELATIONSHIP TO ABRAHAM (JOHN 8:56–59)

It seems as if some of the religious authorities returned to the scene at Jesus' return to teaching the crowd. At this juncture, the image of Abraham was invoked, both as a connection to the Jews and as a connection to Jesus. Like Moses, the Jews would sense a relationship and bond with their ancestor Abraham and would listen to His discourse. Although it is not mentioned in the final verses of chapter 8, Jesus must have included the redemption of the woman in His instruction, as the need for a Messiah was very real. However, in the atmosphere of compassion and faith, Jesus referred to Abraham's terminology of "My Day" and its meaning as the messianic salvation that God promised that "all peoples on earth will be blessed through [Abraham]" (Genesis 12:2). How much about the messianic times God revealed to Abraham is unknown, but it is clear that Abraham knew of the coming salvation, and he rejoiced in knowing about it and expecting it.

The response of these Jews was typically negative, snorting, "You are not yet fifty years old, how could You have seen Abraham?" This was meant not only as a retort but as a criticism against His claim of physically seeing the venerated patriarch. As a precursor to His declaration of being the Son of God, Jesus' response was that He existed before Abraham was born (v. 58). These Jews would understand the significance of Jesus' use of "I am," which boomed from the voice of Yahweh when Moses asked, "Who shall I tell Pharaoh that sent me?" (Exodus 3:14). At this juncture, Jesus revealed that He was with God and that He was God! This is a claim to be Yahweh of the Old Testament. Angered by this latest claim as to His closeness to God, they resorted to what it seems they knew best: they picked up stones (probably the ones that were to be used to kill the woman) in order to kill Jesus. Yet, Jesus escaped their presence and again, for His safety, left the Temple grounds.

THE LESSON APPLIED

As for the affair with the woman, we must remember it was the religious authorities who were bringing charges, not the civil authorities, who were employed by Rome and could not care less about Mosaic Law. There was a group, who the Pharisees labeled as "this crowd," i.e., the *am haarez* (people of the land), who they despised because they no longer observed the minutiae of the Jewish law. This group probably favored Jesus. Jesus' actions and rejection of the Pharisees while supporting the adulterous woman was not an attack or a refutation of the Law of Moses; it was an attack on their hypocrisy. Moreover, Jesus' desire was to show that mercy overrode the Law, which was needed at the time it was given; but now that the Son had been given, forgiveness and redemption was the only avenue for the salvation of humanity.

LET'S TALK ABOUT IT

Is forgiveness really for everyone?

Adults grow in their willingness to forgive the wrongdoing of others, especially if they are Christians who realize that their blessings and grace are provided because Jesus serves as the Savior for the forgiveness of our shortcomings. When Christians are not caught up in attempting to marginalize or look down on others, we are able to realize that "all have fallen short of the glory of God" (Romans 3:23) and understand that God's grace is a gift. The desire of authentic Christians is that the world would be filled with forgiveness and love through Jesus Christ.

GET SOCIAL

Share your views and tag us @rhboydco and use #forgiveness.

Twitter
@rhboydco (#rhboydco)

Instagram
@rhboydco (#rhboydco)

Facebook
@rhboydco (#rhboydco)

www.rhboyd.com

HOME DAILY DEVOTIONAL READINGS
SEPTEMBER 25–OCTOBER 1, 2023

MONDAY	TUESDAY	WEDNESDAY	THURSDAY	FRIDAY	SATURDAY	SUNDAY
Keep God's Laws in Your Heart	Practice Your Piety in Secret	Abide in Christ	God Will Give the Spirit	God Will Repay Each One's Deeds	God Shows No Partiality	God Looks at Your Heart
Deuteronomy 6:4–9	Matthew 6:1–8, 16–18	John 15:1–8	Ezekiel 36:25–30	Romans 2:1–8	Romans 2:9–16	Romans 2:17–29

KEEPING THE LAW INWARDLY

ADULT TOPIC: A MATTER OF THE HEART	BACKGROUND SCRIPTURE: ROMANS 2:1–29 LESSON PASSAGE: ROMANS 2:12–24, 28–29

ROMANS 2:12–24, 28–29

King James Version

FOR as many as have sinned without law shall also perish without law: and as many as have sinned in the law shall be judged by the law;

13 (For not the hearers of the law are just before God, but the doers of the law shall be justified.

14 For when the Gentiles, which have not the law, do by nature the things contained in the law, these, having not the law, are a law unto themselves:

15 Which shew the work of the law written in their hearts, their conscience also bearing witness, and their thoughts the mean while accusing or else excusing one another;)

16 In the day when God shall judge the secrets of men by Jesus Christ according to my gospel.

17 Behold, thou art called a Jew, and restest in the law, and makest thy boast of God,

18 And knowest his will, and approvest the things that are more excellent, being instructed out of the law;

19 And art confident that thou thyself art a guide of the blind, a light of them which are in darkness,

20 An instructor of the foolish, a teacher of babes, which hast the form of knowledge and of the truth in the law.

21 Thou therefore which teachest another, teachest thou not thyself? thou that preachest a man should not steal, dost thou steal?

22 Thou that sayest a man should not commit

New Revised Standard Version

ALL who have sinned apart from the law will also perish apart from the law, and all who have sinned under the law will be judged in accordance with the law.

13 For it is not the hearers of the law who are righteous in God's sight but the doers of the law who will be justified.

14 When Gentiles, who do not possess the law, do instinctively what the law requires, these, though not having the law, are a law to themselves.

15 They show that what the law requires is written on their hearts, to which their own conscience also bears witness; and their conflicting thoughts will accuse or perhaps excuse them

16 on the day when, according to my gospel, God, through Jesus Christ, will judge the secret thoughts of all.

17 But if you call yourself a Jew and rely on the law and boast of your relation to God

18 and know his will and determine what is best because you are instructed in the law,

19 and if you are sure that you are a guide to the blind, a light to those who are in darkness,

20 a corrector of the foolish, a teacher of children, having in the law the embodiment of knowledge and truth,

21 you, then, that teach others, will you not teach yourself? While you preach against stealing, do you steal?

22 You that forbid adultery, do you commit

MAIN THOUGHT: But he is a Jew, which is one inwardly; and circumcision is that of the heart, in the spirit, and not in the letter; whose praise is not of men, but of God. (Romans 2:29, KJV)

King James Version	*New Revised Standard Version*
adultery, dost thou commit adultery? thou that abhorrest idols, dost thou commit sacrilege?	adultery? You that abhor idols, do you rob temples?
23 Thou that makest thy boast of the law, through breaking the law dishonourest thou God?	23 You that boast in the law, do you dishonour God by breaking the law?
24 For the name of God is blasphemed among the Gentiles through you, as it is written.	24 For, as it is written, 'The name of God is blasphemed among the Gentiles because of you.'
• • • • • •	• • • • • •
28 For he is not a Jew, which is one outwardly; neither is that circumcision, which is outward in the flesh:	28 For a person is not a Jew who is one outwardly, nor is true circumcision something external and physical.
29 But he is a Jew, which is one inwardly; and circumcision is that of the heart, in the spirit, and not in the letter; whose praise is not of men, but of God.	29 Rather, a person is a Jew who is one inwardly, and real circumcision is a matter of the heart—it is spiritual and not literal. Such a person receives praise not from others but from God.

LESSON SETTING

Time: Circa AD 57–58
Place: Corinth

LESSON OUTLINE

I. **Condemnation of the Jew Who Keeps the Law (Romans 2:12–16)**
II. **The Jew Must Practice the Law (Romans 2:17–23)**
III. **Using Circumcision to Divide Rather than to Unite (Romans 2:24, 28–29)**

UNIFYING PRINCIPLE

People hold conscious and unconscious assumptions of right and wrong. What motivates the choice of one over the other? Paul teaches that faith can guide our choices and inform our convictions about what is right.

INTRODUCTION

The following account is a condemnation of a moralist set of Jews (Romans 2:1–16). The Jews that Paul responds to are those who publicly identify themselves as just, but only because they believe themselves to be keepers of the Law. In this rebuttal, Paul declares that these Jews wrongly believe that they are superior to the Gentile members of the church and society. In this case, they were oblivious to the judgment of God because they believed that in their embrace of Mosaic Law, they were beyond His wrath. Although the Christian church is established, the Jews had an obligation (because of their heritage) to continue to be God's chosen people. These Jews wanted the privilege but not the responsibility.

EXPOSITION

I. CONDEMNATION OF THE JEW WHO KEEPS THE LAW (ROMANS 2:12–16)

In this set of circumstances, Paul argues that the Gentiles of the Christian church did not have the Law and, therefore, were not bound to the religious practices of the Law.

This is not to say that the Gentiles were not bound by civil and moral laws, i.e., laws against murder, coveting, etc. These laws came from the Ten Commandments and are considered religious laws because of the Mosaic Covenant; therefore, they are examples of what is to guide humanity and set the boundaries that allow people to exist without destroying each other. The Gentiles, however, were not exempt from God's judgment and necessary wrath. Since they did not have the Law to protect them, if guilty, they would perish when judged without the Law. God has other means of judging and protecting the Gentiles. Since God created the world and all of the people included in His artistry, Gentiles are His people, too! Yet, as God's chosen people, the Jews had been placed in a unique situation. Historically, they had had the Law to guide them and also had this same Law to protect them. Therefore, they were "opposite" from the Gentiles in their dependency upon the Law as God's chosen people.

When compared to the Gentiles' lack of receiving the Law, some may think the Law is an unfair gift that God gives to the Jews. For example, when God created all of mankind from the beginning of the world, there was no designation of Jew and Gentile. Originally, God's chosen were "Hebrew," as was demonstrated when a fugitive came and told Abram, the Hebrew, who was living by the oaks of Mamre, about Lot's capture (Genesis 14:12–13). However, the first appearance of the designation of the Jew appears in the account of the death of Gedaliah, who died along with the Jews and Chaldeans at Mizpah (2 Kings 25:25). The first appearance of the designation of "Gentile" is found in Isaiah, e.g., the "Galilee of the Gentiles," in his prophecy about Jesus. However, Israel was given the designation of God's chosen people, as Isaac was the child of promise. The nation was to be bound to God as seen in the lineage that Jesus was a Jew! Nonetheless, Paul writes to the Jew first, then, to the Greek (Gentile). This is not a sign of disrespect but an acknowledgment of the plan of redemption.

Since the Gentiles did not have the Law given to them, they resorted to creating laws that were just in their eyes and served their purposes. Although many of their laws were based on Mosaic Law, the edicts of the Gentiles were not based on a relationship with Yahweh. Recall that the enemies of Israel, such as Nebuchadnezzar, were pagan Gentiles who worshipped idols and gods who are antithetical to Yahweh. The Jews looked down on the Gentiles partly because they did not have the revelation of God's will in the Mosaic Law. However, as Paul pointed out, there were also moral Gentiles who did by nature those things required by the Law. The Law given to Israel is in reality only a specific statement of God's moral and spiritual requirements for everyone. Moral Gentiles have a conscience, but it is not an absolutely trustworthy indicator of what is right. Yet, on a designated day, it will be God who will judge the inner thoughts and secrets of men, based on their relationship and a genuine commitment to Jesus Christ.

II. JEWS MUST PRACTICE THE LAW (ROMANS 2:17–23)

Continuing, Paul places his focus on those who identify themselves as Jews. Herein lies an immediate problem, as witnessed in our contemporary period. As it is with many groups today that identify with a certain movement, the Jews did so because it created self-awareness and made them feel important by belonging to something. The Jews that Paul identifies are, by inheritance, part of the nation, but they cannot make an impact or any contributions because they are non-practicing Jews, which means they may identify as Jewish from an ethnic perspective but not from a religious commitment. In essence, these Jews are out of the arc of God's safety.

Paul notes that these Jews rely solely on Mosaic Law; yet, while true, his statement only applies to a certain degree. These Jews, both ethnic and religious, seem to embrace the Law when it benefits their situations and causes. The issues may be national, such as when the power, prestige, and edicts of Israel's kings created a sense of nationalist pride. However, the punishments that the nation suffered were directly linked to their disobedience to God and their subsequent punishments, such as being conquered by their enemies and exiled into foreign lands. Paul advocates that the people follow the tenants of the Christian movement, which is based on faith in Jesus Christ. The Jews that are identified here are possibly Jewish Christians, who refuse to abandon the Law and commit to Christ because it does not satisfy their selfish and controlling purposes. In this case, their reliance on the Law is not holy but superficial and hypocritical.

Many of these Jews readily identified with their Jewish heritage, which made them comfortable in the knowledge that they were God's chosen people.

Unfortunately, many of these Jews boasted in God because of the history of what God had meant to them during their halcyon days. In many cases, their boasts included national miracles, such as the Red Sea crossing, and the return from Babylonian exile. Unfortunately, these boasts became anemic when they failed to realize that Jesus is the Messiah and God's supreme Gift to the world (both Jew and Gentile). They were relying on the nostalgic memories of the past but failed to embrace the realities of God's present and future plan of salvation.

Since these Jews claimed to be connected to God, Paul declares that they should be confident that they are actually God's chosen, not simply in historical name only. If God's chosen, their lives should be of such greatness that they are confident in their ability to be a light to those (the blind) who are living in darkness and a guide to those who are seeking Christ. Recall that Jesus came to give sight to the blind (John 9:1ff.), and He becomes the ultimate teacher and example of how enlightened men should live, especially those who claim to be God-chosen. Many of these Jews lacked confidence in this declaration because of a lack of faith and a refusal to adhere to the mission of Jesus, all the while, attempting to remain committed to the mission of Moses.

Because these Jews claimed to be of God, Paul declares that they should be just and righteous men who are able to lead but also, to command the respect of the people and correct those who are wayward and misguided. Paul is specific when he lists the foolish and the immature, who may not be evil but have been misled by those who (although charismatic, or serving as family or community leaders) are foolish and immature themselves. In essence, the foolish and immature may be those that society would call "good people;" yet, in their lack of "Jesus-awareness" and knowledge, they create an analogy with the old quip of the "blind leading the blind." Paul argues that knowing the Law but not using it for the reason it was intended becomes sheer folly for the people, especially the leaders of the community. The Law itself embodies all knowledge and truth. Paul declared that he would be a Jew to the Jews and a Greek to the Greeks if it would lead them to Christ.

II. USING CIRCUMCISION TO DIVIDE RATHER THAN TO UNITE (ROMANS 2:24, 28–29)

Here, Paul connects verse 24 as a bridge through verses 28 and 29, saying that these Jews have lowered the prestige of God in the eyes of the Gentiles because of their behavior and lack of commitment to the Law. Since these Jews wished to connect to the act of circumcision to serve their own purposes, Paul uses circumcision to refute their lofty claims. Circumcision was brought into the picture as a clear act of bias against the Gentile members of the church. However, because their so–called faith was questionable and lacking, they sought to usurp the Law to justify their selfish and social desires. Their position was not based upon their faith in Jesus, who is the head of the Christian church to which these Jews had committed. In this case, they were possibly attempting to re–convert the church in a return to the period of Moses. This is another reason that Paul says that Yahweh is blasphemed among the Gentiles because of their actions.

These men from Antioch, who came to the Council at Jerusalem, did not have the right or authority to use circumcision as a qualifier for membership in the body because circumcision is not an indicator of one who keeps and practices the Law. Remember, Peter had learned that no man should be called unclean, not even a Gentile (Romans 10:34), and the Jerusalem church had accepted the first Gentile converts on an equal basis with Jewish converts, without the necessity of being circumcised. These Jews were "imitation Jews" in that they seemed to be ignorant of the rationale for the circumcision covenant. Although an original covenantal sign, by this period, the Christian Jew did not need to show his circumcision to belong to the nation, or to serve as a "badge of honor." Instead, the Jew who is committed to Yahweh has undergone an inward or spiritual circumcision. Their idea of using circumcision as a tool of discrimination was blasphemy in the sight of God.

The notion that a man could not be saved unless he was circumcised should have been eradicated by the council; but Paul is having to address the problem again. These arrogant Jews' walk with God was tarnished and filled with blemishes because of their lack of faith and determination to attempt to move the doctrine, practices, and fellowship away from what Jesus had intended. A Jewish lawbreaker must stand before God in judgment in the same manner as that of a pagan. Paul had to remind them that a redeemed Jew (or Gentile) possesses a circumcised heart that was not performed by the Law but by the Spirit, and any praise that occurred, came from God. Remember, when Jesus declared,

"Upon this rock (petros), I will build My church," He meant that the church belonged to Him and was founded on His principles and authority. Furthermore, Jesus must have anticipated that the gates of hell would seek to destroy His Church because of men such as these; but regardless of the source of the gates of hell, Jesus promised that they would never prevail against His Church (See Matthew 16:18). Had the division over these questions of circumcision (and food) laws prevailed, the unity of the Church would have been shattered from the start.

THE LESSON APPLIED

Circumcision today is a health issue, and in most hospitals, male babies are automatically circumcised. The rationale is not based on religious practice, but rather, it has shown that men may have problems later in life if they remain uncircumcised. Nonetheless, the Jews in this account are using this covenantal practice as a means of segregation, which also, by extension, included dietary laws. Recall at one segment in American history that Blacks could worship in the same church as whites but were relegated to the balcony or some other racially designated area. Regardless of the mechanisms, using the elements of God to divide people who are seeking Him will bring judgment upon those who are guilty.

LET'S TALK ABOUT IT

What happens when we judge others in a self-righteous manner?
Many adults feel self-righteous in relation to those who are different and may condemn them for their beliefs and actions. Unfortunately, our churches are filled with cliques that embrace those who are in the same social and economic strata and reject those who are perceived unworthy. In this case, the people who are hurting and need to be supported in their quest to live a better life under the tutelage of the church are left behind. This is not to say that these people do not have Jesus in their lives; however, we are called to be our brothers' keepers, and the rejection of someone based on their clothes, etc. will bring God's judgment on the unrighteous.

GET SOCIAL
Share your views and tag us
@rhboydco and use #choices.

Twitter
@rhboydco (#rhboydco)

Instagram
@rhboydco (#rhboydco)

Facebook
@rhboydco (#rhboydco)

www.rhboyd.com

HOME DAILY DEVOTIONAL READINGS
OCTOBER 2–8, 2023

MONDAY	TUESDAY	WEDNESDAY	THURSDAY	FRIDAY	SATURDAY	SUNDAY
Living Before God	Living with Others	Who Will Rescue Me?	Outward Piety Earns God's Wrath	Dead to Sin; Alive in Christ	Present Your Bodies to God	Dead to the Law Through Christ
Deuteronomy 5:1–15	Deuteronomy 5:16–22	Romans 7:14–25	Jeremiah 7:1–15	Romans 6:1–12	Romans 6:13–23	Romans 7:1–13

THE LAW REVEALS SIN

ADULT TOPIC:	BACKGROUND SCRIPTURE: ROMANS 7:1–25
FINDING LIFE AND FREEDOM	LESSON PASSAGE: ROMANS 7:1–12

ROMANS 7:1–12

King James Version

KNOW ye not, brethren, (for I speak to them that know the law,) how that the law hath dominion over a man as long as he liveth?

2 For the woman which hath an husband is bound by the law to her husband so long as he liveth; but if the husband be dead, she is loosed from the law of her husband.

3 So then if, while her husband liveth, she be married to another man, she shall be called an adulteress: but if her husband be dead, she is free from that law; so that she is no adulteress, though she be married to another man.

4 Wherefore, my brethren, ye also are become dead to the law by the body of Christ; that ye should be married to another, even to him who is raised from the dead, that we should bring forth fruit unto God.

5 For when we were in the flesh, the motions of sins, which were by the law, did work in our members to bring forth fruit unto death.

6 But now we are delivered from the law, that being dead wherein we were held; that we should serve in newness of spirit, and not in the oldness of the letter.

7 What shall we say then? Is the law sin? God forbid. Nay, I had not known sin, but by the law: for I had not known lust, except the law had said, Thou shalt not covet.

8 But sin, taking occasion by the commandment, wrought in me all manner of concupiscence. For without the law sin was dead.

New Revised Standard Version

DO you not know, brothers and sisters—for I am speaking to those who know the law—that the law is binding on a person only during that person's lifetime?

2 Thus a married woman is bound by the law to her husband as long as he lives; but if her husband dies, she is discharged from the law concerning the husband.

3 Accordingly, she will be called an adulteress if she lives with another man while her husband is alive. But if her husband dies, she is free from that law, and if she marries to another man, she is not an adulteress.

4 In the same way, my friends, you have died to the law through the body of Christ, so that you may belong to another, to him who was raised from the dead in order that we may bear fruit for God.

5 For while we were living in the flesh, our sinful passions, aroused by the law, were at work in our members to bear fruit for death.

6 But now we are discharged from the law, dead to that which held us captive, so that we are slaves not under the old written code but in the new life of the Spirit.

7 What then should we say? That the law is sin? By no means! Yet, if it had not been for the law, I would not have known sin. I would not have known what it is to covet if the law had not said, "You shall not covet."

8 But sin, seizing an opportunity through the commandment, produced in me all kinds of covetousness. For apart from the law sin lies dead.

MAIN THOUGHT: But now we are delivered from the law, that being dead wherein we were held; that we should serve in newness of spirit, and not in the oldness of the letter. (Romans 7:6, KJV)

Romans 7:1–12

King James Version	New Revised Standard Version
9 For I was alive without the law once: but when the commandment came, sin revived, and I died.	9 I was once alive apart from the law, but when the commandment came, sin revived
10 And the commandment, which was ordained to life, I found to be unto death.	10 and I died, and the very commandment that promised life proved to be death to me.
11 For sin, taking occasion by the commandment, deceived me, and by it slew me.	11 For sin, seizing an opportunity in the commandment, deceived me and through it killed me.
12 Wherefore the law is holy, and the commandment holy, and just, and good.	12 So the law is holy, and the commandment is holy and just and good.

LESSON SETTING
Time: Circa AD 57–58
Place: Corinth

LESSON OUTLINE
I. Are Believers Under the Law? Or Limited Dominion of the Law?
(Romans 7:1–6)
II. Is the Law Evil? Or Does the Law Create Sin?
(Romans 7:7–12)

UNIFYING PRINCIPLE

Laws are created for the mutual benefit of society, to give clear guidelines for "right" and "wrong." Why do some people insist on breaking the law? In Romans, Paul wrestles with the reality that while God's Law guides us to do right, sin uses that very same law to bring disobedience and death.

INTRODUCTION

Here, Paul introduces a new metaphor, that of a faithful marriage. The Christian, because of his death with Christ, is free from his marriage to the Law and is brought into a new marriage with Christ. Although it seems that Paul never marries, for him, marriage is a sacred union in the eyes of the Lord. Following the illustra-tions of marital laws, which are civil legal principles, not Mosaic Law—which is understood as a guiding set of principles for setting order and living in a civilized society—Paul shifts to the law of coveting and how it aroused the sin in him. Scholars suggest that Paul's personal experience of this may have taken place around the time of his Bar Mitzvah when he became, as the term translates, "a son of the Law." As his sharp young mind grappled with the concept, he began to see that his inner life was filled with coveting.

EXPOSITION

I. ARE BELIEVERS UNDER THE LAW? OR LIMITED DOMINION OF THE LAW?
(ROMANS 7:1–6)

Paul has previously explained that believers that have been bonded to God are granted the benefit of having been freed from sin, which results in sanctification and eternal life. To press this point, Paul adds that the "wages of sin is death, but the free gift of God is eternal life in Christ Jesus, our Lord" (Romans 6:22–23). Now, he issues an option, asking if the brethren (who supposedly know the Law) understand that the Law has jurisdiction over a person, though, only as long as he lives. However, upon death, a man is freed from his obligation to the Law. Civil laws were set by rulers of the various countries where Paul traveled, and the Roman Empire continued to dominate Paul's world through power and non-sectarian politics.

The first example offered by Paul is how the Law governs marriage. This is a conditional analogy that, according to the Law(s), a woman is bound to her husband, but only as long as he is alive. Marriage was based on solemn obligations, as was written from Edenic times, that a man shall leave his father and mother and be joined to his wife and they shall become one flesh (Genesis 2:24), or as expressed in Malachi, that a married woman is a man's companion and his wife by covenant (Malachi 2:14). The Law has references to the marital responsibilities of the man and the prohibitions against outsiders, such as a neighboring man interfering in the marriage. These marital laws were based on ownership, i.e., the wife was considered property of the husband, suggesting a monogamous union.

In normal situations, these marital laws were designed to keep the woman in the marriage as long as the husband is alive. If the husband dies, the woman is then released from the marriage and is free to remain single or to re-marry. Yet, if the wife enters into a relationship with another man while her husband is alive, she is considered an adulteress. Many of the divorce laws were designed to protect Hebrew women who were totally dependent on the husband for their livelihoods (see Deuteronomy 22:19, 29). There are, however, provisions for divorce that exist under certain circumstances, where the husband may issue a certificate of divorce (see Deuteronomy 24:1-4). Nonetheless, in Paul's analogy, about which he reflects on civil law, the woman who becomes a widow is not an adulteress and is free to enter a new marriage without the stigma of being viewed as a harlot.

Following Paul's illustration on the civil concepts of a normal marriage, he applies the argument to the life of the believer and her relationship to the Law. In this case, the believer takes on the role of the woman, whereas, the husband becomes the Law. Yet, because the Law cannot die, the believer (the woman) does not have the natural ability to live forever, and she must die. Although Paul's application of the marriage analogy is not altogether perfect, the meaning is clear. As death breaks the bond between husband and wife, so death—the believer's death with Christ—breaks the bond that formerly yoked him to the Law, and now, he is free to enter into union with Christ. Here, Paul equates death in the Law as a rebirth into the body of Christ where a new life begins. The Christian's death and renewal can be thought of as a baptism, where the old man enters a "watery" grave and emerges as a new creature. Moreover, the renewed Christian is granted new life in order to "bear fruit" or find himself in the service of the Lord. Remember, the Church is the bride of Christ for whom the Bridegroom will one day return, in a seminal event for which believers must be ready!

Therefore, for Paul, the believer who has died with Christ is released from bondage to the Law and hence, from bondage to sin, and is free to experience the abundant life of Christ. Paul notes that believers were formerly subject to forces of darkness that created a barrier to their union with Christ. When Paul speaks of being in the flesh, he is describing our status prior to being saved. However, Paul declares that sinful passions, which were aroused by the Law, were at work in the members of our bodies (v. 5). How can this occur? Paul's argument is that the edicts of the Law actually made people aware of the actions that were prohibited, such as coveting. One only has to think of the reverse effects that instruction has on some people when they are encouraged not to break the Law. This is Paul's analogy to Mosaic Law, in that it arouses curiosity and passions that usurp the commandments. For Paul, while in the flesh, we bore bad fruit that ended in death, both physical and spiritual. Our lifestyles worked to accomplish tangible treasures, but they soon became items that encouraged death. However, by dying in Christ, we were released from the shackles that made us slaves to the needs and desires of this world and not of heaven. Now, being identified with Christ, believers are dead to the Law. Like a widow released from marital obligations, so believers are released from the Law and its arousal to sin.

II. Is the Law Evil? Or Does the Law Create Sin? (Romans 7:7–12)

Continuing his discourse, Paul posed two questions, asking, "Is the Law sin?" and how do we adequately respond to or explain the concepts of the Law as creating sin? He must have known that this would be a controversial theory, yet, here,

presents a plausible argument. The first question asked is whether he is suggesting that the Law of God is sinful. Answering his question, Paul declares, "Of course not!" For Paul, it was the Law that revealed his weaknesses and sin. Paul bases his vulnerability on his attempt to keep the tenth Commandment, which declares that "you shall not covet" (Exodus 20:17). Paul singles out this commandment, although it is the last of the Ten (Decalogue), because it serves as a warning that failure to obey this command will cause one to commit other transgressions, such as murder, adultery, theft, and lying. For Paul, it was not so much that the Law created sin and caused him to do wrong but that God's Law reveals our sin.

However, Paul argues that it was sin that, in him, invaded the commandment of coveting, producing opportunities to test his abilities to overcome or sidestep the edict, while fulfilling his desires or cravings [of the flesh]. In the phrase "sin found its chance" (opportunity), the word *chance* translates a term that originally was used by the military to mean "a base of operation." But in New Testament times, the word was used frequently in a metaphorical sense with the meaning of "opportunity (to do something)." Here, Paul is revealing his personal experiences of grappling with an inability to resist the attraction to things that do not belong to him, or are not part of his personal blessings, as his desire to obtain these things is overwhelming. The meaning of the last sentence in this verse, for sin is a dead thing apart from law, is difficult. Paul seems to mean that apart from law, sin is inactive, that is, powerless. In some languages, sin is a dead thing apart from law may be expressed as "if there is no law, sin has no power," or "where the Law does not exist, sin can do nothing." As Paul concluded, apart from the Law, sin is dead. This does not mean that sin has no existence without the Law but that without the Law, sin is less active, for the Law arouses "sinful passions." Paul's argument of fighting the commandment is not to indicate that the tenth Commandment is flawed; it means instead that Paul sees in the edict his failure to adhere to its guidelines without the guidance of the Lord.

Moreover, Paul realizes that these commandments were given by the Lord and by breaking them, he is worthy of death; therefore, this specific commandment was given to preserve life. However, rejection and disobedience of His laws brings death upon the offender. Paul had previously included this warning to the lawbreakers of the Corinthian church, where he declared that apart from God, humans are inadequate. Paul writes that it is God who also made us adequate as servants of a new covenant, not of the letter but of the Spirit; for the letter kills, but the Spirit gives life (2 Corinthians 3:5–6). Here, Paul contrasts life versus death in his example of the need to actively maintain the tenants of the Law. Although breaking the commandments will cause a physical demise, here, Paul is concerned with his spiritual death, which in this case, would be the death of rejecting the commandments, which would result in him being alive.

Recall that the earlier examination of the phrase "sin found its chance (opportunity) and its understanding as a base of operation" indicates that the specter of sin is a cancer that creates a nuclear foundation or home base that allows its tentacles to spread into other parts of the body, creating destruction and mayhem, while continuing to retain its power in the nucleus. To care for the cancer, the doctor is forced to treat the affected areas; however, to destroy the malignancy, the surgeon must remove the evil core. In this case, Paul continues to express that it was through the base of operations that sin deceived him into believing that he could live apart from the Law (and the Lord) by coveting or doing anything else that would cause harm to his existence. Here, we must not misunderstand his theory; he does not postulate that the Law killed him but that sin misused the Law to destroy him.

In his conclusion, Paul believes that the Law is fundamentally good. Technically, laws consist of a body of regulations that are enforced by society, while a commandment is a specific order that is enforced by the individual who gives it. The commandments, which were given by God, became the Law of the people, and they were enforced by sanctions imposed by Hebrew or Jewish society. In order to indicate the contrast between Law and commandment in verse 12, one may speak of the Law as being the "laws" and the commandment as being "each commandment" or "each command" [given by God]. Since the commandment(s) are given by God, these commandments are holy. The basic definition of holy describes someone who is exalted or worthy of complete devotion, as one perfect in goodness and righteousness. In addition, this person is divine, which could only be definitive of the person of Yahweh. Moreover, everything that is blessed by Yahweh is to be considered consecrated, hallowed, and sacred. Furthermore, the commandment(s) are righteous, meaning that they are just and are given by a God who is invested in His creation, especially, mankind. For Paul, the commandments are fair and are not beyond Israel's interpretation or their ability to obey. Therefore, its commandment(s) are good, and they produce joyous feelings in the hearts of men who are dedicated to serving the Lord. The Law was given so that people could live productive lives and govern a society that would not destroy itself.

THE LESSON APPLIED

Several scholars suggest that when Paul speaks of "not being under the law," he is relating this to the period before Moses and specifically, the period of the fall, when sin became a factor in mankind's horrendous decision to separate themselves from God. Moses urged Israel to obey the laws of God, stating, "What great nation is there that has statutes and judgments as righteous as this whole law which I am setting before you today?" (Deuteronomy 4:8). In his day, Moses is instilling in Israel the objective impartiality of Yahweh that reveals His love for His people. That day has not changed, as God continues to love His people.

LET'S TALK ABOUT IT

Why does humankind seem to enjoy breaking rules?

Adults understand that laws can either be observed or ignored, obeyed or denied. Many humans have an issue with the word "don't." Recall the myriad of occasions and situations where warnings are issued for humans (caution: "coffee is hot" labels, etc.). Moreover, the social media giant TikTok is filled with how-to-break-the-rules videos. At the time of this writing, a spate of car thefts that target a certain make of automobiles is occurring. The video visibly instructs the interested party how to use components of a cell phone to start the intended vehicle, without a key. Unfortunately, human nature can be drawn to the challenge of breaking the law just because we are knowledgeable of the law.

HOME DAILY DEVOTIONAL READINGS
OCTOBER 9–15, 2023

MONDAY	TUESDAY	WEDNESDAY	THURSDAY	FRIDAY	SATURDAY	SUNDAY
The Lord Preserves the Faithful	Your Faith Has Made You Well	My Heart Trusts in God	The Gospel Sets Us Free	God Demands Justice, Kindness, and Humility	The Gospel for All People	We Are Justified in Christ
Psalm 31:1-5, 19–24	Mark 10:46–52	Psalm 28	Acts 15:22–35	Micah 6:1–8	Galatians 2:1–10	Galatians 2:11-21

JUSTIFIED BY FAITH NOT LAWS

| ADULT TOPIC: | BACKGROUND SCRIPTURE: GALATIANS 2:11–21 |
| ONE'S FAITH IS THE KEY | LESSON PASSAGE: GALATIANS 2:11–21 |

GALATIANS 2:11—21

King James Version

BUT when Peter was come to Antioch, I withstood him to the face, because he was to be blamed.

12 For before that certain came from James, he did eat with the Gentiles: but when they were come, he withdrew and separated himself, fearing them which were of the circumcision.

13 And the other Jews dissembled likewise with him; insomuch that Barnabas also was carried away with their dissimulation.

14 But when I saw that they walked not uprightly according to the truth of the gospel, I said unto Peter before them all, If thou, being a Jew, livest after the manner of Gentiles, and not as do the Jews, why compellest thou the Gentiles to live as do the Jews?

15 We who are Jews by nature, and not sinners of the Gentiles,

16 Knowing that a man is not justified by the works of the law, but by the faith of Jesus Christ, even we have believed in Jesus Christ, that we might be justified by the faith of Christ, and not by the works of the law: for by the works of the law shall no flesh be justified.

17 But if, while we seek to be justified by Christ, we ourselves also are found sinners, is therefore Christ the minister of sin? God forbid.

18 For if I build again the things which I destroyed, I make myself a transgressor.

New Revised Standard Version

BUT when Cephas came to Antioch, I opposed him to his face because he stood self-condemned,

12 for until certain people came from James, he used to eat with the Gentiles. But after they came, he drew back and kept himself separate for fear of the circumcision faction.

13 And the other Jews joined him in this hypocrisy, so that even Barnabas was led astray by their hypocrisy.

14 But when I saw that they were not acting consistently with the truth of the gospel, I said to Cephas before them all, "If you, though a Jew, live like a Gentile and not like a Jew, how can you compel the Gentiles to live like Jews?"

15 We ourselves are Jews by birth and not Gentile sinners,

16 yet we know that a person is justified not by the works of the law but through the faith in Jesus Christ. And we have come to believe in Christ Jesus, so that we might be justified by the faith in Christ and not by doing the works of the law, because no one will be justified by the works of the law.

17 But if, in our effort to be justified in Christ, we ourselves have been found to be sinners, is Christ then a servant of sin? Certainly not!

18 But if I build up again the very things that I once tore down, then I demonstrate that I am a transgressor.

MAIN THOUGHT: I am crucified with Christ: nevertheless I live; yet not I, but Christ liveth in me: and the life which I now live in the flesh I live by the faith of the Son of God, who loved me, and gave himself for me. (Galatians 2:20, KJV)

King James Version	*New Revised Standard Version*
19 For I through the law am dead to the law, that I might live unto God.	19 For through the law I died to the law, so that I might live to God. I have been crucified with Christ;
20 I am crucified with Christ: nevertheless I live; yet not I, but Christ liveth in me: and the life which I now live in the flesh I live by the faith of the Son of God, who loved me, and gave himself for me.	20 and it is no longer I who live, but it is Christ who lives in me. And the life I now live in the flesh I live by the faith in the Son of God, who loved me and gave himself for me.
21 I do not frustrate the grace of God: for if righteousness come by the law, then Christ is dead in vain.	21 I do not nullify the grace of God; for if justification comes through the law, then Christ died for nothing.

LESSON SETTING
> Time: Circa AD 49
> Place: Antioch

LESSON OUTLINE
> I. Peter's Duplicity
> (Galatians 2:11–13)
> II. Paul's Rebuke of Peter
> (Galatians 2:14–17)
> III. Christ Lives in Paul
> (Galatians 2:18–21)

UNIFYING PRINCIPLE

Some people behave a certain way with their friends and behave differently with coworkers or those they want to impress. Is there anything that can override our inconsistencies? Paul rebukes Peter's inconsistency with regard to welcoming Gentiles, as a way of encouraging the Galatians to rely on faith in Christ above works of the Law.

INTRODUCTION

At some point in the development of the "Way" (i.e., the term used before "Christianity" became the official identification of the followers of Jesus), the church at Antioch had replaced Jerusalem as the number one Christian city and the center of missionary activity. One of the central aspects of the letter is to demonstrate that men who are sinful by nature can come to God who is holy by nature through the redeeming grace that is available through the resurrection of Jesus Christ. In this lesson, Paul rebukes Cephas (Peter) because of the latter's conduct toward the Gentile group that he had befriended. Peter had come to Antioch, and although the time of Peter's visit remains obscure, it possibly occurred after Paul attended the Jerusalem conference (Acts 12:25).

EXPOSITION

I. PETER'S DUPLICITY (GALATIANS 2:11–13)

Our account begins with Peter's visit to Antioch, where Paul challenged Peter because of his stance on dietary laws and what Paul felt was a modicum of hypocrisy toward Gentile converts. Verse 11 of the NASB reads that Paul opposed Peter "to his face because he stood condemned," which is quite strong and aggressive language. In our contemporary interpretation, this language suggests that Paul was in Peter's face while condemning or denouncing him for his stance on the subject. The language portrays more than a criticism but suggests a tense standoff. The translation of the Greek term *kataginosko* is to detect something in a bad sense that leads to denunciation and disapproval, which is serious. This rebuke should be translated in such a way to avoid the suggestion of scolding, such as "Paul says that Peter was wrong," as some languages have translated. However, this is not to indicate any hostility or hatred between the two. Nonetheless, Paul is adamant that Peter is wrong in his actions and conduct.

When Peter was living and preaching in Jerusalem, he had developed a relationship with the Gentile converts. Previously, Peter had an issue with the dietary laws that decreed certain foods to be clean and others to be avoided (unclean). While in Joppa, he stayed with Simon the Tanner (Acts 9:43) and received a vision from Yahweh about eating animals that he once considered unclean. Moreover, the Lord commanded that Peter eat from these animals, saying, "What God has cleansed, no longer consider unholy" (Acts 10:15). At this juncture, Peter is being converted. First, staying with Simon was considered unclean because he worked with the skins of dead animals (Leviticus 11:40). Second, Peter's staying with Simon was also a preparation for preaching to the Gentiles, who he initially considered unclean.

In the communal worship of the period, Peter joined in the meals between the believers, which included both Jews and Gentiles. It was the perfect example of unity and the common bond both groups shared in their quest to be a part of the new church. However, when some of the emissaries of James (the brother of Jesus and head of the Jerusalem church) visited, Peter stopped his fellowship around the meals with his Gentile friends. It would appear that Peter was afraid that he would be criticized by the men from the church in Jerusalem and had decided to revert to indifference toward the Gentiles. Members of the Jerusalem church were overt Jewish converts who continued to cling to the Law while attempting to embrace the concept that Jesus had died for all men. It seemed that Peter wanted to be "safe rather than sorry" by deciding to shield himself from their opinions. Sadly, it looked as if Peter was reverting back to the person who denied Jesus at a very crucial hour.

As a result of his actions, the men of Jerusalem joined in with Peter (including Barnabas, who had been a partner with Paul during his first missionary journey). Ironically, Barnabas was carried away by the hypocrisy of Peter and the other Jewish men, which was alarming to Paul. This situation in Antioch caused a rift between Paul and Peter; and Paul and Barnabas soon parted company (very possibly because of this situation). However, the pressure must have been great for Barnabas to succumb in this situation because he was from Cyprus, a Gentile center, and was involved in a missionary program with Paul to reach Gentiles with the Gospel. It seemed incredible that Barnabas would shrink from the principles that had guided their evangelism. All of them—Peter, the other Jewish Christians, and Barnabas— were guilty of hypocrisy. The Gospels are filled with Jesus' condemnation toward those who practiced hypocrisy, calling them actors who display feelings and opinions that they actually do not hold, in order to conceal their real feelings and motives. In this situation, Cephas (Peter) was not preaching heresy; yet, neither was he consistently practicing the Gospel of grace.

II. PAUL'S REBUKE OF PETER (GALATIANS 2:14–17)

Paul felt compelled to rebuke and condemn Peter for his actions, thus, defending the Gospel and demonstrating again his own independence and equality as an apostle. It quickly became obvious that the actions of Peter and the other men of Jerusalem did not line up with the principles of the Gospel, which were supposed to reflect upon believers and non-believers alike. Paul challenges Peter directly by asking why Peter (a Jew), who had been comfortable living and ministering among the Gentiles, had (when convenient) resorted to distancing himself from these Gentiles? Paul accuses Peter of demanding that the Gentiles adhere to Jewish norms, which in this case was requiring these Gentiles to accept the Law. Since God had released Peter from the shackles of the Law—especially in his conflict with dietary laws—he could not have it both ways. In Paul's theology, God does not work like this, as He sent Jesus to reclaim all men! When Peter withdrew from fellowship with Gentile believers, he was rejecting the truth of the Gospel by not accepting Jews and Gentiles equally.

When Paul speaks of being "Jews by nature," he is stating that he and Peter are Jews by birth; and when he refers to the Gentiles as sinners (by birth), he is speaking of their separation from God and lack of the birthright of His Chosen. From another perspective, it is possible that Paul is unconsciously ranking the two groups, which results in placement of the Jew first in line to receive God's blessings, protection, and plan of salvation. Remember that when Paul would journey to a town or city, upon his arrival, he would first visit the local synagogue. Additionally, Paul acknowledges the importance of the two, writing, "To the Jew first and then to the Greek" (See Romans 1:16). Nonetheless, all men, Jew and Gentile, are justified by their faith in Jesus, not by the letter of the Law. In this case, for Paul, justification means to be vindicated because one decides to follow the edicts of the Lord. In addition, justification is equated with righteousness, as the person that is justified through faith is set right with God. Moreover, having been justified by faith, believers have peace through our Lord Jesus Christ (Romans 5:1). The theology advocated by Paul creates a difficult tension and will become a seed that will bloom for the new faith. Paul insists that the crucifixion (not the Mosaic Law) is central to the redemption of humanity because the Law did not cover the inception of the new era of Jesus. For Paul, the fate of humanity is steeped in the grace of Jesus, and these new Gentile believers must not be disrespected by a tradition that cannot save!

However, Paul's next question asks if (in their seeking to be justified in Christ) the Jews find that they are also among the sinners, does that mean that Jesus is likewise a minister of sin (v. 17)? In this case, if the term *sinners* is used to define those persons who identify as Gentile (who were thought of as evil because they were not given the Law), could Jesus be a minister or agent of sin, since belief in Christ is based on faith and not the Law? The answer is obviously no; but this verse serves as an answer to Paul's critics toward believers who are in harmony with God by placing their faith in Jesus, which (in their assessment) reduces Jesus to a minister of sin. Paul's critics felt that being loyal to and worshiping Jesus amounted to the sin of rejecting God.

III. CHRIST LIVES IN PAUL (GALATIANS 2:18–21)

In this section, Paul presents a compelling question by asking why he should rebuild what was once destroyed. Although he refers to himself as the one who was the author of this destruction and restoration, he actually gives credit to Jesus and the Spirit for destroying what was his old self and restructuring the new. Because the Law opened his eyes to his sin, his embrace of the Spirit allowed him to become a new person in Christ. Paul acknowledges that for him to make the mistake of returning to the Law, he would resort to being a transgressor against the Spirit, which would be contrary to the grace of God. Paul realizes that if a believer would return to the Law after trusting Christ alone for salvation, that Law would only demonstrate that he was a sinner, a lawbreaker.

Paul declares that since he has been crucified with Christ, his old self has died. This means that he has removed himself from the old nature, his weakness of possible coveting, and his lifestyle that kept him from being united with the Lord.

Paul declares that he lives for Christ because Jesus has completely wrapped Himself in the person of Paul, and through faith, Paul will be able to retain the spirit of the Lord in his life. This grasp of the spirit of Jesus allows Paul to become a vessel and witness for the faith, without losing his persona. On the contrary, however, the believer must ignore the negative connotations that, for example, being saved makes one a stiff, aloof person that loses his/her zest for life. Paul would argue vehemently against this thought, as living with the Lord brings unbridled joy to the believer and creates a clearer perspective on the beauty of God's world. Therefore, in living for the Son of God (Jesus), Paul is grateful for the opportunity for a blessed life of sanctification from the One who died (but was resurrected) to redeem him from the vestiges of sin, where only damnation and eternal separation from heaven is an option.

In conclusion, Paul summates his argument by returning to the weakness in the Law. In the defense of his case against Peter, Paul asks, "Why did Christ have to die" if the Law could provide righteousness and grace? In this case, Paul declares that he does not ignore or overlook the power of the grace of God, which is the power and the pathway to salvation. Remember, Paul is addressing the church at Galatia, who he rebukes for attempting to nullify grace by wanting to hold onto the Law. Further, such insistence on legal obedience rests on the theory that Christ died for nothing! If righteousness comes by keeping the Law, the cross was a futile gesture, the biggest mistake in the universe. This disagreement between Paul and

Peter has been overblown, and attempts have been made to place the men as antagonistic rivals. However, their friendship developed when Paul visited Jerusalem, where Paul stayed with Peter for fifteen days (Galatians 1:18). These men, while having different apostolic platforms, remained friends. They both believed in the Jesus Movement and the new direction guided by the Holy Spirit. Both men were fully committed to the Gospel, and Paul recognized Peter's mission to the people as similar to his mission to the Gentile nation.

THE LESSON APPLIED

One detriment to the growth of Christians is that in many cases, adults tend to return to former habits when in the presence of old friends. It is difficult to walk with the Lord when attempting to "hang out with the boys," when the lifestyle of "the boys" is contrary to the lifestyle of Jesus. For example, because of your commitment to the faith, you do not drink or smoke anymore; but your old friends insist that "one drink [or one hit] won't hurt," and you find yourself succumbing to the values of your old friendships. Resistance to these temptations can be found if the believer trusts in their faith and the ability to resist in the Lord. In the end, your walk with Jesus will be respected more by your old friends than any weakness displayed by trying to align with the crowd.

LET'S TALK ABOUT IT

Do you fall back into old habits when you reunite with old friends?

Adults are capable of influencing others for either right or wrong. In this lesson, Peter is influenced by certain men of Jerusalem, which caused him to act differently toward those that were supposed to be his friends. Can you remember having a friend that acted differently toward you when the two of you encountered their other friend? Unfortunately, this happens when people place differences between each other based on their moods and the convenience of "who" is actually the friend. In a day when influencers are praised and rewarded, they must be accountable for the direction of their influence.

GET SOCIAL

Share your views and tag us @rhboydco and use #FaithNotLaws.

Twitter
@rhboydco (#rhboydco)

Instagram
@rhboydco (#rhboydco)

Facebook
@rhboydco (#rhboydco)

www.rhboyd.com

HOME DAILY DEVOTIONAL READINGS
OCTOBER 16–22, 2023

MONDAY	TUESDAY	WEDNESDAY	THURSDAY	FRIDAY	SATURDAY	SUNDAY
So Great a Salvation	Christ Destroys the Power of Death	Delight in the Law of the Lord	Blessed with Every Spiritual Blessing	The Hope to Which We're Called	Receiving the Spirit	Redeemed from the Law's Curse
Hebrews 2:1–9	Hebrews 2:10–18	Psalm 1:1–6	Ephesians 1:3–14	Ephesians 1:15–23	Galatians 3:1–5	Galatians 3:6–18

THE SUPERIORITY OF THE GOSPEL

ADULT TOPIC: BACKGROUND SCRIPTURE: GALATIANS 3:1–18
ALL OR NOTHING AT ALL   LESSON PASSAGE: GALATIANS 3:1–14

GALATIANS 3:1—14

King James Version

O foolish Galatians, who hath bewitched you, that ye should not obey the truth, before whose eyes Jesus Christ hath been evidently set forth, crucified among you?

2 This only would I learn of you, Received ye the Spirit by the works of the law, or by the hearing of faith?

3 Are ye so foolish? having begun in the Spirit, are ye now made perfect by the flesh?

4 Have ye suffered so many things in vain? if it be yet in vain.

5 He therefore that ministereth to you the Spirit, and worketh miracles among you, doeth he it by the works of the law, or by the hearing of faith?

6 Even as Abraham believed God, and it was accounted to him for righteousness.

7 Know ye therefore that they which are of faith, the same are the children of Abraham.

8 And the scripture, foreseeing that God would justify the heathen through faith, preached before the gospel unto Abraham, saying, In thee shall all nations be blessed.

9 So then they which be of faith are blessed with faithful Abraham.

10 For as many as are of the works of the law are under the curse: for it is written, Cursed is every one that continueth not in all things which are written in the book of the law to do them.

11 But that no man is justified by the law in the sight of God, it is evident: for, The just shall live by faith.

New Revised Standard Version

YOU foolish Galatians! Who has bewitched you? It was before your eyes that Jesus Christ was publicly exhibited as crucified!

2 The only thing I want to learn from you is this: Did you receive the Spirit by doing the works of the law or by believing what you heard?

3 Are you so foolish? Having started with the Spirit, are you now ending with the flesh?

4 Did you experience so much for nothing?—if it really was for nothing.

5 Well then, does God supply you with the Spirit and work miracles among you by your doing the works of the law, or by your believing what you heard?

6 Just as Abraham "believed God, and it was reckoned to him as righteousness,"

7 so, you see, those who believe are the descendants of Abraham.

8 And the scripture, foreseeing that God would justify the Gentiles by faith, declared the gospel beforehand to Abraham, saying, "All the Gentiles shall be blessed in you."

9 For this reason, those who believe are blessed with Abraham who believed.

10 For all who rely on the works of the law are under a curse; for it is written, "Cursed is everyone who does not observe and obey all the things written in the book of the law"

11 Now it is evident that no one is justified before God by the law; for "The one who is righteous will live by faith."

MAIN THOUGHT: This only would I learn of you, Received ye the Spirit by the works of the law, or by the hearing of faith? (Galatians 3:2, KJV)

GALATIANS 3:1—14

12 And the law is not of faith: but, The man that doeth them shall live in them.

13 Christ hath redeemed us from the curse of the law, being made a curse for us: for it is written, Cursed is every one that hangeth on a tree:

14 That the blessing of Abraham might come on the Gentiles through Jesus Christ; that we might receive the promise of the Spirit through faith.

12 But the law does not rest on faith; on the contrary, "Whoever does the works of the law will live by them."

13 Christ redeemed us from the curse of the law by becoming a curse for us—for it is written, "Cursed is everyone who hangs on a tree"—

14 in order that in Christ Jesus the blessing of Abraham might come to the Gentiles, so that we might receive the promise of the Spirit through faith.

LESSON SETTING
  Time: Circa AD 49
  Place: Antioch

LESSON OUTLINE
  I. Paul Argues from His Experience (Galatians 3:1–5)
  II. Paul Argues from the Perspective of Abraham (Galatians 3:6–9)
  III. Paul Argues from the Perspective of the Law (Galatians 3:10–14)

UNIFYING PRINCIPLE

When trying to make positive changes in our lives, there is a tendency to be pulled back into old habits. How can we embrace change when it is in our best interests? With faith in Jesus Christ, we are strengthened in our resolve to embrace new and better possibilities and promises.

INTRODUCTION

Bible scholars must not overlook one of the central reasons for this letter from Paul to the Galatians, which was to correct the false teaching that one cannot be a Christian without obeying Jewish law, particularly the rite of circumcision. Paul's purpose was to speak against salvation by any other means but Jesus. And to lead the Galatian Christians back to true freedom in Christ. It was imperative that the Galatian believers follow the statutes and commandments of the new Church and resist the temptation and wrongheaded persuasions of the Judaizers to return to Mosaic Law. This lesson serves as a continued remonstration that the Law does not have salvific powers and that only through faith in Jesus Christ are men saved.

EXPOSITION

I. PAUL ARGUES FROM HIS EXPERIENCE (GALATIANS 3:1–5)

Paul begins this missive by calling the Galatians foolish. He is addressing particular Galatians, saying that they are "not using their heads" or "not thinking right." It is a rhetorical statement to reveal the opinions of the unbeliever for Christians. The Greek term *moros* indicates one who is stupid or nonsensical and, in this case, represents Paul's perspective of these

Galatians who were acting as if they were the victims of an evil spell or a bewitching by someone who practiced the dark arts. Paul had preached the reality of "Jesus crucified" in a very public manner, but because of the various negative influences that were present, it now appeared that the Galatian church had forgotten or felt that His crucifixion was not important. For Paul, it is disappointing that although the church had been taught about the crucified Jesus and the glorified implications of His death, these Galatians were deeming it as unnecessary or unholy.

Continuing the probe, Paul asks of the Galatians only one thing: "Did you receive the Spirit by the work of the Law or by faith upon hearing the truth?" Note the contrasting adverbial phrases and their implications on the members of this body. The members of the Galatian church were stymied here because their adherence to the Law forced them into the faction that would never accept salvation through any other means except the provisions of the Law. These members were juxtaposed with those who were convicted by the preaching and hearing of the Gospel and relied upon their embracing of salvation through faith in Jesus. For the Galatians to have been taught about the power of the Spirit, and then return to the aspects of the Law was a regression for the church. In obtaining the Spirit, Paul contrasts the ability of the Law against that of faith and which one would produce fruit. Herein lies the problem: to return to the Law reduces Jesus to a condemned man who was crucified for some unforgivable crime, and if that was the case, the strictness and austerity of the Law could never be associated with Jesus. However, if one receives the Spirit by hearing the Gospel, then, that person has been granted grace because he has embraced the gift by stepping out on his faith. The works of the Law are rendered inadequate and insufficient to grant the Spirit to the Church; therefore, the Spirit can only be received by faith.

Again, Paul asks if the Galatians are negatively foolish. These people knew better because Paul had convincingly preached and taught them, which resulted in these converts receiving the Spirit. But now, for some reason, they were regressing, reverting to the flesh, or depending upon the interpretation of man with what may be considered a hope that a combination of faith (Spirit) and works (flesh) would be better. Paul asked if they were foolish enough to think they could begin the Christian life in one way (by faith) and move on to spiritual maturity in another (by works). There was no provision under the Law for the Holy Spirit to do a work of sanctification. The Galatian believers probably thought that keeping the old Law would aid them in their spiritual lives, but it would not. In this case, if one receives the Spirit, there cannot be any substitute for the works of faith.

Paul notes that all believers suffer because of situations of some type; however, he rhetorically asks if the Galatians had suffered many things in vain, and then, questions whether their suffering was indeed futile. What he is referring to is the persecution the apostles and new believers experienced in the region of Galatia. After preaching, Paul was stoned, dragged outside of the city, and left for dead, where the dogs were to eat his body (Acts 14:19).

Paul would warn the Galatian converts that they also would suffer as Christians (Acts 14:21–22). If then, the Galatians returned to following the Law while rejecting grace, their suffering would have been in vain.

Verse 5 refers to the miracles that were produced by the power of the Spirit and faith, not by the Law. Paul wishes to know if the Galatians understand that it is "He who provides you with the Spirit and works miracles among you, do it by the works of the Law, or by hearing with faith." What Paul is asking is on what basis did God perform miracles among the Galatians by divine power, which was recorded in the book of Acts (14:3). It was clear that these supernatural works were not the result of the works of the Law but from their hearing, which leads to faith. The Galatians did not know the Law, and Paul's message was that of justification by faith.

II. Paul Argues from the Perspective of Abraham (Galatians 3:6–9)

To bolster his argument of appealing to faith rather than the Law, Paul referred to the account of Abraham, who entered into a covenant with Yahweh and received the blessings and an everlasting promise of being a great nation. Recall that a childless Abram was called out of the land of the Chaldeans to be the bedrock of this new family. What is important in this account is that Abraham could have rebuffed God's call; yet, he left his homeland and entered into a new region, based on his faith in Yahweh, who reckoned it to him as righteousness. Abraham believed in and trusted God, willing to be bound to a covenant based on this trust. Abraham would produce physical descendants through the

progeny of Isaac and Jacob who would represent the foundation of the Jewish nation. However, Paul argues that the heirs of this family are the spiritual descendants who believe in God and trust Him for their salvation. These are men and women of faith who accept their inheritance through the grace of God. Contrasted with the idea that works could produce salvation (and the concept that circumcision is required for justification), Paul argues the contrary and promotes the need for the believer to embrace a life of faith in the Lord, the author and giver of life, based on the gift of grace. Remember, Paul harmonizes his argument with God's declaration that "all nations will be blessed through Abraham" (Genesis 12:2). In this case, all people who are believers are descendants (sons) of Abraham because they are the progeny of his faith and dedication to Yahweh.

Therefore, the scriptural account foretells the time when God would justify and incorporate the Gentile into His Holy Family because of their faith—not because of a ritual that had been rendered obsolete by the advent of Jesus Christ. In this situation, the Gentile is not to be excluded from the Church because he was not given the Law, nor penalized because his culture was not exposed to it. When Paul states that the Gospel was preached to Abraham, it could be interpreted that it was the "Good News" (Gospel) that Abraham received, or the realization that Jesus was present when Abraham received the declaration of the blessing and promise. In receiving promises, Abraham, by faith, received the promise, which is the gift of salvation. This may not have been seen as the promise of the Messiah in the language that, per se, the contemporary church would be accustomed to; yet, the promise of the Messiah was present as evident in the genealogy of Jesus, the Messiah (see Matthew 1:1–17).

III. PAUL ARGUES FROM THE PERSPECTIVE OF THE LAW (GALATIANS 3:10–14)

Paul has now clarified that although the Jews had a connection to Abraham, that connection is not capable of providing saving grace. Moreover, he points out the danger of holding onto the Law that covered a bygone era and now, through the gift of Jesus, was rendered powerless. Paul then directs their attention to a segment of the Law that pronounces a curse on the people who continue to cling to its traditions. To highlight this component of his argument, Paul noted that Moses pronounced a series of curses from Mount Ebal (Deuteronomy 27:11–26), with the last curse stating, "Cursed is the one who does not confirm all the words of this Law," and (in a prepared response), "all the people shall say, Amen" (Deuteronomy 27:26).

Paul contrasts this idea with the words of James, who states that the one who is a keeper of the Law but stumbles at one point is guilty of breaking all the entirety of the Law. From this perspective, Paul argues that man alone cannot possibly keep all the laws, hence, his bondage. The summary nature of the twelfth curse, however, indicates that God desires a wholehearted obedience to the Law, both in public and in private. Paul used this verse to teach that no one could find eternal life by obeying the Law (Galatians 3:10). Eternal life is received only through God's grace when one places his faith in Jesus Christ as his substitutionary Sacrifice for sin (Romans 3:24–25; Ephesians 2:8–9). Paul quotes from Habakkuk 2:4 to stress that the righteous man shall live by faith. Paul will later write to the Roman church that a man is justified by faith apart from the deeds of the Law (Romans 3:28), which echoes the words from Hebrews 10:38 that declare "the just shall live by faith." This argument emphasizes that it is by faith (not works) that both Jews and Gentiles shall govern their lives.

Therefore, the Law is not based on faith, and one who adheres to the Law will be subject to the aforementioned inadequacies of the Law. However, those who live by faith and are called according to these principles shall bask in their resplendent benefits. Remember, Mosaic Law had a purpose for the era during which it was given: to counter the laws of Egypt and provide a structure of governance for a newly freed people who had no law of their own. Moses was told to speak to the children of Israel and tell them that they were not to walk in the ordinances of the Egyptians but to observe "My" (Yahweh's) judgments and statutes. Moreover, God said, "I am the Lord your God" (Leviticus 18:1–5), which is the foundation of the Law.

However, what Paul explains is that the Law brings a curse, but Jesus rescues the believer from this curse (e.g., "Cursed is everyone who hangs [being executed] on a tree," Deuteronomy 21:23). When Jesus was crucified, he was not only condemned by the Romans but also condemned by the Law. For Paul, the crucifixion was not a curse but a blessing in that it served as an act of redemption and restoration that allows justification and the promise of salvation for all believers. The destiny of the Christian nation is based on that which God transformed from "a curse" into "a care." This transformation created a scenario where the gift of Jesus Christ and the promises of Yahweh are available to all men, Jew and Gentile alike. The idea of the Gentiles receiving these blessings should not be misunderstood as God taking away Abraham's blessings to give to the Gentiles because the common denominator that bonds all men to the promise is faith in and through Jesus Christ. Moreover, the curse of "hanging from a tree" is removed because Christ is the Redeemer for all believers.

THE LESSON APPLIED

One of the more direct goals of this lesson is to understand that following Mosaic Law does not justify us. For contemporary Christians, much of the Law given to Moses is not applicable to modern society and is definitely not part of our culture. However, this lesson teaches us that many of the new converts to the faith of Paul's era attempted to cling to concepts that were not congruent with the concept of justification through faith in Jesus. Christians will often experience conflicting demands on their loyalty in their walk by faith. Yet, authentic Christian believers must eschew persons or situations that are determined to undermine the loyalty of the believer. To whomever is faithful to God, God will remain faithful, and to whomever is loyal to the Lord, the Lord will remain loyal.

LET'S TALK ABOUT IT

Have you ever felt rejected by society due to your Christian beliefs?

In our contemporary society, adults may be condemned for their faithfulness to high ideals. In many cases, when someone tries to live by certain moral standards, they are referred to as "goody two–shoes" or some other derogatory label that marks them as someone who is not to be part of the club (or even someone not to be trusted). Unfortunately, while some may exhibit these non-stellar attributes, true Christians realize that living a wholesome and holy life means exhibiting the very traits of a disciple of Jesus. We must continue our faithfulness to the practice of life within the "higher calling."

GET SOCIAL

Share your views and tag us
@rhboydco and use #Gospel.

Twitter
@rhboydco (#rhboydco)

Instagram
@rhboydco (#rhboydco)

Facebook
@rhboydco (#rhboydco)

www.rhboyd.com

HOME DAILY DEVOTIONAL READINGS
OCTOBER 23–29, 2023

MONDAY	TUESDAY	WEDNESDAY	THURSDAY	FRIDAY	SATURDAY	SUNDAY
A Promise to Abram's Offspring	An Imperishable Inheritance	God Chose the Poor to Be Heirs of the Kingdom	The Lord Is My Portion	God's Inheritance Is God's People	Heirs of God's Promise	Children of God
Genesis 12:1–9	1 Peter 1:3–12	James 2:1–7	Psalm 16	Deuteronomy 32:1–14	Hebrews 11:8–19	Galatians 3:23–4:7

FREED TO BECOME AN HEIR

ADULT TOPIC:	BACKGROUND SCRIPTURE: GALATIANS 3:19–4:7
FREE TO LIVE A MATURE LIFE	LESSON PASSAGE: GALATIANS 3:23–4:7

GALATIANS 3:23—4:7

King James Version

BUT before faith came, we were kept under the law, shut up unto the faith which should afterwards be revealed.

24 Wherefore the law was our schoolmaster to bring us unto Christ, that we might be justified by faith.

25 But after that faith is come, we are no longer under a schoolmaster.

26 For ye are all the children of God by faith in Christ Jesus.

27 For as many of you as have been baptized into Christ have put on Christ.

28 There is neither Jew nor Greek, there is neither bond nor free, there is neither male nor female: for ye are all one in Christ Jesus.

29 And if ye be Christ's, then are ye Abraham's seed, and heirs according to the promise.

• • • • • •

1 Now I say, That the heir, as long as he is a child, differeth nothing from a servant, though he be lord of all;

2 But is under tutors and governors until the time appointed of the father.

3 Even so we, when we were children, were in bondage under the elements of the world:

4 But when the fulness of the time was come, God sent forth his Son, made of a woman, made under the law,

5 To redeem them that were under the law, that we might receive the adoption of sons.

New Revised Standard Version

NOW before faith came, we were imprisoned and guarded under the law until faith would be revealed.

24 Therefore the law was our disciplinarian until Christ came, so that we might be reckoned as righteous by faith.

25 But now that faith has come, we are no longer subject to a disciplinarian,

26 for in Christ Jesus you are all children of God through faith.

27 As many of you as were baptized into Christ have clothed yourselves with Christ.

28 There is no longer Jew or Greek, there is no longer slave or free, there is no longer male and female; for all of you are one in Christ Jesus. .

29 And if you belong to Christ, then you are Abraham's offspring, heirs according to the promise.

• • • • • •

1 My point is this: heirs, as long as they are minors, are no better than those who are enslaved, though they are the owners of all the property,

2 but they remain under guardians and trustees until the date set by the father.

3 So with us; while we were minors, we were enslaved to the elemental spirits of the world.

4 But when the fullness of time had come, God sent his Son, born of a woman, born under the law,

5 in order to redeem those who were under the law, so that we might receive adoption as children.

MAIN THOUGHT: For ye are all the children of God by faith in Christ Jesus. (Galatians 3:26, KJV)

GALATIANS 3:23—4:7

<table>
<tr><td>King James Version</td><td>New Revised Standard Version</td></tr>
</table>

King James Version

6 And because ye are sons, God hath sent forth the Spirit of his Son into your hearts, crying, Abba, Father.

7 Wherefore thou art no more a servant, but a son; and if a son, then an heir of God through Christ.

New Revised Standard Version

6 And because you are children, God has sent the Spirit of his Son into our hearts, crying, "Abba! Father!"

7 So you are no longer a slave but a child, and if a child then also an heir through God.

LESSON SETTING
Time: Circa AD 49
Place: Antioch

LESSON OUTLINE
I. **Custody Under the Law (Galatians 3:23–25)**
II. **Sons of God Through the Promise (Galatians 3:26–29)**
III. **Guardianship Before Belief (Galatians 4:1–3)**
IV. **Sonship Through Christ (Galatians 4:4–7)**

UNIFYING PRINCIPLE

Young people look forward to growing up and making decisions without having to ask their parents' permission. What guides us in making responsible choices? In Galatians, Paul describes the Law as a disciplinarian (or parent) but now, on account of Christ, we are released from the Law to become children of God.

INTRODUCTION

In this lesson, Paul argues for the inheritance of God that is given to believers once they reach the proper stage of spiritual maturity and responsibility. Again, he argues against the Law and its weaknesses, including the paradigm of how birthrights are passed from the father to the son(s). Included in Paul's illustrations is Abraham and how he was the foundation of the promise of Yahweh. Paul notes that the Law served as a custodial master (to those who were not of age) to receive the inheritance prior to being ready to be sons of God through the promise. Additionally, Paul will demonstrate that the legal restrictions of guardianship would encompass the novice before he realized his system of belief. Nonetheless, once the new believer is accepted into the faith, he (or she) would receive the blessings of sonship through Christ.

EXPOSITION

I. CUSTODY UNDER THE LAW (GALATIANS 3:23–25)

Paul begins this section by arguing that before faith came, we were kept in custody under the Law, which, depending upon the interpretation of the term, may not be such a bad thing. The Greek term *phrouréō* may mean to guard, as from a military or jailer's perspective, or it can mean to preserve and keep spiritually, as one's guarding his own faith! However, here, Paul's interpretation is that the Law is keeping the believer from accessing the knowledge of faith in Jesus, which had not yet been revealed. God's revelation to His people is not always given in the period or timeframe that they would desire; however, His revelation is always accurate, true, and appropriate for the time in which it is needed. Faith was present and active in the Old Testament, and it would be a grave mistake to believe otherwise.

In verse 24, Paul softens his previous stance against the Law by embracing its benefits, noting that it has become a tutor that leads the believer to Christ. The term used for tutor, *paidagōgós*, is defined as an instructor of children, or a schoolmaster, originally referring to the slave who conducted the boys from home to the school. Yet, the word used here does not mean a "teacher" but an "attendant, custodian, or guardian," which was usually a slave whose job it was to accompany, train, and discipline the child. In this manner, the Law was such a disciplinarian until Christ, the Teacher, came. However, a better understanding of this concept is to understand that the Law did not actually lead us to Christ; it was the disciplinarian until Christ came. Through Jesus the Messiah, believers were given the opportunity to be justified by faith.

II. SONS OF GOD THROUGH THE PROMISE (GALATIANS 3:26–29)

The key to understanding the revelation and gift of faith in Jesus Christ is that believers become the sons of God, meaning that Christians are adopted into the Holy Family of God, where all rights and privileges of inheritance are bestowed. Just as a child is adopted into a loving family, privileges may be automatic because of the desires of the parents;

however, the adopted child must adapt to the rules and regulations of the house. In this case, there is a warning: believers who are adopted into the family of the Lord must embrace the edicts of Christianity; otherwise, the union will fail. The aforementioned believers, however, are ones who have reached spiritual maturity, as contrasted with the child that needed the guidance of the tutor. Now, as adults, they are able to utilize the gifts of their inheritance and may delight in the riches as mature Christians. Since many believers were not originally committed to the faith, they had to undergo a transformation to become one of God's sons. However, it must be noted that the changed agent is one's faith in Jesus Christ. To identify as a believer, these persons would follow the ordinance and example of Jesus and be baptized by water. Yet, it must be understood that the water baptism itself is not the saving agent; salvation comes from being baptized by the Spirit, which connects the believer to Jesus. Because of the Spirit, the former convert becomes a new creature and a new creation whose transformation is "lifesaving."

In verse 28, Paul returns to the idiom that identifies the Jew and the Greek. However here, rather than to speak of God's redemption to the Jew first, then, to the Greek (Gentile), Paul declares that there is no distinction or separate identity for believers who are in God's Holy Family. Furthermore, he expands upon those who are eligible to be in the family, noting that there is no dissimilarity or prejudice among slaves and freedmen, or males and females. When reading the Scriptures, many passages only identify "man," such as, "The righteous man shall live by faith" (Romans 1:17). In other cases, the sexes are defined, such as when Moses issued a command that "no man or woman will perform the work of contributions for the sanctuary" (Exodus 36:6). In the first example, "man" is used to identify both man and woman to explain the rules of this command. However, when God blesses "man" in the Scriptures, women (and children, by default) are included. Therefore, in His goal of redemption, God shows personal favoritism to no one (Galatians 2:6), but rather, favors the believer who is committed to the faith. The oneness of all Christians does not mean that people are robotic clones because there is inherent beauty in the individual who is part of the body of Christ.

III. GUARDIANSHIP BEFORE BELIEF (GALATIANS 4:1–3)

Being in a "sonship" in Christ must not be thought of as a problem. We have been taught to see our kinship with Jesus in the family unit as a brother. Here, Paul is illustrating a connection to the inheritance that has been granted to the believer and the dependency provided for the spiritually immature. Moreover, this passage will be easier understood when we think of Jesus as being God the Father, who is the provider of the adoption process. To illustrate the spiritual immaturity of those who lived under the Mosaic Law, Paul reminded the Galatian believers of certain characteristics of an heir as a minor child (*nēpios*, "infant, young child," in contrast with *huios*, "son"). As previously mentioned, the child —although he may be the heir of all of the property and wealth of his father—does not differ from the slave because he (and the slave) has a guardian that makes decisions for the child until the son reaches what is considered to be the age of a responsible adult. During ancient times, there are several accounts of boy rulers, such as Ptolemy XIII, who became pharaoh at age eleven and was overshadowed by his famous sister Cleopatra; or the young Pharaoh Tutankhamen (King Tut), who ascended to the throne at the tender age of nine. These rulers were too young and physically immature to have led the armies of their respective nations; they did not know the scope of world affairs nor the resources of their nations. Recall that in ancient societies, the king also served as the commanding general of the armies, which by default, often placed these children in the position to have to lead the battles, while fighting with or ahead of their men. Therefore, they were guided by counselors (i.e., guardians and managers) until they reached the day when they could realistically assume the throne. In many cases, when the boy-king reached adulthood, he had severe disagreements with the coalition of these managers and councilors, wanting his "own team" because these councilors were appointed by someone else.

While it can be proved from Roman law that property was transferred to a son only upon the death of the father, a literal reading of this understanding cannot be applied here. It would create serious difficulties, particularly with the application of the illustration later in this section, for it would imply that God had died. It is more likely that Paul has in mind a situation where the father, for some reason, establishes a guardianship while he is still alive.

Therefore, before we became believers, humanity was as children, who were not ready to assume the inheritance of the Father because our immaturity would not allow us to understand and embrace the knowledge and wisdom of the kingdom. Like the young pharaohs, we were guided by managers, under the domain of the guardians of this world, who probably did not have our best interests at heart (while all the while, benefiting from their appointed positions). Although our wealth and inheritances were held in the form of trusts, there are many who will never realize their wealth because of the "glittery shackles" of this world. It is only through our faith in Jesus that Christians are able to inherit the wealth of those protected trusts.

When Paul speaks of the elemental things of this world, he is recognizing the bondage of the legalistic practices of Judaism or (for the Gentiles) the bondage of heathenism. This notion will cause Paul to pose this question: "But now that you have come to know God, or rather to be known by God, how is it that you turn back again to the weak and worthless elemental things, to which you desire to be enslaved all over again?" (Galatians 4:9). At this juncture, it is important to understand the elemental things as the fundamental or foundational practices of both society and the Law, which can be restrictive or liberating. Believers must obviously choose to embrace the guidance of our managers (the Spirit) that will navigate us through the snares of illicit captivity as we pursue the goodness of the Father.

IV. SONSHIP THROUGH CHRIST (GALATIANS 4:4–7)

However, Paul interjects that all things happen according to the will of God, noting that when the fullness of time came, God sent forth His Son. This statement is based on the fulfillment of the Old Testament prophecies that are foundational to the coming Messiah. The fullness of time was not an afterthought, nor did it span a short window, but God's gift of Jesus into the world occurred over centuries of planning. God is a God of human history, and although the advent of the Messiah occurred during the era of Roman oppression, the period possibly served as a platform for what would become the new religion. This period of the first century was under Roman domination, which did bring a great measure of stability that allowed the faith to grow and eventually flourish. Ironically, the Romans who would allow Jesus to be crucified would mandate Christianity as the state religion under Constantine (AD 312–325) Here (v. 4), Paul uses the image of a child coming of age to say that Jesus came at a point in human history when the time was ripe and released humanity from bondage to the Law.

As sons (now that the adoption process is complete), we are able to receive the Spirit from the Son into the center of our being, the heart, which allows us to call out to the Father. Note that the term used here (v. 6), *Abba*, is the Aramaic word for "father," which was used in the everyday, spoken language among the people during Jesus' era. Because of the acceptance of God, believers are no longer slaves who are powerless and incapable of understanding their positions in the faith but are adult sons who are able to function and live as heirs of God. Believers are blessed because God laid plans for our inclusion into the Holy Family from the beginning of the epoch, as "He predestined us to adoption as sons through Jesus Christ to Himself, according to the kind intention of His will to the praise of the glory of His grace, which He freely bestowed on us in the Beloved" (Ephesians 1:5–6). In conclusion, Paul reminds his readers that each one of them, as a son, enjoys the full privileges of sonship and will receive from God everything that He promised to Abraham. The addition of the expression "through God" reminds Paul's readers of two things: (1) their sonship is a gift from God alone, not through any effort or merit on their part; and (2) since it is all from God, then, God will certainly see to it that whatever He has promised to His sons will be realized.

THE LESSON APPLIED

Adults become aware of the limited value of the Law as they better understand their freedom in Christ. Because of our lack of understanding about the culture of Paul's era, we are far removed in our consideration of the traditions and impact of the Law upon the people. Although the Law was primarily given to the Jews, many of its civil and moral aspects affected the Gentile nations. Since contemporary Christians do not have a connection to the Law, it is imperative that we understand and embrace the gift of the Spirit and grace, which allow us to be free in our relationship with Jesus Christ. As God's chosen people, we must model a free and faithful life.

LET'S TALK ABOUT IT

How can there be unity in an increasingly intolerant world?

Adults acknowledge those who are different from them as sisters and brothers in Christ. We live in a society that has become increasingly anti-Jesus, and is producing overwhelming groups of non-believers, atheists, and those who are indifferent. Yet, we must celebrate the diversity of the faithful segment of Christians from diverse faiths and denominations who are our brothers and sisters.

GET SOCIAL

Share your views and tag us @rhboydco and use #heirs.

Twitter
@rhboydco (#rhboydco)

Instagram
@rhboydco (#rhboydco)

Facebook
@rhboydco (#rhboydco)

www.rhboyd.com

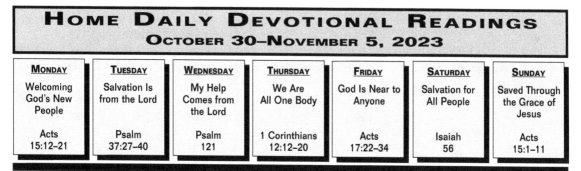

HOME DAILY DEVOTIONAL READINGS
OCTOBER 30–NOVEMBER 5, 2023

MONDAY	TUESDAY	WEDNESDAY	THURSDAY	FRIDAY	SATURDAY	SUNDAY
Welcoming God's New People	Salvation Is from the Lord	My Help Comes from the Lord	We Are All One Body	God Is Near to Anyone	Salvation for All People	Saved Through the Grace of Jesus
Acts 15:12–21	Psalm 37:27–40	Psalm 121	1 Corinthians 12:12–20	Acts 17:22–34	Isaiah 56	Acts 15:1–11

WHAT IS REQUIRED FOR SALVATION?

ADULT TOPIC: ENLARGING OUR VISION	BACKGROUND SCRIPTURE: ACTS 15:1–21 LESSON PASSAGE: ACTS 15:1–11

ACTS 15:1–11

King James Version

AND certain men which came down from Judaea taught the brethren, and said, Except ye be circumcised after the manner of Moses, ye cannot be saved.

2 When therefore Paul and Barnabas had no small dissension and disputation with them, they determined that Paul and Barnabas, and certain other of them, should go up to Jerusalem unto the apostles and elders about this question.

3 And being brought on their way by the church, they passed through Phenice and Samaria, declaring the conversion of the Gentiles: and they caused great joy unto all the brethren.

4 And when they were come to Jerusalem, they were received of the church, and of the apostles and elders, and they declared all things that God had done with them.

5 But there rose up certain of the sect of the Pharisees which believed, saying, That it was needful to circumcise them, and to command them to keep the law of Moses

6 And the apostles and elders came together for to consider of this matter.

7 And when there had been much disputing, Peter rose up, and said unto them, Men and brethren, ye know how that a good while ago God made choice among us, that the Gentiles by my mouth should hear the word of the gospel, and believe.

8 And God, which knoweth the hearts, bare them witness, giving them the Holy Ghost, even as he did unto us;

New Revised Standard Version

THEN certain individuals came down from Judea and were teaching the brothers, "Unless you are circumcised according to the custom of Moses, you cannot be saved."

2 And after Paul and Barnabas had no small dissension and debate with them, Paul and Barnabas and some of the others were appointed to go up to Jerusalem to discuss this question with the apostles and the elders.

3 So they were sent on their way by the church, and as they passed through both Phoenicia and Samaria, they reported the conversion of the Gentiles and brought great joy to all the brothers and sisters.

4 When they came to Jerusalem, they were welcomed by the church and the apostles and the elders, and they reported all that God had done with them.

5 But some believers who belonged to the sect of the Pharisees stood up and said, "It is necessary for them to be circumcised and ordered to keep the law of Moses."

6 The apostles and the elders met together to consider this matter.

7 After there had been much debate, Peter stood up and said to them, "My brothers, you know that in the early days God made a choice among you, that I should be the one through whom the Gentiles would hear the message of the good news and become believers.

8 And God, who knows the human heart, testified to them by giving them the Holy Spirit, just as he did to us,

MAIN THOUGHT: And God, which knoweth the hearts, bare them witness, giving them the Holy Ghost, even as he did unto us; And put no difference between us and them, purifying their hearts by faith. (Acts 15:8–9, KJV)

ACTS 15:1–11

<table>
<tr><td>King James Version</td><td>New Revised Standard Version</td></tr>
<tr><td>

9 And put no difference between us and them, purifying their hearts by faith.

10 Now therefore why tempt ye God, to put a yoke upon the neck of the disciples, which neither our fathers nor we were able to bear?

11 But we believe that through the grace of the Lord Jesus Christ we shall be saved, even as they.

</td><td>

9 and in cleansing their hearts by faith he has made no distinction between them and us.

10 Now therefore why are you putting God to the test by placing on the neck of the disciples a yoke that neither our ancestors nor we have been able to bear?

11 On the contrary, we believe that we will be saved through the grace of the Lord Jesus, just as they will."

</td></tr>
</table>

LESSON SETTING
Time: Circa AD 49–50
Place: Antioch–Jerusalem

LESSON OUTLINE
I. The Dissension
(Acts 15:1–5)
II. The Discussion
(Acts 15:6–11)

UNIFYING PRINCIPLE

Some laws become obsolete and, like scaffolds, no longer serve the purpose for which they were originally designed. How can we discern which laws are obsolete? Peter rightly asserts that faith in Jesus Christ eliminates the need for slavish adherence to former laws, such as circumcision, for salvation.

INTRODUCTION

This lesson focuses on an argument of dissension that morphed into an agreement of discussion. The events lead to the climax of the lesson, which is the Council of Jerusalem, consisting of the Pharisees and elders of the Jerusalem church. At stake are the new converts, who are being directed to follow Mosaic Law versus the guidance of faith in Jesus through the Holy Spirit. The Council at Jerusalem is important because its ruling, erroneous or correct, could have

had lasting implications for the new church and Paul's missionary ventures. It was a blessing that the assembly rejected the old ways of the Law and embraced faith in Jesus Christ. One added benefit was that James, the brother of Jesus, was the leader of the church. The account happens between the first and second missionary journeys.

EXPOSITION

I. THE DISSENSION
(ACTS 15:1–5)

Luke begins the report by noting that some men came down from Judea to Antioch. While he was staying with Simon the Tanner (Acts 10:5), the Lord revealed to Peter that what God had cleansed and considered clean would be purified and acceptable for his consumption. However, this revelation had further implications, as it also indicated that both Jew and Gentile believers were acceptable to the Lord. Nonetheless, Peter, who had participated in the common meals and fellowshipped in the worship with Gentiles, now (upon their arrival to Antioch) distanced himself from them because they were preaching cultural divisions of food laws and that circumcision was necessary to be saved. Recall that circumcision served as a foundational principle for Jewish men, in that it signified the acceptance of the original covenant between Abraham and the Lord. This ritual of cutting away the foreskin was to be performed on Hebrew males on the eighth day following their birth; however, Abraham was an adult when the covenant was formed. Many Jews were possibly afraid that they were breaking the Law—and would be punished—by not being circumcised or allowing uncircumcised males into the movement (church). While the agreement between Abraham and Yahweh commanded circumcision, the Law also contained a warning that an uncircumcised male who is not circumcised in the flesh of his foreskin "shall be cut off from his people [because] he has broken My covenant" (Genesis 17:14). Herein lies the problem of the cultural divide that Yahweh had bridged: no man is clean, and the Jerusalem church had accepted these Gentile converts without the circumcision requirement; so, why should the church return to this unjust Law and custom that Yahweh had corrected? These Pharisees who continued to embrace the legalism of the Law did so when it was convenient and served their purposes. They had come to create a division that they could not repair by rejecting the mandates of the new faith that were given by God.

Paul and Barnabas had been great friends and co-laborers on the First Missionary Journey, and now, it seems disheartening that this issue of dietary laws and circumcision for the Gentile converts could possibly create dissension between the two men. Yet, both men rejected the overtures of these Pharisees and were asked to go to Jerusalem to address the Council in rejecting these issues that were dividing the new church. As previously mentioned, Barnabas, also known as Joseph, was a Gentile of Cyprian birth, who was given his known name by the apostles, which when translated, means "son of encouragement." Barnabas had earlier demonstrated his commitment to the movement by selling a tract of land and giving the proceeds to the apostles (Acts 4:36–37). Barnabas was what we would call "all in" and would support the inclusion of Gentile converts into the faith without having to adhere to the old customs required by the Law. The seriousness of the problem presented here is that the Pharisees (and some other apostles) continued to reject the directives of the Lord and were bringing harm to the church by pulling away from the doctrine of grace. Along with some others who possibly served as unbiased witnesses, Paul and Barnabas were qualified for this task as they embraced the method of receiving salvation through grace.

Antioch is located some 300 miles north of Jerusalem, and as Paul and Barnabas journeyed toward the city, they had ample time to share in the joy over the conversions of their Gentile brothers and the methods that had been deemed successful. Additionally, what may have weighed on their minds is that they had the burden of realizing the task of addressing the Council and attempting to convince many of the conservative members of the assembly to move to the concept of grace. Nevertheless, they made their way toward Jerusalem, filled with resolve that the Lord was with them. Notice that Luke mentions the route of their trip, especially, Phoenicia and Samaria. Coming from Antioch in the north, the road traveled would take them along the coast through Berytus, Tyre, and Sidon, which at this time were places of great importance, as it was evident that there were Christian communities in Phoenicia, as well as in Samaria. Therefore, their journey was not without the deliberate spreading of the Gospel and the continued evangelizing and conversion of new converts to the faith.

Finally, the group of travelers reached Jerusalem. We are not told of the time of their arrival, or the days spent in Phoenicia and Samaria; however, they were well-received by the Jerusalem church and her apostles and elders. The report was well received, which completely frustrated the men who had instigated the conflict during their sojourn to Antioch. Remember, all of Paul's antagonists were not Pharisees, but included a segment of unnamed apostles unknown by Paul, who were appointed by the elders of the Jerusalem church.

Paul distinguished true from false apostles (2 Corinthians 11:13; cf. Revelation 2:2), and he acknowledged "signs of a true apostle," apparently including "signs and wonders and mighty works" (2 Corinthians 12:12). Paul may also have thought about his having seen the risen Jesus as sufficient for his being an apostle (1 Corinthians 9:1). At any rate, some people in Corinth and Galatia had challenged Paul's apostleship (cf. Galatians 2:8), perhaps on the grounds that he had not followed the pre-resurrection Jesus. Paul insisted that he was an apostle through Jesus Christ and God the Father, not through human means (Galatians. 1:1). However, the Council was

joyous in knowing that additional souls had been added to the fellowship, which served as confirmation that all who were involved and dedicated to the new faith ultimately had the support of the Lord. Remember, the leader of the Jerusalem church is James, the brother of Jesus, and he and the Jerusalem elders must have been jubilant that Paul and Barnabas were able to introduce converts to the faith in and around Antioch and especially in the cites en route to Jerusalem.

Nonetheless, the joy of the assembly was short-lived because some of the Pharisees stood up upon hearing their report, shouting, "It is necessary to circumcise Gentiles and force them to follow the Law of Moses" (v. 5). Again, the argument over the method of justification is being put to the test. Paul had been arguing that the stoic Law inhibits the believer's path to justification because only the grace of the Lord has saving power. This sect of Pharisees, with their aversion to following the new concept, are reminiscent of the Pharisees who opposed Jesus during His earthly ministry. Seemingly, these men could not reconcile their cultural "Jewishness," with its prejudices and customs, to the new all-inclusive faith. By clinging to the rigidity and unyielding principles of the Law, these Pharisees are outrightly rejecting Jesus and the movement to which they are supposedly committed.

II. THE DISCUSSION (ACTS 15:6–11)

After hearing all sides of the issue, and not to be dissuaded, the apostles and elders may have gone into what we would call an "executive session" to reach a conclusion to the problem (and possibly, others). That the members had much debate has provided several perspectives among scholars, as the term *zétēsis* (debate) may indicate a general or terse discussion. Rather, the term suggests a word used by the Greeks to indicate philosophical inquiry. In the New Testament, however, it indicates an exchange of (heated) words, rather than a true search. An example of this dissension is found in the strife between the disciples of John and the Jews who argued over ceremonial washing and purification (i.e., John's practice of baptism, John 3:25).

The similarity of the Jews wanting to cling to the older ways had occurred in previous situations. Peter, however, stood among the assembly and declared, "Brethren, you know that in the early days God made a choice among you, that by my mouth the Gentiles would hear the word of the gospel and believe." Peter was resolute in his stance that it was God that had made the choice, meaning that it was Yahweh who had sent Peter on the mission to evangelize the Gentiles; it had not been something that Peter decided to do on his own. Therefore, if the directive of God was obeyed, then, why should it not be followed in this current situation? Sharing with the assembly, Peter reflected that he stood up in the midst of the brethren (a gathering of about one hundred and twenty persons), including the women, Mary, the mother of Jesus, and His brothers. At that time, Peter declared that the Scripture concerning the arrest of Jesus had to be fulfilled (Acts 1:15–16). Peter (who, in his hour of despair, had abandoned Jesus) could now speak with conviction because he knew, even in his fear, that Jesus had not abandoned him. Nonetheless, through the preaching of the Word of the Lord, these Gentiles received the Gospel and believed in Jesus and His mission.

Peter's argument for the Council to "search their hearts" is an appeal to the faith of the assembly, that their thoughts and decisions would be guided by the Holy Spirit. For Peter, the guidance of the Holy Spirit is crucial and indispensable to the success of this Council. Peter understands that any rules and edicts that emanate from the decisions of those who are gathered could have either meaningful or disastrous consequences for the movement and the faith. Peter's discourse is a personal testimony about the gift of the Holy Spirit. Peter has had his issues, among them, denying his acquaintance to Christ during Jesus' arrest and the distancing of himself with his Gentile friends. However, because of the grace of God and the forgiveness therein, Peter can easily argue that it is the same gift of the Holy Spirit he had received that is now given to the Gentiles. Peter declares that he and all additional believers have had their hearts cleansed by their faith in Jesus Christ. Peter reminds the Council that the Spirit has not made any distinction between "us" (Jews) and "them" (Gentiles) because the gift of the Spirit is not discriminatory.

Therefore, Christians believe that we are saved through the grace of the Lord Jesus (v. 11). Here, Peter argues his conviction, that all believers, Jew and Gentile, are saved through grace and faith without the act of circumcision or the yoke of the Law. The statement, "We are saved, just as they are," is amazing because a Jew under the Law would say the opposite, and in reverse order ("They are saved as we are"); however, one who knew God's grace as Peter did would not say that. Salvation for anyone—Jew or Gentile—is by God's grace (v. 11) and is by faith. This declaration is not meant to be confined to the present time but is futuristic, knowing that God will save and justify future believers who dare to embrace the call of Jesus through their faith. The lesson concludes with the impact of Peter's speech and his argument for the need to eschew the traditions of the Law that serve to shackle the movement of the new church in the mission of Jesus Christ. The silence of the assembly confirmed the power and direction of the Holy Spirit.

The Lesson Applied

One of the main points of this lesson chronicles Peter's change of heart and mind on the spiritual requirements of the need for physical circumcision. Whereas Peter had initially embraced Gentile converts who did not have to meet the circumcision requirement forwarded by the Judaizers, he later waffled on his belief. As God revealed his error, Peter redeemed himself by supporting Paul and advocating for the need to embrace the faith through Jesus Christ. Christians who walk with the Lord must constantly work to cultivate an awareness of the Holy Spirit in the discernment process. This account must not be taken as Peter's vacillating on the issue but should be seen as his being directed by the Spirit of the Lord.

Let's Talk About It

Why must we respect all denominations, even those that practice faith differently?

Adults grow as they learn respect for all who manifest faith in Jesus Christ. Adults or mature Christians have grown beyond denominationalism or the need to place one group's religious practice above others. Mature Christians must not be found in the position of judging which evangelical group with its specific ordinances and practices are guaranteed a place in heaven. Mature Christians should only be concerned that how we are living is satisfactory in the eyes of the Lord.

Get Social

Share your views and tag us @rhboydco and use #Salvation.

Twitter
@rhboydco (#rhboydco)

Instagram
@rhboydco (#rhboydco)

Facebook
@rhboydco (#rhboydco)

www.rhboyd.com

Home Daily Devotional Readings
November 6–12, 2023

Monday	Tuesday	Wednesday	Thursday	Friday	Saturday	Sunday
Let Us Love One Another	Perfect Love Casts Out Fear	Love and Serve the Lord	Faith Working Through Love	The Greatest Commandment Is Love	Loving Deeds	Fulfill the Law Through Love
1 John 4:7–13	1 John 4:14–21	Deuteronomy 10:12–22	Galatians 5:1–6	Matthew 22:34–40	Leviticus 19:11–18	1 Corinthians 13:8-13; Romans 13:8–10

LOVE FULFILLS THE LAW

1 CORINTHIANS 13:8–13; ROMANS 13:8–10

King James Version

CHARITY never faileth: but whether there be prophecies, they shall fail; whether there be tongues, they shall cease; whether there be knowledge, it shall vanish away.

9 For we know in part, and we prophesy in part.

10 But when that which is perfect is come, then that which is in part shall be done away.

11 When I was a child, I spake as a child, I understood as a child, I thought as a child: but when I became a man, I put away childish things.

12 For now we see through a glass, darkly; but then face to face: now I know in part; but then shall I know even as also I am known.

13 And now abideth faith, hope, charity, these three; but the greatest of these is charity.

• • • Romans 13:8–10 • • •

8 Owe no man any thing, but to love one another: for he that loveth another hath fulfilled the law.

9 For this, Thou shalt not commit adultery, Thou shalt not kill, Thou shalt not steal, Thou shalt not bear false witness, Thou shalt not covet; and if there be any other commandment, it is briefly comprehended in this saying, namely, Thou shalt love thy neighbour as thyself.

10 Love worketh no ill to his neighbour: therefore love is the fulfilling of the law.

New Revised Standard Version

LOVE never ends. But as for prophecies, they will come to an end; as for tongues, they will cease; as for knowledge, it will come to an end.

9 For we know only in part, and we prophesy only in part,

10 but when the complete comes, the partial will come to an end.

11 When I was a child, I spoke like a child, I thought like a child, I reasoned like a child; when I became an adult, I put an end to childish ways.

12 For now we see in a mirror, dimly, but then we will see face to face. Now I know only in part; then I will know fully, even as I have been fully known.

13 And now faith, hope, and love remain, these three, and the greatest of these is love.

• • • Romans 13:8–10 • • •

8 Owe no one anything, except to love one another; for the one who loves another has fulfilled the law.

9 The commandments, "You shall not commit adultery; You shall not murder; You shall not steal; You shall not covet;" and any other commandment, are summed up in this word, "You shall love your neighbor as yourself."

10 Love does no wrong to a neighbor; therefore, love is the fulfilling of the law.

MAIN THOUGHT: For this, Thou shalt not commit adultery, Thou shalt not kill, Thou shalt not steal, Thou shalt not bear false witness, Thou shalt not covet; and if there be any other commandment, it is briefly comprehended in this saying, namely, Thou shalt love thy neighbour as thyself. (Romans 13:9, KJV)

LESSON SETTING
Time: Circa AD 55–57
Place: Corinth and Ephesus

LESSON OUTLINE
I. **The Supremacy of Love Over Gifts (1 Corinthians 13:8–13)**
II. **Love Fulfills the Law (Romans 13:8–10)**

UNIFYING PRINCIPLE

We desire to follow rules and practices that lead to a rightful and satisfying way of life. When there are so many choices before us, how do we know what is the best and most pleasing way of living? Paul asserts that the whole of the Mosaic Law is summed up and fulfilled in the act of love.

INTRODUCTION

In this lesson, we will survey Paul's argument for the supremacy of love and the unlimited power that it wields. In his discourse, Paul reflects on the many other gifts that are given to the believer and notes that these entities will one day become extinct. While listing several characteristics of love, Paul connects the source of love to Jesus, who is the embodiment of love and the gift of love to humanity. Moreover, to illustrate the power of love, Paul focuses on the commandment (Law) that humans must love one another as we love ourselves. In his writings to both the churches at Rome and Corinth, Paul is pleading for the need to embrace the gift of love. In both cases, Paul argues that love is not some fleeting emotion; it is a permanent attribute and gift because it is foundational to the gift of Jesus in God's redemption of the world. In this lesson, we are reminded that gifts, even spiritual gifts, are temporary and will expire in due season, especially at the second coming of Jesus. However, Paul lists three gifts —faith, hope, and love—that will never perish because they are grounded in Jesus' mission and the fact that He and His people (the Church) are eternal.

EXPOSITION
I. THE SUPREMACY OF LOVE OVER GIFTS (1 CORINTHIANS 13:8–13)

Paul begins this section by espousing the idea of the permanency of love. For Paul, love is the most important human element of all the Christian graces because of its Source. Paul declares that love is eternal and trustworthy (i.e., love never fails). In verse 8, Paul uses the term *agape*, which is understood as a sacrificial love, versus *phileo*, which is a brotherly love. In his comparison, Paul notes that God gave additional gifts, but none compare to the gift of love. First, he notes that prophecy (which was a mainstay for the direction and encouragement of Israel) will one day have served its purpose.

If Old Testament prophecy is surveyed, outside of its warnings and predictions, it points toward the coming of the Messiah, who brought a new method to justification and salvation. Because of Jesus, the gift of New Testament prophecy will shift to include Gentile believers who are grounded in the foundation of the apostles and prophets—the Body of Christ. The "prophets" are of the New Testament era, not the Old Testament. These men received the revelation of the mystery of the Church in the present age, which had been hidden in days past, that is, in Old

Testament times (Colossians 1:26). Paul notes that the gift of tongues will also one day have served its purpose and no longer exist. Recall that "tongues" can be simplified as speaking in different languages, and "spiritual tongues" are a gift because believers are able to understand and share in these diversely divine vernaculars. The day of Pentecost serves as a focal point regarding the believers from many regions having been given the ability to celebrate the arrival of the Holy Spirit, which signaled the birth of the Church. In our contemporary period, the "gifts of tongues" continue to exist to whom God provides the utterances; however, Paul points to a time when tongues will not be necessary, as all believers will share a permanent heavenly language.

Every gift is linked in some way to the building up of the church through maturity—some gifts (such as tongues), functioning in the early years of the Church Age and others, continuing on until the church is perfected. When that perfection is achieved, the gifts will have served their purposes and be rendered obsolete; but this will not happen to love. Additionally, if the gift of knowledge remains, it, too, will cease to exist, along with prophecy (which is usually connected to knowledge), although it is essential for the life of the Church. This is the essence of Paul's saying that "we know in part and prophesy in part" (v. 9) because with the coming of the perfect age, there will not be a need to "know in full and prophesy in full," removing any gift that is incomplete, i.e., "the partial will be done away" (v. 10). This concept will occur because of the coming of the One Paul refers to as the Perfect, which is representative of the second coming of Christ. Some understand this to refer to the completion of the canon of Scripture, but that would mean that we now see more clearly than Paul did. Though perfection remains the goal for Christians in this life, and a relative perfection can be achieved, Paul envisioned an eventual state of entire perfection for those who are in Christ. He argues that even the most impressive spiritual gifts fall short of God's final intention for His people. Although much debated, Paul declares that the church will reach its state of perfection upon Christ's return.

Continuing, Paul alludes to the aspect of Christian maturity, relating to his personal experiences of speaking, thinking, and reasoning as one who is a child. In one of the more recognizable verses of Scripture, Paul explains, "When I was a child, I used to speak like a child, think like a child, reason like a child; when I became a man, I did away with childish things" (1 Corinthians 13:11). This ideology does not refer to a numerical age, as children mature at different levels. Here, Paul encourages the believers to move toward the awareness of a "higher calling," which will bring them closer to an understanding of their decisions during their walk with the Lord. Their maturity will also create a more dynamic sense of ecstasy in their worship! Notice that in his child-man comparison, Paul alludes to a mature man, not a person who has reached a certain societal age. In addition, the church at Corinth was hampered by childish internecine battles that weakened the body. Paul notes his own childlike experiences, which could refer to his days of being a persecutor of the church; however, when he became a man (as he grew in the spirit and grace of the Lord), he put away childish things. In verse 11, Paul lists three reasons for "putting away childish things" that would erode his ministry and his ability to spread the Gospel. First, Paul does not want to speak like a child because as an apostle, the phonetic voice of a child is usually high-pitched, as the male child has not gone through puberty. Moreover, a child will not have a developed vocabulary and due to the lack of experience, will not be able to explain things reasonably.

This facet is important because the audience must be able to understand the message if one is going to be a messenger for the Lord. Second, thinking like a child means performing immature and unreasonable actions that only serve the interests of the child. The sweetest of children are by nature selfish and self-centered. Have you witnessed children fighting over a toy, or having a "fit," while screaming, "Mine"?

Sadly, due to their lack of reasoning, the world is inundated with carjackings, shootings, and murders committed by children who rely on emotion to solve interpersonal conflicts. Paul's thoughts had to focus on the message of Jesus, with a deep awareness of his calling, which would allow him to evangelize God's people. Third, Paul had detractors and faced enemies of the Gospel and, as a messenger of Christ, was subjected to facing his battles with love and reason. If he were to attempt to use child-like reasoning, he would not be able to realize the art of conflict resolution, which would be needed to guide and hold the churches together when the influences of Satan were trying to rip them apart.

The child lacks the experiences and viewpoint of the world and life, which would not allow the child to foster any correct decisions. Moreover, children cannot take care of themselves, and Paul knew he was constantly under God's care. In this scenario, the Church must move beyond the simplicity of an immature nature and become adults in their quest for perfection.

A city like Corinth, famous for its bronze mirrors, would have particularly appreciated Paul's final illustration. Here, Paul notes that the image in the mirror happens to be dim, probably because ancient mirrors were made of polished metal and therefore, gave a generally less-clear reflection. This prompts Paul to declare that in order to fully appreciate and submit to God's will, he clearly sees God face-to-face. While it is generally known that a man could never survive seeing the actual face of God, the imagery that Paul presents describes his spiritual encounter with God. The phrase "face-to-face" is not found elsewhere in the New Testament, but its meaning is plain, as Numbers 12:8 similarly refers to God and Moses speaking "mouth to mouth." This phrase should be understood as Paul's understanding the activities or directives of God and knowing that "God fully understands [him]." The term *abide* (*ménō*), may be defined as "to remain," to "dwell," or to "live" (in place); however, a more precise understanding of the declaration is that the three gifts are to continue in the lives of the believer. Since these three virtues remain after all the gifts have ceased, they should be cultivated.

Love is the greatest, since it expresses God and Calvary. Nonetheless, the triad of faith, hope, and love are currently the priority of all of the gifts, as faith and hope will result in love, which is eternal and will reign supreme in Jesus Christ.

II. LOVE FULFILLS THE LAW (ROMANS 13:8–10)

In our move to Romans 13:8, it seems as if Paul has segued to another topic by declaring that one should owe nothing to anyone. However, he begins this illustration by connecting it to the prominent theme of loving one another. Initially, Paul's command is, literally, not to continue in debt. However, love is a debt one can never fully discharge. The thought here should not be read literally as to forbid the taking of any loans; the point is that debts incurred should be paid. Believers are summoned to pay the debt of love to others, which in this case, is a debt that never comes to an end. In this illustration, Paul compares the Law, which commands that we honor our debts, while also noting that we are commanded to love our neighbor, which is a fulfillment of the Law. However, the Law is not an agent of salvation for the Christians in the church at Rome.

The illustration here is that we not be indebted to another in the form of money, land, or any other commodity. Being a debtor places a person under unnecessary stress and creates a certain dependence upon the borrower to the one who is owed. Borrowers must be committed to repaying their debt or face the consequences from raised interests, forfeiture of property, or even time in jail. Here, Paul is speaking of being in debt to love, where there is a commitment that one should not default nor be able to relinquish. The most positive assessment of this image is that the debt remands the debtor to the one who holds the mortgage, and the illustration here is that believers are in perpetual debt to the "One who paid it all."

For Paul to have seemingly railed against the Law—considering it a yoke and possible stumbling block to the believer trying to access the concepts of faith, grace, and the Spirit—here, Paul returns to the strictness of the Law, which serves as a guide to moral living. Highlighting verse 9, Paul returns to the weakness of coveting, which has a direct influence upon the sixth, seventh, and eighth commandments. Yet, his return to these aspects of the Law supports Paul's continued argument for the power of love. Paul notes that the commandment to love is central to Yahweh's Gift to humanity. Here, Paul may have referred to Yahweh's command as the people were not to hate their fellow countrymen, nor commit any form of vengeance, nor bear any grudges, but they were to "love [their] neighbor as [themselves]" (Leviticus 19:18–19). The foundation for this command is, "You shall love the LORD your God with all your heart, with all your soul, and with all your strength" (Deuteronomy. 6:5). The New Testament is filled with commands to love one's neighbor and also one another, "as you would love yourself."

Therefore, love will never bring harm to our neighbors nor to ourselves. Additionally, in order to have love for oneself, we must first love God! The Law is filled with commands to love (hahab), specifically, to love God, as in this example from Deuteronomy: "You shall diligently keep all these commandments which I am commanding you to do, to love the LORD your God, to walk in all His ways and hold fast to Him" (Deuteronomy 11:22). World history has shown that humanity has failed to first love God because of the lack of love that people have for each other. As believers who have accepted love as a prominent instrument of humanity, we have embraced the gift of Jesus (and fulfilled the Law), while living within a moral compass. In this case, Christian believers who love the Lord obey the whole commandment, not a part thereof. Therefore, believers have a duty to love our neighbors and to be committed to our best interests because it sets the status and stability of the entire community, and the Church, where the benefits are obvious.

THE LESSON APPLIED

Mature Christians become more and more aware that love is superior to all the commandments and laws of the human community. While the meaning of the word "love" and its intentions are mostly misused, the world would be edified if humanity would seek to demonstrate and live by its true applications. To love someone because of what can be gained is not true love, and the result will be as

pretentious as the method by which it was given. However, in a world that needs true love, the command to love our neighbors reaches far beyond the next driveway or yard next door. The community of believers must not be afraid to carry the banner of authentic love.

LET'S TALK ABOUT IT

In what ways do you experience God's love daily?

Mature Christians grow in their love for God as they become aware of God's gracious love for them. Christians must not limit God's love to the "things" He provides, the tangible items, but must realize that the greatest aspects of His love are found in a daily walk with Him. Things such as cars, houses, and money will fade and go away, but God's love is eternal and will never vanish. It is the mature Christian who realizes that we operate in a comfort zone dominated by God's love. For the believers who have been called according to His purpose and who strive to become men and women of goodwill, God's love is unlimited and will never fail. Therefore, what have you to lose?

GET SOCIAL

Share your views and tag us @rhboydco and use #Love.

Twitter
@rhboydco (#rhboydco)

Instagram
@rhboydco (#rhboydco)

Facebook
@rhboydco (#rhboydco)

www.rhboyd.com

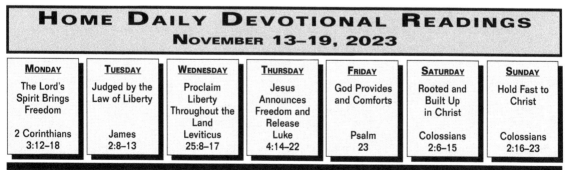

HOME DAILY DEVOTIONAL READINGS
NOVEMBER 13–19, 2023

MONDAY	TUESDAY	WEDNESDAY	THURSDAY	FRIDAY	SATURDAY	SUNDAY
The Lord's Spirit Brings Freedom	Judged by the Law of Liberty	Proclaim Liberty Throughout the Land	Jesus Announces Freedom and Release	God Provides and Comforts	Rooted and Built Up in Christ	Hold Fast to Christ
2 Corinthians 3:12–18	James 2:8–13	Leviticus 25:8–17	Luke 4:14–22	Psalm 23	Colossians 2:6–15	Colossians 2:16–23

LIFE IN CHRIST BRINGS FREEDOM

ADULT TOPIC:	BACKGROUND SCRIPTURE: COLOSSIANS 2:6–23
LIVE AS YOU WERE TAUGHT	LESSON PASSAGE: COLOSSIANS 2:16–23

COLOSSIANS 2:16—23

King James Version

LET no man therefore judge you in meat, or in drink, or in respect of an holyday, or of the new moon, or of the sabbath days:

17 Which are a shadow of things to come; but the body is of Christ.

18 Let no man beguile you of your reward in a voluntary humility and worshiping of angels, intruding into those things which he hath not seen, vainly puffed up by his fleshly mind,

19 And not holding the Head, from which all the body by joints and bands having nourishment ministered, and knit together, increaseth with the increase of God.

20 Wherefore if ye be dead with Christ from the rudiments of the world, why, as though living in the world, are ye subject to ordinances,

21 (Touch not; taste not; handle not

22 Which all are to perish with the using;) after the commandments and doctrines of men?

23 Which things have indeed a shew of wisdom in will worship, and humility, and neglecting of the body: not in any honour to the satisfying of the flesh.

New Revised Standard Version

THEREFORE, do not let anyone condemn you in matters of food or drink or of observing festivals, new moons, or Sabbaths.

17 These are only a shadow of what is to come, but the body belongs to Christ.

18 Do not let anyone disqualify you, insisting on self-abasement and worship of angels, initiatory visions,[b] puffed up without cause by a human way of thinking,

'19 and not holding fast to the head, from whom the whole body, nourished and held together by its ligaments and tendons, grows with a growth that is from God.

20 If with Christ you died to the elemental principles[d] of the world, why do you live as if you still belonged to the world? Why do you submit to regulations,

21 "Do not handle! Do not taste! Do not touch!"?

22 All these regulations refer to things that perish with use; they are simply human commands and teachings.

23 These have indeed an appearance of wisdom in promoting self-imposed piety, humility, and severe treatment of the body, but they are of no value in checking self-indulgence.

MAIN THOUGHT: As ye have therefore received Christ Jesus the Lord, so walk ye in him: Rooted and built up in him, and stablished in the faith, as ye have been taught, abounding therein with thanksgiving. (Colossians 2:6–7, KJV)

LESSON OUTLINE

I. **Paul Argues Against Colossian Philosophy (Colossians 2:6–8)**

II. **Paul Argues Against Legalism (Colossians 2:9–14)**

III. **Paul Argues Against Mystical Teaching (Colossians 2:15–19)**

IV. **Paul Argues Against Asceticism (Colossians 2:20–23)**

UNIFYING PRINCIPLE

People may submit to legalistic practices for a variety of reasons. How can we break free of practices that ensnare us? Paul persuades us that such practices are a human entrapment from which Christ frees us through grace.

INTRODUCTION

Paul writes this letter to the church in Colossae from Rome during his first imprisonment. Tychicus was apparently the bearer of the letter (Ephesians 6:21). Paul was probably personally unacquainted with the believers there (v. 1), but Epaphras may have reported on the conditions of the church when he visited Paul in prison. Additionally, Epaphras played a major role in the evangelism and growth of the Colossians, where gnosticism and heresy presented a serious set of challenges. Paul argues for the exaltation and superiority of Christianity over philosophy, legalism, mystical teachings, and asceticism (abstinence). Located about one hundred miles from Ephesus, Colossae was an ancient but declining commercial center.

EXPOSITION

I. PAUL ARGUES AGAINST COLOSSIAN PHILOSOPHY (COLOSSIANS 2:6–8)

Paul begins this missive by declaring a common trait in the believer, in that we must "walk with Him." In our walk, we must also "live in Him" by the direction and power of our "faith in Him." Moreover, by walking with Him, believers acknowledge their total dependence on the management of the Lord in our lives. By living in Him, our walk is considered in "lockstep" or in union with Him. Although an exhortation to "live in Christ" seems to be directed toward others, Paul based this encouragement on the personal experience of his walk with the Lord. Paul received Jesus at a point in his life when he was conflicted, being a Pharisee who was determined to destroy the new church, or being at a crossroads where he could accept or reject Jesus' call. Consequently, by faith, Paul accepted his call from the Lord, and he explained that the Colossians' faith was based on the Gospel and they must not forsake its divine authority for any form of worldly sophistication or convention. Nevertheless, our connection to the Lord runs deep, and through faith and a total commitment, grateful Christians that are anchored in Jesus will not succumb to any random wind and will be able to weather the "storms of life" that may come our way.

Therefore, Paul admonishes the Colossians to see to it that no one takes them captive through philosophy and empty deception (v. 8). Paul does not condemn philosophy in general, as he is a great philosopher himself. *Philosophy* is defined as "a search for wisdom or the search for truth through logical reasoning rather than factual observation." Hence, philosophy is the love of wisdom. In addressing the Colossians, Paul does not argue against all philosophy but against false philosophy, false religion, and false teachers. The wisdom of the Colossians was based on many wrongheaded traditions of their culture and the elemental principles of the pagan world. One of the more alarming issues was the spread of gnosticism, which taught that a person must work his or her way up a long series of lesser gods (called emanations) before reaching the ultimate god. Here, false Jewish teachers combined Hebrew rites and ascetic regulations with their philosophy, as a better way to move up the spiritual ladder. It was all very mysterious, complicated, astrological, and snooty. This was presented as "something more," which would elevate the ignorant Colossian Christians from their crude baby-faith to the truly deep things of God.

II. PAUL ARGUES AGAINST LEGALISM (COLOSSIANS 2:9–14)

Although Paul returns to the act of circumcision in this illustration, he speaks of it as a command of the Law (which he argues against); but since Jesus was a circumcised Jew, Paul argues that we have been circumcised in Him, having undergone not a physical circumcision but one that is spiritual. When one is physically circumcised, the process removes the foreskin of the organ, which imagines the removal of the flesh of the old nature and our constant state of rebellion against God.

This is illustrated in the rite of circumcision and the ordinance of baptism but is accomplished by a spiritual circumcision and Spirit baptism. Now, as the believer has been buried or crucified with Him through our baptism, we have also been raised from the dead, as our breaking forth through the waters signals a resurrection of the new person. In this case, the connection to Jesus' resurrection is uncomplicated because, as He was raised from the tomb, Jesus had a glorified body and a new mission, with His earthly journey complete. For the believer, our baptism in Him must signal that we have a new spiritual body, mind, and heart, and our Christian mission is not dead but is very much new and alive!

Continuing the illustration, Paul notes that when the believer was dead in his or her rebellion (transgressions) against God and living a lifestyle that was inverse and diametrically opposed to the will of God, it was the same God (who loves us more than we can love ourselves) that redeemed us by bringing us into His domain, where we would live according to His purposes. In order to bring us into this sphere with Him, He had to first forgive us of our transgressions and offenses against Him and heaven. For centuries, humans languished in their sin and separation from God, and the principles of the Law condemned mankind. However, because of Jesus, Paul wrote that "the law of the Spirit of life in Christ Jesus has set you free from the law of sin and of death" (Romans 8:2). God forgives those who are faithful and determined to walk with Him. Therefore, the debt is canceled, and the believer realizes that the debt of sin was hostile and debilitating to our past, present, and even future.

III. Paul Argues Against Mystical Teaching (Colossians 2:15–19)

In His glory, Jesus stripped the earthly rulers and kings of their power and authority, although Israel had believed the Messiah would be a political king in the mold of David and Solomon, who would return Israel to her former military glory. Jesus' mission, however, was as He described His Kingdom, i.e., "not of the world." Jesus actually demonstrated that He was above all earthly rulers. Recall the exchange between Jesus and Pilate when Pilate asked if Jesus was a king. In this civil line of questioning, Jesus acknowledged that He was King and that His reason for coming into the world was to bear witness to the truth, and that all earthly kings would recognize His kingship (by truthfully hearing His voice) (John 18:37). His arrest and interrogation by Pilate served as a public display of the power of the earthly rulers, and through the cross, His triumph was complete.

Biblical festivals ordained by Yahweh were periods of religious celebration that called for a cessation from ordinary workday activities, replacing them with communal activities that were special to the religious occasion and community. Additionally, Israel's festivals were crucial to national unity; however, these celebrations were religious observances and not to be viewed as religious carnivals. Warnings existed about perverting these festivals, as Malachi reveals the crime of neglect, during which the people offered blind, lame, or sick animals in the place of unblemished ones. Above all, the theme of Israelite festivals was to celebrate their commitment to the Lord. In this case, believers should not have subjected themselves to the customs of false teachers who initiated certain food and drink laws to align with their pagan festivals. In many ancient agnostic cultures, new moon festivals were dedicated to gods of agriculture and fertility, which ran counter to a belief in Yahweh. These cultic practices and celebrations were deceptive and misleading because the reality of the universe rested in the person of Jesus Christ. One of the popular festivals of the era was the Roman bacchanal, in which the festivities were dedicated to several from the pantheon of Roman gods.

Paul insists that the Colossian believers reject the fraud perpetrated by these false teachers and diviners, who injected into the believer a sense of self-abasement or shame, resulting in a false sense of humility. Paul declares that no one should defraud or deceive you in your relationship with Christ by taking away from you that which is rightfully yours. Additionally, these diviners promoted the worship of angels and claimed special mystical insights. The Scriptures strictly forbid the worship of angels (Exodus 20:3–4; cf. Revelation 22:8–9). Among other issues that served to detract evangelism was that Paul and the early church had to fight gnosticism, which purported that humans were understood to be in a state of blindness, sleep, and drunkenness. The inner spirit was prisoner to the fleshly body, which was prisoner to the material cosmos, both created by an inferior lower god sometimes said to enslave his creation with time, laws, and lust. Humans would then have to seek the true and highest god who lived in the highest heaven. Mankind had to reach a state of true knowledge in order to obtain acceptance into the highest heaven. The Colossians were not to be deluded into these gnostic cults because the gnostics were driven by their obsession with the flesh, not by their realization of the Spirit. To be a true believer, one must be a part of the entire body of Christ, not holding onto one part while rejecting another. Believers must be totally connected to receive the growth and maturity that can only come from God.

IV. PAUL ARGUES AGAINST ASCETICISM (COLOSSIANS 2:20–23)

For Paul, Christ freed the Colossians from the taboos of asceticism, which can only give a pretense of wisdom, promote a self-made religion, and hinder the natural instincts of the person. Yet, the strictness of this type of abstinence would limit humanity of their emotions of joy and love in the worship of the Lord. Because many of the Colossians were falling victim to the gnostics, Paul asked why they submitted themselves to decrees of "not tasting or touching" that which was a necessary part of living. These gnostic values run counter to God, where ascetic worldliness presents a different set of values. For example, ascetic worldliness is living by the world's rules (including those that have a show of humility) and some alleged "angelic" source. On the contrary, true spirituality is living by the power of the Spirit, in union with Christ, by whom the believer has died to sin.

In Paul's example, all of the physical gnostic items, such as food and drink, will cease to exist once they are used or consumed. Therefore, what value will they have in the course of longevity? If the Colossians fail to understand this principle, it will be because they have fallen for the deceptive teachings and decrees of these imitators of the faith. For Paul, these actors only teach what they have created, and their wisdom is "self-made." Additionally, their idea of depriving the body of what is needed to live goes beyond the physical body. The gnostics' mission is actually meant to deprive the body of Christ of what the believer needs to survive! The Colossians must be in a position to discern between the influence of false teachers and their faith in Jesus.

When believers walk with Christ, it is like unto a university marching band that creates visual patterns for their shows, where all of its members march simultaneously, with the left and right feet moving to the precision of a designated cadence. All of the band members must be united and together under the direction of the director. So must the Colossian believers be united under the direction of the Lord because they are a target of gnosticism that is designed to lead the people away from the teachings of Jesus. Gnosticism was very dangerous and not to be ignored because it mixed some of the truths of Hebrew religion with the delectably enticing mysteries of Eastern mysticism and Greek philosophy. Paul fights this movement with all that he has and never wavers in his commitment to Christ. Paul preaches a Christ-crucified message and strongly states that it is through the human Jesus and the centrality of the cross that we live, breathe, and have our very being

(Acts 17:28). This aspect of the human Jesus refutes the gnostic idea that His fullness came through some other process, such as through angelic intervention and human worship. Finally, the power of Jesus' kingship must never be understated.

THE LESSON APPLIED

Christians must be able to evaluate or understand the difference between legalistic salvation and freedom in Christ. Probably because most Christians today do not identify with Jewish culture, the Mosaic Law is not attractive. Gnosticism, which occurred during the period of Gentile conversion, is also not understood. Paul challenges the Judaizers and false teachers who are determined to sabotage the new Church (especially the neophyte Gentile converts) to a religion that is foreign to the teachings of Jesus. In this account, Christians are warned not to allow concepts of outdated legalism (or as in this lesson, gnosticism) or any other dated perceptions and practices that have invaded the modern Church to succeed in complicating our walk with the Lord.

LET'S TALK ABOUT IT

How is your life a witness for Christ each day?

Adults continue to seek new ways to proclaim the freedom they have in Christ in the world. Christians who are not ashamed of the Gospel of Jesus Christ are those who physically, emotionally, and spiritually "get into" our worship services and can be seen demonstrating their joy in the Lord. Additionally, these Christians exude the freedom to share the Gospel and serve as witnesses for the Lord in the manner that they live their lives. Moreover, these believers will not be swayed from their Christian principles when in the company of non-believers or lukewarm Christians. Mature Christian believers acknowledge the kingship of Jesus in a society that values politics and presidents! Recall that the titular or placard that was nailed above Jesus' head, stating, "Jesus, King of the Jews," was meant to be demeaning but was quite explicit and correct in all three languages: Hebrew, Latin, and Greek. Mature Christians are free to declare that Jesus is King!

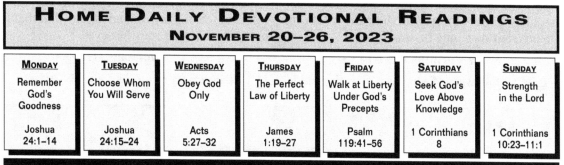

HOME DAILY DEVOTIONAL READINGS
NOVEMBER 20–26, 2023

MONDAY	TUESDAY	WEDNESDAY	THURSDAY	FRIDAY	SATURDAY	SUNDAY
Remember God's Goodness	Choose Whom You Will Serve	Obey God Only	The Perfect Law of Liberty	Walk at Liberty Under God's Precepts	Seek God's Love Above Knowledge	Strength in the Lord
Joshua 24:1–14	Joshua 24:15–24	Acts 5:27–32	James 1:19–27	Psalm 119:41–56	1 Corinthians 8	1 Corinthians 10:23–11:1

LIBERTY, NOT LICENSE

ADULT TOPIC:	BACKGROUND SCRIPTURE: 1 CORINTHIANS 8; 10:23–11:1
DO WHAT IS HELPFUL	LESSON PASSAGE: 1 CORINTHIANS 10:23–11:1

1 CORINTHIANS 10:23–11:1

King James Version

ALL things are lawful for me, but all things are not expedient: all things are lawful for me, but all things edify not.

24 Let no man seek his own, but every man another's wealth.

25 Whatsoever is sold in the shambles, that eat, asking no question for conscience sake:

26 For the earth is the Lord's, and the fulness thereof.

27 If any of them that believe not bid you to a feast, and ye be disposed to go; whatsoever is set before you, eat, asking no question for conscience sake.

28 But if any man say unto you, this is offered in sacrifice unto idols, eat not for his sake that shewed it, and for conscience sake: for the earth is the Lord's, and the fulness thereof:

29 Conscience, I say, not thine own, but of the other: for why is my liberty judged of another man's conscience?

30 For if I by grace be a partaker, why am I evil spoken of for that for which I give thanks?

31 Whether therefore ye eat, or drink, or whatsoever ye do, do all to the glory of God.

32 Give none offence, neither to the Jews, nor to the Gentiles, nor to the church of God:

33 Even as I please all men in all things, not seeking mine own profit, but the profit of many, that they may be saved.

• • • 1 Corinthians 11:1 • • •

1 Be ye followers of me, even as I also am of Christ.

New Revised Standard Version

"All things are permitted," but not all things are beneficial. "All things are permitted," but not all things build up.

24 Do not seek your own advantage but that of the other.

25 Eat whatever is sold in the meat market without raising any question on the ground of conscience,

26 for "the earth and its fullness are the Lord's."

27 If an unbeliever invites you to a meal and you are disposed to go, eat whatever is set before you without raising any question on the ground of conscience.

28 But if someone says to you, "This has been offered in sacrifice," then do not eat it, out of consideration for the one who informed you and for the sake of conscience—

29 I mean the other's conscience, not your own. For why should my freedom be subject to the judgment of someone else's conscience?

30 If I partake with thankfulness, why should I be denounced because of that for which I give thanks?

31 So, whether you eat or drink or whatever you do, do everything for the glory of God.

32 Give no offense to Jews or to Greeks or to the church of God,

33 just as I try to please everyone in everything I do, not seeking my own advantage but that of many, so that they may be saved.

• • • 1 Corinthians 11:1 • • •

11 1 Be imitators of me, as I am of Christ.

MAIN THOUGHT: All things are lawful for me, but all things are not expedient: all things are lawful for me, but all things edify not. (1 Corinthians 10:23, KJV)

UNIFYING PRINCIPLE

To take a stand for "freedom" challenges us to relate to others in a responsible way. How can our freedom lead us to respect and accept the freedom of others? The first letter to the Corinthians encourages Christians to honor and respect others in their choices and glorify God in whatever we do.

INTRODUCTION

Paul writes the first of possibly three letters to the church at Corinth. In this section of the first letter, he presents several metaphors that have a reversed meaning. For example, he will speak of entities that are components of the Law but yet, these laws do not adequately serve the citizens of the community, either civil or religious. Additionally, he will write about the freedom of conscience and offenses against a weaker believer. The use of these reverse metaphors can be problematic, as Paul does not provide more lucid examples, such as citing a specific law and its effects on society and the Church. However, the apex of this section is to cement the need to be our brother's keeper and imitators of Christ.

EXPOSITION

I. LAWFUL BUT NOT PROFITABLE (1 CORINTHIANS 10:23–26)

Paul has been writing about the constraints of the Law, especially concerning the issues of circumcision and its hampering Gentile believers, versus following the mandates of the Spirit and faith in Jesus. In this case, Paul is speaking of all types of law, civil as well as religious, that form a framework of guidance in all manners of society. Paul had previously used the saying that "everything is permissible for me" (1 Corinthians 6:12), which had become a slogan to cloak the immorality of some in Corinth. In his rationale between what is lawful and what is profitable, Paul notes a contrast that could be misused by the members of the church. Paul's statement that all things "are lawful" (from the word, *éxesti*) means "to be lawful." Used in verse 23, the term is translated as "it is possible," referring to moral possibility or propriety meaning it is lawful, right, permitted, can, or may. The term *profitable* (*sumphérō*) is understood by the combination of the word *sum*, meaning "together with," and *phérō*, meaning "to bring;" and (in this case) the definition is to bring together to be advantageous, or to contribute or bring together for the benefit of another. However, Paul could have referred to Jesus' comment on what is profitable when Jesus asked, "For what will it profit a man if he gains the whole world and forfeits his soul?" (Matthew 16:26).

Paul, however, continues by saying that "not all things are profitable" because this would favor acceptable behavior for all quarters, which would cause total chaos.

To have unbridled opportunities for unregulated freedom, the city of Corinth would face severe problems. Additionally, the specter of there not being any laws to govern the body would be very destructive in the church. Moreover, Paul relates that not all lawful things edify because many laws are meant to favor one group while oppressing another. In this case, Paul wishes to enlighten and educate the Corinthians, that unjust laws will not serve as their master; instead, their actions and approach to life must be determined by love. Again, the concept of "neighbor" remains an important structure in the unity of the nation of Israel but also in the composition of the body of Christ. In the Scriptures, the instances of the need for, concern for, and care for, as related to the term "neighbor," are found in Genesis, in the Law, in Jesus' verbiage, and beyond.

In verse 24, the observance of treating one's neighbor well is not a novel idea. When Paul writes that "one should not seek his own good but that of his neighbor," he is not asking the Corinthians to limit themselves at the expense of their neighbor; instead, Paul insists that the people (especially those of the church) follow the truism of being their (my) brother's keeper (Genesis 4:9). In this sense, the members of the Corinthian church (and beyond) should know about the needs of the brethren, the state of their households, and the stability of their dedication to the church and to Jesus. In a period when there did not exist a police force, neighbors had to depend and rely on one another for protection. However, here, "neighbors", their families, and the community were collectively protected by the Lord. In his argument, love must dominate the lifestyle of the believer, especially when it comes to loving one's neighbor. This language is clearly reminiscent of Jesus' teachings of "loving your neighbor as yourself" (Luke 10:27).

Continuing, Paul frames an argument that acknowledges the complete sovereignty of the Lord. To shape his line of reasoning, Paul refers to the Lord's complete ownership of the world and all it contains. To better understand this passage, it is prudent to "reverse" verses 25 and 26, to underscore the dominion of the Creator of the world. Therefore, Paul's illustration of "everything that is sold in the meat market" emanates or is a product of God's world; yet the evil misuse of these commodities occurs because of the deeds of evil men.

II. ALL THINGS MUST GLORIFY GOD (1 CORINTHIANS 10:27–31)

In the construct that Paul proposes, he focuses on the purchases from the meat market that are used for the sacrifices and rituals of pagan feasts, as compared to meat purchased from the same shops that is served at normal dinners. His point here is that because of our walk with the Lord, our intuition should allow us the liberty of eating foods, even in the company of a non-believer. It is important to understand that Paul does not wish to segregate himself from the opportunity to evangelize the non-believer. The concept of "breaking bread" or having dinner with someone remains an opportunity during which love and concern can be demonstrated and, also, where opposing forces can "drop their guard" and reason together in a platform of neutrality. Yet, Paul notes the reverse of this thought by stating to the believer that if he is invited to a pagan festival, or offered meat (items) sacrificed to idols, he must abstain from participation or the eating of these foods. Here, Paul poses an illustration that is visual in its presentation, as well as being founded in all aspects of one's commitment to the Lord. The meat is not a series of leftovers that was supposed to be sacrificed to idols, the remains of which are part of a dinner party. The meat in question (v. 28) is meat that was destined to be sacrificed and, for whatever reason, never made it to the altar. In this case, the meat itself remains unblemished; however, for Paul, it is the mere thought that the meat was originally readied for idol sacrifice that brings his judgmental opinion.

The idea of eating meat that was cut for idol sacrifice in a dinner setting, either public or private, is not a good visual representation of the believer's commitment to the Lord. The meat may not be tainted, but it is the appearance and example of the believer that matters, as this act should represent his thoughts and place in the church. For Paul, eating meat meant for idols was akin to advertising that one is a Christian but does not know how to refrain from aligning with pagan concepts. Again, he notes that the believer will be led in the right decision because of his or her conscience or the direction of the Holy Spirit. By refusing to be part of something tainted by man's dalliances (with anything pagan or evil), believers will not embarrass themselves before God.

Additionally, Paul notes that another person could be involved in this example, that is, the person that may have informed the believer that the meat they were about to consume was left over from a pagan ritual. In this case, the believer must identify with the conscience of the informant who does not want to cause the believer to be "unclean." In this case, the believer must recognize the morality of the other person in his attempt to be just. Paul asks two rhetorical questions: (1) "Why is Paul's freedom being judged or (better yet) influenced by the conscience of this other man?" and (2) "If Paul is thankful for the other man's intervention and concern, why should he be slandered?"

Both of these questions are answered by the notion that people have the liberty to make decisions, and, in this illustration, no one should be able to say that their liberty or freedom of choice should be determined by someone else's sense of morality. Paul, however, believes that Christians should discern the morality of a good person and must be sensitive to the weaknesses of others who may not be as strong in the Lord. For example, weaker brothers and sisters will look to the examples of the mature Christian for guidance in all matters, not just in this food example. Furthermore, this paradigm is not about individual freedom as much as it is about the use of personal freedom because of the edification and "spirit" gained by walking with the Lord. As to emphasize his thoughts, Paul declares that whatever the believer does—whether it falls within the examples of eating and drinking—Christian knowledge must be paramount, as all that we do must be done in the name of the Lord.

III. BE IMITATORS OF CHRIST (1 CORINTHIANS 10:32–11:1)

To conclude this segment of the lesson, Paul illustrates the power of being an example to the believers and the civil population in Corinth. Here, Paul lovingly admonishes the Corinthians to "give no offense to the Jews or the Greeks, or to the church of God." The Greek term used here to not cause stumbling is *apróskopos*, which can be defined as "to strike at" or "to trip." Paul's desire is that the believers in Corinth are sensitive to the plight of their fellow believers in society and especially in the church (of God). These members are to live above the worthless "flotsam and jetsam" that fills the lives of the unconcerned and unconnected. Paul wishes the Corinthian church will live in such a manner as to not become a stumbling block or cause any trouble to their fellow believers. Paul uses this term when declaring, "I myself always strive to have a [clear] conscience without offense toward God and men" (Acts 24:16), and in admonishing the Philippians to "be sincere and without offense till the day of Christ" (Philippians 1:10), where the word means "undamaged" in the path of duty and religion. In verse 32, it means "not causing [moral or spiritual] damage to anyone else."

Continuing, Paul declares that he is very deliberate in his attempts to please men in all things. This does not mean that Paul is timid or a coward who is bullied into baseless submission; instead, it reveals a clearer image of one who lives for Jesus while not seeking any type of profit for himself. For Paul, the profit for many is based in the reward for many, and that is to be a disciple of Jesus Christ. In a "true walk" with Jesus, many will be drawn to the faith, and many will be saved. "That all men might be saved" is a definitive position of Paul's ministry to the churches, her people, and the respective communities.

First, Paul realizes that his salvation was a gift from Jesus, and without that act of grace, Paul may have been dead. However, in his evangelistic efforts, the knowledge of being saved reverberates in his heart, mind, and soul. The imperative of "to save" (*sōzō*) is so important that it occurs fifty-four times in the Gospels that relate to deliverance from disease or demon possession, the rescue of physical life from some impending peril or instant death, and the reference to spiritual salvation from eternal death, sin, and the punishment and misery consequential to sin. Therefore, "to save" (by implication) is "to give eternal life," especially of Christ as the Savior of the world. Therefore, Paul urges the believers to "become imitators of me, just as I am in Christ" (1 Corinthians 11:1). Part of the imitational walk with Christ is to understand self-sacrifice, compassion, and love for the Church and the Lord. The Corinthians are not to believe they can "be" Christ but are urged to be "Christlike." Being Christlike will attract and develop converts, which will allow the church and the body to grow in faith and grace. The Corinthians must know that God will bless their efforts of devotion and steadfastness. Contemporary Christian believers must also become imitators of Christ, while refuting the atheists that believe the task is impossible in a world filled with hate, violence, and strife. As the light of Jesus shines through the life and disposition of the believer, others will be drawn to that light, as men naturally seek Jesus. As the expression says, "like a moth to a flame," men actually have a desire to be attached to Jesus; however, since Eden, the sting of the evil one has placed a barrier between

God and man. Paul uses several metaphors and illustrations, such as "all things are lawful," which may seem unrealistic; yet, he uses these statements to point toward a loving God and our being His ambassador.

THE LESSON APPLIED

One of the messages that stems from this lesson is that of wrestling with the discord that emerges from the differences between what is lawful versus what is beneficial. Initially, Paul seems guilty of what is known as "double-speak," in which the statements are usually backward or have a dual meaning. Paul is not trying to be evasive or ambiguous when he speaks about what is lawful, profitable, or what can be used to edify. In his sometimes "quirky" manner of style, he contrasts these opposing forces to clarify that lawful acts do not always benefit the believer and that his position is to embrace the things that edify the Lord. When Paul declares that he is an imitator of Christ, he is not restricting his lifestyle to the church, but he intones that his walking with the Lord is more powerful in his witness to the world.

LET'S TALK ABOUT IT

How can you imitate Christ in your day-to-day living?

Adults increase in faith as they exercise newfound Christian freedom in daily life. Christians must be open to discern opportunities to glorify God and honor others in our religious liberty. In our quest to be like Jesus, opportunities abound to honor God and serve as a witness to the faith. There are opportunities in our places of employment, if done in a manner that does not run counter to the rules and decorum of the workplace.

We have opportunities to honor the Lord in our societal journeys, again, if done in a manner that does not run counter to the rules and decorum of a world that separates church and state. We have opportunities to honor God within our family structures, and in this case, there should be no boundaries or rules that would limit our families from being taught about God and our service to Him. Our homes and churches must not erect barriers that would hinder our opportunities to honor the Lord.

GET SOCIAL

Share your views and tag us @rhboydco and use #ImitatorsofChrist.

Twitter
@rhboydco (#rhboydco)

Instagram
@rhboydco (#rhboydco)

Facebook
@rhboydco (#rhboydco)

www.rhboyd.com

HOME DAILY DEVOTIONAL READINGS
NOVEMBER 27–DECEMBER 3, 2023

MONDAY	TUESDAY	WEDNESDAY	THURSDAY	FRIDAY	SATURDAY	SUNDAY
Faith-based Friendship	Peter's Test of Faith	Hear God's Voice	Faith in Action	God Honors Genuine Faith	Naomi Becomes a Grandmother	Ruth's Compassionate Faith
Proverbs 17:17-22	Matthew 26:31-35	Hebrews 3:7-19	Leviticus 19:30-37	Acts 10:34-48	Ruth 4:13-22	Ruth 1:6-18, 22

Second Quarter

December

January

February

THE FAITH OF RUTH

ADULT TOPIC:	BACKGROUND SCRIPTURE: RUTH 1; 4:13–22
CHANGING IDENTITY	LESSON PASSAGE: RUTH 1:6–18, 22

RUTH 1:6–18, 22

King James Version

THEN she arose with her daughters in law, that she might return from the country of Moab: for she had heard in the country of Moab how that the Lord had visited his people in giving them bread.

7 Wherefore she went forth out of the place where she was, and her two daughters in law with her; and they went on the way to return unto the land of Judah.

8 And Naomi said unto her two daughters in law, Go, return each to her mother's house: the Lord deal kindly with you, as ye have dealt with the dead, and with me.

9 The Lord grant you that ye may find rest, each of you in the house of her husband. Then she kissed them; and they lifted up their voice, and wept.

10 And they said unto her, Surely we will return with thee unto thy people.

11 And Naomi said, Turn again, my daughters: why will ye go with me? are there yet any more sons in my womb, that they may be your husbands?

12 Turn again, my daughters, go your way; for I am too old to have an husband. If I should say, I have hope, if I should have an husband also to night, and should also bear sons;

13 Would ye tarry for them till they were grown? would ye stay for them from having husbands? nay, my daughters; for it grieveth me much for your sakes that the hand of the Lord is gone out against me.

New Revised Standard Version

THEN she started to return with her daughters-in-law from the country of Moab, for she had heard in the country of Moab that the Lord had considered his people and given them food.

7 So she set out from the place where she had been living, she and her two daughters-in-law, and they went on their way to go back to the land of Judah.

8 But Naomi said to her two daughters-in-law, "Go back each of you to your mother's house. May the Lord deal kindly with you, as you have dealt with the dead and with me.

9 The Lord grant that you may find security, each of you in the house of your husband." Then she kissed them, and they wept aloud.

10 They said to her, "No, we will return with you to your people."

11 But Naomi said, "Turn back, my daughters, why will you go with me? Do I still have sons in my womb that they may become your husbands?

12 Turn back, my daughters, go your way, for I am too old to have a husband. Even if I thought there was hope for me, even if I should have a husband tonight and bear sons,

13 would you then wait until they were grown? Would you then refrain from marrying? No, my daughters, it has been far more bitter for me than for you, because the hand of the Lord has turned against me."

MAIN THOUGHT: And Ruth said, Intreat me not to leave thee, or to return from following after thee: for whither thou goest, I will go; and where thou lodgest, I will lodge: thy people shall be my people, and thy God my God. (Ruth 1:16, KJV)

Ruth 1:6–18, 22

King James Version	*New Revised Standard Version*
14 And they lifted up their voice, and wept again: and Orpah kissed her mother in law; but Ruth clave unto her.	14 Then they wept aloud again. Orpah kissed her mother-in-law, but Ruth clung to her.
15 And she said, Behold, thy sister in law is gone back unto her people, and unto her gods: return thou after thy sister in law.	15 So she said, "See, your sister-in-law has gone back to her people and to her gods; return after your sister-in-law."
16 And Ruth said, Intreat me not to leave thee, or to return from following after thee: for whither thou goest, I will go; and where thou lodgest, I will lodge: thy people shall be my people, and thy God my God:	16 But Ruth said, "Do not press me to leave you or to turn back from following you! Where you go, I will go; where you lodge, I will lodge; your people shall be my people, and your God my God.
17 Where thou diest, will I die, and there will I be buried: the Lord do so to me, and more also, if ought but death part thee and me.	17 Where you die, I will die—there will I be buried. May the Lord do thus and so to me, and more as well, if even death parts me from you!"
18 When she saw that she was stedfastly minded to go with her, then she left speaking unto her.	18 When Naomi saw that she was determined to go with her, she said no more to her.
• • • • • •	• • • • • •
22 So Naomi returned, and Ruth the Moabitess, her daughter in law, with her, which returned out of the country of Moab: and they came to Bethlehem in the beginning of barley harvest.	22 So Naomi returned together with Ruth the Moabite, her daughter-in-law, who came back with her from the country of Moab. They came to Bethlehem at the beginning of the barley harvest.

LESSON SETTING

Time: 1380 BCE

Place: Moab

LESSON OUTLINE

I. **Naomi Plans to Leave Her Daughters-in-law (Ruth 1:6–9)**

II. **Naomi Begs Her Daughters-in-law to Leave Her (Ruth 1:10–13)**

III. **The Loyalty of Ruth (Ruth 1:14–18, 22)**

UNIFYING PRINCIPLE

It takes courage to face significant changes in life. When the odds are against us, where do we find this courage? Ruth found strength in her relationship with Naomi and in faith committed to Naomi's God, family, and culture.

INTRODUCTION

During the period of the judges, a severe famine had crippled Bethlehem and the neighboring regions. In a scene reminiscent of the account of Joseph, a certain man named Elimelech decided to leave his city and move to the land of Moab where there was plenty of grain. Relocating with Elimelech was his wife, Naomi, and their two sons, Mahlon and Chilion. Unfortunately, while the family was living in Moab, Elimelech died suddenly, leaving Naomi a widow. At some point, the sons married Moabite women; Chilion wed Orpah, and Mahlon, Ruth. They lived in Moab approximately ten years, when another disaster struck the family. Both of the sons died, leaving Naomi with only her two daughters-in-law. The account in the lesson is one of faith, ultimately in Yahweh, who will bless the widows, especially Naomi and Ruth. Additionally, the book reveals that becoming a child of God (in this case, an Israelite) is not by physical birth but by obeying God's Word.

EXPOSITION

I. NAOMI PLANS TO LEAVE HER DAUGHTERS-IN-LAW (RUTH 1:6–9)

Naomi and her two daughters-in-law prepared to journey from Moab and return to Bethlehem. Moab is located some 300 miles southeast of Bethlehem, which would make the arduous trip approximately 30 days long, if the group could average 10 miles per day. It is not known if Naomi and her family traveled with a larger group, as it was unsafe for smaller parties, who were vulnerable to bandits. Outside of the tragedy of losing her husband and sons, Naomi had heard that the dreaded famine that had driven her family to Moab had abated and there was now relief from the catastrophe, with the land once again flowing with "milk and honey." When the author speaks of "visiting His people giving them food," the meaning is that Yahweh has restored the land to its agricultural prosperity. In this case, Naomi attributes relief from the famine to God. This is one of several hints that a divine hand is guiding the events in the story. Naomi had heard that Yahweh had indeed visited His people, and this highlights the interesting fact that what Yahweh has done in Israel has become well-known in Moab. Thus, what has happened in Israel had been so dramatic that it was newsworthy elsewhere—even in Moab, which had its own deity, Chemosh. When God blessed His people, the Israelites, they acknowledged that their change in fortunes were not just good luck but the result of the direct intervention of God in their affairs.

Trusting God, those that remained of the family began their journey toward Judah (Bethlehem). Naomi was not a selfish woman, and she loved her two daughters-in-law unconditionally. Although she had grown accustomed to their place in her family before the calamity, she only wanted what was best for these young women who had a future beyond this situation. Therefore, Naomi, destitute of husband and sons (for heirs), repeatedly urged her daughters-in-law to return to their Moabite homes (also, vv. 12 and 15). Displaying her faith in Yahweh, her encouragement was that "the Lord would deal kindly with [them]," in His protection and guidance. The Hebrew word *hesed* ("deal kindly," as also, in Ruth 2:20 and 3:10) expresses Naomi's prayer that the Lord (literally, Yahweh, the covenant name of God with Israel) would show His faithful, covenant-keeping love to these two Moabite widows. Additionally, Naomi remembered that Yahweh comforted her through her grief in the loss of the deceased members of her family (v. 8). Naomi implored the young widows to return home to their mother's house and not to journey with her to Bethlehem. Moreover, Naomi displays her understanding of Yahweh's faithfulness as she places her trust in Him.

Continuing her prayer, Naomi asked that the Lord grant the widows rest, each in the house of her husband (v. 9). This is not to be misunderstood as referring to their husbands that were deceased; instead, this phrase means that Naomi is praying that they both find second husbands and create a new life in their households. Attempting to get the women to leave, Naomi kissed them as an act of affection, but also in a parting emotional display. The pain of this situation must have been excruciating, as the women, including Naomi, cried uncontrollably while clinging to each other with a last desperate embrace. Again, they had grown so close in this family unit, but now, it had been unpredictably destroyed by the ravages of death. What was to be their future?

II. Naomi Begs Her Daughters-in-law to Leave Her (Ruth 1:10–13)

However, the daughters-in-law disagreed with Naomi saying, "We will return [to Bethlehem] with you to be with your people." Consider the agony and sorrow they felt by breaking up their homes. You may recall the distress that families face after the funeral of loved ones, especially parents, and how it changes the dynamics of what had been a stable household. Did they have household goods and land that they now had to liquidate and abandon? The women were facing some serious challenges. Again, Naomi pleaded with the daughters to return to their homeland and families. Maintaining that moving to Bethlehem with her did not give them a future, she literally asked the daughters why they would wish to stay with her, as she did not have any sons in her womb that could replace their deceased husbands (v. 11). This metaphorical phrase is meant to convey that she was beyond childbearing years and, although her sons had been married to these women, Naomi did not have the means to provide the daughters with other sons of her blood.

Again, Naomi pleads with the daughters to return to Moab, saying that she is too old for a husband, acknowledging her advanced age, saying that even if she could bear sons, would the widows be able to wait for the sons to reach the age of marriage? Even if this was possible, could they have enough discipline to ignore their physical and emotional needs and wait for the sons to mature? Stressing an impossible situation, Naomi declares that the daughters are facing an easier time than what is Naomi's fate. These girls are obviously young, attractive, and vibrant, and have the best of their lives ahead of them, including obtaining husbands and bearing children, especially, the valued sons. When Naomi says that "the hand of the Lord is against me" (v. 13), she does not mean that Yahweh has abandoned her or has placed a punishment against her. It simply means that she believes that (unlike Sarah) she will not be able to bear children, and more than likely, she will remain a widow for the rest of her life. In this case, Naomi had very fixed ideas about how a woman could acquire security or rest. Influenced by her knowledge of the patriarchal societies in which she had spent all her life, she believed that the only way a woman could find rest was to find a husband. This meant that she felt personally that there could be no "rest" for her since she was too old to find another husband. Bordering on despair herself, she wanted the very best for her daughters-in-law.

III. THE LOYALTY OF RUTH (RUTH 1:14–18, 22)

Naomi's pleas that they separate, and the thought of the daughters' return to Moab, continues to instigate the women's bouts of crying. It seemed as if Naomi had convinced the daughters that this move was best for their future; yet the separation that occurred may not have been what was predicted. Unexpectedly, Orpah, the widow of Chilion, kissed Naomi, but it was not the normal kiss of a greeting or that of a temporary departure. This kiss was the kiss of a permanent goodbye. Some scholars have equated this kiss (*nashaq*) with the action of Judas (*phileo*) because both kisses were that of affection; however, the kiss that Judas planted on Jesus signified a betrayal, whereas Orpah's demonstration was one of resignation and regret. Orpah decided to return to Moab. One should not be critical of Orpah's decision to return to her homeland because Naomi had convinced her that it was the more prudent thing to do.

However, Ruth, the widow of Mahlon, clung to Naomi, overcome with emotion, refusing to let go of her mother-in-law. Ruth's attachment to Naomi is reminiscent of Genesis 2:24, which refers to the "clinging" of husband to wife. The connotation here is probably not sexual but rather signifies Ruth's unswerving devotion to Naomi. Naomi continued to reason with Ruth, saying that since Orpah had decided to return to Moab, Ruth should follow her lead. Verse 15 suggests that the events happened in sequence and not all at once. Naomi declared to Ruth that her "sister-in-law has gone back to her people and her gods; [therefore] return after your sister-in-law."

Here is recorded Ruth's answer to Naomi's request to have the daughters return to their homeland. This moving plea is among the best-known lines in the book, as it expresses Ruth's devotion and loyalty to Naomi (v. 16). Rabbinical literature views Ruth's passionate declaration of allegiance as the point at which Naomi instructs Ruth in a formal process of conversion. Ruth's oath of asking that the Lord punish her if anything but death separated them underscores the seriousness of her declaration. It has been interpreted to mean "only death will part us" or "not even death will part us."

Naomi now realized that Ruth was determined to remain with her, even going as far as her moving to Bethlehem and embracing Naomi's God, Yahweh. At this juncture, Ruth has passed the threefold exam of discouragement for following Naomi to Judea. Naomi never wanted Orpah or Ruth to leave; however, Naomi probably wanted to make sure their conversion was solid. In this case, Orpah failed but Ruth passed the test and would accompany Naomi to Bethlehem, her newly adopted homeland.

Naomi returned to her precious Bethlehem, having Ruth with her, who vowed to remain with Naomi. The author notes that they arrived in Bethlehem at the time of the barley harvest, which was toward the end of April. This is associated with the Passover Festival. When they reached the city, the women asked, "Is this Naomi?" Naomi asked the women not to call her "Naomi," which means "pleasant," but to call her "Mara," meaning "bitter." It was perhaps that the women of the city saw that Naomi had left with a husband and sons, but had returned empty (except for Ruth), that made Naomi embittered.

Nevertheless, she then remembered Yahweh, who she calls "El Shaddai, the Almighty God," who she decided was her protector and Lord. Although the central character in this opening section is Naomi, it is appropriate to have named the book "Ruth" because it is actually her character that becomes the inspiration and example for having faith in God. Ruth will become a focal point in the latter stages in the book, and her commitment to God is rewarded, as she becomes an ancestress of David and thus, Jesus.

The Lesson Applied

Christians trust God's guidance during times of major life losses. At the time of this writing, a famine of sorts had crippled the land. This lesson's aim is to analyze the situation in which Ruth and Naomi find themselves. During a period when women had to depend on their husbands (and sons) for survival, these women were in a tenuous situation. Land was owned by men, and sons became the heirs, not widows. This record does not account for the possessions that were owned by the family; however, it seems as if their family holdings were meager. Hence, the women were faced with an uncertain future. Despite this, they trusted in Naomi's God and committed their lives to Him.

Let's Talk About It

How can believers maintain their faith despite their hardships?

A statement of Ruth's faith can be justified by imitating Ruth's model of courage and faithfulness when facing the hardships of life. One massive adversity that people face is death. In this account, death has seemingly destroyed Naomi's family. Death has the capacity to destroy a family that lacks faith and trust in the Lord to guide them through such a period of uncertainty. However, the hardships faced by these women (such as the death of their husbands) did not weaken their resolve to remain alive and committed to Yahweh. Death changes the familial dynamic; yet those who walk with the Lord are blessed by the Lord. This still holds true for us today!

Get Social
Share your views and tag us @rhboydco and use #rhboydco.

Twitter
@rhboydco (#rhboydco)

Instagram
@rhboydco (#rhboydco)

Facebook
@rhboydco (#rhboydco)

www.rhboyd.com

Home Daily Devotional Readings
December 4–10, 2023

Monday	Tuesday	Wednesday	Thursday	Friday	Saturday	Sunday
Faith Expressed through Courage	David's Son Came to Serve	Ask in Prayer with Faith	Prophets Speak God's Word	Rekindle God's Gift and Stand Firm	Israel's Wavering Faith	Faith That God Will Act
Joshua 1:1–9	Matthew 20:25-34	Matthew 21:18-22	Psalm 27	2 Timothy 1:3–14	1 Samuel 17:1, 3–4, 8, 20–30	1 Samuel 17:31-37, 45, 48-50

FACING LIFE WITH CONFIDENCE

ADULT TOPIC:	BACKGROUND SCRIPTURE: 1 SAMUEL 17:1–58
THE FAITH OF DAVID	LESSON PASSAGE: 1 SAMUEL 17:31–37, 45, 48–50

1 SAMUEL 17:31–37, 45, 48–50

King James Version

AND when the words were heard which David spake, they rehearsed them before Saul: and he sent for him.

32 And David said to Saul, Let no man's heart fail because of him; thy servant will go and fight with this Philistine.

33 And Saul said to David, Thou art not able to go against this Philistine to fight with him: for thou art but a youth, and he a man of war from his youth.

34 And David said unto Saul, Thy servant kept his father's sheep, and there came a lion, and a bear, and took a lamb out of the flock:

35 And I went out after him, and smote him, and delivered it out of his mouth: and when he arose against me, I caught him by his beard, and smote him, and slew him.

36 Thy servant slew both the lion and the bear: and this uncircumcised Philistine shall be as one of them, seeing he hath defied the armies of the living God.

37 David said moreover, The Lord that delivered me out of the paw of the lion, and out of the paw of the bear, he will deliver me out of the hand of this Philistine. And Saul said unto David, Go, and the Lord be with thee.

• • • • • •

45 Then said David to the Philistine, Thou comest to me with a sword, and with a spear, and with a shield: but I come to thee in the name of the Lord of hosts, the God of the armies of Israel, whom thou hast defied.

New Revised Standard Version

WHEN the words that David spoke were heard, they repeated them before Saul; and he sent for him.

32 David said to Saul, "Let no one's heart fail because of him; your servant will go and fight with this Philistine."

33 Saul said to David, "You are not able to go against this Philistine to fight with him; for you are just a boy, and he has been a warrior from his youth."

34 But David said to Saul, "Your servant used to keep sheep for his father; and whenever a lion or a bear came, and took a lamb from the flock,

35 I went after it and struck it down, rescuing the lamb from its mouth; and if it turned against me, I would catch it by the jaw, strike it down, and kill it.

36 Your servant has killed both lions and bears; and this uncircumcised Philistine shall be like one of them, since he has defied the armies of the living God."

37 David said, "The Lord, who saved me from the paw of the lion and from the paw of the bear, will save me from the hand of this Philistine." So Saul said to David, "Go, and may the Lord be with you!"

• • • • • •

45 ut David said to the Philistine, 'You come to you with sword and spear and javelin; but I come to you in the name of the Lord of hosts, the God of the armies of Israel, whom you have defied.

MAIN THOUGHT: David said moreover, The Lord that delivered me out of the paw of the lion, and out of the paw of the bear, he will deliver me out of the hand of this Philistine. And Saul said unto David, Go, and the Lord be with thee. (1 Samuel 17:37, KJV)

1 SAMUEL 17:31–37, 45, 48–50

King James Version	New Revised Standard Version
• • • • • •	• • • • • •
48 And it came to pass, when the Philistine arose, and came, and drew nigh to meet David, that David hastened, and ran toward the army to meet the Philistine.	48 When the Philistine drew nearer to meet David, David ran quickly toward the battle line to meet the Philistine.
49 And David put his hand in his bag, and took thence a stone, and slang it, and smote the Philistine in his forehead, that the stone sunk into his forehead; and he fell upon his face to the earth.	49 David put his hand in his bag, took out a stone, slung it, and struck the Philistine on his forehead; the stone sank into his forehead, and he fell face down on the ground.
50 So David prevailed over the Philistine with a sling and with a stone, and smote the Philistine, and slew him; but there was no sword in the hand of David.	50 So David prevailed over the Philistine with a sling and a stone, striking down the Philistine and killing him; there was no sword in David's hand.

LESSON SETTING
Time: 930–550 BCE
Place: Unknown

LESSON OUTLINE
I. **David is Prepared to Fight Goliath**
(1 Samuel 17:31–37)
II. **David Defeats Goliath**
(1 Samuel 17:45, 48–50)

UNIFYING PRINCIPLE
We need confidence to face the challenges before us—especially when others doubt our abilities. What is the source of this confidence? David's faith in God gave him the confidence he needed to defeat the giant Goliath in battle.

INTRODUCTION
According to the battle customs of the time, many clashes were fought during the day between one mighty man for each of two armies. These "mighty men" were defined as the best and most valiant warriors of their respective armies. These individual battles were designed to provide relief from the general slaughter that came as a result of the men throwing themselves at each other in a primitive frontal assault. While the remainder of the two armies "stood down," the men would place bets as to which one would be the victorious gladiator, who was promised rewards, such as land, money, or even the hand of the daughter of the king! Following the battle, the two armies would then retreat to their respective camps, comforted by the loss of only one man instead of many from both armies. This is the account of a young shepherd boy that God had designated to be the victor in this battle.

EXPOSITION

I. DAVID IS PREPARED TO FIGHT GOLIATH (1 SAMUEL 17:31–37)
Prior to the battle, David addressed the men of the Israelite army who were standing around him, as Goliath taunted the Israelites by calling them an array of

despicable names. Additionally, Goliath defamed the Holy Name of Yahweh, while daring anyone from Saul's army to stand up for Yahweh's honor by fighting him. David was prepared to answer Goliath's insults in a fight that seemed unrealistically one-sided. In this culture, it was common for a warrior to address his men or the crowd, who may serve as witnesses to the battle. David's address to the men was meant to inspire and bolster their courage and provide them with a psychological inducement that they were invincible in their quest for victory. Moreover, the motivational speech would include the reasons for their fight, e.g., protection of their homeland, defeat of despots, and in biblical situations, upholding the honor of the name of the Lord.

At some point, Saul was made aware of David's address and sent for him before the battle actually begun. It seems as if Saul attempted to dissuade David from entering battle with the Philistine giant. Yet, David was firmly "psyched" that he would prevail against the Philistine and declared to Saul that his "heart" would not fail because of Goliath's reputation and size. In this case, David's heart is a reflection of his courage and strength to encounter who he considered the enemy. Saul continued to try to convince David that this was a suicide mission, as none of the other "mighty men" of Israel (including Saul himself) dared to confront Goliath. Saul pleaded with David not to enter the fight, saying, "You are not able to go against this Philistine to fight with him; for you are but a youth while he has been a warrior from his youth" (v. 33). Saul noted that this was normal for Goliath: that he had killed many men and had been groomed for moments such as this in the culturally warrior state of Philistia.

David, however, challenges Saul with a declaration of his valor—if not his manhood—noting that as a shepherd, he has had to protect his father's herd from an array of challenges, especially, marauding wild animals. Observers of the David story should not romanticize the account of this shepherd boy by assuming that this is some idyllic story about a shepherd protecting a few lambs. Jesse was a wealthy man, and his animal holdings would have been large. Therefore, David's exploits in the protection of the herd cannot be overstated. As David relayed to Saul, he had to defend the flock from lions (although not currently found in Palestine, in David's time, lions were plentiful and dangerous). Lions not only attacked flocks in the presence of the shepherd, but also laid waste of towns and villages (2 Kings 17:25–26) and devoured human beings (1 Kings 13:24–25). Shepherds, sometimes single-handedly, encountered lions and slew them (1 Samuel 17:34–35; Amos 3:12). Bears were also dangerous to the flocks and the populace. David bravely faced these animals, in several cases, taking the lambs out of the mouths of the hunters before they had time for the kill.

This declaration was meant to prove that although David did not have the military background of Goliath, he had been tempered in another battleground in the grazing land of his father's estate. Therefore, David declared that he would kill Goliath, just as he did the lion and the bear. David reminds Saul that it was Yahweh who delivered him from the "paw" of both the lion and the bear, and Yahweh will ultimately deliver him from the "hand" (paw) of Goliath. At that point, Saul had to give David his blessings, saying, "May the Lord be with you" (v. 37).

Indeed, the Lord will be with David as is declared that "the battle is the Lord's and He will give you [the victory] into our hands" (v. 47). In this case, God prepares David to fight the enemy in a manner that eclipses human knowledge and understanding. Therefore, the battle is the warfare against God's enemy, both spiritual and physical. To David, as to Paul, this battle was fundamentally spiritual in nature (see Ephesians 6:12). Therefore, the Lord's battle is not the same as a "just war" (warfare justified by human judgment) or a so-called "holy war" (a war between two opposing deities and their human armies).

II. DAVID DEFEATS GOLIATH (1 SAMUEL 17:45, 48–50)

The scene now shifts to the battlefield in the valley of Elah. David is now facing Goliath, the Philistine champion who had defied the Israelite army for forty days. With the two armies anxiously watching from opposing sides of the mountains, the two men met in this most famous fight. Goliath was resplendent in his battle array: large armor, breastplate, shield, spear, and massive sword. His armaments had been crafted in the best foundries, by the best weapon makers of Gath. His helmet and shield probably shone like the rays of the sun. The image of this massive man, who supposedly stood over nine feet, dressed in armor weighing 125 pounds, was definitely frighting! Saul had provided David with his armor, but it was too large and bulky for David, who needed to be mobile if he was to succeed in this fight.

David preferred the simple implements of a shepherd. Again, outside of the guidance of the Lord, mobility was his best ally. He had five smooth stones that he had taken from a brook and his favorite weapon, the sling. It is important that David's weapon not be confused with the slingshot toy of our modern era, as they are totally different in their design and use. David's sling consisted of a strip of cloth or leather folded double, in the center of which a stone was placed. The sling is held at the ends and rotated, then, one end is released, which causes the stone to fly with great force toward its target. However, exactly hitting the mark requires considerable dexterity. Additionally, David chose smooth stones rather than those that were uneven or jagged because the aerodynamic properties of the smooth stone would increase its speed and velocity, resulting in a greater impact to its target. Although Goliath was armed with the best weapons of the Philistine army, David's ordinance was superior because he was armed by the power of Yahweh.

As David approached the giant Philistine, Goliath laughed at the sight of such a young boy, who was the champion of Israel. The warrior from Gath was actually insulted that the army of Israel did not send someone who at least looked the part of a worthy adversary. Goliath shouted at David, saying, "Am I a dog, that you come to me with sticks?" The Philistine cursed David by his Philistine gods and said that he would feed his body to the birds of the sky and the beasts of the field (vv. 43–44). Goliath came at David; however, David, with his unbridled mobility, avoided any thrusts or movement by the giant from Gath. Keeping his distance and out of the grasp of Goliath, David reached into his pouch and placed one of the stones in his sling. Whirling it above his head to increase its force, David then launched the projectile toward the massive Goliath, striking the Philistine in the forehead, probably between the eyes. Goliath "never knew what hit him" and crumpled to the ground, falling face first into the dust. David then grabbed the giant's sword and severed his head, which was a common practice of the period, raising Goliath's bloody head above his head, while the two armies remained stunned! Actually, the Philistines were in a state of disbelief, as were the Israelites, except for different reasons. Goliath's larger-than-life weapons were rendered useless by the sling and stone because the latter were the weapons of Yahweh and His invested power in David. Now, the headless giant from Gath lay motionless on the valley floor of Elah, unable to utter curses against Yahweh and His people. Israel now understood that the power of Yahweh was unlimited and that He possesses many methods concerning the protection of His chosen.

The more well-known account of the placement of the stone, which is the Hebrew term 'eben (eh·ben), has David hurling the stone into the forehead of Goliath. However, Old Testament scholar David Tsumara examines another translation of verse 49, replacing forehead metsach (may·tsakh) with the Hebrew term mitschah (mits·khaw). The latter is translated as "greave" instead of forehead, which would render the verse "And the stone sank into his greave, so that he fell on his face to the ground" (1 Samuel 17:49). In this translation, the suggestion is that the stone hit the upper shin or knee at the place left open and unprotected so the knee could move. But this probably would not have knocked a giant down, and certainly would not have left him helpless when David came and took his sword.

In this case, there may have been a mistake in translation as these two Hebrew terms, metsach and mitschah could have been mistakenly misread or copied incorrectly. Nonetheless, the traditional account is probably closer to the truth as the stone that hit Goliath brought the giant down where David was able to reach Goliath's sword and sever his massive head. The severing of Goliath's head was not simply a way to kill the enemy but was part of the culture that maintained that the head (and also the hands) was to be severed to be displayed in prominent areas, such as the gates of the city, to serve as a physical announcement to the public that the enemy was vanquished. Although the Scriptures do not detail what happened to Goliath's head, the sight of the decapitation was enough to terrorize the Philistine army and fortify the Israelites.

The outcome is not what the Philistines suspected would happen. They could not believe their eyes—their mighty champion Goliath had fallen. Upon coming to their senses, the Philistines fled in terror, with the Israeli army chasing in close pursuit. The Israelites caught up with their opponents and defeated them on the same day. The army gave Saul a great victory but, although they won this battle, they did not win the war. The Philistines would remain a nemesis of Israel for many years. This powerful tribe made frequent incursions against the Hebrews, as there was almost perpetual war between them. These hostilities did not cease until the time of Hezekiah (2 Kings 18:8), when they were entirely subdued. To this day, Israel is still a place of civil unrest.

THE LESSON APPLIED

A central goal of this lesson is to analyze David's confidence in defeating Goliath. Although the details of the battle are quite explicit, believers should not allow these details to mask the confidence David had in Yahweh. It may seem as if David was confident in his own abilities, and while true to a great extent, he never wavers in his trust that God will deliver him from defeat and grant him the victory. The battle is an exercise of faith in that Yahweh is ordering the steps of David, as history will later validate. Without this confidence and trust, David could have never faced Goliath, nor would he have been anointed as the future king of Israel.

LET'S TALK ABOUT IT

Have you experienced a time when you were forced to place your faith in the Lord's hands?

Adult Christians may gain an increase in faith when they witness the bravery of others in dangerous situations. Recently, an account was shared by several veterans of the Vietnam War, whose particular division consisted of some men of faith and others of no faith. These troops were involved in a serious battle during which the Viet Cong enemy ambushed them from all sides. They had received faulty intelligence and were thus outnumbered because the planning was greatly flawed. Some of the men panicked and threw down their guns or froze in the midst of the battle, while others fought bravely and even ran through enemy fire to rescue their fallen comrades.

When asked from where they got their courage, one soldier said that he placed his trust and life in God's hands. As he led by example, other soldiers gained confidence and joined in the fight, turning a defeat into a victory. The bravery of the Christian soldier passed to the others, though, whether they were believers (or not) is not important. God won the battle that day, and the Christian soldier who led by example testified to that truth.

GET SOCIAL

Share your views and tag us @rhboydco and use #Confidence.

Twitter
@rhboydco (#rhboydco)

Instagram
@rhboydco (#rhboydco)

Facebook
@rhboydco (#rhboydco)

www.rhboyd.com

HOME DAILY DEVOTIONAL READINGS
DECEMBER 11–17, 2023

MONDAY	TUESDAY	WEDNESDAY	THURSDAY	FRIDAY	SATURDAY	SUNDAY
Tamar's Risk-taking Faith	Rahab's Faith	Patient Faith	God's Grave Overflowed	Bathsheba's Challenged Faith	God, the Stronghold for the Oppressed	A Family Tree Characterized by Faith
Genesis 38:6-11, 13–18, 24–26	Joshua 2:1–6, 8–16	James 5:1–11	1 Timothy 1:12–17	2 Samuel 11:1–5, 26–12:1, 4–7,15–16, 24	Psalm 9:1–14	Matthew 1:1–17

THE FAMILY OF FAITH

ADULT TOPIC: BACKGROUND SCRIPTURE: Matt. 1:1–17, Gen. 38; Josh. 2; 6:22–25, 2 Sam. 12:24, Ruth 4:13–22
GOD BRINGS "OUTSIDERS" IN   LESSON PASSAGE: MATTHEW 1:1–16

MATTHEW 1:1–16

King James Version

THE book of the generation of Jesus Christ, the son of David, the son of Abraham.

2 Abraham begat Isaac; and Isaac begat Jacob; and Jacob begat Judas and his brethren;

3 And Judas begat Phares and Zara of Thamar; and Phares begat Esrom; and Esrom begat Aram;

4 And Aram begat Aminadab; and Aminadab begat Naasson; and Naasson begat Salmon;

5 And Salmon begat Booz of Rachab; and Booz begat Obed of Ruth; and Obed begat Jesse;

6 And Jesse begat David the king; and David the king begat Solomon of her that had been the wife of Urias;

7 And Solomon begat Roboam; and Roboam begat Abia; and Abia begat Asa;

8 And Asa begat Josaphat; and Josaphat begat Joram; and Joram begat Ozias;

9 And Ozias begat Joatham; and Joatham begat Achaz; and Achaz begat Ezekias;

10 And Ezekias begat Manasses; and Manasses begat Amon; and Amon begat Josias;

11 And Josias begat Jechonias and his brethren, about the time they were carried away to Babylon:

12 And after they were brought to Babylon, Jechonias begat Salathiel; and Salathiel begat Zorobabel;

New Revised Standard Version

AN account of the genealogy of Jesus the Messiah, the son of David, the son of Abraham.

2 Abraham was the father of Isaac, and Isaac the father of Jacob, and Jacob the father of Judah and his brothers,

3 and Judah the father of Perez and Zerah by Tamar, and Perez the father of Hezron, and Hezron the father of Aram,

4 and Aram the father of Aminadab, and Aminadab the father of Nahshon, and Nahshon the father of Salmon,

5 and Salmon the father of Boaz by Rahab, and Boaz the father of Obed by Ruth, and Obed the father of Jesse,

6 and Jesse the father of King David. And David was the father of Solomon by the wife of Uriah,

7 and Solomon the father of Rehoboam, and Rehoboam the father of Abijah, and Abijah the father of Asaph,

8 and Asaph the father of Jehoshaphat, and Jehoshaphat the father of Joram, and Joram the father of Uzziah,

9 and Uzziah the father of Jotham, and Jotham the father of Ahaz, and Ahaz the father of Hezekiah,

10 and Hezekiah the father of Manasseh, and Manasseh the father of Amos, and Amos the father of Josiah,

11 and Josiah the father of Jechoniah and his brothers, at the time of the deportation to Babylon.

12 And after the deportation to Babylon: Jechoniah was the father of Salathiel, and Salathiel the father of Zerubbabel,

MAIN THOUGHT: The book of the generation of Jesus Christ, the son of David, the son of Abraham. (Matthew 1:1, KJV)

King James Version	New Revised Standard Version
13 And Zorobabel begat Abiud; and Abiud begat Eliakim; and Eliakim begat Azor;	13 and Zerubbabel the father of Abiud, and Abiud the father of Eliakim, and Eliakim the father of Azor,
14 And Azor begat Sadoc; and Sadoc begat Achim; and Achim begat Eliud;	14 and Azor the father of Zadok, and Zadok the father of Achim, and Achim the father of Eliud,
15 And Eliud begat Eleazar; and Eleazar begat Matthan; and Matthan begat Jacob;	15 and Eliud the father of Eleazar, and Eleazar the father of Matthan, and Matthan the father of Jacob,
16 And Jacob begat Joseph the husband of Mary, of whom was born Jesus, who is called Christ.	16 and Jacob the father of Joseph the husband of Mary, of whom Jesus was born, who is called the Messiah.

LESSON SETTING
   Time: 4 BCE
   Place: Jerusalem

LESSON OUTLINE
   I. **Abraham to David (Matthew 1:1–6)**
   II. **David to the Babylonian Exile (Matthew 1:7–11)**
   III. **From Babylon to Christ (Matthew 1:12–17)**

UNIFYING PRINCIPLE

People want to research their family of origin. How does knowing or understanding the genealogy of one's family provide insight into who we are? The Gospel of Matthew highlights surprising twists in Joseph's genealogy by the nontraditional mention of Gentiles and women, and in so doing, demonstrates God's faithfulness to and inclusion of all people.

INTRODUCTION

This pericope of Scripture is a part of a larger unit that describes the circumstances of the birth of Jesus Christ (Matthew 1:1–4:25). The fuller unit describes in detail the genealogy of Jesus from Joseph's side of the family. The appearance of the angel Gabriel to Mary, the visit of the Magi and Herod's response to their refusal to comply with God's revelation to them, the preaching of John the Baptist and Jesus' identification by him as the Son of God (as the One whose shoelaces he was not worthy to unloose), and His test in the wilderness are all included in the larger unit.

Matthew is the writer of the first Gospel account. He notates his call in Matthew 9:9. Matthew is also a despised publican (tax collector). As a Jew, he writes to fellow Jews about the Messiah and His birth, the greatest Person of the age and the most significant event in Jewish history, except for the resurrection ("The Gospel According to Matthew" in *The New Oxford Annotated Bible, New Revised Standard Version*, Edited by Bruce Metzger and Roland Murphy. New York: Oxford University Press, 1994, p. 1 NT). We know very little of the man himself behind the book. We do know that one of his major purposes was to "demonstrate that all of the prophecies of the Old Testament are fulfilled in Jesus, and that therefore he must be the Messiah" (*The*

Gospel of Matthew, Volume 1, Revised Edition. Translated by William Barclay. Philadelphia: Westminster Press, 1975, pp. 5–8).

Our text links the story of Jesus to the Old Testament and to the promise God made to Abraham (Genesis 12–18). The theme of this textual passage is that Jesus is the fulfillment of the Messianic promise and the predicted heir to the Davidic Kingdom that will stand forever (see Genesis 12:1 ff. 18:18; 2 Samuel 7:16). Initially, Matthew begins this description with Israel's heritage (see Genesis 12:1) and slowly builds it into the story's implications for the entire world in the Great Commission (Matthew 28:18–29). Matthew records the linage of Jesus first to show the purity of the Jewish heritage that establishes Jesus as both King of the Jews and as a son of Abraham and David. The other references to this commission listed in the other Gospel accounts—Mark, Luke, and John—also verify this point. Three things are important in this text. First, we shall examine the era from Abraham to David, the twilight of the heritage of Israel. Second, we shall examine the decline of Israel's ancestry history. Finally, we shall discover the elevation of Israel's legacy and worldwide impact through the birth of Jesus Christ.

EXPOSITION

I. ABRAHAM TO DAVID (MATTHEW 1:1–6)

The story of Jesus begins in Matthew with two prominent names in Jewish history, Abraham and David, the king of Israel. Jesus is listed as the son of both figures. That is because Matthew follows Abraham's lineage, of which David is a part. In Jewish custom, the words "son of" identifies the person as belonging to a certain family. It is the line of ancestry or of family development and formation. This story of Jesus for Matthew begins with Abraham. The lineage traces an ancestral line of Jesus. Of course, it includes the patriarchs, Abraham, Isaac, and Jacob, and passes on through Judah until it reaches Obed and Jesse, the grandfather and father of David. The patriarchs are well-known entities, for their stories take up the majority of the books of Genesis and Exodus, but many of the personages are not well-known at all. For example, very little is known about Perez, the father of Hezron or Ram, the father of Aminnadab, and Nahshon, the father of Salmon (Stagg, Frank, *The Broadman Bible Commentary*. Vol. 8, General Articles, Matthew—Mark, Broadman Press: Nashville, pp. 80–83).

What is remarkable is that within the lineage of Jesus are four women named, Tamar, Rahab, Ruth, and the wife of Uriah, Bathsheba. The culture of the times often ignored the contribution of women and considered women to be second-class citizens. However, in this record, these women are recognized as historical figures in Jesus' lineage. Rahab, a harlot from Jericho and a Canaanite, assisted the invading Israelites as they sought to penetrate the defenses of Jericho. Tamar, a widowed Canaanite woman, outwitted her father-in-law, Judah, Jacob's son, who had promised to provide for her. She disguised herself as a harlot and tricked the aged Judah into fathering her son, thus enabling the continuation of the bloodline (see Genesis 38:3–30). Bathsheba is called the wife of Uriah. She was the mother of Solomon, David's son. Ruth was from Moab. Theologian Frank Stagg does not believe that Matthew seeks to contrast these women with Mary, but to illustrate that God used outsiders or people from all stands of humanity to develop or restore the divine-human fellowship (Stagg, *The Broadman Bible,* pp. 81–82). Matthew seems to be saying that one's background is unimportant in terms of one's eternal destination. Jesus' ancestral line bore no significance in Him being the Messiah.

Verses 1–7 could be deemed as the highlight of the Israelite empire or nation. God's salvation began with the call of Abram, later known as Abraham. God established His covenant with Abraham. He promised that He would give the patriarch the fertile land of Canaan, innumerable descendants, and provide for him and his family throughout all generations. Abraham's faith led him to acknowledge and accept God as his Lord and Creator. Abraham accepted God's call and obeyed Him by looking for a city whose builder and maker was God (Hebrews 11:8–12). Isaac inherits the promise of God from Abraham, and the tribes and nations truly begin their quest from the sojourn of Jacob to David. Israel joined the elite group of nations under David's reign as king and continues to be in the mix until the Babylonian Exile.

II. DAVID TO THE BABYLONIAN EXILE (MATTHEW 1:7–11)

The stress here, however, lies partially on Jesus as a son of Abraham and as a son of David. Both fall within the ancestral line of the original patriarch. Yet the birth of Jesus relates to the entire world, as indicated earlier. Matthew presents Jesus as both, while later suggesting that Jesus is David's Lord (see Matthew 22:41–46; see also Acts 2:25–42. Also, see Peter's sermon in the *New Oxford Annotated Bible*, New Revised Standard Version. Edited by Bruce Metzger and Roland E. Murphy New York: Oxford University Press, 1994).

The genealogy of Jesus is composed of a list of men and four women that continues for several generations that lead from Abraham to the birth of David, from David to the Exile, and from the Exile to the birth of Jesus.

The total number of each equals fourteen generations for each section. Fourteen may be a reference in code to Jesus as "David." According to Stagg, "Gematria was an ancient practice of assigning a number to a person (cf. Revelations 13:18), computed by totaling the number value of each letter in one's name. The first letter in the alphabet had the same number value of one, the second letter two, etc. The name David in Hebrew would have the number value of fourteen (DVD = 4+6+4). Matthew may have attended thus to have written 'David' across each section of the genealogy." Unlike Matthew, the genealogy in Luke follows the ancestry of Nathan because Luke's intent is to show the much wider impact of Jesus in the relationship to the whole human race. Matthew is more concerned with the royal descent and fulfillment of Israel's heritage and hopes (*Ibid*. See Stagg, *The Broadman Bible*, p. 81). Furthermore, the number of names in the Matthean and Lukan accounts also differ because there are some omissions of names between Solomon and David (v. 5) and between Joram and Uzziah and Jehoiakim (v. 11). From this difference, one may reasonably assume that the two genealogies are not to be harmonized, nor are the references to "father of" meant to indicate direct progenitorship, but rather, progenitorship in general.

III. FROM BABYLON TO CHRIST (MATTHEW 1:12–17)

It was during the reign of Rehoboam that the kingdom of Israel split into two independent nations, the Northern Kingdom and the Southern Kingdom (Judah). The Northern Kingdom was destroyed in 722 BC when it came under assault by the mighty Assyrian Empire. The Southern Kingdom hung on until 587 BC, when it folded beneath the military power of the Babylon Empire. Deliverance from Babylonian captivity involves a study of several Old Testament books, such as Nehemiah, Ezra, the Minor Prophets, the Chronicles, Kings, and Isaiah. The Servant Songs of Isaiah (Isaiah 52–66) provide a great deal of information concerning the reign of the Servant and His importance to the restoration of Israel and her return to prominence in world affairs. The elevation of Israel has to do with Jesus coming to be the Messiah, bringing with Him truth and justice, which are predicated on Him as Lord and Savior of the world. Recovery from the Exile, in a sense, restores Israel to a high level of prominence that the nation had not experienced since the years of the Davidic Kingdom.

THE LESSON APPLIED

This text is to shows us that Jesus is the fulfillment of God's promise to Abraham.

As a Jewish writer whose purpose was to minister to the Jewish community, Matthew wholeheartedly succeeds as he demonstrates time and time again that Jesus is the Messiah. Not only does the genealogy establish Jesus as the promised Messiah, but through it, Matthew also establishes Him as the legal heir to the throne of David, who was a descendant of Abraham. The writer also points out in this pericope of Scripture his confirmation of the virgin birth of Jesus. For Matthew's Jewish audience, this is important because it also affirms and confirms His divine Sonship. He is Joseph's son legally, but He is God's Son in every other way that matters (by birth, by appointing, by anointing, etc.).

The text represents the three stages of Israelite life. The first stage takes the history down to King David. David was the king who forged Israel into a world power. The second stage takes the story down to the exile in Babylon. It tells of the nation's shame and tragedy. The third period takes the story down to Jesus Christ. He is the One who liberated the people from its slavery to sin and who turned their tragedy into triumph.

That is to say that these three periods symbolized the goodness of God and His eternal presence with humankind, through observance of the Jewish way of life. Humanity was born for greatness. It was created in the image and likeness of God. However, that greatness was lost through denial of God and the act of depraved living. Humanity became a slave to sin. Left to itself, humanity frustrated the plan of God for itself and fell into a state of lostness. Its fall and failure is quite similar to that of the prodigal son. The younger son had it made while abiding at home with his father and elder brother. It was for sure a blessed and honorable life. But soon he wanted to exercise his options, and demanded the goods he had coming to him and left his father's home. He lived a life of riotous living and squandered his advantages. He did whatever he was big and bad enough to do. Soon, his sinful and extravagant lifestyle had helped to deplete him of his funds and he would have eaten the slop that the swine did eat, but no one gave him any. He was at the lowest point of his life, and that is when he determined that he would arise and go back to his father. What a great fall he had, but oh, what a greater recovery he had as well. When he arose and went to his father, he experienced a great blessing. The father gave him a ring, a robe, and prepared the fattened calf to welcome and celebrate the son's return. He, like Israel, had reached his lowest point and had now risen to his highest point. His decline modeled Israel's experience in the Babylonian Exile, as noted in the genealogy, but he reached his highest confession of Jesus Christ as the Messiah, thus allowing Israel to reach the pinnacle of its life through the truth that Jesus Christ has elevated all humankind to experience the glory of God in His offer of divine salvation to the world.

LET'S TALK ABOUT IT
Why are the three stages important for Matthew?

These stages are important because they show that Matthew believed that Jesus was the fulfillment of God's promise to Abraham and to all of the Jewish people. The genealogy shows His lineage as the son of Abraham and as the son of David. Humanity recovers through Jesus Christ the glorious intention of God to elevate the Jewish people, as well as the whole of humanity, to the glory God intended for them to have before they exercised dominion over their own lives. In Jesus, they both reached their highest level of success and righteousness to exemplify God's salvation. In Jesus, the Messianic Servant, Israel became all that God intended humanity to be.

HOME DAILY DEVOTIONAL READINGS
DECEMBER 18–24, 2023

MONDAY	TUESDAY	WEDNESDAY	THURSDAY	FRIDAY	SATURDAY	SUNDAY
Contentment in Every Situation	God Is My Refuge	The Lord Has Done Great Things!	The Annunciation to Zechariah	Zechariah Doubts but Elizabeth Rejoices	Believe!	Mary and Elizabeth Express Faith
Philippians 4:10–19	Psalm 91:1–16	Joel 2:18–27	Luke 1:5–17	Luke 1:18–25	John 20:19, 24–29	Luke 1:36–45, 56

SHARING HOPE AND COURAGE

ADULT TOPIC: THE FAITH OF ELIZABETH AND MARY	BACKGROUND SCRIPTURE: LUKE 1:1–25, 39–45, 56–60 LESSON PASSAGE: LUKE 1:36–45, 56

LUKE 1:36–45, 56

King James Version

AND, behold, thy cousin Elisabeth, she hath also conceived a son in her old age: and this is the sixth month with her, who was called barren.

37 For with God nothing shall be impossible.

38 And Mary said, Behold the handmaid of the Lord; be it unto me according to thy word. And the angel departed from her.

39 And Mary arose in those days, and went into the hill country with haste, into a city of Juda;

40 And entered into the house of Zacharias, and saluted Elisabeth.

41 And it came to pass, that, when Elisabeth heard the salutation of Mary, the babe leaped in her womb; and Elisabeth was filled with the Holy Ghost:

42 And she spake out with a loud voice, and said, Blessed art thou among women, and blessed is the fruit of thy womb.

43 And whence is this to me, that the mother of my Lord should come to me?

44 For, lo, as soon as the voice of thy salutation sounded in mine ears, the babe leaped in my womb for joy.

45 And blessed is she that believed: for there shall be a performance of those things which were told her from the Lord.

• • • • • •

56 And Mary abode with her about three months, and returned to her own house.

New Revised Standard Version

AND now, your relative Elizabeth in her old age has also conceived a son; and this is the sixth month for her who was said to be barren.

37 For nothing will be impossible with God."

38 Then Mary said, "Here am I, the servant of the Lord; let it be with me according to your word." Then the angel departed from her.

39 In those days Mary set out and went with haste to a Judean town in the hill country,

40 where she entered the house of Zechariah and greeted Elizabeth.

41 When Elizabeth heard Mary's greeting, the child leaped in her womb. And Elizabeth was filled with the Holy Spirit

42 and exclaimed with a loud cry, "Blessed are you among women, and blessed is the fruit of your womb.

43 And why has this happened to me, that the mother of my Lord comes to me?

44 For as soon as I heard the sound of your greeting, the child in my womb leaped for joy.

45 And blessed is she who believed that there would be a fulfillment of what was spoken to her by the Lord."

• • • • • •

56 And Mary remained with her about three months and then returned to her home.

MAIN THOUGHT: And it came to pass, that, when Elisabeth heard the salutation of Mary, the babe leaped in her womb; and Elisabeth was filled with the Holy Ghost: And she spake out with a loud voice, and said, Blessed art thou among women, and blessed is the fruit of thy womb. (Luke 1:41–42, KJV)

LESSON SETTING

Time: Circa 7 BCE

Place: Judea

LESSON OUTLINE

I. Gabriel Visits Mary
   (Luke 1:36–38)
II. Mary Visits Elizabeth
   (Luke 1:39–42)
III. Mary's Joy in God's Favor
   (Luke 1:43–56)

UNIFYING PRINCIPLE

We need people with whom we can share our joys and struggles in life. Who do we turn to when we need to process major life events? Just as Mary found a kindred spirit in her relationship with Elizabeth, so also can we find spiritual encouragement and support from those who share our faith in God.

INTRODUCTION

The lesson is about Mary's visit to see her relative, Elizabeth, and the inclusion of the message that both women were pregnant with male children who were gifts from God. The Scriptures do not say if this was Mary's first visit to Elizabeth's, as she would certainly not be traveling alone, or who Mary was traveling with; however, Joseph must not have been present, as he is not mentioned in the account. Although Zacharias is the husband of Elizabeth and the master of the house, neither is he mentioned during the visit of Mary. Her visit may have occurred during the days that Zacharias was in service in the Temple; though, the term of his service would have lasted for only about two weeks. Zacharias should have been at his house to interact with Mary because Luke records that after the days of his priestly service had ended,

he went back home (Luke 1:23). Mary would remain with Elizabeth for three months, then, return home to Nazareth.

EXPOSITION

I. GABRIEL VISITS MARY (LUKE 1:36–38)

We must begin this section with the declaration that "nothing is impossible with God" (v. 37). The lesson begins with a visit from the angel Gabriel who informs Mary that her cousin, Elizabeth (some scholars refer to her as an aunt), has also "conceived a son in her old age." Mary is probably at her parents' home in Nazareth when Gabriel appears, as Joseph had not yet taken her into his home. Luke does not indicate whether it was a day or night visit, but it seems as if he appeared to Mary when she was alone because there is no indication of any witnesses to the angel's presence. Mary was excited because Elizabeth had previously been barren, as was the motif of other women in Israel's history.

Elizabeth attributed her conception to the favor of the Lord upon her, saying, "This is the way the Lord has dealt with me in the days when He looked with favor upon me, to take away my disgrace among men" (Luke 1:25). Luke uses the term *óneidos*, meaning "disgrace," or better yet, "reproach," which caused men and women to literally revile a barren woman, who was thought of as cursed by the Lord. The significance of Luke's noting that Elizabeth was in her sixth month provides a timeline that reveals that John would be six months older than Jesus, and that the two men, who are close in age, would realistically encounter each other and have similar movements at the same time. Again, the chorus of "nothing is impossible with God" is exclaimed by Gabriel, although he could have been joined by the angelic hosts that would later herald the birth of Jesus to the shepherds (Luke 2:8–14). Luke reinforces the power of God over all forces in the natural as well as the spiritual realm. This is the reoccurring theme that functions as a foundation for the faith and gratitude that Mary and Elizabeth had in God.

Buoyed with exuberance and confidence over the angel's revelation, Mary's response was to declare that she was a bondslave or bondservant of the Lord. The word used here is *doúlēs* (the feminine of *doúlos*- servant), denoting a female servant or bondwoman. The language of being a bondservant to the Lord is not to be viewed as a negative position, as it actually reflects a person's dedication to the Lord. The plea, "May it be done to me according to your word," (v. 38) reflects Mary's pledge in that as a servant of the Lord, she accepted His decision, that whatever her fate be in life, she would willingly agree and submit to His will. Satisfied with Mary's embrace of the "Good News," Gabriel departed and left the young woman to bask in the message of God's favor.

II. MARY VISITS ELIZABETH (LUKE 1:39–42)

Mary decides to visit her relative, Elizabeth, and sets forth to leave her home in Nazareth to journey to the hill-country city in Judah, or in the region of Judea. This was close to Jerusalem, which would allow Elizabeth's husband, Zacharias, to serve and perform his duties in the Temple. Zacharias (who is also known as Zechariah) was a priest of Abijah's division and one of the men chosen to represent his division in its yearly appointed session of service in the Jerusalem Temple (the priests of Israel were divided into twenty-four orders, each being assigned an annual two-week period of service in the Temple). Mary would journey for several days (as Elizabeth lived about 100 miles from Nazareth), probably taking a similar route that the Holy Family would follow when they were forced to travel to Bethlehem to report for the Roman census (Luke 2:1–5).

When Mary entered the home of Elizabeth and Zacharias, she was probably greeted with the affectionate *shalom*, the traditional Hebrew term for "peace [be with you]," which carries the fundamental wish of welfare, prosperity, or wholeness, as well as the absence of hostility. What is most important is that the highlight of this greeting was the increased activity of the baby Elizabeth was carrying. During pregnancy, it is quite normal for a child to move while in the womb. However, in this case, Luke reports that the baby leaped in Elizabeth's womb, which was beyond its normal movement. It is probable that, through the Holy Spirit, the baby in Elizabeth's womb reacted to the Child that had begun to form inside of Mary. Although invisible to the naked eye, the Holy Spirit created a bond between the two cousins, who never seemed to meet again until Jesus' baptism, yet, recognized each other. Additionally, the Holy Spirit revealed to Elizabeth that Mary was pregnant, prompting Elizabeth to cry out in a loud voice, "Blessed are you among women [or above all women], and blessed is the fruit of your womb!" (v. 42). This "fruit" could also be indicative of the gift of God that is manifested as evidence in one who possesses a life through which God is alive and reigning. Detractors often claim that Mary knew that Elizabeth was pregnant before she made her visit to her older cousin. However, God is developing the narrative behind the scenes. Mary has not requested a sign but, as often in scenes of this kind, she is given one. She receives what is for her new information; Elizabeth has just come out of seclusion, where she hid herself for a period of five months (See Luke 1:24), so Mary could not have known of her pregnancy. The repetition of this information also serves to emphasize again the trustworthiness of Gabriel's words and the heightened sense of the miraculous already penetrating this story.

III. MARY'S JOY IN GOD'S FAVOR (LUKE 1:43–56)

Verse 43 confirms that the person speaking is Elizabeth, i.e., "the mother of my Lord coming to me." The phrase "mother of my Lord" refers to Elizabeth's realization that Mary's unborn Child is the Messiah ("my Lord"). Apparently, Mary's visit was unexpected and a pleasant surprise; Elizabeth, already astonished that she is pregnant in her advanced age, wonders how she deserved a visit from Mary. However, Mary's surprise visit should not be misunderstood as if Elizabeth did not receive Mary well; to the contrary, Elizabeth was overjoyed with Mary's coming to her house, especially with the results —thanks to the Holy Spirit—of this visit. Mary would later be called the *theotokos,* or mother of God, "child-bearer." In the fifth century, Nestorius, the Archbishop of Constantinople, stated that Mary should not be called Theotokos, which sounded like the "mother of pagan deities," but Christotokos, the "one who gave birth to Christ." Importantly, Elizabeth uses the term "mother of my Lord" and not "Mother of God," which denotes that Mary would be the mother of Yahweh. This latter phrase is not found in Scripture.

Mary's visit to see Elizabeth was so exciting that Elizabeth reiterated that, although in her womb, the baby leaped for joy! Elizabeth made that claim accurately, not out of speculation or emotional delight but through the aid of the Holy Spirit. Mary agrees that she is blessed because she is convinced that there will be a fulfillment of what had been spoken to her by the Lord through the angel Gabriel. Mary would not know the exact circumstances that she would experience after her visit with Elizabeth; however, Luke makes it quite clear that Mary is ready to embrace her gift and responsibilities. Luke does not indicate if Mary was aware of the Scriptures and prophecies, such as in Isaiah and the Psalms, which predicted the advent of Jesus the Messiah, yet her excitement and dedication to being a servant of the Lord is indicative to her commitment and faith.

Luke does not indicate as to whether Mary had any traveling companions during her journey. In this period of the first century, it would nearly be impossible and improbable for a young woman of Mary's age and distinction to have traveled alone to the home of Zacharias and Elizabeth. Recall that under arduous circumstances, a very pregnant Mary would later travel from Nazareth to Bethlehem where she would give birth to a son named Jesus. However, then she was accompanied by her husband. The record here is silent about any other characters in the account; however, if any additional persons were part of Mary's traveling party, Luke does not include them in the record and their contributions, if any, remain nil. Mary and Elizabeth lived in uncertain times in a land that was occupied by the Romans, who could be cruel and oppressive in their treatment of the populace. Women and children were especially vulnerable to the soldiers stationed in their towns and villages. However, Mary and Elizabeth trusted God to guide their lives and that of their children.

Mary stayed with Elizabeth about three months, and then returned to her home in Nazareth. One can only imagine the bonding that occurred between these two women, spiritually selected by God to make an impact on the redemption and salvation of Israel and the world. More than likely, there were giddy conversations during their dinners and walks together, as the women described and compared their situations and conditions. Following the Hebrew lunar calendar, if Jesus was born in the month(s) of Nisan (March/April), Mary would have visited Elizabeth nine months prior, during the month(s) of Abu (July/August), which places John's birth in the month(s) of Heshvan (October/November). Weather conditions during Abu were warm and dry, whereas, the rainy season would begin during Heshvan, which would have compelled Mary's party to leave for Nazareth, before the conditions would render it difficult or impossible to return home. Additionally, Mary had to later travel to Bethlehem from Nazareth for the fulfillment of prophecy. Moreover, when Mary left Elizabeth, she would have been in the third month of her pregnancy. Her three-month stay would coincide with the time Elizabeth (ninth month) would give birth, making it probable that Mary stayed to assist or to comfort Elizabeth in the delivery of her son, allowing Mary to meet John, the cousin of Jesus.

In chronicling this account about God blessing women from the embarrassment and humiliation of barrenness, recall that God promised Israel no infertility, if they obeyed His laws (Deuteronomy 7:14). Ironically, unique among ancient writings is the concept here that barrenness could be a result of male infertility, when it was usually directed as a fault or a curse borne by women! Finally, as bad as barrenness was, Jesus would tell the women of Jerusalem that barrenness and dry breasts would be better than what they were going to go through (Luke 23:29). He was teaching that our physical problems are never ultimate; only spiritual ones are. Mary was not in a position to experience infertility; however, the contrast exists with her older cousin, Elizabeth. Mary is so overjoyed with God's favoring of her that she sang or recited a loving dedication to God that is often called the "Magnificat" (Luke 1:46–56). There are fifteen discernible quotations from the Old Testament in this poem, showing how much the Old Testament was known and loved in the home in which Jesus was reared.

THE LESSON APPLIED

One of the important themes in our lesson today is to make connections between the lives of two women, Elizabeth and Mary, who faced extraordinary circumstances in God's grand scheme of salvation. Both women were pregnant with servants of God, the first, who would declare the coming of the Messiah by "preparing the way," and the second, Jesus the Messiah. In the eyes of non-believers, both pregnancies are controversial; Elizabeth is advanced beyond her child conception years, and Mary has not experienced copulation with a man. Yet, because of the grand design of the Lord, both women are pregnant with two of the most important men in Christendom. The grand scheme is God's plan of redemption, that of providing a guide to eternal life.

LET'S TALK ABOUT IT
How does the story of Mary and Elizabeth affect parenthood now?

The faith of Mary and Elizabeth are on display and their trust that God will grant them parenthood. In our society, some adults experience sorrow because they are unable to become parents due to biological factors that inhibit one or the other persons from contributing to the union. Yet, in many situations, a by-product of parenting happens to be anxiety and stress, occurring especially when the child is exposed to influences outside of the protection of the home, such as childcare, the school system, and their being exposed to and playing with other children. These challenges may influence couples to decide whether or not to have children or possibly, to delay the starting of their families until they feel they have better solutions to the outside forces that can affect their children.

Nonetheless, children, whether conceived or adopted, deserve a chance to live, and no greater blessing can have afforded them than that of a Christian home. Christians should gain strength to face the future when they hear of the faith of Elizabeth and Mary. Moreover, Christian parents should look at the accounts of Mary and Elizabeth to know that God has a plan and design for our children and that, through faith—and our rearing them in a Christian home, church, and environment—we will be successful, as long as we lean on Him.

GET SOCIAL
Share your views and tag us
@rhboydco and use #Hope.

Twitter
@rhboydco (#rhboydco)

Instagram
@rhboydco (#rhboydco)

Facebook
@rhboydco (#rhboydco)

www.rhboyd.com

HOME DAILY DEVOTIONAL READINGS
DECEMBER 25–31, 2023

MONDAY	TUESDAY	WEDNESDAY	THURSDAY	FRIDAY	SATURDAY	SUNDAY
Christ the Savior Is Born	Mary's Exultant Faith	Reject Abhorrent Imitations of Faith	Make Disciples in Faith	God's Salvation for All the Earth	Arise, Shine; Your Light Has Come	Worship the King of the Jews
Matthew 1:18–25	Luke 1:46–55	Deuteronomy 18:9–14	Matthew 28:16–20	Isaiah 49:1–6	Isaiah 60:1–6	Matthew 2:1–12

THE FAITH OF THE WISE MEN

ADULT TOPIC:	BACKGROUND SCRIPTURE: MATTHEW 2:1–12
TAKING RISKS AND REAPING REWARDS	LESSON PASSAGE: MATTHEW 2:1–12

MATTHEW 2:1–12

King James Version

NOW when Jesus was born in Bethlehem of Judaea in the days of Herod the king, behold, there came wise men from the east to Jerusalem,

2 Saying, Where is he that is born King of the Jews? for we have seen his star in the east, and are come to worship him.

3 When Herod the king had heard these things, he was troubled, and all Jerusalem with him.

4 And when he had gathered all the chief priests and scribes of the people together, he demanded of them where Christ should be born.

5 And they said unto him, In Bethlehem of Judaea: for thus it is written by the prophet,

6 And thou Bethlehem, in the land of Juda, art not the least among the princes of Juda: for out of thee shall come a Governor, that shall rule my people Israel.

7 Then Herod, when he had privily called the wise men, enquired of them diligently what time the star appeared.

8 And he sent them to Bethlehem, and said, Go and search diligently for the young child; and when ye have found him, bring me word again, that I may come and worship him also.

9 When they had heard the king, they departed; and, lo, the star, which they saw in the east, went before them, till it came and stood over where the young child was.

10 When they saw the star, they rejoiced with exceeding great joy.

New Revised Standard Version

IN the time of King Herod, after Jesus was born in Bethlehem of Judea, wise men from the East came to Jerusalem,

2 asking, "Where is the child who has been born king of the Jews? For we observed his star at its rising, and have come to pay him homage."

3 When King Herod heard this, he was frightened, and all Jerusalem with him;

4 and calling together all the chief priests and scribes of the people, he inquired of them where the Messiah was to be born.

5 They told him, "In Bethlehem of Judea; for so it has been written by the prophet:

6 'And you, Bethlehem, in the land of Judah, are by no means least among the rulers of Judah; for from you shall come a ruler who is to shepherd my people Israel.'"

7 Then Herod secretly called for the wise men and learned from them the exact time when the star had appeared.

8 Then he sent them to Bethlehem, saying, "Go and search diligently for the child; and when you have found him, bring me word so that I may also go and pay him homage."

9 When they had heard the king, they set out; and there, ahead of them, went the star that they had seen at its rising, until it stopped over the place where the child was.

10 When they saw that the star had stopped, they were overwhelmed with joy.

MAIN THOUGHT: Saying, Where is he that is born King of the Jews? for we have seen his star in the east, and are come to worship him. (Matthew 2:2, KJV)

MATTHEW 2:1–12

King James Version	New Revised Standard Version
11 And when they were come into the house, they saw the young child with Mary his mother, and fell down, and worshipped him: and when they had opened their treasures, they presented unto him gifts; gold, and frankincense and myrrh.	11 On entering the house, they saw the child with Mary his mother; and they knelt down and paid him homage. Then, opening their treasure chests, they offered him gifts of gold, frankincense, and myrrh.
12 And being warned of God in a dream that they should not return to Herod, they departed into their own country another way.	12 And having been warned in a dream not to return to Herod, they left for their own country by another road.

LESSON SETTING
Time: 4 BCE
Place: Jerusalem

LESSON OUTLINE
I. **Where Is He That Is Born King of the Jews?** (Matthew 2:1–2)
II. **Herod's Response** (Matthew 2:3–9)
III. **The Wise Men's Faith** (Matthew 2:10-12)

UNIFYING PRINCIPLE

We may choose to pursue things that take us out of our comfort zones. What makes these pursuits worth the risk? The wise men in Matthew's Gospel took the risk of following a star that led them to Christ.

INTRODUCTION

This is a passage of true faith. It is the story of belief by a group of astrologers who believed that Jesus Christ was born King of the Jews and was the new King of divine salvation. They made known their belief by journeying to Jerusalem from somewhere in the East that pointed to a newborn King. It was the result of a long-awaited expectation that a world redeemer would come. Matthew, like the Apostle Paul, believed that the Gospel must come by way of the Jews and then to the Gentile nations of the world (see Matt. 8:10–12; 12:18–21; 15:24–28; 24:14; 28:19; and Rom 1:16). From the beginning of the Gospel, the implication is that One would come, and He would not be recognized by His own people (see John 1:4–13), but would receive homage from comers or sojourners from the East (Frank Stagg, *The Broadman Commentary* [Vol. 8], General Article, Matthew–Mark. Broadman Publishers, Nashville, pp. 80–84.).

The Magi, or the astrologers, of the East came with an interesting inquiry, "Where is He that is born King of the Jews?" The sentence reads as an assumption or as a event that has already taken place. It upsets the equilibrium of the Jewish palace. Any king would have been worried at hearing such news come off the press, but Herod was deeply troubled. He was half Jew and half Idumaean. There was Edomite blood in his veins. He was given the title by the Roman Senate with the backing of Mark Antony and Octavius in 40 BC.

Scholars believe the Magi were actually Persian soothsayers who watched the stars. The word *Magi* is Indo-European, its root appearing in many languages and carrying the meaning of "greatness." The magi were originally a priestly caste among the Medes, later recognized as teachers of religion and science among the Medo-Persians, with special interest in astrology and medicine. They were Gentiles. There are also listed as three in number, according to the gifts that they brought to the newborn king: gifts of gold, frankincense, and myrrh. However, the number of gifts do not necessarily pertain to the number of people who came to pay homage to Jesus. The verse that deals with the opening of their treasure means "caskets" from the verb "receptacle for valuables." In the ancient writings, it meant "treasury" as in 1 Maccabees 3:29. So a "storehouse" as in Matthew 13:52. Then it means the things laid up in store, treasure in heaven (Matthew 6:20), in Christ (Colossians 2:3). In their caskets, the Magi had the three treasures mentioned above.

Three things are important here. First, the question the Magi asked of the king was important. They went to the most direct source to discover what the star meant. Second, their question was a good one for it revealed a lack of observation in the political and theocratic empire of Herod. No one locally had given any thought to the meaning of the star or thought to pursue its theological implications. Third, it revealed the faith of the Magi, who had evidently traveled many miles to uncover the contents of their discovery. The coming of the Magi with their question, however, is more than an ordinary inquiry. It is an act of faith. For some reason, their inquiry prompts them to action that goes beyond curiosity. Furthermore, they defy the king who occupied the throne and listened to the voice of another. They dared to disobey a contingency of the Roman government and return home another way.

EXPOSITION

I. WHERE IS HE THAT IS BORN KING OF THE JEWS? (MATTHEW 2:1-2)

It is safe to say that their initial inquiry startled King Herod. Their question was unexpected and seemingly caught the king off guard. Would they take on such an expedition to discover the origin of a star simply because of curiosity? First and foremost, the evidence pointed to how incredible the event was. It was the equivalent of Moses' sight in the wilderness of the burning bush in Exodus 3. He felt compelled to step aside to see the incredible sight of the burning but unconsumed bush because it was a phenomenon. There are other incredible sights in the biblical record that causes us to get hold of our bearings (see Exodus and the talking donkey of Balaam, Exodus 14; Numbers 22). It is fair to say that the star, its size, shape, and movement, precipitated the interest in it, both the research interest and the travel. That Jerusalem was caught unaware of its presence and location is also interesting. The Jews were surprised by its reality. It is apparent, however, that King Herod misunderstood the threat to his kingdom by Jesus. The description of Bethlehem as the place where Jesus was to be born has a reference to Jesus as a ruler, but He rules from the standpoint of governing the people as a shepherd. The word interpreted as "govern" (*poimanei*) is also in Micah 5:2. This points out that Jesus was king not in the traditional fashion, but that He was the Shepherd King. Jesus termed Himself as the Good Shepherd. Also in Hebrews 13:20, He is called the great "Shepherd of the Sheep." In 1 Peter 2:25, Peter calls Him the chief Shepherd. Revelation 7:17 says that "the Lamb which is in the midst of the throne shall be their shepherd." In John 21:16, Jesus told Peter to shepherd the lambs. Our word "pastor" means to shepherd, to care for and protect the sheep.

II. HEROD'S RESPONSE (MATTHEW 2:3–9).

Needless to say, Herod had to be embarrassed by it all. There was a star indicating kingly activity at the very least in his own backyard, yet it went unnoticed. The text says that he was disturbed. It is clear how such a man would feel when the news reached him that a child was born who was destined to be king. Herod was troubled and all Jerusalem with him. The city residents knew full well what this meant. Herod would stop at nothing to eliminate the young child. Jerusalem knew and shivered as it waited for his inevitable reaction. The writer indicates it was more because of jealously than anything else. He sought to hide it as a point of worship when his real intentions were to kill the young child. History shows Herod as a killer of his own people; he even killed his own wife and sons. When the Magi did not return as promised, he went on a killing spree, slaying all of the children under his rule aged two years and under. He was quite calculating in his determination to take the life of the young child (Matthew 2:16–18). The deceit of Herod seems plausible enough and might have succeeded but for God's intervention to protect His Son from the jealous rage of Herod.

The prophetic presence (*gennatai*) is given, the very words of Herod retained by Matthew's report. It suggests that Herod inquired repeatedly of the leaders gathered together—both Sadducees (chief priests) and Pharisees (scribes), if Herod actually called together all the Sanhedrin and probably "he could have asked the question of a single scribe," because he had begun his reign with a massacre of the Sanhedrin (see Josephus XIV. ix. 4). But that was over thirty years ago at this point, and Herod was desperately in earnest to learn what the Jews really expected about the coming king. Herod probably gathered together not the entire Sanhedrin since elders are not mentioned, but certain leaders, a free assembly of leaders, for a conference. He had heard of this expected king and he would swallow plenty of pride to be able to compress and defeat these hopes of "the Messiah." According to the scribal records, the event was to take place in a small town seven miles to the northwest called Bethlehem of Judah, which means "House of Bread." It was the home of Ruth and Boaz, and King David. Then there was the reaction or response of the chief priest and others in the kingdom. They were indifferent; they were so engrossed in their temple rituals that it did not matter what was about to happen with Herod the Great. They were so involved in their legal discussions that Jesus did not matter at all. The question comes what did matter and to whom did it matter?

III. THE WISE MEN'S FAITH (MATTHEW 2:10–12)

It mattered to the Magi. Their response to the star is noteworthy. They obeyed and followed it in faith. They had more than a passing interest in Jesus. The star got their attention; they followed it. When it led them to Herod's palace, they inquired about it. Their activity forced the scribes to discover what its theological implications were. They finally acknowledged Herod as dishonest and avoided him as they returned home. They ignored his request to let him know where the Christ Child had been born and returned home another way. Their action was an act of faith. They took the voice of God in their dreams as the essential truth. Faith is listening to the voice of truth. It is to be actively engaged in something beyond yourself. Dreams were acceptable forms of divine communication in the ancient world. Matthew found his own way to express what he believed to be real and authentic. It was a faith that "passeth understanding." Why did the wise men not return to share what they had discovered to be true with Herod? What lead them to avoid Herod's deception? The biblical record is true and speaks for itself. It was Matthew's way of saying that God acted in such a way to preserve this event as one of the greatest miracles of all time. The Magi believed and so they acted accordingly.

THE LESSON APPLIED

This passage of Scripture confirms the birth of Jesus and the Magi's faith in God by going home another way. Matthew records it as heavenly evidence that a miracle of God has taken place. Several things are important in this text. First, it confirms that the phenomenon was an authentic and true revelation from God. The star was not a made-up elaboration or fiction. The naming of historical figures as witnesses to the event further authenticates it. The activity of Herod the Great and the facts surrounding the killing of children in the Jerusalem massacre weighs heavily as truth in the story as told by Matthew.

Second, the element of surprise revealed the reality that Herod's government was absorbed in other things. It sets up the idea of homage paid to Jesus by foreigners, while Jesus incurred hostility from His own people (see John 1:4-13). He was to be a "man of sorrows." He came unto his own, but His own did not receive Him. It was a part of Herod's ignorance that the birth of the Christ Child was taking place right in the king's own backyard and went unnoticed. The chief priest and scribes' interest was elsewhere until the Magi asked them where the newborn king would be born. They saw only an enemy lurking or arising out of the darkness. They saw God as an enemy of humanity ready to upset the tranquility of their lives, rather than as One who was coming to provide the assistance they needed to live abundant lives.

Third, the passage displays another opportunity for the purpose of God to be revealed. The star arising in the East was of divine concoction. It was God making His presence known in human affairs, keeping the promise He had made in the Garden of Eden (see Genesis 3:15–20). It was His announcement that salvation had come to humanity. The long-awaited day had occurred.

LET'S TALK ABOUT IT

1. **Does God often intervene in world affairs?**

God does intervene in world affairs— the star arising in the East is one of

His divine interventions. The miracle of the Christ birth is another, the miracles Jesus performed are others, and the event called the Resurrection is yet another. In the Old Testament, the incident at the Tower of Babel is another and so was God revealing Himself to Moses at the burning bush, as well as the Exodus from Egypt, among other examples. God still performs miracles today as well, but it takes a lot of prayer and faith for humanity to see them. We take so many things for granted that we often dismiss His special interventions as accidents of nature or as sporadic occasions in our history.

2. Who decides when we are to be faithful or to express faith in the works of God?

Faith is a matter of our personal choice. We have the luxury to call things as we see them. For some, we respond to a happening in faith and, for others, it may be seen as a product of our circumstances. How we respond to an issue is an individual matter that we attribute to God working in our lives. At times, Jesus was genuinely convinced that He had not seen so great of a faith in Israel and at other times, He called for them to be not faithless, but to believe. Consider a time when you could exercise greater faith.

3. Does faith limit God's capacity to do great things?

No! It allows us to see the great things God is doing in our lives. God is God Almighty and sovereign, whether we believe in Him or not. Our faith does not limit God. The people of Nazareth could not witness His miracles because they blinded themselves to His physical presence among them. They refused to fathom that God was among them. It was too impossible for them to believe that God was living with them in their small neighborhoods. The lack of faith illustrates that they, and sometimes us too, need a fresh vision of God and what He does among us. Let us wake up and obtain a new fresh vision of God.

HOME DAILY DEVOTIONAL READINGS
JANUARY 1–7, 2024

MONDAY	TUESDAY	WEDNESDAY	THURSDAY	FRIDAY	SATURDAY	SUNDAY
The Heavenly King Rewards the Righteous	Promises and Praises for Righteousness	The Faith of Israel's Ancestors	The Victory of Faith	Despite Sin, God's Covenant Prevails	Righteousness through Jesus Christ	Assurance and Conviction through Faith Hebrews 11:1–
Isaiah 33:15–22	Psalm 106:1–12	Hebrews 11:20–29	Hebrews 11:32–40	Psalm 106:13, 26–27, 42–48	Romans 5:12–21	4, 7–8, 17–18, 20-23, 32, 39–40

FAITH AND RIGHTEOUSNESS

ADULT TOPIC: BACKGROUND SCRIPTURE:
NOT SEEING BUT BELIEVINGLESSON PASSAGE: HEB. 11:1–4, 7–8, 17–18, 20–23, 32, 39–40

HEBREWS 11:1–4, 7–8, 17–18, 20–23, 32, 39–40

King James Version

NOW faith is the substance of things hoped for, the evidence of things not seen.

2 For by it the elders obtained a good report.

3 Through faith we understand that the worlds were framed by the word of God, so that things which are seen were not made of things which do appear.

4 By faith Abel offered unto God a more excellent sacrifice than Cain, by which he obtained witness that he was righteous, God testifying of his gifts: and by it he being dead yet speaketh.

• • • • • •

7 By faith Noah, being warned of God of things not seen as yet, moved with fear, prepared an ark to the saving of his house; by the which he condemned the world, and became heir of the righteousness which is by faith.

8 By faith Abraham, when he was called to go out into a place which he should after receive for an inheritance, obeyed; and he went out, not knowing whither he went.

• • • • • •

17 By faith Abraham, when he was tried, offered up Isaac: and he that had received the promises offered up his only begotten son,

18 Of whom it was said, That in Isaac shall thy seed be called:

• • • • • •

20 By faith Isaac blessed Jacob and Esau concerning things to come.

21 By faith Jacob, when he was a dying, blessed both the sons of Joseph; and worshipped, leaning upon the top of his staff.

New Revised Standard Version

NOW faith is the assurance of things hoped for, the conviction of things not seen.

2 Indeed, by faith our ancestors received approval.

3 By faith we understand that the worlds were prepared by the word of God, so that what is seen was made from things that are not visible.

4 By faith Abel offered to God a more acceptable sacrifice than Cain's. Through this he received approval as righteous, God himself giving approval to his gifts; he died, but through his faith he still speaks.

• • • • • •

7 By faith Noah, warned by God about events as yet unseen, respected the warning and built an ark to save his household; by this he condemned the world and became an heir to the righteousness that is in accordance with faith.

8 By faith Abraham obeyed when he was called to set out for a place that he was to receive as an inheritance; and he set out, not knowing where he was going.

• • • • • •

17 By faith Abraham, when put to the test, offered up Isaac. He who had received the promises was ready to offer up his only son,

18 of whom he had been told, "It is through Isaac that descendants shall be named for you."

• • • • • •

20 By faith Isaac invoked blessings for the future on Jacob and Esau.

21 By faith Jacob, when dying, blessed each of the sons of Joseph, "bowing in worship over the top of his staff."

MAIN THOUGHT: Now faith is the substance of things hoped for, the evidence of things not seen. (Hebrews 11:1, KJV)

HEBREWS 11:1-4, 7–8, 17–18, 20–23, 32, 39-40

King James Version	*New Revised Standard Version*
22 By faith Joseph, when he died, made mention of the departing of the children of Israel; and gave commandment concerning his bones.	22 By faith Joseph, at the end of his life, made mention of the exodus of the Israelites and gave instructions about his burial.
23 By faith Moses, when he was born, was hid three months of his parents, because they saw he was a proper child; and they were not afraid of the king's commandment.	23 By faith Moses was hidden by his parents for three months after his birth, because they saw that the child was beautiful; and they were not afraid of the king's edict
• • • • • •	• • • • • •
32 And what shall I more say? for the time would fail me to tell of Gedeon, and of Barak, and of Samson, and of Jephthae; of David also, and Samuel, and of the prophets:	32 And what more should I say? For time would fail me to tell of Gideon, Barak, Samson, Jephthah, of David and Samuel and the prophets–
• • • • • •	• • • • • •
39 And these all, having obtained a good report through faith, received not the promise:	39 Yet all these, though they were commended for their faith, did not receive what was promised,
40 God having provided some better thing for us, that they without us should not be made perfect.	40 since God had provided something better so that they would not, apart from us, be made perfect.

LESSON SETTING
Time: 70 CE
Place: Jerusalem

LESSON OUTLINE
I. **Faith in What We Do Not See (Hebrews 11:1–23)**
II. **Hope for the Future (Hebrews 11:32–40)**

UNIFYING PRINCIPLE
Frequently, we have to act without complete information. How do we make wise decisions in the face of uncertainty? Hebrews 11 lifts up the exemplary faith of many who demonstrate confidence in God's promises even in the absence of a tangible, seeable basis for doing so.

INTRODUCTION
The book of Hebrews was written during the persecution of Jewish Christians who lived in Rome, and likely the members of the church at Rome. The author of the book of Hebrews interestingly is not known; however, scholars believe that it was written before the destruction of the temple in Jerusalem in 70 CE (*Zondervan Life Application Study Bible*, p. 2,798).

In Hebrews 11, we see examples of individuals who had such great confidence in God, they burned all their bridges behind them, risking their whole future on what God said. Throughout Hebrews 11, we are reminded of what faith in action looks like through the exemplary lives of Abel, Enoch, Noah, and Abraham.

The book of Hebrews was written in a time when the early church was evolving and some Jews had converted to Christianity. As time went on, they found themselves reverting back to Judaism. The author is writing his letter to the Jewish Christians who were very well-versed in the Scriptures, and they were in danger and undergoing severe persecution. They largely relied on the study of the Old Testament and on the old covenant. Although they had professed Christ, they tended to go back to the teachings of the Old Testament and eventually rejected Jesus as the Messiah that was prophesied.

EXPOSITION

I. FAITH IN WHAT WE DO NOT SEE (HEBREWS 11:1–23)

What is faith? The author of Hebrews begins to unpack the definition of faith by describing what faith is. He asserts that faith is confidence or assurance of the things hoped for. Faith is trust in God. Though we have not seen God, faith in God helps us to know without seeing. Having faith is ultimately the evidence or proof of the existence of that which we do not see (*Wycliffe Bible Commentary*, p. 1,422). We know that God made the world by His word because we believe that God exists.

The author of Hebrews makes a strong case for what faith is and sets forth his arguments in defense of the possibilities of living a life of faith. He reminds the reader of people who lived out their faith in exemplary ways as proof or evidence that living a life of faith is entirely possible. Men of old such as Abel, Enoch, Noah, and Abraham had such great confidence and absolute resolve in God that they gained approval of God and their faith was counted to them as righteousness.

Through their faith, these great men of the Old Testament experienced God. They learned that their confidence in God is a surety for what they hoped for. Abel, the son of Adam who became a shepherd, offered the firstborn of his flock as a blood sacrifice. God was pleased with his sacrifice, and it was counted to him as righteousness. Abel's sacrifice "established blood sacrifice as the basis of entrance into the life of faith" (Wycliffe, p. 1,422). His offering pointed to the ultimate sacrifice of Jesus when He shed His blood for the remission of our sins.

Enoch was a prophet who preached about the coming judgment upon the ungodly generations and called them to repentance. His faith was both vocal and visible. He lived for 300 years and spent his life living out his active, visible faith. Enoch's singular purpose in life was to please God, and he spared nothing to accomplish this because his faith in God was deeply imbedded in his heart. Enoch spent his entire life walking with God and had the good reputation as being a man who walked with God. Enoch did not just walk with God one time in his life; he walked with God every day of his life. His faith in God was his way of life.

Enoch lived in fellowship and communion with God as he preached and prophesied messages of warning, judgment, and repentance to the ungodly generations of his time. Hebrews 11:5 states that Enoch pleased God. The Greek word for "pleased" is *euaresteo*, which means "pleases to gratify entirely" (*Hebrew-Greek Bible*, p. 2,136). It also comes from the Greek word *euarestos*, which means "well-pleasing." Enoch's faith was so entirely gratifying and well-pleasing to God that God just simply transferred him to heaven. His faith was counted to him as righteousness so much so that he was taken up to heaven and did not see death. Before he was taken to heaven, Enoch was commended as one who pleased God. The Greek word for "commended" is *maretureo*, which means "to have a reputation; to speak well of; to bear witness" (*Hebrew-Greek Keyword Bible*, p. 2,195).

The generations that existed during Noah's time were corrupt, and violence filled the world (Genesis 6:11). When God saw that all of humanity had corrupted their ways and were full of violence, He decided to bring an end to all flesh. He told Noah to build an ark because He saw that Noah was righteous. By faith, Noah believed God and started building an ark after God showed him that the world was going to be destroyed by a flood. The day he took the first saw to cut the first piece of timber to build the ark was an act of faith. Noah believed God and his faith was expressed by his actions. When the flood came, he was 600 years old (see Genesis 7:6). Noah's faith saved his family and repopulated the whole earth.

Abraham was an ancestor of Jesus. Abraham was also the father of the Jewish nation. God wanted to set apart a nation unto Himself to tell the world about Him. He chose Abraham, who was a man of faith. He believed in God's promises, even though he did not have his son until he was well past his childbearing age. Abraham followed God and God blessed him because of his faith. God called Abraham to move out of the land of Ur and to go to inherit a city he had not seen. By faith, Abraham obeyed God and sojourned as a tent dweller, in search of this city. He did not know where he was going or how long it would take to get there. God promised Abraham that he would be the father of many nations. Abraham continued believing God even though he and his wife were well past the childbearing age. God gave Sarah the power to have a son. When she conceived, she considered God to be faithful. When God blessed Abraham and his wife with Isaac, Abraham, by faith, was willing to offer his only son as a sacrifice to God. Abraham showed his faith, despite his circumstances and despite his trials and testing. God could count on Abraham to follow Him. God called Abraham His friend because Abraham believed God.

We learn from the fathers of faith that faith is whole-hearted commitment to God. Faith is pleasing God. Faith is demonstrated through actions. God confers righteousness upon those who truly believe and trust in Him.

II. HOPE FOR THE FUTURE (HEBREWS 11:32–40)

So what is faith? According to Hebrews 11:1, faith is confidence. The word *confidence* means "assurance;" the word *faith* comes from the Hebrew word *pistus*, which means "persuasion, moral conviction, reliance upon Christ for salvation." It also means "assurance and belief" (*Hebrew-Greek Bible*). The noun form of *pistus* is *pthreitho,* and it means "to win over or persuade; firm persuasion; confiding belief in the truth; veracity reality of any person or thing." Faith is assurance and confidence in the things that we hope for and the conviction of what we do not see.

Hope comes from the Greek word *elpizo*,

which means "to expect with desire." It more explicitly relates to those who put their trust in God. Having hope is a result of putting your trust in God. The fathers of our faith were highly commended or highly regarded because of their faith.

It is because of faith that we come to appreciate that the world was formed by God as He commanded it to come forth. Everything that we see around us wasn't made from anything that's visible. By faith, we breathe air. By faith, we experience gravity. By faith, we wake up every day. Faith is having the assurance and confidence in God. Faith is having the desire to please God. Our desire to please God comes out of our relationship with God.

Hebrews 11:6 says "Without faith it is impossible to please God and so anyone who comes to God must believe that He is; that He exists; and that He rewards those who earnestly seek Him."When we look at Abraham, Noah, Enoch, and all of the fathers of faith, we can see the threads of consistency in their faith. They all walked with the Lord. They all obeyed the Lord. Because they all kept their faith, they kept their confidence in God, and it was counted to them as righteousness. They all wanted to please God, and they trusted God.

Abraham didn't mind living in tents, journeying through life while searching for the land of his inheritance because God told him he was going to be the father of many nations. Noah didn't mind building an ark for years and years because he was pleasing God. The fathers of our faith had one central focus, one vision, and one purpose and that was they wanted nothing more of this life than to please God. Their goal was to be with God forever.

God created the world out of nothing, and by His word, the world came into being, and this we believe by faith. We also believe that God has no equal and that He is sovereign. Because He is sovereign, we can rest our faith and our hope in the One who created everything.

Having faith in God is believing first that He exists, but we also understand that even the devils believe that God exists, so a mere knowledge of God or a mere acknowledgement of the fact that He does exist is not enough. What God desires is to be one with us in relationship. We see this in the prayer of Jesus when He prayed that we would become one just as He and the Father are one. Having faith in God is having a commitment to God, and is the outcome of having a deep abiding relationship with God. Our human reasoning will not help us to understand God. Our relationship with God will privilege us to have the companionship of God.

The fathers of our faith had hope for the future because they had hope in God. God's delight and blessing is not contingent on God's people's ability to do everything well, or even correctly, but it is based on how their actions reveal a heart that completely trusts in God's heart and God's authority. Although Abraham sinned in trying to force the fulfillment of God's promise by sleeping with Sarah's handmaiden, God forgave him and still honored the promise He'd made to give Abraham a son and make him a father of innumerable children.

Our actions reveal our faith; God's actions reveal God's heart. God's sovereignty helps our faith to grow. Abraham is the epitome of faith because his relationship with the Lord exemplifies the situation with the Church. Abraham (the father of many and the nation of Israel) entered into a covenant with God. This covenant was based on faith. Abraham did not experience the fulfillment of all of God's promises, yet he remained faithful to God. Today, as followers of Jesus, we are looking for our eternal home. Abraham never questioned God. He assumed that God would fulfill His word. Abraham trusted God's character absolutely both in risk and sacrifice to resolve the situation in a way consistent with who God is. His example is one that we can follow today. Even though we may not see the fulfillment of every promise in our lifetime, we trust that God will do what He says.

THE LESSON APPLIED

Believing that God exists is the beginning of having faith in God. God wants to have an intimate relationship with each of us. Abiding in God is trusting Him with every part of our lives. Walking in faith is a daily commitment. Our faith must go beyond acknowledging that God exists. To please God, we must be deeply committed to doing so. Faith begins in the heart and is carried out in the actions. Faith is knowing that God will work things out even when we don't see Him working.

LET'S TALK ABOUT IT

Do you really have faith in God?

It is one thing to say that we have faith, yet another to be able to stand in faith. The fathers of our faith did not "see" things work out before they had faith in God, yet they trusted God and took Him at His word because they knew God.

When trials and adversity come, they often build our faith in God. Second Corinthians 13:5 says we should examine ourselves to see whether we are in the faith. Despite what pressures we face, one day, every knee will bow and every tongue will confess that Jesus is Lord. Make a commitment to God to walk in faith. May all of heaven commend you as one who walked with God.

GET SOCIAL
Share your views and tag us @rhboydco and use #faith.

Twitter
@rhboydco (#rhboydco)

Instagram
@rhboydco (#rhboydco)

Facebook
@rhboydco (#rhboydco)

www.rhboyd.com

HOME DAILY DEVOTIONAL READINGS
JANUARY 8–14, 2024

MONDAY	TUESDAY	WEDNESDAY	THURSDAY	FRIDAY	SATURDAY	SUNDAY
God's Word Lights My Path	Rest to the Weary	I Put My Trust in God	Trust in the Unchanging Lord	I Will Not Leave You Orphaned	God's Surpassing Wisdom	Trust in the Lord
Psalm 119:97–112	Matthew 11:25–30	Psalm 56	Hebrews 13:5–16	John 14:18–27	1 Corinthians 2:6–16	Proverbs 3:1–12

FAITH AND TRUST

ADULT TOPIC: WISE BEYOND YOUR YEARS	BACKGROUND SCRIPTURE: PROVERBS 3:1–12 LESSON PASSAGE: PROVERBS 3:1–8

PROVERBS 3:1–8

King James Version

MY son, forget not my law; but let thine heart keep my commandments:

2 For length of days, and long life, and peace, shall they add to thee.

3 Let not mercy and truth forsake thee: bind them about thy neck; write them upon the table of thine heart:

4 So shalt thou find favour and good understanding in the sight of God and man.

5 Trust in the Lord with all thine heart; and lean not unto thine own understanding.

6 In all thy ways acknowledge him, and he shall direct thy paths.

7 Be not wise in thine own eyes: fear the Lord, and depart from evil.

8 It shall be health to thy navel, and marrow to thy bones.

New Revised Standard Version

MY child, do not forget my teaching, but let your heart keep my commandments;

2 for length of days and years of life and abundant welfare they will give you.

3 Do not let loyalty and faithfulness forsake you; bind them around your neck, write them on the tablet of your heart.

4 So you will find favor and good repute in the sight of God and of people.

5 Trust in the Lord with all your heart, and do not rely on your own insight.

6 In all your ways acknowledge him, and he will make straight your paths.

7 Do not be wise in your own eyes; fear the Lord, and turn away from evil.

8 It will be a healing for your flesh and a refreshment for your body.

LESSON SETTING

Time: 900 BCE

Place: Unknown

LESSON OUTLINE

I. **Wisdom Through God's Word**
   (Proverbs 3:1–2)

II. **God's Wisdom**
   (Proverbs 3:3–4)

III. **Seeking God's Direction**
   (Proverbs 5:12)

UNIFYING PRINCIPLE

We get into trouble when we think we have all the answers. Where can we look for trustworthy guidance? The writer of Proverbs calls us to humility, acknowledging God's authority in our lives instead of relying solely on our own instincts.

INTRODUCTION

Proverbs is a book of instruction on morality and ethical principles. Using wise sayings, poetry, parables, questions, cou-

MAIN THOUGHT: Trust in the Lord with all thine heart; and lean not unto thine own understanding. (Proverbs 3:5, KJV)

plets, and contrasts between what is right and wrong, and what is good and evil, Proverbs provides guidance and wisdom for godly living. Proverbs was written by the wisest man who ever lived—King Solomon. He wrote the majority of Proverbs during the early part of his reign. Solomon also authored the books of Ecclesiastes and Song of Songs. Through all of his books, we gain practical insights for applying godly principles to our everyday lives (*Zondervan Life Application Bible*, page 1,325–1,326).

Proverbs provides godly wisdom, timely warnings, and advice on how to walk in relationship with God and how to govern our relationship with man (*Zondervan Life Application Bible*, p. 1,325–1,326). Almost every aspect of human life is addressed in the book of Proverbs—everything from guidance for youth, self-discipline, self-control, family, business, taming our tongues, our relationship with God, marriage, wealth, poverty, immorality, and wisdom are all referenced. Proverbs provides guidance for everyday life; therefore, we should not just read it, but apply the principles to our lives and thus walk closer with the Lord.

Proverbs is a Hebrew word that means "to rule or to govern." The guidance provided in the book of Proverbs helps us to govern our lives. The author of Proverbs hinges success on maintaining an accurate perspective on God's place as authority and source of wisdom, and on our own role as responding to God in the active trust of obedience and submission. The core foundational message of Proverbs is the fear of the Lord. Proverbs 1:7 states, "The fear of the Lord is the beginning of knowledge, but fools despise wisdom and instruction." Those who choose to obey God will benefit by having wisdom. When we walk in a trusting relationship with God, He grants us wisdom. He leads us and helps us to make good decisions in all areas of our lives. No matter our age, race, gender, or economic status, we all gain wisdom from God through our relationship with Him (*Zondervan Life Application Bible*, p. 1,325).

EXPOSITION

I. WISDOM THROUGH GOD'S WORD (PROVERBS 3:1–2)

The book of Proverbs teaches us how to have good relationships in all areas of our lives with friends, family, colleagues, and coworkers. Through our relationship with God, we are empowered to live a life of high moral standards. Our relationships with others should be guided by high moral standards that are in alignment with God's standards (*Zondervan Life Application Bible*).

Proverbs teaches us how to be wise with our words; for example, "The tongue has the power of life and death, and those who love it will eat its fruit" (Proverbs 18:21, NIV). Out of the abundance of the heart, the mouth speaks. Proverbs teaches us how to be wise in our speech and to have self-control in our words. Proverbs also provides guidance for our work life. As Christians, we are accountable to God to work with diligence, discipline, and integrity. We are accountable to God to also work purposefully and to use our skills to glorify God.

Proverbs also teaches us how to be successful in life. God's definition of success is not the same as our definition of success; God sees success as having high moral character, spiritual devotion and obedience to Him, and having a good reputation among our peers. The most important relationship we will ever have in this life is our relationship with God. Our relationship with God is for eternity; everything in this life will fade away eventually. Everything we have comes from God, including our time, our resources, and our talents (*Zondervan Life Application Bible*, p. 1,326). The Word of God is the authority for our very being.

This is why Solomon emphasizes in the first verse of today's passage to not forget the teaching of the Lord; it is vital to our physical and spiritual health. When Solomon became king, God instructed him to ask for whatever he wanted. Instead of asking for riches, Solomon asked for wisdom to know how to judge his people (1 Kings 3: 5–14): "Now, O Lord my God, You have made Your servant king in place of my father David, yet I am but a little child; I do not know how to go out or come in. Your servant is in the midst of Your people which You have chosen, a great people who are too many to be numbered or counted. So, give Your servant an understanding heart to judge Your people to discern between good and evil. For who is able to judge this great people of Yours?"

Solomon dared not lead God's people without God's guidance, which proved how humble and wise he already was. We will find ourselves encountering many situations in life where we need God's wisdom and guidance. Our first response in any situation should always be to seek God's guidance. This cultivates reliance on God, which is the beginning of wisdom.

Proverbs 3 begins with a call to the reader to not forget the teachings of God and to keep His commandments. The Hebrew word for *teaching* refers to the Torah or instruction from God (*Hebrew-Greek Bible*, p. 1,981). The Bible is the inspired Word of God. Holy men of God spoke and wrote down these teachings as they were moved by the Holy Spirit (see 2 Peter 1:21).

As a father speaking to a son, Solomon then admonishes the reader to "Let your heart keep my commandments" (v. 1). The Hebrew word for *heart* refers to the will or intellect; understanding, and usually refers to the inner self or inner nature; the mind. (*Hebrew-Greek Bible*, p. 1,766). We are to submit our will, our mind, and our inner self to honor and keep God's commandments. Wisdom and understanding go hand in hand. We should not seek to be independent of God or to do things without seeking His guidance first. Reliance on God enables us to go forward in life. Instead of seeking to be independent and doing life on our own, we should seek to live a life that is dependent on God and keep His commandments. The word "commandment" used in this verse does not refer to the laws of Moses. It refers to the Lord's Word — His divine commandments (*Hebrew-Greek Bible*). Respecting God, learning His principles, and keeping His commandments all come with the promise of a long life and peace, according to verse 2 (*Wycliffe Bible Commentary*, 559–560). The life described in Proverbs 3:2 is, according to the Hebrew term used, not one of material success, but rather a life that is relationally, spiritually, and physically healthy (see also Proverbs 3:8).

II. GOD'S WISDOM (PROVERBS 3:3–4)

We are also admonished to be steadfast in love and faithfulness. We should bind them (love and faithfulness) around our neck, and write them on the tablets of our hearts. For the ancient Israelites, the heart was the center of the will, while the throat represented the life of a person. What is in a person's heart is expressed in his life. "For out of the abundance of the heart the mouth speaks. A good man out of the good treasure of his heart brings forth good things, and an evil man out of the evil treasure brings forth evil things" (Matthew 12:34–40, NKJV). It is no accident that the author addresses the state of the heart (Proverbs 3:3) after introducing the goal of life (Proverbs 3:1–2) and before describing its actions: wise and healthy actions that are the fruit of the heart that is focused on God and God's character.

Proverbs 3:3 thus claims truth and mercy as the guardian and guide for life and decision making. Divine wisdom is not like human wisdom. We never want to forget what God commands us to do. Love and faithfulness require actions. Our actions are the result of what is in our hearts. Those who truly love God will act responsibly toward others, and will work to help others to be treated fairly. What we do in terms of our actions shows what is in our hearts.

In Proverbs 3:4, we see the benefit of being steadfast in love and faithfulness is that we will gain favor and a good name (reputation) with God and people. The reference to "name" or "good repute" in Proverbs 3:4 is an outcome of faithfulness to God. The Hebrew word for "favor" is *chen*, which means "unmerited favor in God's sight; special standing or privilege with God or people" (*Hebrew-Greek Bible*, p. 1,709). It means that those around you will recognize the wisdom and healthiness of your choices and actions.

One may wonder, "How do I live this life and how can I be happy in this world?" The way to happiness is to live our lives fully dependent upon God. The fathers of the faith were known for their reliance and dependance on God. We should never lose our fear or respect for God because it helps us to have a fulfilling life in this world, and prepares us for eternal life to come. We must dedicate all that we have (materially) to God and use it to His glory. All that we desire in life, we may gain as we govern ourselves by the rules of wisdom and respect for God (*Wycliffe Bible Commentary*, p. 560).

What does wisdom in action look like? "A person who has wisdom is loving, faithful, trusts God, puts God first, turns away from evil, knows right from wrong, listens and learns, and does with is right" (*Zondervan Life Application Study Bible*, p. 1,332). The benefits of having wisdom include a long, prosperous life, favor with God and man, having a reputation for good judgment, success, health, vitality, riches, honor, pleasure, peace, and protection. We also gain riches, honor, justice, righteousness, life, God's favor, lifelong learning, and understanding from walking in wisdom (*Zondervan Life Application Study Bible*, p, 1,332).

Wisdom comes from God; therefore, in all our getting in this life, we must ensure that we get God. As we are steadfast in love and faithfulness, we will find favor and good success in the sight of God and man. "A good name is more desirable than great riches; to be esteemed is better than silver or gold" (Proverbs 22:1, NIV).

III. SEEKING GOD'S DIRECTION (PROVERBS 3:5–12)

In this technological age, we have access to information like never before. One click of the finger and we can find information on almost anything, anywhere in the world. Yet, with all the information that we can gain from the internet, there is no technology that can give us wisdom like the wisdom that comes from God.

We are admonished to "Trust in the Lord with all your heart and lean not on your own understand; in all your ways, submit to him, and he will make your paths straight" (Proverbs 3:5–6). "To lean" means to "support oneself, rely on, rest on." We are to lean upon the Lord for support. It also means to trust in another person or God for help or counsel. Not everything or everyone in this life can provide the support that we need, even though we may try to make it work. For some, they may rely on a relationship for wholeness. Others may turn to a vice like drugs or alcohol to fill the void in their soul. Others try to drown themselves in work and busyness to feel fulfilled. All of those things, and others not mentioned, will end in disappointment sooner or later. Ultimately, we are to trust God and lean upon Him as our first response in any given situation (*Hebrew-Greek Bible*, p. 1,969). Oftentimes when assailed by trials or circumstances that are overwhelming, our first reaction is to reach out to our friends and family and to lean on them for support. This is not necessarily a bad thing, unless you only seek their assistance and don't also seek support from the Lord. Tragedies happen in life that leave us feeling wounded and helpless—even hopeless. At times, we may have weighty decisions to make and choose to seek the counsel of friends without taking the matter to God. While many may offer comfort, guidance, and assistance, which may all be needed, no one can be to us what God can be to us. He is the ultimate Source that we can and should lean on, in addition to seeking help from others (*Zondervan Life Application Study Bible*, p. 1,332). While we should carefully consider the situation from all aspects, we should not rely on the advice of others above God's Word or guidance. God can provide trusted wisdom and guidance needed to navigate life and often He will speak through or use others to help us. When we make an important decision, we should bring it before God and also seek godly guidance from trusted believers. Read Scriptures that relate to the situation and humbly submit the issue to God. He will provide the guidance to help protect you and keep you.

THE LESSON APPLIED

According to Psalm 111:10, "The fear of the Lord is the beginning of wisdom; all who follow his precepts have good understanding. To him belongs eternal praise." The foundation of all wisdom comes out of an abiding relationship with God.

Proverbs provides practical guidance for daily living. It is not just enough to read the Proverbs, but to take the gems of guidance to heart and to implement it in our lives. Proverbs offers the recipe for a good, long, healthy, and prosperous life—all of which comes out of our obedience to God. Regardless of our age or circumstances, as we learn to trust God, we grow in wisdom and understanding. As we apply the Word of God to our lives daily, and practice it, we benefit exponentially. What if you are not hearing from God? According to Solomon, in order to hear from God, we must first submit to Him in all our ways. "Submit yourselves, then, to God. Resist the devil , and he will flee from you" (James 4:7, NIV). If you want to live a prosperous life, "Submit to God and be at peace with Him; in this way prosperity will come to you" (Job 22:21, NIV).

Proverbs 3: 5–7 is the key to understanding wisdom. It centers wise living in a trusting and faithful relationship with God. The author admonishes us to trust in the Lord. "Trust in the Lord with all your heart and lean not on your own understanding; in all your ways submit to Him, and He will make your paths straight" (Proverbs 3:5–6). We are to shun evil and as we do so, God will make our paths straight.

Today, there may be more temptations than ever before and you may feel more pulled in different directions that any other time previously. Everything in the world screams for your attention and promises you satisfaction, but these are all false promises. There is only one place that true hope and satisfaction can be found and that's in the Lord God.

LET'S TALK ABOUT IT
Do you struggle with trusting God?

Sometimes, it can be difficult to trust in Someone that we do not see, especially when adversity creates all kinds of doubts and fears. Noah, Abraham, Moses, and other fathers of our faith encountered many trials. They trusted and obeyed God regardless of the pressures of life, rejection, and circumstance. In all cases, they gave up everything to have God. What will it take for you to trust God like that? It might not be easy, and don't expect it to happen overnight. But day by day, when you exercise trusting Him, He will prove that He is trustworthy.

GET SOCIAL

Share your views and tag us
@rhboydco and use #FaithandTrust.

Twitter
@rhboydco (#rhboydco)

Instagram
@rhboydco (#rhboydco)

Facebook
@rhboydco (#rhboydco)

www.rhboyd.com

HOME DAILY DEVOTIONAL READINGS
JANUARY 15–21, 2024

MONDAY	TUESDAY	WEDNESDAY	THURSDAY	FRIDAY	SATURDAY	SUNDAY
Praise the God Who Comforts	God Delivers Me from My Fears	God's Eyes Are on the Righteous	Encourage One Another	Rejoice, Pray, and Give Thanks	Remember God's Power and Might	Do Not Be Dismayed
2 Corinthians 1:3–11	Psalm 34:1–10	Psalm 34:11–22	1 Thessalonians 5:1–15	1 Thessalonians 5:16–28	2 Chronicles 20:5–12	2 Chronicles 20:13–20

FAITH AND ENCOURAGEMENT

ADULT TOPIC: OVERCOMING FEAR	BACKGROUND SCRIPTURE: 2 CHRONICLES 20:5–20 LESSON PASSAGE: 2 CHRONICLES 20:13–20

2 CHRONICLES 20:13–20

King James Version

AND all Judah stood before the Lord, with their little ones, their wives, and their children.

14 Then upon Jahaziel the son of Zechariah, the son of Benaiah, the son of Jeiel, the son of Mattaniah, a Levite of the sons of Asaph, came the Spirit of the Lord in the midst of the congregation;

15 And he said, Hearken ye, all Judah, and ye inhabitants of Jerusalem, and thou king Jehoshaphat, Thus saith the Lord unto you, Be not afraid nor dismayed by reason of this great multitude; for the battle is not yours, but God's.

16 To morrow go ye down against them: behold, they come up by the cliff of Ziz; and ye shall find them at the end of the brook, before the wilderness of Jeruel.

17 Ye shall not need to fight in this battle: set yourselves, stand ye still, and see the salvation of the Lord with you, O Judah and Jerusalem: fear not, nor be dismayed; to morrow go out against them: for the Lord will be with you.

18 And Jehoshaphat bowed his head with his face to the ground: and all Judah and the inhabitants of Jerusalem fell before the Lord, worshipping the Lord.

19 And the Levites, of the children of the Kohathites, and of the children of the Korhites, stood up to praise the Lord God of Israel with a loud voice on high.

New Revised Standard Version

MEANWHILE, all Judah stood before the Lord, with their little ones, their wives, and their children.

14 Then the spirit of the Lord came upon Jahaziel son of Zechariah, son of Benaiah, son of Jeiel, son of Mattaniah, a Levite of the sons of Asaph, in the middle of the assembly.

15 He said, "Listen, all Judah and inhabitants of Jerusalem, and King Jehoshaphat: Thus says the Lord to you: 'Do not fear or be dismayed at this great multitude; for the battle is not yours but God's.

16 Tomorrow go down against them; they will come up by the ascent of Ziz; you will find them at the end of the valley, before the wilderness of Jeruel.

17 This battle is not for you to fight; take your position, stand still, and see the victory of the Lord on your behalf, O Judah and Jerusalem.' Do not fear or be dismayed; tomorrow go out against them, and the Lord will be with you."

18 Then Jehoshaphat bowed down with his face to the ground, and all Judah and the inhabitants of Jerusalem fell down before the Lord, worshiping the Lord.

19 And the Levites, of the Kohathites and the Korahites, stood up to praise the Lord, the God of Israel, with a very loud voice.

MAIN THOUGHT: And they rose early in the morning, and went forth into the wilderness of Tekoa: and as they went forth, Jehoshaphat stood and said, Hear me, O Judah, and ye inhabitants of Jerusalem; Believe in the Lord your God, so shall ye be established; believe his prophets, so shall ye prosper. (2 Chronicles 20:20, KJV)

2 CHRONICLES 20:13—20

King James Version	New Revised Standard Version
20 And they rose early in the morning, and went forth into the wilderness of Tekoa: and as they went forth, Jehoshaphat stood and said, Hear me, O Judah, and ye inhabitants of Jerusalem; Believe in the Lord your God, so shall ye be established; believe his prophets, so shall ye prosper.	20 They rose early in the morning and went out into the wilderness of Tekoa, and as they went out Jehoshaphat stood and said, "Listen to me, O Judah and inhabitants of Jerusalem! Believe in the Lord your God and you will be established; believe his prophets."

LESSON SETTING
Time: 430 BCE
Place: Unknown

LESSON OUTLINE
I. **Jehoshaphat's Prayer (2 Chronicles 20:5-12)**
II. **Moving Beyond Immobilizing Fear (2 Chronicles 20:13-17)**
III. **Inviting God's Presence (2 Chronicles 20:18-20)**

UNIFYING PRINCIPLE
When we face opposition, we are tempted to give up because of fear. How do we loosen the grip of fear? The faith demonstrated by Jehoshaphat encourages us to overcome fear through trust in God.

INTRODUCTION
The central message of 2 Chronicles is to remind people of their past and to call them back into a right relationship with God. The book was written by Ezra to the exiles who had returned from Babylonian captivity. First and Second Chronicles are commentaries on the kings of Judah. The Chronicles were originally one book, written around 430 BCE. They record events from the start of King Solomon's reign in 970 BCE to the start of the Babylonian captivity in 587–586 BCE. It highlights the importance of the temple, which was in Jerusalem, as a symbol of the importance of serving and obeying God (*Zondervan's Life Application Study Bible*, p. 812–813).

The Canaanites had many gods. Among them were Baal, the god of rain, and Ashtoreth, the goddess of fertility. The religious altars of the Canaanites remained in Judah and Israel, although God's people had taken over the land. Therefore, the pagan beliefs of the Canaanites gradually seeped into the religious practices of the people of God. The kings of Israel and Judah did not destroy the high places of the worship of Baal. The worship of Baal intermingled with the worship of God was an egregious sin and led to all forms of wickedness among God's people. The wicked kings of Israel and Judah led the people to rebel against God. The practice of idolatry in all its forms is sin; God will not tolerate sharing His throne with another.

The Babylonian empire, under King Nebuchadnezzar, became the next global power superpower. Because of Judah's idolatry, God allowed the Babylonians to capture Jerusalem. Under King Nebuchadnezzar, Jerusalem was sieged, the temple was destroyed, and the articles of the temple were plundered and brought to Babylon (*Zondervan's Life Application Study Bible*, p. 812–813). Second Chronicles primarily focuses on Judah. Throughout the reign of each of the kings of Judah, God sent prophets to warn Judah about their unfaithfulness. Since they did not turn entirely away from their wicked ways, God allowed them to go into captivity. Prophets such as Ezekiel and Daniel were also taken into captivity. God allowed His chosen people to be exiled and go into slavery to get their attention and to turn their hearts toward Him. Throughout the history of Judah, most of the kings did not follow God wholeheartedly and did not tear down the high places of the worship of Baal and Ashtoreth (See 1 Kings and 2 Kings).

EXPOSITION

I. JEHOSHAPHAT'S PRAYER (2 CHRONICLES 20:5–12)

Jehoshaphat, son of Asa, succeeded the throne and strengthened himself against Israel (2 Chronicles 17:1). The Lord was with Jehoshaphat because he followed the ways of David. He did not consult with Baals (gods of water and fertility), but consulted with the Lord God. Instead of following the practices of the wicked kings before him, Jehoshaphat followed the Lord. The Lord established a kingdom under his control in Judah. When the people of Judah saw that he was a godly king, they brought gifts to Jehoshaphat. Because his ways were devoted to the Lord, Jehoshaphat increased in wealth and honor. King Jehoshaphat also removed the high places of the worship of Baals and the

Asherah poles from Judah (2 Chronicles 17:3–6). God was with Jehoshaphat because he was submitted to God. He instituted an educational system to ensure teaching of the Torah to the people. Throughout Judah and the surrounding towns, some of the Levites taught the Book of the Law of the Lord (2 Chronicles 17:9).

Although Jehoshaphat followed the Lord, he made a poor decision by allowing his son to marry Athalia, the daughter of the wicked king Ahab and his wife Jezebel. Athalia was just as wicked as her parents. The marriage essentially was an alliance between the two nations of Israel and Judah. King Ahab was the king over Israel. Jehoshaphat made a military alliance with King Ahab by allowing his son to marry King Ahab's daughter. King Ahab convinced Jehoshaphat to join with him to attack Ramoth Gilead. King Ahab's prophets predicted victory, but God's prophet Micaiah predicted defeat. In the end, both kings were defeated, and King Ahab was killed. God was angry when Jehoshaphat formed his alliance with King Ahab (See 2 Chronicles 18). He should have never sought protection from humanity. God fought a major battle for him; therefore, he should have trusted God for everything from that day forward.

After the death of king Ahab, Jehoshaphat appointed judges to rule in each of the fortified cities of Judah (2 Chronicles 19:5). After this, the Moabites, Ammonites, and some of the Meunites waged war against Jehoshaphat. He received word that they were coming against him from Edom and from the other side of the Dead Sea, and that they were already in Hazon Tam (En

Gedi). With several armies bearing down on Judah, Jehoshaphat was frightened and turned to the Lord for help. He immediately proclaimed a fast for all of Judah. All the people came together to seek help from the Lord. Jehoshaphat stood up in the assembly of the people of Judah in Jerusalem at the temple and he prayed to God. He entreated the Lord to hear their prayer and to save them. He realized that they had no power to face the army that was about to attack them and that he didn't know what to do. However, he said to the Lord; "our eyes are on you" (2 Chronicles 20:1–12).

All the men of Judah, along with their wives and children, stood before the Lord. The Spirit of the Lord fell on Jahaziel, who was the son of Zachariah. Jahaziel prophesied and said to King Jehoshaphat and all the people of Judah in Jerusalem; "Do not be afraid or discouraged because of this vast army. For the battle is not yours, but God's" (2 Chronicles 20:15, NIV). He told them that tomorrow they should "march down against them. They will be climbing up by the Pass of Ziz, and you will find them at the end of the gorge in the Desert of Jeruel. You will not have to fight this battle. Take up your positions; stand firm and see the deliverance the Lord will give you, Judah and Jerusalem. Do not be afraid; do not be discouraged. Go out to face them tomorrow, and the Lord will be with you" (2 Chronicles 20:15–17, NIV).

When Jehoshaphat heard this prophecy, he bowed down and worshiped the Lord, and all of Judah and Jerusalem bowed down and worshiped the Lord in response. Then some of the Levites stood up with a very loud voice, giving thanks to God (2 Chronicles 20:18). As they began to sing praises to the Lord, the Lord sent ambushes against the men of Ammon and Moab and Mount Seir to annihilate them. Essentially, the Ammonites and Moabites revolted against the men from Mount Seir and destroyed them, and then they destroyed one another. When the men of Judah came out and saw them, they saw a sea of dead bodies. Jehoshaphat and his men were able to carry out the plunder, equipment, clothing, and articles of value. There was so much plunder that it took three days to collect it (2 Chronicles 20:22–26).

On the fourth day, they assembled in the Valley of Berakah, and they praised the Lord. Then they returned to Jerusalem "for the Lord had given them cause to rejoice over their enemies" (2 Chronicles 20:26–28, NIV) and they immediately went to the temple of the Lord with harps, lyres, and trumpets (2 Chronicles 20:28, NIV). As a result of this great victory, the fear of the Lord fell on the surrounding kingdoms. Jehoshaphat's reign was at peace for God had given him rest on every side.

II. Moving Beyond Immobilizing Fear (2 Chronicles 20:13–20)

When Jehoshaphat learned that he was about to be attacked, he immediately called on the Lord and called his people together to fast to seek the Lord together. During his fast, the people were to reflect on their sins, repent, and pray to God for help. Fasting helps us to recognize our weakness and our dependence upon God. When faced with danger, Jehoshaphat immediately turned to God and committed the situation to God. He acknowledged that only God could help him. Jehoshaphat sought God's favor on grounds that the people were God's people. Jehoshaphat knew the problem was so big that only God's sovereignty could overhaul the situation. He professed that he was completely dependent upon God and didn't know what to do. Instead of focusing on his own power, Jehoshaphat focused on God's power. Jehoshaphat bought his case to the courts of heaven and laid out the facts and he pleaded with God to judge them.

In the middle of their praying, while the army was bearing down on Judah, God used a prophet Jahaziel to encourage Jehoshaphat. Whatever our battles may be, whatever situation we find ourselves in, we all know when we are in over our heads. It's sometimes easier to see God when the situation is beyond our ability and capabilities. This was the case with Jehoshaphat. He understood that the people that he led were just ordinary people, and they were no match for the surrounding armies of the Ammonites, Moabites, and Meunites.

God told Jahaziel to tell the people not to be afraid because He was going to fight this battle. They had no idea how this fight was going to be won. Jahaziel told them to go out the next day and march out to the battlefield. He told them that they were never going to have to fight, but they still had to show up for the battle. Basically, he said to just take your position and stand firm, and don't be afraid because God was going to deliver them that day.

What should we do in situations where the difficulty requires a God-sized solution? It is often easier to trust God when a situation is impossible or seems impossible, but less easy to trust God when we think we have the solution. For example, it may be easy to trust God when a loved one is sick and clearly only God can heal them or keep them alive. But how often do we go into our day-to-day work life or home life or school life experiences without bringing God into our plans? How often do we forge ahead and make decisions without consulting God? For example, decisions such as career choices, marital partners, friendships, allegiances, and business partnerships without inviting God into those relationships or those challenges could end in disaster.

THE LESSON APPLIED

God will fulfill His promises no matter what our circumstances may be. Jehoshaphat was in great danger and it was obvious that seeking God for the answers was the only way to victory. Jehoshaphat and the people of Judah humbled themselves before God by fasting in prayer, and trusting in God and His sovereignty and providence to bring relief. Who should we go to when we need help? We should always first run to God and humbly submit our case to Him.

When confronted by those whose intentions are evil toward us, we may trust that God will see us through. Jehoshaphat encouraged his army to hold fast to their faith in God and to have courage. Firm belief in God's power and His mercy will give us courage through the most trying times. Jehoshaphat was careful to worship God and ensured that his people also worshiped God. As a result of Jehoshaphat's godly leadership, God gave him a great victory.

LET'S TALK ABOUT IT

Are you confronted by an impossible situation currently?

King Jehoshaphat was confronted by three powerful armies and he became overwhelmingly afraid. He did not have power within himself to accomplish a victory on his own. Jehoshaphat sought the Lord and called all the people together to fast and pray for God's guidance and God's help. God heard Jehoshaphat's prayer and responded by letting Jehoshaphat know that the battle was not his; but that the battle belonged to the Lord. We may not always know what to do in any given situation. Whenever adversity overwhelms us and when the problems of life seem bigger than life, we may always turn to God for help. As Jehoshaphat took the case to the courts of heaven, he recognized God's sovereignty, and he recognized that the people of Judah were God's people. He implored God to act on behalf of His people. What we learned from the story of Jehoshaphat is: 1) to acknowledge God's sovereignty over-all; 2) to acknowledge that we are God's people; 3) to acknowledge our complete dependence upon God. We also learn from Jehoshaphat that the problems that we face in life do belong to the Lord and as His children, when we humbly submit ourselves to His leadership, He will lead us safely to victory.

In today's lesson, Jehoshaphat and the people of Judah did not have to deploy one weapon; all they had to do was submit to God and show up with faith and courage in God. They won the war that day because of their faith in God, and because God fought the war for them, they benefited by getting the victory. When problems seem bigger than you, or bigger than life, remember the problems belong to the Lord and so do you. He will always hear the humble prayer of any repentant sinners "who are kept by the power of God through faith unto salvation ready to be revealed in the last time," according to 1 Peter 1:5. Take comfort in that promise this week.

GET SOCIAL

Share your views and tag us
@rhboydco and use #Encouragement.

Twitter
@rhboydco (#rhboydco)

Instagram
@rhboydco (#rhboydco)

Facebook
@rhboydco (#rhboydco)

www.rhboyd.com

HOME DAILY DEVOTIONAL READINGS
JANUARY 22–28, 2024

MONDAY	TUESDAY	WEDNESDAY	THURSDAY	FRIDAY	SATURDAY	SUNDAY
A New Spirit and Heart	A Transforming Testimony	Be Holy, for God Is Holy	A Prayer for Transformation	God Breathes New Life	From Death to Life	God Gives Different Gifts
Ezekiel 11:17–21	John 9:17–25	Leviticus 20:22–26	Psalm 51:1–15	Ezekiel 37:1–14	1 John 3:14–24	Romans 12:3–8

FAITH AND TRANSFORMATION

ADULT TOPIC: USING OUR UNIQUE GIFTS	BACKGROUND SCRIPTURE: ROMANS 12:3–8 LESSON PASSAGE: ROMANS 12:3–8

ROMANS 12:3–8

King James Version

FOR I say, through the grace given unto me, to every man that is among you, not to think of himself more highly than he ought to think; but to think soberly, according as God hath dealt to every man the measure of faith.

4 For as we have many members in one body, and all members have not the same office:

5 So we, being many, are one body in Christ, and every one members one of another.

6 Having then gifts differing according to the grace that is given to us, whether prophecy, let us prophesy according to the proportion of faith;

7 Or ministry, let us wait on our ministering: or he that teacheth, on teaching;

8 Or he that exhorteth, on exhortation: he that giveth, let him do it with simplicity; he that ruleth, with diligence; he that sheweth mercy, with cheerfulness.

New Revised Standard Version

FOR by the grace given to me I say to everyone among you not to think of yourself more highly than you ought to think, but to think with sober judgment, each according to the measure of faith that God has assigned.

4 For as in one body we have many members and not all the members, have the same function,

5 so we, who are many, are one body in Christ, and individually we are members one of another.

6 We have gifts that differ according to the grace given to us: prophecy, in proportion to faith;

7 ministry, in ministering; the teacher, in teaching;

8 the exhorter, in exhortation; the giver, in generosity; the leader, in diligence; the compassionate, in cheerfulness.

LESSON SETTING

  Time: 57 CE
  Place: Corinth

LESSON OUTLINE

  I. **Living by Faith**
     (Romans 12:3–5)
  II. **Gifted by God**
     (Romans 12:6–8)

UNIFYING PRINCIPLE

We all face pressure to conform to the world. How can we recognize our unique giftedness and withstand pressure to conform? Paul reminds us that through faith, God transforms us by renewing our minds so we can discern God's will.

MAIN THOUGHT: Having then gifts differing according to the grace that is given to us, whether prophecy, let us prophesy according to the proportion of faith. (Romans 12:6, KJV)

INTRODUCTION

The book of Romans was written in 57 CE in Corinth by the Apostle Paul for the Christians who lived in Rome. The intent of the book is to introduce the Gospel to the Romans before Paul's arrival. The Christian Church in Rome was comprised largely of Jewish and also Gentile believers. The church at Rome was developed during the Pentecost (see Acts 2) and was started by Jews who experienced the Pentecost. They likely returned to Rome and spread the Gospel. The church in Rome began to grow even before Paul visited them. He wrote the book of Romans as an introduction before his arrival. In this letter to the Romans, he declares his faith and presents a firm case for the Gospel. The New Testament was not yet written during Paul's time, so this letter provides guidance and instructions for living a life of faith in Christ. He says that the Gospel is available to everyone, regardless of their identity or background, and that we are saved by grace through faith in Christ.

Paul discusses unity as a foundation for believers from different backgrounds to live together and worship together, especially between the Jews and Gentiles. These two groups had long been enemies who steered clear of each other, but now they were being united under the banner of Christianity. While this was wonderful news, it also meant some growing pains and adjustments as they learned to coexist. Paul's letter clearly helps us to examine what we believe as the foundation of our faith as followers of Jesus Christ and how to live it out. It helps us to understand that when Christ died, His death made us right with God through faith, and allows us to have a personal relationship with God. Paul also provides practical guidelines for believers and teaches believers what it means to be a follower of Jesus Christ, and to allow Christ to transform our lives in every way. Paul's goal in visiting the Christians in Rome was to further establish them in the faith, and from there, he planned to carry the Gospel to Spain (*The Life Application Study Bible*, p. 2,538–2,540).

In Romans 12, we see a turn from Paul's theology of salvation to the behavioral and ethical implications of that salvation for the believer. He asserts that the only reasonable, true response to God's mercy is to submit one's life as a sacrifice, wholly entrusted to Christ who sacrificed Himself for us. In the Old Testament, the remission of sins required a blood sacrifice. Unlike sacrifices in the Old Testament and first century, the sacrifice of a believer is not to death but to a new kind of life that is foreign and even directly opposed to what the world believes and practices. A new life in Christ requires self-restraint, and the actions of a believer come from a surrendered heart and exemplifies oneself as a product of the fruits of the Spirit.

EXPOSITION

I. LIVING BY FAITH (ROMANS 12:3–5)

In Romans chapter 12, Paul begins to exhort the believers in Rome about how to walk out or live out their faith. He provides practical guidelines of being a believer in everyday life. He discusses practical ways to live our faith by obedience to our government, loving our neighbors, and taking care of one another. In so doing, we give expression to our faith. In this chapter, Paul also discusses our duty to God and our duty to man (*The Life Application Study Bible*, p. 2,573).

He makes an appeal to the believers in Rome to present their bodies as a living sacrifice to God. As followers of Jesus Christ, we are partakers in His suffering and as such, we are to render ourselves, all that we do, and all that we are, fully to God as an expression of our love for Him. Since Christ gave His life for us, this is our reasonable expression of gratitude. We demonstrate our full surrender to God by giving Him our wholehearted service and allowing the Holy Spirit to renew our minds and re-educate us on how to follow Christ. Through sanctification, we daily surrender to Christ, and our characters will become more and more like Him. When we give our bodies as a reasonable sacrifice, in essence, we are dying to our carnal nature to sin, and we are living in righteousness increasingly each day (*The Life Application Study Bible*).

Sanctification is a process that renews our mind, and it happens over time, not overnight. Presenting ourselves as a living sacrifice means not conforming to this world or its ways. It means not giving in to the pressures of the culture and its demands. It also means not giving in to the ideologies of the world. As followers of Jesus Christ, we are not to be attached to this world. We are to wear it as a loose garment, being ready always to make personal sacrifices to live out our faith in God. Instead of walking in the lust of the flesh and being focused on the things of this world, we should allow the Holy Spirit to sanctify our will, our affections, and our conversations. The closer we get to Christ, the more our affections will grow for Him and the more we become like Him in our character. To be a true follower of Jesus Christ is to give up ourselves completely to Him (*Matthew Henry's Concise Commentary on the Whole Bible*, p. 1,086.). We belong to God because He created us and ordained our lives to exist in this world. We also belong to God because Christ died for us.

Being a living sacrifice is about being unselfish with God. It is our reasonable expression of loving God. Because we belong to God, we are not our own. Our time is not our own. Our money is not our own. Any material thing that we have is not our own. We are mere stewards of God's material world. Since we belong to God, we are kept by the power of God; therefore, the problems that we face must be presented to the One who owns us, just as a child brings their concerns to their parent. Our reasonable service is to be available to God; therefore, regardless of what we list in our daily planner, or what we "must" have to be happy, His will for us has to take priority. This is definitely a sacrifice because our human nature would rather be selfish and only do the things that we want to do. Our flesh desires to do the things that make us feel good, even if it means someone else getting less, getting hurt, or missing out entirely. That's because our flesh is self-seeking. But when we surrender ourselves to the will of God, we start doing what He wants instead of what our human desires want, and that's how we become more Christlike. It takes more effort to choose God's will over our own, but in the end, the reward is much greater than anything our flesh could imagine here on earth.

Worshiping God is more than just going to church each week. It is about being fully surrendered to Him in all areas of our lives to do His will and to seek to please Him in every way (*The Life Application Study Bible*, p. 2,573). You are able to worship Him in your car on the way to work. You can worship from the comfort of your own home. You can worship in the way you steward your money or raise your children. When you are a child of God, everything you do in His service is an act of worship.

God's plans for us are perfect in every way. He has a plan for every day of our lives that will bring glory to His name. As mere humans, it's impossible to always see the greater picture of the plan that God is trying to bring to fruition. Oftentimes, we have to walk by faith blindly and trust that He knows what He's doing, even if we don't understand it. But we can daily surrender our circumstances over to Him and be consistent in our prayer walk.

When our minds are renewed, we live to honor and obey God because we want to please Him. Jesus made a new life in God possible for each one of us, and in return, we should happily offer ourselves to Him in humble service.

The central foundation of a sanctified life is obedience to God. We lay aside our own desires and our own plans to follow Christ. When we make Christ our priority, we will consider His will above ours. This demonstrates our complete trust in Him (*The Life Application Study Bible*, p. 2,573.). "Let us examine ourselves to see whether we're in the faith. We do not belong to ourselves but we are in Christ" (2 Corinthians 13:5). Jesus modeled a life that is fully surrendered to God, "Saying, Father, if thou be willing, remove this cup from me: nevertheless not my will, but thine, be done" (Luke 22:42, KJV).

In Romans 12:2, Paul admonishes us not to be conformed to the pattern of this world but to be transformed by the renewing of our minds. So while we're not to follow the customs and the beliefs or ideologies of the world, we must also guard against being proud, selfish, stubborn, and arrogant. The Holy Spirit can renew our minds and teach us how to walk in obedience with God.

Paul further discusses that we should not think of ourselves more highly than we ought. We should not overestimate ourselves and think we're better than others, but we should have an honest and accurate evaluation of ourselves based on our identity in Christ. Without Christ, we can do nothing; therefore, evaluating ourselves by worldly standards of success and achievement may give us a false sense of our worth or value. If we compare ourselves to others, we might think we're better based on the newness of our car or the size of our house. We might compare salaries or job titles. But these things are meaningless in the sight of God. Our true value is how God sees us. He gave His Son as a sacrifice for our sins in order that we may have eternal life. God sees in us more worth than we would ever see ourselves and values us more than we would ever value ourselves (*The Life Application Study Bible*, p. 2,573).

II. GIFTED BY GOD (ROMANS 12:6–8)

As Christians, we should strive to work together in harmony. We have been given different gifts to edify the body of Christ. Each of us have something to offer in service to God. There are many gifts such as prophesying, teaching, encouraging, giving, leadership, being merciful, etc. When we operate in our gifts, we contribute to the effective ministry of the body of Christ. We are not all gifted the same way, and typically, we don't all possess all of the gifts. The church needs the variety of gifts in order to meet a variety of needs. Think of it this way. If we all had the gift of encouragement, and none of the other gifts, we would all constantly say nice things to one another, but nothing would actually be accomplished. And that can be said of any of the gifts; they're all necessary for God's kingdom. God wants each of us to take responsibility for the gifts He has given us and find ways to serve others.

The hallmark of the believer's life is love. Paul emphasizes that love must be sincere. People generally know when we are being genuine. Even if they are fooled, God never is because He looks directly at your heart. He knows when you're being sincere and when you're just going through the motions. God wants us to be fully engaged in being expressions of His love. We should also practice hospitality. This can look like inviting one another over for fellowship, sharing a meal or coffee, hosting out-of-town guests or missionaries, etc. Paul encourages us to be devoted to each other in love, practice hospitality, and honor one another above ourselves. We should also do right by others.

Another aspect of Paul's letter admonishes us to hate what is evil and cling to what is good (v. 9), and avoid what is evil. While this sounds simple, it is becoming increasingly difficult in this gray world we live in. Issues and concerns used to be much more black and white, but nowadays, things have become much more complicated. This means we need to be on our guard even more than before, and avoid any temptation that might give the devil a foothold in our lives.

Paul even addresses the attitude and disposition that should govern our devotion to God. We should always be full of zeal or energy, excitement for the Lord. We should be fervent for the Lord, joyful in hope, and patient in affliction. When we truly consider what He's done for us and take a moment to acknowledge the magnitude of His sacrifice, how can we do anything less than praise Him all day? We should be bursting to share this good news with everyone who will listen. It truly is too good to keep to ourselves. As we never know when the Lord will return for the second time, we don't know how long we have left to share this news with others. The clock will eventually run out, and we want as many people as possible to be rejoicing in heaven with us for eternity!

THE LESSON APPLIED

As the Gospel spread, new believers needed guidance on how to be a follower of Jesus Christ. Paul wrote his letter to the believers in Rome as a way to introduce himself and to provide some theological and practical guidance for living out their faith in God. Our first responsibility toward God is to surrender our heart to Him. In a world where the culture tends to be about me and mine, surrendering ourselves means surrendering our hearts, minds, will and emotions to God. In order to surrender to God, we must understand that we do not belong to ourselves; we belong to God.

As we live out our lives as believers, we should make every effort to seek first the kingdom of God. "But seek ye first the kingdom of God, and his righteousness; and all these things shall be added unto you" (Matthew 6:33, KJV). The second thing to keep in mind is to offer our bodies as a living sacrifice. As followers of Jesus Christ, we are in service to God. We are supposed to live and work to please Him. The third thing to keep in mind is we are to renew our minds. As we read the Bible, pray, worship God, and educate ourselves about His perfect will, we give way to the Holy Spirit to renew our minds. This is something that must be done repeatedly and often; once a month or less often simply won't cut it. Christ wants our character to be just like His. Allowing the Holy Spirit to guide us in all areas of life will help us to be transformed into His likeness each day.

Since we are imperfect, there will absolutely be times when we slip up and make mistakes. Jesus doesn't expect perfection from us. What He wants is our wholehearted devotion and commitment to becoming more like Him each day. This means that when we make mistakes, we repent and try to do better next time, instead of shrugging it off and saying "that's just the way I am."

LET'S TALK ABOUT IT
What does living our faith look like?

When we first accept Christ as our personal Savior, we tend to think that we have signed up for a trouble-free life. However, following Christ often has tribulation along the way. In fact, Jesus says in John 16:33, "I have told you these things, so that in me you may have peace. In this world, you will have trouble. But take heart! I have overcome the world." Living by faith allows the Holy Spirit to take full control of our lives. Trust God, even when we don't see Him working things out on our behalf. Living a life of faith means sitting with the Lord and hearing His guidance. It also means being patient in tribulation. Trusting the Lord will help us to have peace, even in the midst of the storms of life.

GET SOCIAL
Share your views and tag us
@rhboydco and use #LiveYourFaith.

Twitter
@rhboydco (#rhboydco)

Instagram
@rhboydco (#rhboydco)

Facebook
@rhboydco (#rhboydco)

www.rhboyd.com

HOME DAILY DEVOTIONAL READINGS
JANUARY 29–FEBRUARY 4, 2024

MONDAY	TUESDAY	WEDNESDAY	THURSDAY	FRIDAY	SATURDAY	SUNDAY
Gentiles Become Fellow Heirs	Sing of God's Might	Rely on God	God Reigns in Power	The Power of God for Salvation	Be Strong in the Lord	Wait on God, Who Gives Strength
Ephesians 3:14–21	Psalm 89:1–13	1 Chronicles 16:8–22	Revelation 11:14–19	Romans 1:8–17	Ephesians 6:10–18	Isaiah 40:12–13, 25–31

FAITH IN THE POWER OF GOD

ADULT TOPIC: BACKGROUND SCRIPTURE: ISAIAH 40:12–31
POWER WITHOUT EQUAL   LESSON PASSAGE: ISAIAH 40:12–13, 25–31

ISAIAH 40:12–13, 25–31

King James Version

WHO hath measured the waters in the hollow of his hand, and meted out heaven with the span, and comprehended the dust of the earth in a measure, and weighed the mountains in scales, and the hills in a balance?

13 Who hath directed the Spirit of the Lord, or being his counsellor hath taught him?

• • • • • •

25 To whom then will ye liken me, or shall I be equal? saith the Holy One.

26 Lift up your eyes on high, and behold who hath created these things, that bringeth out their host by number: he calleth them all by names by the greatness of his might, for that he is strong in power; not one faileth.

27 Why sayest thou, O Jacob, and speakest, O Israel, My way is hid from the Lord, and my judgment is passed over from my God?

28 Hast thou not known? hast thou not heard, that the everlasting God, the Lord, the Creator of the ends of the earth, fainteth not, neither is weary? there is no searching of his understanding.

29 He giveth power to the faint; and to them that have no might he increaseth strength.

30 Even the youths shall faint and be weary, and the young men shall utterly fall:

31 But they that wait upon the Lord shall renew their strength; they shall mount up with wings as eagles; they shall run, and not be weary; and they shall walk, and not faint.

New Revised Standard Version

WHO has measured the waters of the sea in the hollow of his hand and marked off the heavens with a span, enclosed the dust of the earth in a measure and weighed the mountains in scales and the hills in a balance?

13 Who has directed the spirit of the Lord or as his counselor has instructed him?

• • • • • •

25 To whom then will you compare me, or who is my equal? says the Holy One.

26 Lift up your eyes on high and see: Who created these? He who brings out their host and numbers them, calling them all by name; because he is great in strength, mighty in power, not one is missing.

27 Why do you say, O Jacob, and assert, O Israel, "My way is hidden from the Lord, and my right is disregarded by my God"?

28 Have you not known? Have you not heard? The Lord is the everlasting God, the Creator of the ends of the earth. He does not faint or grow weary; his understanding is unsearchable.

29 He gives power to the faint and strengthens the powerless.

30 Even youths will faint and be weary, and the young will fall exhausted,

31 but those who wait for the Lord shall renew their strength, they shall mount up with wings like eagles, they shall run and not be weary, they shall walk and not faint.

MAIN THOUGHT: He giveth power to the faint; and to them that have no might he increaseth strength. (Isaiah 40:29, KJV)

LESSON OUTLINE
   I. God is Supreme
      (Isaiah 40:21–24)
   II. Who Can Be Compared
       to God?
       (Isaiah 40:25–26)
   III. God's Strength and
        Our Strength
        (Isaiah 40:27–31)

UNIFYING PRINCIPLE

The power of nature can make us feel small and insignificant. What thoughts ensue in the presence of such awesome power? Isaiah reminds us that the God who created everything around us is worthy of our trust.

INTRODUCTION

As stated earlier, the book of Isaiah is typically divided into two sections by commentators. The first section (chapters 1–39) warns Israel and Judah of impending destruction due to their disobedience. It is primarily concerned with judgment upon Israel and Judah, to be sure, but also upon the nations around them. The second half of the book (chapters 40–66) looks ahead to the time when God's people are in Babylonian captivity. Having languished in captivity for several years, many of the people had lost hope that they would ever be delivered. These chapters speak words of hope and comfort, reminding the people that God has not forgotten them and that He will act on their behalf.

According to Jeremiah 25:9–11, God's people were in captivity in Babylon for seventy years. Isaiah, as just mentioned, was written in anticipation of that, during a time when Israel and Judah were prospering. Because they would not heed the Word of the Lord in the midst of their prosperity, they eventually found themselves captive in a strange land. But even though they did not listen, the Word of the Lord will stand forever (see Isaiah 40:6–8).

In today's text, God brings comfort to the people in exile, reminding them that He is still in control and there is none like Him. After warning the people of what was going to happen to them, He now speaks to them in captivity, telling them how He would eventually restore their land, rebuild the temple, and restore the walls of the city.

EXPOSITION

I. GOD IS SUPREME
   (ISAIAH 40:21–24)

Since Isaiah 40 represents such a significant change in the flow of the book of Isaiah, it will be helpful to briefly survey the chapter as a whole before diving into today's text. It begins with words of comfort and strength: "Comfort, O comfort my people, says your God. Speak tenderly to Jerusalem, and cry to her that she has served her term, that her penalty is paid, that she has received from the LORD's hand double for all her sins" (vv. 1–2, NRSV). God has not forgotten His people. His Word will stand forever, as will His manifold promises. Isaiah attempts to demonstrate this by reminding the people of just how awesome their God is (see vv. 9–20). Even though they suffered in captivity, they should not lose hope. Instead, they should "lift up [their] voices[s] with strength" (v. 9, NRSV); they are not to worry because the nations are "like a drop from a bucket" (v. 15, NRSV).

Perhaps, though, the people were skeptical of this, given what they had suffered. At the outset of today's text, Isaiah addresses the people directly: "Have you not known? Have you not heard? Has it not been told you from the beginning?" (v. 21, NRSV). Even though they were in captivity in Babylon, God was in fact still present with them. At times, they may have felt they could only experience the presence of God back home in Judah. The psalmist hints at this when he writes of their misery in captivity: when mockingly asked to sing one of the songs of Zion, their reply was, "How could we sing the LORD's song in a foreign land?" (Psalm 137:4, NRSV).

But their assumption was not accurate; God is in control in every place. Isaiah uses vivid imagery to depict the sovereign God, looking down upon and controlling the whole world from His heavenly throne (see Isaiah 40:22). He has a panoramic view, which allows Him to observe all that is happening to His people. Whenever He desires to focus on any particular area, He can do so (see vv. 22–23).

God controls history and every human claim to rule or authority (see vv. 23–24). "The one who sits over the earth," John Oswalt observes, "and stretches out the heavens also brings rulers to nothing. The verb here, the common *natan* (lit. 'give'), is the same one used to speak of appointing someone to an official position (cf. Ezra 8:20). Thus, a double irony is at work. These weighty people whom someone has appointed to an important task are really appointed to nothingness in comparison to the authority and weightiness

of God. [*shofetim*] is the usual term for 'judges,'...[referring] to those leaders who are expected to establish right order and conditions for and among their people (the same meaning found in the book of Judges)" (*The Book of Isaiah*, Chapters 40–66 [Grand Rapids: Eerdmans, 1998], 67; emphasis in original).

God can bring princes to nothing, regardless of who they think they are. No matter how firmly established they believe themselves to be, all the Lord has to do is blow, and their efforts will be blown away. He sits high and looks low, observing and controlling all the affairs of the world. He is present, anywhere, and everywhere.

II. WHO CAN BE COMPARED TO GOD? (ISAIAH 40:25–26)

Verses 25–26, structurally speaking, are the final part of the second section (i.e., vv. 12–26) in the chapter and speak more directly to the needs and fears of the Jews in exile in Babylon. As John Oswalt points out, the question addressed in verses 1–11 was "Does God want to deliver us?" The question now, however, is "Can God deliver [us]?" (*The Book of Isaiah,* 57, emphasis in original). The question asked by God in verse 25—"To whom then will you compare me, or who is my equal?" (NRSV)—is the same question asked in verse 18. Understood against the background of the triumphal statements made by the Babylonians about their gods, the insistence upon God's absolute transcendence in this passage makes a great deal of sense.

In verse 25, Isaiah refers to God as "Holy One." Despite the decision by all of the major translation committees (KJV,

NIV, NRSV) to attribute the question to "the Holy One," there is no definite article in the Hebrew text, suggesting that "Holy One" (Heb. *qadosh*) might be understood as a personal name, not as an adjective. The importance of describing God as "holy" cannot be overstated. Oswalt notes that Isaiah uses this word or a derivative of it sixty-nine times throughout the book. Of those, "Holy One" as a way to refer to God occurs thirty-five times (*The Book of Isaiah,* 68).

As we turn to verse 26, Isaiah invites his readers to look up in the sky: "Lift up your eyes on high and see: Who created these? He who brings out their host and numbers them, calling them all by name" (NRSV). Here it is helpful to recall the importance of astrology in Babylonian religion. Isaiah's indirect way of referring to the stars, sun, moon, and planets is seen in his use of the word "these." As John Goldingay points out, this term "downgrades their significance and counteracts the overestimate of them in Babylonian thinking, where they were the entities that determined what happened on earth" (*The Message of Isaiah 40-55: A Literary-Theological Commentary* [London: T&T Clark, 2005], 59). The use of the word "host," though, gives a clear clue as to the prophet's meaning. "Host" (Heb. *tsabia*) is a military term. But this is not a rival army to God; He controls them and "call[s] them all by name" (v. 26, NRSV).

As Oswalt explains, "to him they are not numberless; more than that, he knows them each by name. In the ancient world, to know the name of something was to know its essence, and thereby have power over it" (*The Book of Isaiah,* 70). God is, thus, the Lord of all creation, even the stars the Babylonians worshiped.

III. GOD'S STRENGTH AND OUR STRENGTH (ISAIAH 40:27–31)

In verse 27, Isaiah addresses the people: "Why do you say, O Jacob, and speak, O Israel, 'My way is hidden from the LORD, and my right is disregarded by my God?'"(NRSV). Knowing what we know about God's purposes, this is a ridiculous claim. Even in exile, God has not forgotten His people or abandoned them. He is certainly aware of what is happening to them. His justice has not passed over them. He sees exactly what is happening to them.

Isaiah then repeats the question he first asked in verse 21, "Have you not known? Have you not heard? The LORD is the everlasting God, the Creator of the ends of the earth. He does not faint or grow weary; his understanding is unsearchable" (v. 28, NRSV). In other words, has it not been proclaimed, as though by a messenger running through the streets with much-needed news, that the everlasting God has come to vindicate His people? There is no searching of His understanding. God is not like the idols of the pagans. He does not sleep, neither is His strength undermined by others in any way.

Even the strongest among us, "even youths will faint and be weary, and the young will fall exhausted" (v. 30, NRSV). But when we compare the endurance of youth with that of the eternal God, there is no comparison. Even the young will get tired, and they will grow weary and weak, but the Creator of the world, the One who spoke the entire world into existence, is never weary or weak.

Therefore, He can help or assist those who are in need, especially those who are feeling weary and weak. He offers sustaining power to those who wait on Him. "But those who wait for the LORD shall renew their strength, they shall mount up with wings like eagles, they shall run and not be weary, they shall walk and not faint" (v. 31, NRSV). Some commentators have pointed out that there is a definite article preceding the word "eagles," thus "they shall mount up with wings like the eagles." Oswalt, citing Edward J. Young, observes that the definite article, "the eagles," denotes the class—as eagles are wont to do. Far from being crushed to earth by their own helplessness, those who depend on God can stretch their wings in the effortless way of eagles and sail off on the wind" (75).

THE LESSON APPLIED

In today's lesson, we have studied some of the most famous, as well as most encouraging, words in all of Scripture. We have also come to understand something of the original setting in which these words were spoken. So, what do we do now? The critical issue—both for the original audience and for us—is hope. As John Oswalt has pointed out, "it is into a setting just like ours that Isaiah speaks by inspiration. He speaks to people who have lost hope. The impossible has happened. They were sure their nation could not fall, that their temple could not be destroyed, and that their God would not let them down. Yet all that happened" (*The NIV Application Commentary: Isaiah* [Grand Rapids: Zondervan, 2003], 454).

So, it is for us. There are so many aspects of life on this earth that seem impervious to change. Perhaps it is an illness, a financial situation, or a broken family relationship. Perhaps it is conflict with a brother or sister, or the presence of a stubborn sin in our lives. Sometimes life seems so hopeless and not at all yielding to change. But this is not true. "We can believe," Oswalt writes, "that God can change our circumstances. There can be real change for the better. This is, there can be if we believe in a God who is both outside of the inside of history…But so much depends on our faith…a life of faith in God, a life where we truly release ourselves into his hands without any reservation, a life where we are constantly giving ourselves and our concerns into the caring Creator's hands" (*ibid.*). But just as with the remnant that God led out of captivity, we have to trust that He is able to do this, that He is stronger than any of the demons that assail us. Let us "wait for the LORD" with confidence and trust, knowing that He can bring us through any situation we face (v. 31, NRSV).

LET'S TALK ABOUT IT

Is there a difference between one who is "weary" and one who is "faint" (Isaiah 40:28, NRSV)?

Strictly speaking, there is little difference between these two words. It is a mistake to suggest otherwise. The poetry of Isaiah 40 calls for a more nuanced understanding of verse 31 than a surface reading would reveal. The matter is very simple. The verses of Isaiah 40:27–41, as laid out in the NRSV, form a unit of poetry commonly called a *strophe*. Looking more narrowly at verse 31, we see an example of what is typically called *parallelism* in Hebrew poetry. Notice the phrases: "they shall run and not be weary" and "they shall walk and not faint" (NRSV). The final phrases are synonymous; they complement each other, and each helps to illuminate the meaning of the other. They cannot be artificially distinguished for the purpose of making a catchy preaching or teaching point.

That said, this text—these repeated statements—is a powerful testimony to God's utter and unassailable strength. Quite often, the challenges that we face threaten to overwhelm us. (Recall Martin Luther's lyric; "And though this world, with devils filled, should threaten to undo us" [*New National Baptist Hymnal, 21st Century Edition* #37].) Indeed, they would overwhelm us if left to our own strength. All of our financial troubles, all of our worries about our jobs or our children, all of our concern for the direction of society, all of our worries about the future of the Church as a whole or our local congregation—all of these things will undo us if we allow them to overpower us. But God is never worn out. He "gives power to the faint, and strengthens the powerless" (v. 29, NRSV). Because

He is never weak or weary, we ought to wait on Him. He does not get confused when He is dealing with our headaches or heartaches. He is never baffled by our failures because He is always concerned with our deliverance. This can be such a comforting sentiment for even the most seasoned believer.

One thing is guaranteed: this world will give us trouble, but we know God is greater. There is no better summary of this in the Christian tradition than the one found in Martin Luther's "A Mighty Fortress Is Our God"; "A mighty fortress is our God, a bulwark never failing; our helper He amid the flood of mortal ills prevailing. For still our ancient foe doth seek to work us woe; his craft and power are great, and, armed with cruel hate, on earth is not his equal. Did we in our own strength confide, our striving would be losing, were not the right Man on our side, the Man of God's own choosing. Dost ask who that may be? Christ Jesus, it is He; Lord Sabaoth, His name, from age to age the same, and He must win the battle" (*ibid.*).

GET SOCIAL

Share your views and tag us @rhboydco and use #WaitonGod.

Twitter
@rhboydco (#rhboydco)

Instagram
@rhboydco (#rhboydco)

Facebook
@rhboydco (#rhboydco)

www.rhboyd.com

HOME DAILY DEVOTIONAL READINGS
FEBRUARY 5–11, 2024

MONDAY	TUESDAY	WEDNESDAY	THURSDAY	FRIDAY	SATURDAY	SUNDAY
Seductive Song	Defying an Immoral Command	Works That Proclaim the Truth	When Faith Comes under Fire	We Must Obey God Alone	You Will Not Be Burned	Delivered from the Flames
Daniel 3:1–7	Daniel 3:8–18	John 10:24–38	Acts 4:7–20	Acts 5:17–29	Isaiah 43:1–7	Daniel 3:19–28

FAITH AMIDST THE FIERY FURNACE

ADULT TOPIC:	BACKGROUND SCRIPTURE: DANIEL 3:1–30
WORTH RISKING OUR LIVES	LESSON PASSAGE: DANIEL 3:19–28

DANIEL 3:19–28

King James Version	*New Revised Standard Version*
THEN was Nebuchadnezzar full of fury, and the form of his visage was changed against Shadrach, Meshach, and Abednego: therefore he spake, and commanded that they should heat the furnace one seven times more than it was wont to be heated.	THEN Nebuchadnezzar was so filled with rage against Shadrach, Meshach, and Abednego that his face was distorted. He ordered the furnace heated up seven times more than was customary.
20 And he commanded the most mighty men that were in his army to bind Shadrach, Meshach, and Abednego, and to cast them into the burning fiery furnace.	20 and ordered some of the strongest guards in his army to bind Shadrach, Meshach, and Abednego and to throw them into the furnace of blazing fire.
21 Then these men were bound in their coats, their hosen, and their hats, and their other garments, and were cast into the midst of the burning fiery furnace.	21 So the men were bound, still wearing their tunics, their trousers, their hats, and their other garments, and they were thrown into the furnace of blazing fire.
22 Therefore because the king's commandment was urgent, and the furnace exceeding hot, the flames of the fire slew those men that took up Shadrach, Meshach, and Abednego.	22 Because the king's command was urgent and the furnace was so overheated, the raging flames killed the men who lifted Shadrach, Meshach, and Abednego.
23 And these three men, Shadrach, Meshach, and Abednego, fell down bound into the midst of the burning fiery furnace.	23 But the three men, Shadrach, Meshach, and Abednego, fell down, bound, into the furnace of blazing fire.
24 Then Nebuchadnezzar the king was astonished, and rose up in haste, and spake, and said unto his counsellors, Did not we cast three men bound into the midst of the fire? They answered and said unto the king, True, O king.	24 Then King Nebuchadnezzar was astonished and rose up quickly. He said to his counselors, "Was it not three men that we threw bound into the fire?" They answered the king, "True, O king."
25 He answered and said, Lo, I see four men loose, walking in the midst of the fire, and they have no hurt; and the form of the fourth is like the Son of God.	\25 He replied, "But I see four men unbound, walking in the middle of the fire, and they are not hurt, and the fourth has the appearance of a god."

MAIN THOUGHT: Nebuchadnezzar said, "Blessed be the God of Shadrach, Meshach, and Abednego, who has sent his angel and delivered his servants who trusted in him. They disobeyed the king's command and yielded up their bodies rather than serve and worship any god except their own God." (Daniel 3:28, KJV)

King James Version	*New Revised Standard Version*
26 Then Nebuchadnezzar came near to the mouth of the burning fiery furnace, and spake, and said, Shadrach, Meshach, and Abednego, ye servants of the most high God, come forth, and come hither. Then Shadrach, Meshach, and Abednego, came forth of the midst of the fire.	26 Nebuchadnezzar then approached the door of the furnace of blazing fire and said, "Shadrach, Meshach, and Abednego, servants of the Most High God, come out! Come here!" So Shadrach, Meshach, and Abednego came out from the fire.
27 And the princes, governors, and captains, and the king's counsellors, being gathered together, saw these men, upon whose bodies the fire had no power, nor was an hair of their head singed, neither were their coats changed, nor the smell of fire had passed on them.	27 And the satraps, the prefects, the governors, and the king's counselors gathered together and saw that the fire had not had any power over the bodies of those men; the hair of their heads was not singed, their tunics were not harmed, and not even the smell of fire came from them.
28 Then Nebuchadnezzar spake, and said, Blessed be the God of Shadrach, Meshach, and Abednego, who hath sent his angel, and delivered his servants that trusted in him, and have changed the king's word, and yielded their bodies, that they might not serve nor worship any god, except their own God.	28 Nebuchadnezzar said, "Blessed be the God of Shadrach, Meshach, and Abednego, who has sent his angel and delivered his servants who trusted in him. They disobeyed the king's command and yielded up their bodies rather than serve and worship any god except their own God.

LESSON SETTING
    Time: 605–590 BC
    Place: Babylon

LESSON OUTLINE
  I. **Defiance**
     (Daniel 3:19–25)
  II. **Consequences of Defiance**
     (Daniel 3:26–27)
  III. **Faith Wins Out**
     (Daniel 3:28)

UNIFYING PRINCIPLE

It is problematic to stand by personal convictions when we are threatened by extreme consequences for doing so. For what, or whom, are we willing to stand even at risk to our lives? Shadrach, Meshach, and Abednego declared their faith in God despite Nebuchadnezzar's angry threats.

INTRODUCTION

Daniel 1:19–30 is a part of a larger unit (Daniel 3:1–30), which outlines the strength and power of faith over one of the most powerful regimes recorded in human history. The kingdom of Babylon was known for its riches and dominance over world affairs. It brought the Assyrian Empire to an end. It was a totalitarian type of government (see Sinclair Ferguson, *The Communicator's Commentary, Daniel Volume 19,* Word Books, Publisher, Waco, 1988, pp. 69–86). Holding all of the cards, the government of Babylon with Nebuchadnezzar at its helm was quite vicious, rich, and known for its authoritarianism throughout the world as it was known then. It defeated Israel in 587-86 BC and held the land captive for approximately 70 years. Babylon participated in a melting pot type of government. It allowed the captive nation to be a part of governmental affairs as long as the people acknowledged who was in power. In the midst of defiance by the conquered party, retribution was swift and quite assertive.

In the story before us, Babylon took from the captive nation the best and brightest minds and incorporated these personalities into the kingdom. They went as far as renaming the captives with Babylonian names and sought to disrupt their cultural identity as well. (see Daniel 1:6–7). These Jewish exiles were placed in both administrative and clerical government positions. Among these exiles were Daniel and three of his friends. Their Hebrew names were Belteshazzar, Hananiah, Mishael, and Azariah. The three friends are better known, due to the popularity of the Hebrew story, as Shadrach, Meshach, and Abednego, their Chaldean names.

The three came to the king's attention because they performed their jobs well and displayed personal integrity as they carried out their responsibilities. It is also highly probable that the Babylonian officials did not care for captives holding government authority and devised schemes to get them removed from their occupation in the new government. The three Jewish exiles were among the list of Hebrews who performed their jobs well and were set up to fall underneath the Babylonian system. Learning that the Jews were highly religious, they convinced the king to erect a statue over ninety feet high and nine feet wide and ordered the Hebrews to pay homage to it. The erection of the statue was probably due to the king's dream of power in chapter 2; however, the Jewish exiles refused.

Their refusal to worship the statue set into motion a series of events that escalated the fury of the king and landed them into a furnace that was made seven times hotter than normal. To go against such great power showed the extent of their defiance, to which the king reacted badly. He held them accountable for refusing to pay homage to the statue and for refusing to recant their position and had them thrown into the fiery furnace. However, things did not turn out as planned for the Babylonians as the faith of the three is recognized by the king, who later neutralized the edict by proclaiming the exiles' God as the supreme Lord of heaven and earth. Their defiance and determination to press forward with their Jewish faith offered a great reward to the faithful.

EXPOSITION

I. DEFIANCE (DANIEL 3:19–25)

Then the king was filled with anger. This verse is the king's reaction to the turn of events that unfolded in previous verses. The Jewish exiles had refused to obey the force of the edict and the king had reacted terribly to the news. It was the equivalent of him declaring, "Who do they think they are to defy my order? I will show them!" Yet the trio stood unmoved by the threat and dug their heels in deeper by re-committing themselves to reject the king's edict. They truly believed that God was greater than the king, so they stood fast in their faith. The opening verses of chapter 3 mention the statue at least six times as a way to show its centrality to power and authority. The question was: "How could they refuse to obey such an order?" It was because of their defiant faith in God. They were committed Jews, who believed in the power of God to deliver them from the awesome might of the Chaldeans. The episode sprung from a dream that the king had, which none of his staff members were able to interpret. Daniel heard of the king's problem and volunteered to help resolve the issue (see Daniel 2:1–49). After praying to the Lord his God, Daniel was given the ability to recall and interpret the king's dream that the Chaldeans would eventually be overtaken by an inferior power (see Daniel 2:31–49). In return, the king promoted Daniel and gave his friends special opportunities to help administer to his kingdom.

Daniel 3:9–12 show the accusation brought by a number of Chaldeans. In fact, the very form of this chapter heightens the drama because it is the first mention of the Jewish exiles by name (their Chaldean names). They got word of their defiance to the king. He was outraged! The Jews were the point of scorn, and this story illustrates the jealous mindset of the Chaldeans.

II. CONSEQUENCES OF DEFIANCE (DANIEL 3:26–27)

The second warning was intended to let the Jewish exiles know (if they had not realized it before) that this was no laughing matter. The burning fiery furnace was made seven times hotter than normal to get their attention. After giving them an ultimatum, the king arrogantly asked, "What god will be able to rescue you from my hand?" (v. 15, NIV). The king thought his authority and power could only be overturned by a divine source, or he was rhetorically poking fun at the exiles as to the impossibility of their need to be res-

cued. Yet, what was impossible for human hands was possible for divine ones. The Lord God of heaven and earth had heard the order and He deliberately lowered the temperature. It was hot enough to take the lives of the men who threw the exiles into the furnace, but it was cool enough so that the three Hebrews' bodies were not scorched, nor did their clothing even smell of smoke (Daniel 3:19–24).

It appears that due to the commanding presence of God that the fire refused to act like fire and took on the characteristics of an air conditioner. Furthermore, what is astonishing is that the king rewarded Daniel for being able to tell him his dream and to interpret it (see Daniel 2). He even honored Daniel's God as the true God of heaven and earth, but did not initially believe in His ability to deliver the three Jewish exiles. Nebuchadnezzar later discovered that Daniel's God was not only able to solve the mysterious, but that He also possessed the power to deliver the faithful trio from the burning fiery furnace.

III. FAITH WINS OUT (DANIEL 3:28)

The unbeliever might have thought the Hebrews were crazy for being so determined to resist the king's decree and threat. Their lives were at stake. Yet they were so determined that they would not be persuaded otherwise. They knew their God would deliver them and just in case God didn't exercise His sovereignty, they were prepared for the alternative, "We still will not serve or bow down before the golden statue" (v. 18). It was a bold expression of faith in the power of God. The three Hebrews were willing to die for their faith.

They refused to be convinced otherwise. They acknowledged Nebuchadnezzar as king, yet they stood in defiance of him in honor of a greater King, Yahweh, the Creator of the Universe. As subordinate and powerless captives before the mighty emperor, the three men stood firm in their allegiance to God. What kind of thing did these three men possess that they would be willing to die? What on earth could have made them to take such a stand? It was their faith and trust in the goodness of God. They were obedient to the first four of the Ten Commandments (see Exodus 20). Faith is the act of keeping our commitment to God.

Feeling somewhat uncomfortable with his decision to have thrown the Hebrews into the fiery furnace, Nebuchadnezzar approached the furnace and inquired about the condition of the three men. Surprisingly, the king peered into the furnace and saw four people in the furnace and he inquired, "Didn't we put three people in the furnace?" His eyes had not deceived him. He called out to them by name. They responded positively that they were okay and had survived the ordeal due to the power of their God. Their faith in God had protected them. The king then decreed that the God of the three Hebrews be reverenced as the God above all others and anyone who spoke against Him would be torn limb from limb. Their deliverance had led the king to reverse his decision. Initially, the three were to be punished with death for refusing to bow before the statue; now others would be punished if they defied the name of the Hebrew God. The king then promoted them to a place of high honor in the province of Babylon.

THE LESSON APPLIED

Faith pays off. This account starts by looking at the impossibility of escape from the king's hands, but ends by displaying the power of God to thwart the king's decision to execute three men for their faith in God. God is even seen as being in the midst of the furnace exercising authority over the flames. Look at the contrast between the two things. The king ordered the furnace to be heated seven times hotter than usual, but instead of it acting like fire, it took on the properties of an air conditioner. The text says they did not even smell like smoke.

One can conclude that in the hands of God, the elements reflect His will. God has ultimate authority over the elements and over life. He did not relinquish control to the king. Humanity has authority to make decisions, but this text indicates that all human decisions can be overridden by God. The three Hebrews believed that God could and would deliver them, but they were also prepared for the possibility that He could exercise His Sovereignty and might not act according to what they believed. In that instance, they expressed that they still would not serve the statue or bow down before it. Either option was an outgrowth of their faith.

LET'S TALK ABOUT IT

1. Does one have to believe in miracles in order to have faith?

The Bible says that faith is the assurance of things hoped for, the conviction of things not seen (Hebrews 11:1). That is to say, one has to believe in the power of God that He can do anything, in order to have faith. Faith says God can do anything despite the odds against Him.

2. What is the relationship between faith, hope, and love?

These three things are actually sisters, but the greatest of these is love. Faith is the conviction that something is real or authentic. Hope is the expectant part of faith. We expect to receive something from it that reflects or points to our hope in it. Love is the means by which we do what we do. It is an event that is a deliberate, self-sacrificing action of goodwill toward another.

3. What is the extent of God's love for humankind?

God's love for humanity is fully seen in the crucifixion of Jesus Christ. God gave all He had to give in the sacrifice of His Son. He was the ultimate gift of eternal life who erased sin as a barrier to have a beautiful relationship with God. Jesus' death on the cross wipes away sin and brings us into a closer and a personal relationship with God. This relationship gives us affinity with His presence so that He becomes a Resource that helps and guides us on how to live to please God. He answers our prayers and communicates with us in blessed ways that keeps us or allows us to receive spiritual resources from our Savior. The Holy Spirt guides our lives so that we may learn, know, and understand what the Lord God says to us and how we can incorporate His will in our lives. The Spirit cleanses us and sanctifies us so we are set apart and commissioned for Christian service. The Spirit then works with us daily to be sure we as believers hold to God's unchanging hand. He does His transformative work in us to conform us to the Spirit's desires.

Thank God for His goodness and love for us. He is the One who took the risk when we sinned against Him. He absolutely could've left us to our own devices and watched us die from afar, but He loved us too much. He broke through time and space to get to us and save us from eternity in hell. Praise God for His overwhelming love!

GET SOCIAL
Share your views and tag us @rhboydco and use #FaithWins.

Twitter
@rhboydco (#rhboydco)

Instagram
@rhboydco (#rhboydco)

Facebook
@rhboydco (#rhboydco)

www.rhboyd.com

HOME DAILY DEVOTIONAL READINGS
FEBRUARY 12–18, 2024

MONDAY	TUESDAY	WEDNESDAY	THURSDAY	FRIDAY	SATURDAY	SUNDAY
Fear God, Not Pharaoh	Why Are You Afraid?	Do Not Let Your Hearts Be Troubled	Earthly and Heavenly Authority	God Cares for the Flock	Unfazed by a Blasphemous Law	Delivered from the Flames
Exodus 1:8–21	Matthew 8:18–27	John 14:1–11	John 19:1–11	1 Peter 5	Daniel 6:1–15	Daniel 6:10–11, 14, 16, 19–23, 26–27

FAITH IN TIMES OF TROUBLE

ADULT TOPIC: BACKGROUND SCRIPTURE: DANIEL 6:1–28
FACING GREAT DANGER   LESSON PASSAGE: DANIEL 6:10–11, 14, 16, 19–23, 26

DANIEL 6:10–11, 14, 16, 19–23, 26

King James Version

NOW when Daniel knew that the writing was signed, he went into his house; and his windows being open in his chamber toward Jerusalem, he kneeled upon his knees three times a day, and prayed, and gave thanks before his God, as he did aforetime.

11 Then these men assembled, and found Daniel praying and making supplication before his God.

• • • • • •

14 Then the king, when he heard these words, was sore displeased with himself, and set his heart on Daniel to deliver him: and he laboured till the going down of the sun to deliver him.

• • • • • •

16 Then the king commanded, and they brought Daniel, and cast him into the den of lions. Now the king spake and said unto Daniel, Thy God whom thou servest continually, he will deliver thee.

• • • • • •

19 Then the king arose very early in the morning, and went in haste unto the den of lions.

20 And when he came to the den, he cried with a lamentable voice unto Daniel: and the king spake and said to Daniel, O Daniel, servant of the living God, is thy God, whom thou servest continually, able to deliver thee from the lions?

21 Then said Daniel unto the king, O king, live for ever.

22 My God hath sent his angel, and hath shut the lions' mouths, that they have not hurt me: forasmuch as before him innocency was found

New Revised Standard Version

ALTHOUGH Daniel knew that the document had been signed, he continued to go to his house, which had windows in its upper room open toward Jerusalem, and to get down on his knees three times a day to pray to his God and praise him, just as he had done previously.

11 The conspirators came and found Daniel praying and seeking mercy before his God.

• • • • • •

14 When the king heard the charge, he was very much distressed. He was determined to save Daniel, and until the sun went down he made every effort to rescue him.

• • • • • •

16 Then the king gave the command, and Daniel was brought and thrown into the den of lions. The king said to Daniel, "May your God, whom you faithfully serve, deliver you!"

• • • • • •

19 Then, at break of day, the king got up and hurried to the den of lions.

20 When he came near the den where Daniel was, he cried out anxiously to Daniel, "O Daniel, servant of the living God, has your God whom you faithfully serve been able to deliver you from the lions?"

21 Daniel then said to the king, "O king, live forever!

22 My God sent his angel and shut the lions' mouths so that they would not hurt me, because I was found blameless before him; also before

MAIN THOUGHT: My God hath sent his angel, and hath shut the lions' mouths, that they have not hurt me: forasmuch as before him innocency was found in me; and also before thee, O king, have I done no hurt. (Daniel 6:22, KJV)

DANIEL 6:10–11, 14, 16, 19–23, 26

King James Version	New Revised Standard Version
in me; and also before thee, O king, have I done no hurt.	you, O king, I have done no wrong."
23 Then was the king exceedingly glad for him, and commanded that they should take Daniel up out of the den. So Daniel was taken up out of the den, and no manner of hurt was found upon him, because he believed in his God.	23 Then the king was exceedingly glad and commanded that Daniel be taken up out of the den. So Daniel was taken up out of the den, and no kind of harm was found on him, because he had trusted in his God.
• • • • • •	• • • • • •
26 I make a decree, That in every dominion of my kingdom men tremble and fear before the God of Daniel: for he is the living God, and stedfast for ever, and his kingdom that which shall not be destroyed, and his dominion shall be even unto the end.	26 I make a decree, that in all my royal dominion people shall tremble and fear before the God of Daniel: For he is the living God, enduring forever. His kingdom shall never be destroyed, and his dominion has no end.

LESSON SETTING
Time: 539 BC
Place: Babylon

LESSON OUTLINE
I. **The Plot and False Report (Daniel 6:4–7)**
II. **The Plot Carried Out (Daniel 6:10, 16, 19)**
III. **Daniel Was Restored (Daniel 6:21, 25–26)**

UNIFYING PRINCIPLE
At times we endure a political climate in which the laws are in conflict with personal convictions. How do we take a stand against the powers that be? On account of his faith in God, Daniel stood up to King Darius' unjust decree even at risk to his own life.

INTRODUCTION
Before we study our lesson in depth, it would be wise to examine the events leading up to the story. In chapter five, King Belshazzar threw a large party. During the festivities, a hand appeared and wrote on the wall. For the king and all in attendance, this was a frightening event. He called all the astrologers, magicians, and enchanters to interpret what was written. Because they failed to decode the message, the queen advised her husband to retrieve Daniel. God had gifted Daniel earlier to interpret strange occurrences such as Nebuchadnezzar's dream. He was called on to interpret the writing on the wall. The interpretation Daniel gave was not pleasant news to the king. Belshazzar was warned that his kingdom would be divided between the Medes and the Persians. Belshazzar elevated Daniel to the third highest ruler in the kingdom; however, later that night, Belshazzar was killed, and Babylon fell to Cyrus the Great who conquered Babylon. That episode inaugurated the reign of Darius the Mede.

The selected text for today's study has similar substance of the story about the three Hebrew young men who would not bow to the golden image of Nebuchadnezzar. Even though these men stood firm in their faith, there was always someone challenging them. For Daniel, it was the new ruler. Just as Daniel was absent from the fiery furnace story, Hananiah, Mishael, and Azariah were absent in this account.

EXPOSITION

I. THE PLOT AND FALSE REPORT (DANIEL 6:4–7)

Darius had appointed 120 *satraps* to govern the Persian provinces, along with three administrators (some translations say presidents). These administrators were overseers to the satraps. Daniel was one of the three administrators in power. Daniel governed in such an excellent manner that Darius decided to set him over the whole kingdom. Darius was going to elevate a Jewish man second in command over the Medes and Persians. Obviously, Darius' decision did not sit well with the satraps and the administrators.

Because King Darius appointed Daniel over the entire kingdom, the administrators and the satraps plotted to bring him down. Much like the advertisements in a political race, the officials tried to find a blemish in Daniel's career to exploit his character. However, none could be found. Daniel was trustworthy in all things. Finally, they conceded among one another that they could not find any negative press or scandalous things about Daniel. He was indeed a man of integrity.

The conspirators agreed that if there was any fault to find, it would have to be something regarding God's Law. Because the Persian nationals knew the Jews tended to strictly adhere to the Torah, they tried to use that fact against Daniel. If they could force Daniel to choose between the Law of his God and law of the king, then they had a chance to ruin Daniel's standing.

The conspirators approached the king by declaration, saluting him with the customary. "Live forever!" Even though only the administrators and satraps went before the king, they represented a larger consensus.

This unified group consisted of the administrators (overseers of the kingdom), the prefects (governors), the satraps (Persian governors), counselors (ministerial advisers), and the captains (different governors). Before they confronted the king, they assembled together to devise a plan. Whether or not all these officials were consulted with such an idea is unknown; however, it is likely that all the leaders, beside Darius, were troubled with a Jewish man being second in command. The administrators and satraps presented the idea that the king should issue a decree stating that no one should worship or pray to any god or person except the king for thirty days. Whoever failed to adhere to the decree would be thrown into a den of lions. They pleaded with the king to issue the law and put it in writing. By signing off on such a decree (or any decree for that matter), the law could not be overturned during the next thirty days.

The trap for Daniel included conflict between his religion and the law of the land. It is interesting to note that Daniel's habit of praying three times each day was not a requirement of the Law. He would face Jerusalem and pray three times daily, yet that was nowhere mandated in the Torah. The practice of praying in the morning, noon, and evening can be found in later rabbinic tradition as well as among the early church. However, Daniel was not commanded by God's Law to pray a certain number of times in a single day.

The conspirators might have seen the Hebrew God that Daniel worshiped to be in conflict with the Zoroastrian deity Darius worshiped. No matter the reasoning, Darius established the edict and signed it. The Aramaic term for "decree," *ecar*, was related to the terms for "binding" as well as "prison." Thus, the term suggested the law was obligatory, and punishment was connected to violators of the statute. The same scenario was played out in Ezra 6:11–12 as well. Even though the situation seemed bleak for Daniel, God could change what humans considered unalterable.

II. THE PLOT CARRIED OUT (DANIEL 6:10, 16, 19)

The trap had been set; all that the officials needed was evidence against Daniel's disobedience to the king's edict. Daniel heard that the decree had been signed into law by Darius. He had to make a decision based on what he thought was ethically correct. He could have easily stopped praying for the determined time, in order to avoid punishment or demotion as a political leader. However, that was not important to him. He could have prayed in the middle of the night with his windows closed, so no one would catch him; yet he continued to pray toward Jerusalem three times daily in his room.

On his knees with his windows open, Daniel prayed and gave thanks to God as he had done in the past. Daniel was openly disobeying the king's decree by keeping the window of his upper room open. The choice Daniel made was not between life by adhering to the decree or death by ignoring the decree; rather the choice Daniel made was life through obedience to God. It could be plausible that Daniel was taught to follow the Shema his whole life: "Hear, O Israel: The LORD our God, the LORD is one. Love the LORD your God with all your heart and with all your soul and with all your strength" (Deuteronomy 6:4–5, NIV). Because of Daniel's consistency throughout his life, it did not make sense to choose anything over Yahweh.

Even though his action carried severe consequences such as death, Daniel refused to not commune with God. His integrity and character proved his devotion to his Heavenly Father. Regardless of his position and status as a powerful government official in a Persian Empire, he vowed to pledge his allegiance to God alone. Daniel's insubordination appeared to have worked out for those plotting against him. To make matters worse, the conspirators reported the offense to the king. Yet, they did not mention who the offender was. They wanted the king to confirm that punishment would ensue for any perpetrator of the law. After his verbal confirmation, the group revealed the identity of the law breaker—Daniel. Upon hearing the news, the king became troubled. Since the decree was irrevocable, Darius had to carry out the penalty. But Darius began to see that there was something wrong with what was taking place. In fact, Darius tried to find ways of rescuing Daniel from this tribulation.

The next morning at the lions' den, Darius commented to Daniel, "May your God, who you serve continually, rescue you!" (v. 16, NIV). This was not a snide remark but a blessing of hope for his trusted administrator. King Darius realized that he had been tricked; yet, his hands were tied because the law was binding. Daniel was thrown into a den of lions. After sealing the mouth of the den with a stone, King Darius went back to his palace heavy-hearted. That night, he fasted from food and entertainment. His fast may be seen not only as sympathy toward Daniel but also in context of a miraculous delivery from death. One might even say Darius might have been interceding on Daniel's behalf.

The next morning, he ran in haste to check on the fate of Daniel. As Darius neared the den, he cried out, "Daniel, servant of the living God, has your God, whom you serve continually, been able to rescue you from the lions?" (v. 20, NIV). If Darius did not have faith in Daniel's God, why did he call out to someone presumed dead? Daniel's strong witness of faith and integrity impacted the king greatly.

III. DANIEL WAS RESTORED (DANIEL 6:21, 25–26)

When Daniel heard the king's voice, he answered, "O king, live forever!" Daniel had been vindicated; God had proved true to Daniel's prayer. Daniel continued to tell the king about his innocence, saying he had done nothing wrong. His calmness to the situation contrasted to the king's seemingly anxious state of being.

The story concluded with a reversal of fortune. Daniel was immediately pulled from the lions' den. Because they conspired against one of Darius' top officers, the administrators and satraps were thrown into the lions' den in place of Daniel.

Not only did they suffer for their unjust act, but also their families faced the same punishment. The conspirators were faced with the stark reality that they had not only attacked Daniel but also the God he served. This reversal of fortune was similar to the ending in the book of Esther.

Once more, Daniel was considered the hero. After Daniel's miraculous exit from the lions' den, Darius issued a blessing of peace throughout the nations as well as a proclamation among the nations that all should honor and respect the God of Daniel. Darius stated that Daniel's God was alive and concerned about the affairs of His people. He wanted his people to recognize that no other god before God had been involved in the very life of the people like Daniel's God.

THE LESSON APPLIED

The primary discipline displayed throughout the book of Daniel is prayer. Daniel's enemies thought that prayer could be used against him. Prayer can be an underrated element within a believer's life. The power in prayer is not that you pray for power, but you release your will to the will of God. By praying for God's will, we can indeed experience freedom and peace in our lives. We let go of our wants and allow God to shape us into His image. If you make an effort to commune more with God in prayer, then you will begin to see amazing things happen in your life. You will be changed, which gives a whole new insight on the decisions and trials you face.

There are other spiritual disciplines that we see here within the story. In addition to prayer, Daniel also exhibited a life of submission, which is a spiritual discipline. Richard Foster, in *Celebration of Discipline* says, "The cross is the sign of submission" (Foster 1998, 126). Humility is a mark of the discipline of submission. Daniel showed great humility in his life. The freedom in what he did came from his submission to Yahweh. There is indeed freedom in the spiritual disciplines. Daniel chose to submit to Yahweh, and in turn, God allowed him to walk free.

"Stand" is a song that came out in the 1960s by Sly and the Family Stone. The lyrics to their song say, "Stand, in the end, you'll still be you. One that's done all the things you set out to do. Stand, there's a cross for you to bear. Things to go through if you're going anywhere. Stand for the things you know are right. It's the truth that the truth makes them so uptight."

We must stand for what we believe to be true. We must resolve to be more dedicated in our prayer lives. Our help comes from the Lord; that help strengthens us to face whatever obstacles or opposition that may come. Daniel did not look to anyone for his help; rather, he continued in the discipline he practiced daily—prayer.

LET'S TALK ABOUT IT

1. What are some challenges that we face in dong God's work?

We don't face the physical challenges that Daniel did before the lions, but we face a real challenge in ourselves. We are our biggest struggles against God.

2. How can you be more effective in utilizing spiritual disciplines in your life?

Remember, practicing spiritual discipline allows room for God to work in your life. When we practice these things, we submit our lives to Jesus' lordship.

3. Are you placing all your trust in God?

Has God ever told you to turn left, and you continued straight? This week, write down specific examples of things that you are not trusting God for in your life. If you can not trust God in small matters, how can you stand with Him in major ones?

GET SOCIAL
Share your views and tag us @rhboydco and use #StandinFaith.

Twitter
@rhboydco (#rhboydco)

Instagram
@rhboydco (#rhboydco)

Facebook
@rhboydco (#rhboydco)

www.rhboyd.com

HOME DAILY DEVOTIONAL READINGS
FEBRUARY 19–25, 2024

MONDAY	TUESDAY	WEDNESDAY	THURSDAY	FRIDAY	SATURDAY	SUNDAY
God's Plan for Welfare and Hope	In Christ All Things Were Created	God Will Complete God's Work	God Works for Our Good	God Plans Our Steps	God's Consuming Judgment	Living by Faith
Jeremiah 29:8–14	Colossians 1:13–20	Philippians 1:3–11	Romans 8:19–28	Proverbs 16:1–9	Habakkuk 1:5–17	Habakkuk 2:1–5

FAITH IN GOD'S PURPOSE

ADULT TOPIC: WAITING AND TRUSTING	BACKGROUND SCRIPTURE: HABAKKUK 1:5–2:5 LESSON PASSAGE: HABAKKUK 2:1–5

HABAKKUK 2:1–5

King James Version

I WILL stand upon my watch, and set me upon the tower, and will watch to see what he will say unto me, and what I shall answer when I am reproved.

2 And the Lord answered me, and said, Write the vision, and make it plain upon tables, that he may run that readeth it.

3 For the vision is yet for an appointed time, but at the end it shall speak, and not lie: though it tarry, wait for it; because it will surely come, it will not tarry.

4 Behold, his soul which is lifted up is not upright in him: but the just shall live by his faith.

5 Yea also, because he transgresseth by wine, he is a proud man, neither keepeth at home, who enlargeth his desire as hell, and is as death, and cannot be satisfied, but gathereth unto him all nations, and heapeth unto him all people:

New Revised Standard Version

I WILL stand at my watchpost, and station myself on the rampart; I will keep watch to see what he will say to me, and what he will answer concerning my complaint.

2 Then the Lord answered me and said: Write the vision; make it plain on tablets, so that a runner may read it.

3 For there is still a vision for the appointed time; it speaks of the end, and does not lie. If it seems to tarry, wait for it; it will surely come; it will not delay.

4 Look at the proud! Their spirit is not right in them, but the righteous live by their faith.

5 Moreover, wealth is treacherous; the arrogant do not endure. They open their throats wide as Sheol; like Death they never have enough. They gather all nations for themselves and collect all peoples as their own.

LESSON SETTING

Time: 612–588 BCE

Place: Unknown

LESSON OUTLINE

I. **Trusting God in Times of Uncertainty (Habakkuk 1:5–17)**

II. **Waiting on God (Habakkuk 2:1–5)**

UNIFYING PRINCIPLE

We are prone to discouragement when navigating life's hardships. How can we endure the wait and trust that better days are ahead? God's message through Habakkuk encourages us to wait in faith and trust God's timing.

MAIN THOUGHT: For the vision is yet for an appointed time, but at the end it shall speak, and not lie: though it tarry, wait for it; because it will surely come, it will not tarry. (Habakkuk 2:3, KJV)

INTRODUCTION

The author of the book of the Habakkuk is, in fact, the prophet Habakkuk. It was written between 612 and 588 BCE, just prior to when Babylon overthrew the Assyrians and rose in power. In 605 BCE, the Babylonians overthrew Judah and enslaved its inhabitants. The book was written to the people of Judah just prior to the Babylonian overthrow. Habakkuk prophesied during the reign of Jehoiakim. He was troubled by the people of God falling into horrific practices of temple prostitution and child sacrifices. Habakkuk seemed traumatized by the corruption and evil that was unchecked. Habakkuk's urgent cry to God for help in the face of evil seemed to go unanswered. Like Habakkuk, we may also wonder why does the evil that we see in our world today go unchecked? Does God notice that wickedness is all around us, and is God indifferent to our cries?

EXPOSITION

I. TRUSTING GOD IN TIMES OF UNCERTAINTY (HABAKKUK 1:5-17)

Habakkuk became a prophet in 612 BCE, after Jeremiah. His ministry began during a time of political chaos. The Assyrians were losing power and Babylon was becoming the next world leader. After Habakkuk became a prophet, King Josiah died in battle in 609 BCE. In 605 BCE, Babylon overthrew Egypt and Assyria. Daniel was taken into captivity in 605 BCE, and Zedekiah became king in 597 BCE. Habakkuk's ministry ended in 589 BCE, just before the fall of Judah and the destruction of Jerusalem.

The Babylonians had military might, and no respect for humanity. They plundered the nations that they conquered and used violence to gain wealth. There are times when it seems as though the wicked prosper and the godly suffer. Throughout the history of the world, wickedness has often gone unchecked; bad things happen to good people; one country overthrows another at any cost. The evil and wickedness that exist today existed during Habakkuk's time. He was so deeply distressed by how wicked Judah had become, and yet, they were not being punished for their sins. Like Habakkuk, we also wonder why does God allow sin to go on and on?

It could be quite discouraging to see wars and all kinds of injustices to humanity take place in our world. Habakkuk had the same questions that we have today. He cried out to God in his desperation. Habakkuk was so discouraged by what he saw in his time he could not believe that God would allow such things to take place. Maybe you can relate to his sentiments when you look at the world today: overrun with corrupt politicians, human trafficking, wars and disease, rampant violence on the news every day, etc.

Throughout the history of Judah, God sent many prophets to warn Judah of their sins. After hundreds of years of one evil king after another not obeying God, and leading the people to sin against Him, God allowed the Babylonians to overtake Judah as a way of punishing them for their sins. He told Habakkuk that Judah would be overthrown by a heathen nation and be enslaved for their refusal to obey Him. The Babylonians destroyed the temple in Jerusalem and plundered the articles of worship. Habakkuk did not understand why God would allow a wicked nation to attack His people.

It may seem for a time that sin goes unchecked; however, ultimately, there are consequences as God's judgment falls upon humanity. Sin will not continue to be unchecked. God will carry out His plan for salvation and His plan to punish sin.

The book of Habakkuk gives us an insider's view on the prophet's conversations with God. Habakkuk was very saddened at the violence and corruption in Judah. There were temple prostitutes and children were being sacrificed to pagan gods. Although the people of Judah were once God-fearing people, they had descended to depths of horrific measures in sinful behavior.

However, God will always do what is right and what is just to punish sin, according to His perfect timing and will. Almost overnight it seems, Egypt, which was once a global power for centuries, lost its power. The Babylonian Empire rose and became the next world power. Habakkuk prophesied of Judah's destruction, even though it was hard to imagine that Judah would be destroyed. As a prophet, Habakkuk had a platform with God and asked many questions and stated his concerns openly (*The Life Application Study Bible*).

Although Habakkuk complained to God about allowing sin to go unchecked, God's response to him was quite the contrary. God will use even more wicked people to address sin. It was difficult for Habakkuk to understand what God was doing. Habakkuk was frustrated with God because he thought that God was not taking action and just allowing sin to go on and on. The events that came later (the Babylonian invasion) would be the answer to Habakkuk's argument with God. Faith often involves waiting on God. His timing is often vastly different than our own timetables. Especially in our modern world, we are conditioned to expect results instantly. However, even when we do not see God working, it does not mean that He is not working. Oftentimes, we may not understand what God is doing. During such times, we should not lean on our own understanding, but continue to faithfully trust in God and obey Him.

God told Habakkuk that He was going to do something that he would not believe. God told him that He would allow the Babylonians to overtake His people. Habakkuk was confused. How could God allow His nation to be destroyed? Destruction of an entire nation wasn't exactly the solution that Habakkuk was expecting.

Sin is traumatizing to the soul. Living in a world where sin and violence prevail affects those who are serving God. Around the world, the people of God suffer persecution, injustice, and crimes against humanity. God is patient and long-suffering; however, He will not allow sin to run forever. Those who suffer under the weight of injustice will one day be free from such oppression. Sin will be punished and eradicated from the world. Calamities will one day befall those who believe that they can escape God's judgment. When believers are oppressed, God will vindicate them.

God is sovereign; He rules everything. Despite what power the wicked may think they have, no one has more power than God. It may seem as though wicked people prosper and godly people suffer; however, we can be sure that God will one day judge the world and everyone in it. We may see others (or even ourselves) continue in sin as though God is okay with it. Rest assured, that is not the case. Let us each examine our own hearts to see if we are truly for God and with God. Whenever God's patience and long-suffering is abused, the consequences will surely follow. Some may think that they are more clever than God. This is a form of idolatry. Anything that is set up against God or more important than God will be torn down. Those who prey on others will be preyed on themselves. Let none think that they will sin and escape punishment. No matter how long we sin and ignore God's warnings, the day will come when we will meet the consequences of our disobedience. Let us all submit and surrender to God while we still can. Wait on God, and have resilience in your faith that come what may, we will not abandon our post of duty and our walk with the Lord (*Matthew Henry's Concise Commentary of the Whole Bible*, p. 825–826).

II. WAITING ON GOD (HABAKKUK 2:1–5)

Habakkuk prayed for a long time that God would do something about the sins of Judah. He complained of the unchecked violence; things had just simply gotten way out of hand. God told him that He was using the Babylonians to punish His people. Habakkuk was devastated. The problem was that the Babylonians were more wicked than the people of God. How was God going to use wicked to overtake wicked? Divine judgement has a way of using everything to check iniquity. Habakkuk was heartbroken about the cruelty, violence, immorality, and injustice that were practiced by God's own people. He reasoned within himself that since God is holy, He could not just pretend that the evil did not exist. The Law of God was being ignored by the people as though it did not exist. Any judgments that regarded sin were largely powerless. There was no accountability in public life for person or property. Wicked people took advantage of those who were righteous. The righteous were surrounded by lawlessness. Followers of God were outnumbered and overpowered by the wicked. Those who were supposed to defend justice and truth could not be counted on because they were also crooked. This sad state of affairs grieved the prophet Habakkuk (*The Wycliffe Bible Commentary*, p. 871–873). Similar conditions exist today around the world. Christianity is being perverted as vain philosophies and false teachings creep into the church. Those who are believers in public service often do not stand for what they believe.

Many Christians are silently working on their jobs, hoping that no one will discover that they are followers of Jesus Christ for fear of losing their jobs. Others suffer micro-aggressions for their faith, while countless others lose their lives, families, and possessions for their faith. Habakkuk was tired of this system of injustice and violence. How effective could he be in a world where everyone was practicing all levels of debauchery? Frustrated as a prophet, Habakkuk needed some answers from God.

The Lesson Applied

Habakkuk had many questions to ask God. He was frustrated and angry by the evil practices that seeped into the lives of the people of Judah and Jerusalem. The people of God compromised with sin and because everyone was sinning, it seemed normal. Habakkuk was outraged and wanted God to do something about it. Habakkuk was frustrated at the apparent demoralizing practices of evil, injustice, and wickedness among God's people. He, like many believers who are alone in their stand for God, felt alone and angry. When he confronted God, he was surprised that God already had a plan to punish His people. It is okay to ask God questions about things that we do not understand. God is okay with our questions. He is seeking people whom He can trust to live above the culture of sin and walk humbly with Him. Our questions do not bother God. He welcomes our interrogation; He is big enough to withstand it. Ask God to help you to not defy His will. Ask Him to help you to obey Him at all times.

Let's Talk About It

Can we be honest with God about our feelings and concerns, even if they're negative?

God wants us to talk to Him about everything—especially the things that we do not understand. Habakkuk was the watchman for God's people. He wanted to know what God was doing, and why He was (apparently) ignoring the rampant sin of His people. He wasn't afraid to take his questions directly to the Lord. He was honest about his feelings.

Many godly men and women posed questions to God. Peter was the disciple who could be counted on to ask questions and not simply accept what he saw at face value (see Matthew 19:27).

God has appointed each of us to be watchers on the wall of our culture. Can He depend on you to live above the culture of sin? When we do not understand what God is doing, or why He appears to be taking too long to answer our prayers, we should trust that He is always working things together for our good and His glory (see Romans 8:28).

Get Social

Share your views and tag us @rhboydco and use #Purpose.

Twitter @rhboydco (#rhboydco)

Instagram @rhboydco (#rhboydco)

Facebook @rhboydco (#rhboydco)

www.rhboyd.com

Home Daily Devotional Readings
February 26–March 3, 2024

Monday	Tuesday	Wednesday	Thursday	Friday	Saturday	Sunday
The Faith in Which We Stand	Turn Away from the Wicked	Flee from the Presence of Sin	Always Do the Right Thing	Walk with God	Contend for the Unchanging Faith	Remain in God's Love
1 Corinthians 15:1–11	Numbers 16:12–13, 23–34	Genesis 18:20–22; 19:1–5, 15–17, 22–25	1 Peter 2:13–25	Genesis 5:18–24	Jude 3–16	Jude 17–25

THIRD QUARTER

March

April

May

SUSTAINING OUR FAITH

JUDE 17–25

King James Version	*New Revised Standard Version*
BUT, beloved, remember ye the words which were spoken before of the apostles of our Lord Jesus Christ;	BUT you, beloved, must remember the words previously spoken by the apostles of our Lord Jesus Christ,
18 How that they told you there should be mockers in the last time, who should walk after their own ungodly lusts.	18 for they said to you, "In the last time there will be scoffers, indulging their own ungodly lusts."
19 These be they who separate themselves, sensual, having not the Spirit.	19 It is these worldly people, devoid of the Spirit, who are causing divisions.
20 But ye, beloved, building up yourselves on your most holy faith, praying in the Holy Ghost,	20 But you, beloved, build yourselves up on your most holy faith; pray in the Holy Spirit;
21 Keep yourselves in the love of God, looking for the mercy of our Lord Jesus Christ unto eternal life.	21 keep yourselves in the love of God; look forward to the mercy of our Lord Jesus Christ that leads to eternal life.
22 And of some have compassion, making a difference:	22 And have mercy on some who are wavering;
23 And others save with fear, pulling them out of the fire; hating even the garment spotted by the flesh.	23 save others by snatching them out of the fire; and have mercy on still others with fear, hating even the tunic defiled by their bodies.
24 Now unto him that is able to keep you from falling, and to present you faultless before the presence of his glory with exceeding joy,	24 Now to him who is able to keep you from falling and to make you stand without blemish in the presence of his glory with rejoicing,
25 To the only wise God our Saviour, be glory and majesty, dominion and power, both now and ever. Amen.	25 to the only God our Savior, through Jesus Christ our Lord, be glory, majesty, power, and authority, before all time and now and forever. Amen.

LESSON SETTING
   Time: AD 65
   Place: Unknown

LESSON OUTLINE
   I. The Purity and Unity
      of the Church
      (Jude 17–19)

II. "Unity in the Body of Christ"
    (Jude 20–21)

III. What Should We Do about
     False Teachers?
     (Jude 22–25)

MAIN THOUGHT: But ye, beloved, building up yourselves on your most holy faith, praying in the Holy Ghost, Keep yourselves in the love of God, looking for the mercy of our Lord Jesus Christ unto eternal life. (Jude 20–21, KJV)

UNIFYING PRINCIPLE

A "shortcut to success" may persuade some people to compromise their standards. How do people remain true to their values despite enticing trends? Jude writes to the faith community, assuring them of God's promises: to keep us from falling and to make us stand without blemish in God's presence.

INTRODUCTION

The epistle of Jude is short. Jude was the half-brother of James, and possibly the brother of Jesus. There were several men with this name which was a derivative of Judas and Judah. It was important to note that Jude and James did not go around bragging that Jesus was their brother; they wanted to be known as servants of God who were deeply troubled by false teachers who had come into the young Christian church. The letter was written to a general audience of believers, who could have easily become comfortable in their faith and fallen prey to these false teachers. He admonished the Church to hold onto the faith that they have been given. He encouraged the new believers to live godly lives to reflect the message they had received. They are to reflect on how Jesus sacrificed His life for this very faith. Jude did not want those false teachers to taint the message that had been given to these early believers. He knew that these teachers had the ability to undo all that these believers had learned. They promoted immoral behaviors and their actions denied the authority of Jesus. He was protective of them and the faith as an older brother.

EXPOSITION

I. THE PURITY AND UNITY OF THE CHURCH (JUDE 17–19)

Jude was most concerned with the purity and unity of Christ's Church. What makes a church more or less pleasing to God? What kinds of churches should we cooperate with or join? We see that there are "true churches" and "false churches." This fact is evident from a brief comparison of Paul's epistles. When we look at Philippians and 1 Thessalonians, we find evidence of Paul's great joy in these churches and the relative absence of major doctrinal or moral problems (see Phil. 1:3–11; 4:10–16; 1 Thess. 1:2–10; 3:6–10; 2 Thess. 1:3–4; 2:13; cf. 2 Cor. 8:1–5). On the other hand, there were all sorts of serious doctrinal and moral problems in the churches of Galatia (Gal. 1:6–9; 3:1–5) and Corinth (1 Cor. 3:1–4; 4:18–21; 5:1–2, 6; 6:1–8; 11:17–22; 14:20–23; 15:12; 2 Cor. 1:23–2:11; 11:3–5, 12–15; 12:20–13:10). Other examples could be given, but it should be clear that among true churches there are less pure and more pure churches. We may define the purity of the Church as follows: the purity of the Church is its degree of freedom from wrong doctrine and conduct, and its degree of conformity to God's revealed will for the Church. As we shall see in the following discussion, it is right to pray and work for the greater purity of the Church. But purity cannot be our only concern, or Christians would have a tendency to separate into tiny groups of very "pure" Christians and tend to exclude anyone who showed the slightest deviation in doctrine or conduct of life.

Therefore, the New Testament also speaks frequently about the need to strive for the unity of the visible church. This may be defined in the following way: the unity of the Church is its degree of freedom from divisions among true Christians. The definition specifies "true Christians" because, as we saw previously, there are those who are Christian in name only, but have had no genuine experience of regeneration by the Holy Spirit. Nonetheless, many of these people take the name "Christian" and many churches that are filled with such unbelievers still call themselves Christian churches. We should not expect or work for organizational or functional unity that includes all of those people, and therefore, there will never be unity with all churches that call themselves "Christian." But, as we shall also see in the following discussion, the New Testament certainly encourages us to work for the unity of all true believers.

Factors that make a church "more pure" include: 1) Biblical doctrine (or right preaching of the Word); 2) Proper use of the sacraments (or ordinances); 3) Right use of church discipline; 4) Genuine worship; 5) Effective prayer; 6) Effective witness; 7) Effective fellowship; 8) Biblical church government; 9) Spiritual power in ministry; 10) Personal holiness of life among members; 11) Care for the poor; 12) Love for Christ. There may be signs other than these, but at least these can be mentioned as factors that increase a church's conformity to God's purposes. Of course, churches can be more pure in some areas and less pure in others—a church may have excellent doctrine and sound preaching, for example, yet be a dismal failure in her witness to others or in meaningful worship. Or a church may have a dynamic witness and very God-honoring times of worship but be weak in doctrinal understanding and Bible teaching. Most churches will tend to think that the areas in which they are strong are the most important, and the areas where they are weak are less important. But the New Testament encourages us to work for the purity of the Church in all of these areas. Christ's goal for the Church is "that he might sanctify her having cleansed her by the washing of water with the word, that he might present the church to himself in splendor, without spot or wrinkle or any such thing that she might be holy and without blemish" (Eph. 5:26–27).

Paul's ministry was one of "warning every person and teaching each one in all wisdom, that we may present each as mature in Christ (Col. 1:28). Moreover, Paul told Titus that elders must "be able to give instruction in sound doctrine and also to confute those who contradict it" (Titus 1:9), and he said that false teachers "must be silenced" (Titus 1:11). Jude urged Christians to "contend for the faith which was once for all delivered to the saints" (Jude 3). Proper use of the sacraments is commanded in 1 Corinthians 11:17–34, and right use of church discipline to protect the purity of the church is required in 1 Corinthians 5:6–7, 12–13. The New Testament also mentions a number of other factors. We are to strive for spiritual worship (Eph. 5:18–20; Col. 3:16–17), effective witness (Matt. 28:19–20; John 13:34–35; Acts 2:44–47; 1 John 4:7), proper government of the church (1 Tim.3:1–13), spiritual power in ministry (Acts 1:8; Rom. 1:16; 1 Cor. 4:20;

2 Cor. 10:3–4; Gal. 3:3–5; 2 Tim. 3:5; James 5:16), personal holiness (1 Thess. 4:3; Heb. 12:14), care for the poor (Acts 4:32–35; Rom. 15:26; Gal. 2:10), and love for Christ (1 Peter 1:8; Rev. 2:4). In fact, all Christians are to "strive to excel in building up the church" (1 Cor. 14:12), an exhortation that applies not only to an increase in the number of church members, but also (and in fact primarily) to the "edification" or growth of the church toward Christian maturity. The force of all of these passages is to remind us that we are to work for the purity of the visible church.

II. UNITY IN THE BODY OF CHRIST (JUDE 20–21)

What are some ways that Christians can restore the church to a faithful, contagious witness? What are some valid, helpful traditions that you remember? In order for the world to see the church as a viable organism, some policies and notions need to change. The preaching and teaching of the Gospel should remain; however, new teaching methods should be employed. Youth should have proper training for life issues. There should be dialogue between generations. Introduce hymns to youth and Christian rap to seniors. Christians who normally would not agree should be challenged in their approach to social justice. This generation is looking for the church to take a stand on important issues. Also, make church fun and inviting with ministries that meet the needs of everyone. Study the Key Verses, concentrating on the verbs Jude uses in admonishing readers to faithful living. How can you progress toward practices in faithful living? Accountability is key in focusing on right living. The enemy likes to isolate us with temptation to do

wrong. If you share your struggles with a worthy friend, they can pray for you and help to keep you on track in your witness to the world. Of course, if we are to work for the purity of the Church, especially of the local church of which we are a part, we must recognize that this is a process, and that any church of which we are a part will be somewhat impure in various areas. There were no perfect churches at the time of the New Testament and there will be no perfect churches until Christ returns. This means that Christians have no obligation to seek the purest church they can find and stay there, and then leave it if an even purer church comes to their attention. Rather, they should find a true church in which they can have an effective ministry and in which they will experience Christian growth as well, and then should stay there and minister, continually working for the purity of that church. God will often bless their prayers and faithful witness and the church will gradually grow in many areas of purity.

III. WHAT SHOULD WE DO ABOUT FALSE TEACHERS? (JUDE 22–25)

Jude was a leader in the early church, so he had witnessed the devastation of false teachers before, and he was merely warning these Christians before this "entrusted" faith would slip away from them. Have you ever heard false teaching? What was your response? Is there a danger in listening to false teachers today? What is an example of false teaching? There are many false teachings that are prominent today such as the Law of Attraction, the Prosperity Gospel, and New Age philosophies that sometimes shows up in our Christian pulpits! Listening to those teachers and preachers whom God has called and studying the Word for ourselves are ways to not succumb to ungodly messages. It is easy to follow false doctrine when we are not students of the Word ourselves. Be careful to always check any idea or philosophy against the Word of God. But, we must realize that not all churches will respond well to influences that would bring them to greater purity.

Sometimes, in spite of a few faithful Christians within a church, its dominant direction will be set by others who are determined to lead it on another course. Unless God graciously intervenes to bring reformation, some of these churches will become cults, and others will just die and close their doors. But more commonly these churches will simply drift into super liberal social clubs. The conversation and activities of churches will have very little genuine spiritual content—little emphasis on the need for daily prayer for individual concerns and for forgiveness of sins, little emphasis on daily personal reading of Scripture, and little emphasis on moment-by-moment trust in Christ and knowing the reality of his presence in our lives. Where there are admonitions to moral reformation, these will often be viewed as human deficiencies that people can correct by their own discipline and effort, and perhaps encouragement from others, but these moral aspects of life will not primarily be viewed as sin against a holy God, sin that can only effectively be overcome by the power of the Holy Spirit working within. When such humanistic emphases become dominant in a church, it has moved far toward the "less-pure" end of the scale in many of the areas listed above, and it is moving in the direction of becoming a false church.

There is a strong emphasis in the New Testament on the unity of the church. Jesus' goal is that "there shall be one flock, one shepherd" (John 10:16), and he prays for all future believers "that they may all be one" (John 17:21). This unity will be a witness to unbelievers, for Jesus prays "that they may become perfectly one, so that the world may know that you have sent me" and have loved them even as you have loved me" (John 17:23).Paul reminds the Corinthians that they are "called to be saints together with all those who in every place call on the name of our Lord Jesus Christ both their Lord and ours" (1 Corinthians 1:2).

Then Paul writes to Corinth, "I appeal to you, brethren, by the name of our Lord Jesus Christ, that all of you agree and that there be no dissensions among you, but that you be united in the same mind and the same judgment" (1 Corinthians1:10; cf. v. 13). He encourages the Philippians, "complete my joy by being of the same mind, having the same love, being in full accord and of one mind" (Phil. 2:2). He tells the Ephesians that Christians are to be "eager to maintain the unity of the Spirit in the bond of peace" (Eph. 4:3), and that the Lord gives gifts to the church "for building up the body of Christ, until we all attain to the unity of the faith and of the knowledge of the Son of God to mature manhood, to the measure of the stature of the fullness of Christ" (Ephesians 4:12–13).

Paul can command the Church to live in unity because there already is an actual spiritual unity in Christ that exists among genuine believers. He says, "There is one body and one Spirit, just as you were called to the one hope that belongs to your call, one Lord, one faith, one baptism, one God and Father of us all, who is above all and through all and in all" (Ephesians 4:4–6). And though the body of Christ consists of many members, those members are all "one body" (1 Cor. 10:17; 12:12–26).

Because they are jealous to protect this unity of the Church, the New Testament writers give strong warnings against those who cause divisions: "I appeal to you, brethren, to take note of those who create dissensions and difficulties, in opposition to the doctrine which you have been taught; avoid them. For such persons do not serve our Lord Christ, but their own appetites." (Romans 16:17–18) Paul opposed Peter to his face because he separated from Gentile Christians and began eating only with Jewish Christians (Galatians 2:11–14). Those who promote "strife...dissension, party spirit...shall not inherit the kingdom of God" (Galatians 5:20–21). And Jude warns that those who "set up divisions" are "worldly people, devoid of the Spirit" (Jude 19).

THE LESSON APPLIED

How have you grown in your determination to live a faithful life? When we strive to grow in Christ, we will be faced with temptation and even others who are not interested in holiness. Pleasing God in our actions is not easy, but it is possible. The Holy Spirit is there to lead, guide, and direct us through the Scriptures. The Christian life is about sacrifice—the sacrifice of Christ and our sacrifice of worldly ways. We must be willing to reject the self-centered demands of this world. Eternity seems far away, but our reward for faithful living will be worth it in the end.

LET'S TALK ABOUT IT

How do you plan to grow your faith?

If we really believe that Jesus' blood saves, we will do everything we can to please Him. He gave His life and because we love Him, we will give Him our lives. We must be willing to turn from the ways of the world if we want to please Him.

GET SOCIAL

Share your views and tag us @rhboydco and use #SustainingFaith.

Twitter
@rhboydco (#rhboydco)

Instagram
@rhboydco (#rhboydco)

Facebook
@rhboydco (#rhboydco)

www.rhboyd.com

HOME DAILY DEVOTIONAL READINGS
MARCH 4–10, 2024

MONDAY	TUESDAY	WEDNESDAY	THURSDAY	FRIDAY	SATURDAY	SUNDAY
The Testing of Faith Produces Endurance	The Sources of Temptations	God Has Searched and Known Us	God Knows All Things	God's People Boast in Weakness	Strength through Christ Alone	Live by Christ's Power in You
James 1:2–12	James 1:13–18	Psalm 139:1–12	Psalm 139: 13–18, 23–24	2 Corinthians 11:22–33	2 Corinthians 12:1–10	2 Corinthians 13:1–10

TESTING OUR FAITH

ADULT TOPIC: BACKGROUND SCRIPTURE: 2 CORINTHIANS 13:1–11
EXAMINE YOURSELF   LESSON PASSAGE: 2 CORINTHIANS 13:5–11

2 CORINTHIANS 13:5–11

King James Version	New Revised Standard Version
EXAMINE yourselves, whether ye be in the faith; prove your own selves. Know ye not your own selves, how that Jesus Christ is in you, except ye be reprobates?	EXAMINE yourselves to see whether you are living in the faith. Test yourselves. Do you not realize that Jesus Christ is in you?—unless, indeed, you fail to meet the test!
6 But I trust that ye shall know that we are not reprobates.	6 I hope you will find out that we have not failed.
7 Now I pray to God that ye do no evil; not that we should appear approved, but that ye should do that which is honest, though we be as reprobates.	7 But we pray to God that you may not do anything wrong—not that we may appear to have met the test but that you may do what is right, though we may seem to have failed.
8 For we can do nothing against the truth, but for the truth.	8 For we cannot do anything against the truth, but only for the truth.
9 For we are glad, when we are weak, and ye are strong: and this also we wish, even your perfection.	9 For we rejoice when we are weak but you are strong. This is what we pray for, that you may become perfect.
10 Therefore I write these things being absent, lest being present I should use sharpness, according to the power which the Lord hath given me to edification, and not to destruction.	10 So I write these things while I am away from you, so that when I come I may not have to be severe in using the authority that the Lord has given me for building up and not for tearing down.
11 Finally, brethren, farewell. Be perfect, be of good comfort, be of one mind, live in peace; and the God of love and peace shall be with you.	11 Finally, brothers and sisters, farewell. Put things in order, listen to my appeal, agree with one another, live in peace, and the God of love and peace will be with you.

LESSON SETTING
Time: AD 57
Place: Corinth

LESSON OUTLINE
I. **Paul, Christ's Ambassador**
   (2 Corinthians 13:5–6)
II. **Personal Integrity**
   (2 Corinthians 13:7–10)
III. **Check Your Faith**
   (2 Corinthians 13:11)

UNIFYING PRINCIPLE
Everyone has principles they are challenged to uphold. How and where do we find the courage to live authentically, keeping true to our ideals? Paul challenges believers to examine themselves as they rely on the power of Christ in keeping the faith imparted to them.

MAIN THOUGHT: Examine yourselves, whether ye be in the faith; prove your own selves. Know ye not your own selves, how that Jesus Christ is in you, except ye be reprobates? (2 Corinthians 13:5, KJV)

INTRODUCTION

Has there ever been a time in your life when you thought that a long-term goal had been achieved? What do you think that you could have done differently? We often seek to accomplish certain things before we have consulted the Lord. We feel defeated, and others apply pressure in their critique of our wrongdoing. We see how social media, and the media in general, gives us a picture of what a fulfilled life should be; the right weight, earning enough money to brag, a lovely home, healthy marriage, etc. We are harshly judged when we fail to meet the world's standards. Instead of comparing our lives to those around us, or celebrities, we are to look at God's standards. We must be sincere in living for Him, according to His Word. Before we judge others, we must "be on point" with God. Self-examination should be our daily practice, not just in the physical but also in the spiritual aspects of our lives. Our witness in the world matters. The Apostle Paul is encouraging his readers to have Christian integrity. When our outer lives match our inner integrity, we can grow in Christ, and others will take notice and then accept Jesus as their personal Savior. This is the test that Paul believes we can pass.

EXPOSITION

I. PAUL, CHRIST'S AMBASSADOR (2 CORINTHIANS 13:5–6)

Chapter 11 shows that spiritual authority lacks coercive powers. How, then, can Paul warn and punish? The answer is Paul does not. As an apostle and spiritual leader, Paul is Christ's spokesman in a particular way. Christ is speaking through him. Refusal to respond to Paul is a refusal to respond to Jesus. One of the earliest interpreters of Christ's message was the Apostle Paul. He was born a Roman citizen in Tarsus, the major city of Cilicia. He called himself the "chief of sinners." He was the one who relished in the death of Stephen, even holding his cloak. Then on the road to Damascus, he was blinded by a great light, and the Lord Jesus asked him, "Saul, Why are you persecuting me?" (Acts 9) It was his test and call to the apostleship. Consequently, there were those who were questioning the validity of Christ's work through Paul. Remember that there were many who witnessed the actions of Saul as he went persecuting Christians. In this letter, he shares that this is his third and final visit. He is trying to show them he is not the same person they remembered. Has anyone ever questioned your motives after God changed your character? Paul admonishes the young church that they need to reflect upon their own salvation and calling as they question his. He tells them he wants them to be authentic with themselves, too. Paul knew that he was speaking firmly to them; he did this so that he could be calmer when he saw them again. Paul was speaking the truth in Christ's love. Paul shares with them that he is praying for them to stand strong in their faith and the truth and not be weak. He wanted them to trust Jesus for themselves.

II. PERSONAL INTEGRITY (2 CORINTHIANS 13:7–10)

While Paul lacks the power to punish, Jesus does not. He is powerful among you. In his first letter, Paul noted that many Corinthians were ill; some had even died because they corrupted the Lord's Supper. So Paul does not need any coercive power at all. He speaks for Jesus. Jesus will do the disciplining if Christians fail to respond. We don't have to look very far to see how some Christians have failed to follow Christ. It happens when we don't stand up on issues that we know are against the Lord's standards. We also compromise our Christian integrity when we lie, steal, or don't confront family or friends about ways that they can improve their spiritual lives. "Selfish Christianity" says, "I've got Jesus; you need to get Him." This sentiment has allowed the Church to slip away from her rightful place in the world, from saving the lost. What is your reason for belonging to a church? Is saving the lost a high priority? We often fail the test of faithful living because we think "sitting on our salvation" is enough. If Christ was serious about saving the lost, just as Paul was, how much more in this lost world should we be?

Challenge yourself to invite one person to Christ and then bring up the discussion about their salvation. But first, as Paul says, examine yourself. You kill your witness for Christ if that person can point out a public sin that you refuse to surrender. If someone tells you that you need to lose weight and eat healthier, you may dismiss them if you see them eating unhealthily and never exercising at the gym. We realize Christ is in us when our desires change, and we don't excuse our sins. When we don't take His grace for granted and are serious about what concerns the Lord, our appetite for sin will lessen. There is a popular prayer: "Lord, break my

heart with the things that break Yours." When we do this and "delight ourselves in the Lord," we will see the difference from our old ways, just like the Apostle Paul did, and we will not be concerned if others don't believe us.

III. CHECK YOUR FAITH (2 CORINTHIANS 13:11)

What a relief for those in spiritual leadership. Like Paul, we can love and give and let God punish those who do not respond to His Word. If those in the church chronically reject God's words and ways, checking to see if they are saved is not just wise; it is essential. What are some ways that you feel weak in your faith? As you grow, share your experiences with a newer believer and see how you can encourage them. Contrary to the current secular understanding of "faith," true New Testament faith is not something that is made stronger by ignorance or by believing against the evidence. Rather, saving faith is consistent with knowledge and a true understanding of facts. Paul says, "Faith comes from hearing, and hearing by the word of Christ" (Romans 10:17 NASB). When people have accurate information about Christ, they can better put their trust in Him. Moreover, the more we know about Him, and about the character of God that is completely revealed in Him, the more fully we are able to put our trust in Him.

Thus, faith is not weakened by knowledge, but rather, should increase with more true knowledge. In the case of saving faith in Christ, our understanding of Him comes by believing a reliable testimony about Him. Here, the reliable testimony we believe is the words of the Scriptures. Since they are God's words, they are entirely reliable, and we gain true knowledge of

Christ through them. This is why "Faith comes from hearing, and hearing by the word of Christ" (Romans 10:17 NASB). In everyday life, we come to believe many things when we hear testimony from someone we consider reliable or trustworthy. This kind of decision is even more justified when the actual words of God provide that testimony, and we believe it.

Faith and repentance must come together. We may define repentance as follows: Repentance is a heartfelt sorrow for sin, renouncing it, and a sincere commitment to forsake it and walk in obedience to Christ. This definition indicates that repentance can occur at a specific point in time and is not equivalent to a demonstration of change in a person's pattern of life. Repentance, like faith, is an intellectual understanding (that sin is wrong), an emotional approval of the teachings of Scripture regarding sin (a sorrow for sin and a hatred of it), and a personal decision to turn from it (a renouncing of sin and a decision of the will to forsake it and lead a life of obedience to Christ instead). We cannot say that someone has to live that changed life over a period of time before repentance can be genuine, or else repentance would be turned into a kind of obedience that we could do to merit salvation for ourselves. Of course, genuine repentance will result in a changed life. A truly repentant person will begin at once to live a changed life; we can call that changed life the fruit of repentance. But we should never attempt to require that there be a period in which a person lives a changed life before we give assurance of forgiveness.

Repentance occurs in the heart and involves the whole person making a decision to turn from sin. It is important to realize that mere sorrow for one's actions, or even deep remorse over one's actions, does not constitute genuine repentance unless it is accompanied by a sincere decision to forsake sin committed against God. Paul preached about "repentance to God and of faith in our Lord Jesus Christ" (Acts 20:21). He says that he rejoiced over the Corinthians, "not because you were grieved, but because you were grieved into repenting....For godly grief produces a repentance that leads to salvation and brings no regret, but worldly grief produces death" (2 Corinthians 7:9–10).

A worldly sort of grief may involve great sorrow for one's actions and probably also fear of punishment but no genuine renouncing of sin or commitment to forsake it. Hebrews 12:17 tells us that Esau wept over the consequences of his actions but did not truly repent. Moreover, as 2 Corinthians 7:9–10 indicates, even genuine godly grief is one factor that leads to genuine repentance. Still, such grief is not itself the sincere decision of the heart in the presence of God that makes genuine repentance. Scripture puts repentance and faith together as different aspects of the one act of coming to Christ for salvation. It is not that a person first turns from sin and next trusts in Christ, or first trusts in Christ and then turns from sin, but rather that both occur at the same time.

When we turn to Christ for salvation from our sins, we simultaneously turn away from the sins that we ask Christ to save us from. If that were not true, our turning to Christ for salvation from sin could hardly be a genuine turning to Him or trusting in Him. Therefore, it is clearly contrary to the New Testament evidence to speak about the possibility of having true saving faith without having any repentance for sin. It is also contrary to the New Testament to speak about the possibility of someone accepting Christ "as Savior" but not "as Lord," if that means simply depending on Him. Some prominent voices within evangelicalism have differed with this point, arguing that a Gospel presentation that requires repentance, as well as faith, is preaching salvation by works. They argue that the view advocated in this instance, that repentance and faith must go together, is a false gospel of "lordship salvation." They would say that saving faith only involves trusting Christ as Savior and that submitting to Him as Lord is an optional later step that is unnecessary for salvation. For many who teach this view, saving faith only requires an intellectual agreement with the facts of the Gospel.

When Jesus invites sinners, "Come to me, all who labor and are heavy laden, and I will give you rest," he immediately adds, "Take my yoke upon you and learn from me" (Matthew 11:28–29). To come to Him includes taking His yoke upon us, being subject to His direction and guidance, learning from Him, and being obedient to Him. If we are unwilling to make such a commitment, then we have not truly placed our trust in Him. When Scripture speaks of trusting in God or Christ, it frequently connects such trust with genuine repentance. For example, Isaiah gives an eloquent testimony that is typical of the message of many of the Old Testament prophets: "Seek the Lord while he may be found,

call upon him while he is near; let the wicked forsake his way and the unrighteous man his thoughts; let him return to the Lord that he may have mercy on him, and to our God, for he will abundantly pardon" (Isaiah 55:6–7). Here, repentance from sin and coming to God for pardon are mentioned. In the New Testament, Paul summarizes his Gospel ministry as "testifying both to Jews and to Greeks of repentance to God and of faith in our Lord Jesus Christ" (Acts 20:21). The author of Hebrews includes as the first two elements in a list of elementary doctrines "repentance from dead works" and "faith toward God" (Hebrews 6:1). Of course, sometimes faith alone is named as the thing necessary for coming to Christ for salvation (see John 3:16; Acts 16:31; Rom. 10:9; Ephesians 2:8–9, et al.). These are familiar passages, and we emphasize them often when explaining the Gospel to others. But we often do not realize that there are many other passages where only repentance is named, for it is assumed that true repentance will also involve faith in Christ for the forgiveness of sins. The New Testament authors understood so well that genuine repentance and faith had to go together that they often mentioned repentance alone with the understanding that faith would also be included because turning from sins in a genuine way is impossible apart from a sincere turning to God. Therefore, just before Jesus ascended into heaven, he told his disciples, "Thus it is written, that the Christ should suffer and on the third day rise from the dead, and that repentance and forgiveness of sins should be preached in His name to all nations" (Luke 24:46–47).

Saving faith is implied in the phrase "forgiveness of sins," but it is not explicitly named.

THE LESSON APPLIED

Have you ever looked at a person you admire who seems to "have it together" when it comes to walking with the Lord? What makes them seem that way to you? What are some ways that you can be more Christlike? Would others say that you are someone whom they admire for your faith? Our walk with Christ is not to be used to make ourselves look good, but it is to show the power of Christ working in us. At the end of our lives, God is the only One who matters. Regular examinations are key to finding what you need to change in order to grow. The more that Christians do this, the more others will want to know Christ and His mercy. Additionally, it cannot be overstated that consistent prayer and Bible study go together. There are no shortcuts to spiritual maturity. Passing the test is to display the presence of the Spirit of God in our lives in every situation.

GET SOCIAL

Share your views and tag us @rhboydco and use #ExamineYourself.

LET'S TALK ABOUT IT

How can we be more sensitive to the Lord's voice?

The more that we seek after the Lord, it will become the norm, and we will be more sensitive to His voice. We cannot rely upon the testimonies of others; we need a personal relationship with the Lord ourselves. Conviction by the Holy Spirit is uncomfortable, but it is necessary for us to hearken to His presence. Making the necessary changes will draw us closer to Christ and prepare us to meet Him. When we solidify our relationship with the Lord, others will notice, and our witness will be stronger. Then we have the honor of being a disciple-maker in the body of Christ. A chain reaction then happens as "each one reaches one."

Remember, God does the work of enhancing the faith in us. He allows others to see His presence in us and blesses them accordingly, as they accept Him as their Lord and Savior. Continue to be a tool that God can use to appeal to others. Share His Word with others.

Twitter
@rhboydco (#rhboydco)

Instagram
@rhboydco (#rhboydco)

Facebook
@rhboydco (#rhboydco)

www.rhboyd.com

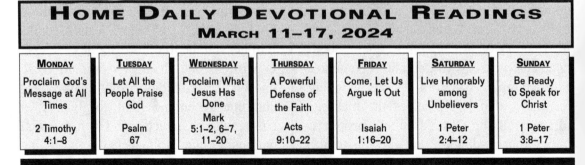

HOME DAILY DEVOTIONAL READINGS
MARCH 11–17, 2024

MONDAY	TUESDAY	WEDNESDAY	THURSDAY	FRIDAY	SATURDAY	SUNDAY
Proclaim God's Message at All Times	Let All the People Praise God	Proclaim What Jesus Has Done	A Powerful Defense of the Faith	Come, Let Us Argue It Out	Live Honorably among Unbelievers	Be Ready to Speak for Christ
2 Timothy 4:1–8	Psalm 67	Mark 5:1–2, 6–7, 11–20	Acts 9:10–22	Isaiah 1:16–20	1 Peter 2:4–12	1 Peter 3:8–17

DEFENDING OUR FAITH

1 PETER 3:8–17

King James Version	New Revised Standard Version
FINALLY, be ye all of one mind, having compassion one of another, love as brethren, be pitiful, be courteous:	FINALLY, all of you, have unity of spirit, sympathy, love for one another, a tender heart, and a humble mind.
9 Not rendering evil for evil, or railing for railing: but contrariwise blessing; knowing that ye are thereunto called, that ye should inherit a blessing.	9 Do not repay evil for evil or abuse for abuse; but, on the contrary, repay with a blessing. It is for this that you were called—that you might inherit a blessing.
10 For he that will love life, and see good days, let him refrain his tongue from evil, and his lips that they speak no guile:	10 For "Those who desire life and desire to see good days, let them keep their tongues from evil and their lips from speaking deceit;
11 Let him eschew evil, and do good; let him seek peace, and ensue it.	11 let them turn away from evil and do good; let them seek peace and pursue it.
12 For the eyes of the Lord are over the righteous, and his ears are open unto their prayers: but the face of the Lord is against them that do evil.	12 For the eyes of the Lord are on the righteous, and his ears are open to their prayer. But the face of the Lord is against those who do evil."
13 And who is he that will harm you, if ye be followers of that which is good?	13 Now who will harm you if you are eager to do what is good?
14 But and if ye suffer for righteousness' sake, happy are ye: and be not afraid of their terror, neither be troubled;	14 But even if you do suffer for doing what is right, you are blessed. Do not fear what they fear, and do not be intimidated,
15 But sanctify the Lord God in your hearts: and be ready always to give an answer to every man that asketh you a reason of the hope that is in you with meekness and fear:	15 but in your hearts sanctify Christ as Lord. Always be ready to make your defense to anyone who demands from you an accounting for the hope that is in you;
16 Having a good conscience; that, whereas they speak evil of you, as of evildoers, they may be ashamed that falsely accuse your good conversation in Christ.	16 yet do it with gentleness and reverence. Keep your conscience clear so that, when you are maligned, those who abuse you for your good conduct in Christ may be put to shame.
17 For it is better, if the will of God be so, that ye suffer for well doing, than for evil doing.	17 For it is better to suffer for doing good, if suffering should be God's will, than to suffer for doing evil.

MAIN THOUGHT: For it is better, if the will of God be so, that ye suffer for well doing, than for evil doing. (1 Peter 3:17, KJV)

LESSON SETTING
Time: AD 65
Place: Jerusalem

LESSON OUTLINE
I. **Be On One Accord and Do Not Repay Evil with Evil (1 Peter 3:8–12)**
II. **Do What is Good with Gentleness and Respect (1 Peter 3:13–15)**
III. **Suffer for Doing Good (1 Peter 3:16–17)**

Unifying Principle

Adhering to dominant norms is a safe and convenient way to live. How do we voice objections to these norms without inviting conflict? In 1 Peter, Christians are encouraged to defend their faith through righteous and humble actions, even at the risk of suffering.

Introduction

Peter was considered the head disciple of Jesus and was part of the trio that accompanied Jesus on special occasions. He is also considered the primary information source behind much of the Gospel of Mark. He is accredited for writing two letters or epistles, 1 and 2 Peter. Their principal objective is encouraging the Church to be faithful to her Lord and Savior, Jesus Christ. He reminds the Church of who she is and her role as the center of the community of faith. She is a chosen generation and a peculiar people, a member of the royal priesthood. She is a force for good and embodies the message of divine faith to the world. In the current text, she suffers for good. Redemptive suffering is this text's major thrust, and the writer informs us it is better than suffering for evil. What comes to mind when you think of suffering? Is it a picture of starving children in a third-world country? Or maybe it is how you try to keep your bank account balance positive. We can suffer in many ways—poverty, hunger, unemployment, illness, rejection, and loss. Do you try to avoid suffering? If so, how? The fact is that suffering is a characteristic of the Christian life. Sadly, we often hear of those who are suffering after they have injured or killed someone. The Lord's plan is not for us to further hurt ourselves or other people, but He does have a purpose for our pain. We can probably recall suffering we brought upon ourselves, but how do you deal with a cancer diagnosis or a sick child? We deal with the consequences of self-inflicted suffering, but even when that occurs, God is gracious. Peter encourages us to suffer for God's will more often than not. Also, the apostles were committed to fellowship with other believers. Find others to share in your grief and struggles in a godly manner. You will discover that you are not alone and that others are dealing with the same similar sufferings. Also, listening to others' testimonies about the faithfulness of God is a sure way to stay in the race! When we are with like-minded individuals, it can lessen the sting of our suffering. Here, Peter encourages us to do three things. First, he employs us not to repay evil for evil. We are encouraged not to give back the sufferings we have received from others who are out to hurt us. Second, according to Peter, the Christian motif must be to practice good. In Matthew's

Gospel (Matthew 5), the Beatitudes in the Sermon on the Mount encourage us not to trade evil for evil but to go about doing good. Third, not only are we to do good, but we are also to be willing to suffer for doing good, if necessary. We are to risk doing good at all costs. The great example to follow is Jesus, who went about doing good, and we know where it got Him. However, the text's point underscores the Christian believer's character. We must, in all situations, emulate our Lord. He will reward us, even when we must suffer the consequences of following Him.

EXPOSITION

I. BE ON ONE ACCORD AND DO NOT REPAY EVIL WITH EVIL
(1 PETER 3:8–12)

Peter's first great advice in this part of the text is for the disciples to be on one accord. Unity is one of their great needs. If they are united they will be able to go on the offensive and defensive together-ness in prayer. In John 13, Jesus plainly instructed the disciples that they were to be defined by His badge and brand of love that would draw them together. The compassion that would indwell their hearts was to be the foundation of their union with Him and with one another. Let's be honest. The world is against Jesus. The Jews and the Romans did terrible things to our Lord and Savior. His life ended in the crucifixion as punishment for the false charge of blasphemy. He was, furthermore, crucified between two thieves. Pilate admitted he found no fault in Jesus. Also, when the Sons of Thunder wanted to call down fire from heaven on the people, Jesus reprimanded them. They were to be identified by their love rather than by their anger, however justified, with the people. When Peter desired to defend Jesus with the sword, Jesus told him that the ones who live by the sword would perish by it also. That is to say, Jesus did not govern His life by retaliation. He did not live to pay people back for how they treated him. Romans 12:9–21 also encourages us to never repay evil for evil. Instead we are summoned to hate what is evil and to love what is good. Therefore, these opposites will never cross paths and allow us to mistake one for the other. We must adhere faithfully to what is good and virtuous. Vengeance belongs to the Lord. This chapter shows Paul's support for Jesus' preachments for transformative living (see Romans 12:1–2). Those who live the transformed life are forgiving in nature. They do not seek revenge. Forgiveness is always the objective. Jesus told Peter to forgive his brother continuously. Thus, we have the model for our reactionary behavior as well. We are never to act offensively or defensively in accordance with evil. We are to forgive. That is the word from Jesus and Paul, and now from Peter. It says a lot about Peter because he was the hotheaded disciple.

Like Paul, the Apostle Peter boldly proclaims giving up retaliation. The command is forcibly given in verses 9–10. There is no allowance for the slightest hint of evil as payment in return for evil. It is anathema! There is even a prohibition on the use of the tongue to utter evil (see. v. 10). Rather, they are instructed to turn. The word "turn," as used here, is the equivalent of the word "repent." They are employed to turn from evil and do good by pursuing peace. Nothing should be done to upset the tide of tranquility set in motion by peaceful endeavors. Peaceful endeavors are elements of reconciliation.

Therefore, they will commence in blessings being poured out upon the adherers. The text is saying that good is worth pursuing. The believer should be in actual pursuit of doing good. It ought to be a very present and vivid activity. The pursuit of goodness is to actively engage with the Spirit of Christ to carry on the way of Christ for His purpose. The situation bears the question of forgiveness. We know that Jesus endured horrible pain and suffering that He did not deserve. If we ponder His responses before and on the cross, we know that His disposition was one of humility and grace for others who doubted and hurt Him. What is your response to false accusations and pain? Also, most of the Twelve died horrible deaths for their commitment to Jesus. Notice that Judas died as a result of his betrayal of Jesus —there is a difference in the precursor to his suffering. They were thrown in jail countless times and treated horribly. What is the most intense suffering that you have experienced/are experiencing? How do we deal with it? What is God teaching you about Him, yourself, or the world around you?

II. DO WHAT IS GOOD WITH GENTLENESS AND RESPECT (1 PETER 3:13–15)

The Scripture calls us to act and to act decisively. We are to do good. Doing good, according to Peter, is to follow in the way or pathway of the Lord Jesus. Verse 13 begins with a question. It deals with one's intent. "Who will harm you if your intention is to go about doing good." "Who will harm you if your motive for operation is pure and clean and not harmful to others?" Be sure and ready to defend yourself and prepared to give your defense of what is right. It will be a blessing to others and to yourself. Defend yourself in all gentleness and respect. Peter warns us in this text to be prepared to ease tensions or lower high tempers. This was great advice from one who experienced bouts of anguish and temper tantrums. Do good. It appears that Peter acknowledged some type of action will take place, so his advice is to do good. The writer of Genesis reminds us also to be angry but do not sin. Our actions are important. Peter soothes us with a comforting voice and calls for gentleness and respect. Respect, as used here, is a call for reverence. It is to do things in a resolute and dignified manner. The reader is urged not to be fearful in one's defense but to be so thoroughly prepared that one's confidence shows with humility. It is the same or similar to the Beatitude expression of blessed, "Be Happy." Happiness goes back to grab the use of the word love, which is in verse eight. Notice the normal word used for the love of God is *agape*, but here we have the word for brotherly love, *philadelphos*. Peter is not suggesting here that we should love one another within the church with a quality of love that is secondary to agape. Instead, he uses familiar vocabulary central in the New Testament to convey how we are to act as a family with Jesus as our Lord and God as our Father. This type of love brings happiness and joy because it builds up the Christian body. Verse 15 tells us to sanctify ourselves. One should exercise caution by cutting oneself off from anything that might defile or corrupt one and make one expendable to the faith. Our faith is positive and sure when it is supported by evidence of a changed person, and the evidence shows that it is of God and not of humanity. The marks of a Christian life will reveal the presence of the faith among the faithful believers.

III. Suffer for Doing Good (1 Peter 3:16–17)

There are at least two types of suffering—suffering for doing good, as in the case of Jesus, and suffering as a just reward for participating in evil. Peter acknowledges that if one has to suffer, he prefers suffering for doing good. Many theologians call this redemptive suffering. In Genesis in the Joseph narratives, Joseph explains to His brother that his suffering was for good and was redemptive because it saved nations from starvation (Genesis 50:20). Likewise, Jesus' death on the cross was redemptive because His blood covered a multitude of sins, and His subsequent resurrection provided hope and new life to many. Suffering for doing good has its own unique set of rewards, whereas suffering for doing evil is a consequence of being deceived by evil and is the growth of evil itself. God will vindicate you when your deeds are good but will punish those whose intent is to spread evil. God's approval of the Resurrection displays the good that can come out of sacrificing oneself for doing good.

The Lesson Applied

This lesson is a picture of the life of Jesus. He was mistreated but refused to retaliate or to repay evil for evil. When he was mistreated, Jesus showered His offenders with love. Are you willing to suffer for the sake of your faith in Christ? American life is filled with modern conveniences and luxuries. What is your idea of suffering for Christ? Is it worth it? We may also be poorly treated in light of how Jesus was ridiculed, beaten, and crucified. Are you ready to face the consequences of your faith in Jesus? We must always commit to doing right, even if it means suffering for our faith.

Let's Talk About It

1. Are there any scriptural examples of Christian suffering for doing good?

Yes. The life of the Lord Jesus is a prime example to use in this light. His entire life was one of good living. He helped the masses, fed multitudes, healed the sick, maimed, and hurt. He made the mute talk, opened up deaf ears, gave sight to the blind, and healed all types of infirmities. Furthermore, He preached a Gospel of love, faith, and hope. Yet despite all His good deeds, the Scriptures list Him as a Man of Sorrows (see the Servant Songs, Isaiah 53; 55; and 61).

During His trial and sentencing, He was subjected to all types of cruelty by the Roman soldiers who mocked Him, spat on Him, beat and whipped Him, and placed on His head a crown of thorns (John 19). The Roman government crucified him, one of the cruelest forms of execution during that time. He did all of these things for the human good. He had no sin. He died for humanity. Let us follow His great example of love so His work will not have been in vain.

2. What does it mean to be faithful to Jesus?

Being faithful to Jesus requires us to keep His commandments. Jesus told His disciple, "If you love me, keep my commandments." Obedience to His Word reveals the content of our hearts and governs the level of our commitment to serve Him. First Samuel 15:22–24 tells us obedience is better than sacrifice. God delights in faithful service to Him rather than in a bunch of praise and offerings that have no purpose but to appease Him verbally. Matthew 15:8 follows after Isaiah 29:13 as it commands the people to serve the Lord with their hearts.

3. How should we relate to others of our faith?

Our faith and trust in Jesus will increase as we get to know Him better, and we are criticized for our beliefs and how we aim to live differently from the world. We can be encouraged by the strength of other believers around us. Our prayer life and Bible study also help us as we suffer righteously. We are to pray for our brothers and sisters around us who are suffering, as well as those in hostile countries overseas.

4. Why is it necessary to be an apologist and to defend our faith?

We must defend our faith against those who would ill-define it. We also must defend it so people will know and understand our doctrine and practice for what they are. For example, a poor reading or understanding of Genesis might encourage one to believe that Christianity involves child sacrifices. But it does not. God tested Abraham's faith by telling him to take his son Isaac to the mountain. God had no intention of the patriarch sacrificing his son. It was a test of faith. The question is would Abraham do it? When Abraham went, God supplied a ram in the thicket. God always provides a ram for us. Thus, we are responsible for going forward in God's name and depending on Him. He has proven over and over again that He will supply our needs.

HOME DAILY DEVOTIONAL READINGS
MARCH 18–24, 2024

MONDAY	TUESDAY	WEDNESDAY	THURSDAY	FRIDAY	SATURDAY	SUNDAY
Blessings of Walking in God's Ways	Let Your Life Match Your Words	Fear God and Gain Knowledge	Refrain from Defiling the Church	Vessels Prepared for Every Good Work	The Ministry of Caring for Others	A Spirit-Empowered Witness
Deuteronomy 28:1–14	Titus 2:1–8	Proverbs 1:1–9	2 Corinthians 5:1–11	2 Timothy 2:8–21	Acts 6:1–6	Acts 6:7–15

LIVING IN FAITH

ADULT TOPIC: BACKGROUND SCRIPTURE: ACTS 6
WHEN THE WORLD IS AGAINST US   LESSON PASSAGE: ACTS 6:7–15

ACTS 6:7–15

King James Version

AND the word of God increased; and the number of the disciples multiplied in Jerusalem greatly; and a great company of the priests were obedient to the faith.

8 And Stephen, full of faith and power, did great wonders and miracles among the people.

9 Then there arose certain of the synagogue, which is called the synagogue of the Libertines, and Cyrenians, and Alexandrians, and of them of Cilicia and of Asia, disputing with Stephen.

10 And they were not able to resist the wisdom and the spirit by which he spake.

11 Then they suborned men, which said, We have heard him speak blasphemous words against Moses, and against God.

12 And they stirred up the people, and the elders, and the scribes, and came upon him, and caught him, and brought him to the council,

13 And set up false witnesses, which said, This man ceaseth not to speak blasphemous words against this holy place, and the law:

14 For we have heard him say, that this Jesus of Nazareth shall destroy this place, and shall change the customs which Moses delivered us.

15 And all that sat in the council, looking stedfastly on him, saw his face as it had been the face of an angel.

New Revised Standard Version

THE word of God continued to spread; the number of the disciples increased greatly in Jerusalem, and a great many of the priests became obedient to the faith.

8 Stephen, full of grace and power, did great wonders and signs among the people.

9 Then some of those who belonged to the synagogue of the Freedmen (as it was called), Cyrenians, Alexandrians, and others of those from Cilicia and Asia, stood up and argued with Stephen.

10 But they could not withstand the wisdom and the Spirit with which he spoke.

11 Then they secretly instigated some men to say, "We have heard him speak blasphemous words against Moses and God."

12 They stirred up the people as well as the elders and the scribes; then they suddenly confronted him, seized him, and brought him before the council.

13 They set up false witnesses who said, "This man never stops saying things against this holy place and the law;

14 for we have heard him say that this Jesus of Nazareth will destroy this place and will change the customs that Moses handed on to us."

15 And all who sat in the council looked intently at him, and they saw that his face was like the face of an angel.

MAIN THOUGHT: Some] stood up and argued with Stephen. But they could not withstand the wisdom and the Spirit with which he spoke. (Acts 6:9–10, KJV)

LESSON OUTLINE
   I. **God Used Stephen**
      (Acts 6:7–8)
   II. **They Argued Against Stephen**
      (Acts 6:9–13)
   III. **They Charged Him**
      (Acts 6:14–15)

UNIFYING PRINCIPLE

People who are falsely accused and persecuted often feel that the whole world is against them. What sustains us in the face of injustice and persecution? The testimony of Stephen encourages us to be obedient to the faith inspired by the grace, power, and wisdom of the Holy Spirit.

INTRODUCTION

On this beautiful Palm Sunday, we remember the upcoming sacrifice of Jesus during Passion or Holy Week. Some opposed Jesus, despite the many miracles He performed and His many teachings. If we follow Christ, there is a target on our backs placed there by the enemy and the world. The suffering that we endure as a result identifies us with Christ. The world was against Him and His followers, like Deacon Stephen of the New Testament. There will always be those who are in defiance of the character of Christ. We see in movies where Jesus is mocked and in music where his beautiful daughters are sometimes spoken of in evil ways. Christians can be accused of wrongdoing when they are innocent, as Jesus was. The temptation to leave the faith will always be with us, but God wants us to remain steadfast because our witness matters in the world, and we ultimately will receive the Great reward of eternal life with Him. These accusations may cost us our jobs, friends, and reputation. God has sent legal and moral help for us, and we must trust Him with our lives and circumstances. This is not easy in a world that does not give credit to God but to the universe, crystals, manifestations, and self-awareness. With the Lord's help, we can overcome the false accusations, isolation, and spiritual bullying of other Christians. We know this because of the victory we have in Jesus.

EXPOSITION

I. GOD USED STEPHEN (ACTS 6:7–8)

Rubin "Hurricane" Carter was a middleweight boxer who gained worldwide attention due to his power in the ring. According to CNN, Ring Magazine named him one of the top middleweight contenders of 1963 after Carter knocked out eleven of his first fifteen major opponents. But then, after losing his title bout in 1964, even worse luck befell the boxing star. In 1966, he was charged with a triple homicide at the LaFayette Bar and Grill and given three life sentences. Allegations of racial bias involved in Carter's trial stirred up immense controversy, and celebrities ranging from Muhammad Ali to Burt Reynolds spoke up about how the courts should free him. Bob Dylan even wrote a song proclaiming Carter's innocence, and the ex-boxer penned an autobiography from prison. It wasn't until 1985 that a federal judge finally ruled that the original

1966 trial had been prejudiced and agreed to release Carter from prison. By then, Carter had spent nineteen years in prison.

How would you have felt having lived the life of Rubin "Hurricane" Carter? Do you think that he had times that he wanted to give up? We can be sure that he felt those feelings. His persistence in stating his case allowed the judge and jury to show mercy to him. Famous Actor Denzel Washington portrayed him in a movie. Many innocent people in prison are awaiting release or for someone to hear and take an interest in their story. The Innocence Project is an organization that hears these stories and helps individuals to transition back into society. God's mercy aids the repentant guilty, but he is present with the innocent. Take time to thank God for extending His mercy to you.

II. THEY ARGUED AGAINST STEPHEN (ACTS 6:9–13)

Living for Christ is not always easy, so what are some possible consequences for sharing your faith? Many people fear talking about Jesus because they fear losing their jobs or being known as a "Bible thumper." Also, because of the separation of church and state laws, people back down from sharing their faith; however, the law is not freedom from religion, but freedom of religion. Christianity also requires boldness; where would we be if not for the courage of Christ? No one forced Him to die, but He did because of His love for us (John 10).

So that the apostles could focus on "weightier matters," Stephen was chosen along with six other men to give out food and serve in different ways. His subservi- ence to this task shows humility and the servant-heart of Stephen. The apostles were then free to preach, teach, pray, and have fellowship with the believers. What do you believe are the long-term results of Stephen's faithful witness? Do you know any "Stephens" in our day? We can point to many civil rights advocates, but how many can be accused of unapologetically proclaiming Christ? The Holy Spirit enabled Stephen to remain faithful when many opposed him. We are still talking about him after 2,000 years. The Apostle Paul was later ashamed of his contribution to Stephen's death, even holding the cloaks of those who stoned him! At the time, he was Saul, the persecutor of Christians. Those who opposed Stephen did not have the legacy he would eventually hold. Stephen was willing to die for his commitment to Christ. Do you have that same conviction? Can Christ count on you to stand for Him in the workplace when there is a gambling pool? Are you generous with your paycheck with abandon? Stephen had the motto "For Christ, I live, and for Christ, I die" stamped on his heart.

III. THEY CHARGED HIM (ACTS 6:14–15)

For some believers, unjust suffering (especially in extreme cases) may lead to doubt, anger, and bitterness in their relationship with God. You may struggle with these emotions as you process pain, grief, and loss. Know that the Lord can handle any emotion you are feeling right now. He isn't expecting us to be superhuman robots without feelings. He is asking us to give these emotions to Him; there is nothing too hard for our Lord.

Find a copy of the song "Only What You Do for Christ Will Last" with the lyrics. Engage in a brief time of worship. Include a hymn and a prayer asking our Heavenly Father for power and strength to remain faithful when threatened with persecution for your faith. Spend some time writing down what you plan to do for Christ and what legacy you plan to leave for others. Palm Sunday is remembered by many as a day when all the people praised God and proclaimed Jesus the Savior (Matthew 21:8–9). Contrast the situations in which it is easy and in which it is hard to profess faith in Jesus. Find a partner or group in your class to discuss what you plan to do.

THE LESSON APPLIED

When we endure unjust suffering, our faith is strengthened if we trust in the power of Christ to fight our battles. It is a time for us to be more committed to Bible study, prayer, and fellowship with other Christians. We need the encouragement that others will give us. We can lean on the promises of God as we suffer wrongdoing. We also have the example of Jesus, who "Never said a mumbling word" as He was unfairly judged at His trials. The strength we receive as we pursue righteousness will equip us to stand for God without regard to personal consequences.

LET'S TALK ABOUT IT

1. What are some ways we can share our faith?

When we are tired of fighting a lost world, we can look to the life of Stephen, who willingly served in humble submis-sion. He was grounded in his faith and commitment to the Lord. Do you have that same conviction? There are times when our suffering will seem unending. We need God's strength and power to stand amid trials and tribulations. Sometimes Christians are afraid to share their faith and testimony with the lost because they feel that they don't know enough about the Bible. If that is you, start studying the Word more. Yes, our testimony can be shared with others, but we are to point people to Christ and share what He has done from our recollection of the Bible. Share your testimony and the Word of God with the world. Role-play with others as you share the Gospel, one acting as the unbeliever and the other sharing Christ. Practice what unbelievers would say to challenge you. Can you witness to a Mormon, Jehovah's Witness, or a Muslim? We know that everyone will not accept Christ's message, or we may not have the spiritual gift of evangelism, but the Lord directs us to share the Good News based on the Great Commission. Ask God to give you the right words to share His truth in love.

2. What does it mean to live the life of faith, as Jesus did?

To live the life of faith like our Lord Jesus means that we must be willing to do the work of the God who sent us. It involves three things. First, it involves a life of Bible study, prayer, and devotion to doing things God's way. Second, it includes a determination to living to please God through a life of obedience to God's divine will. Third, it includes intentional focus to know and understand the spiritual needs of individuals that will draw them closer to the Lord. Stephen had these three qualities and was willing to give his life to share them with others. He knew the Word of God and share it with his enemies. He was determined to share his testimony with others and was not afraid that it might cause him to give up his life. Finally, Stephen knew that they needed what he had to say and he willingly shared the Good News with them. Like Stephen, we must determine the needs of others about us and the Lord's call on us to proclaim the Good News at every opportunity.

3. What does it mean to be a martyr for the Christian faith?

To be a martyr for the Christian faith means that we will give up our life for the cause of the faith. It means to give up everything to see it flourish, live, and grow. Stephen, like the Lord Jesus, gave up his life for what he believed in. Our faith must be one of action or it is not faith at all. Stephen was convicted that what he preached was true and it guided his living. How sure are you that your faith is real and authentic? To what extent will you go to assure others that your testimony, concerning Jesus, is true beyond the shadow of a doubt? You must be willing to give Him your all and go all the way if your testimony is to be valid and become fruitful.

4. Where does obedience add to faith?

Obedience is the flip side of the coin of faith. Jesus told His disciples that if you love me keep my commandments. Additionally, the prophet told the people that obedience is better than sacrifice. Doing God's will is necessary before one can be a true disciple of the faith (Mark 1:14–15; John 14–16). Obedience requires knowing God's will and keeping His truth. It means active engagement with God. At every turn, one could see Jesus living in close affinity with His Father, and that must also be the pattern we set for our lives as well. "Close to Thee, Close to Thee" must be the words that our hearts tell our lips to speak. "Savior, I want to be close to Thee."

GET SOCIAL

Share your views and tag us @rhboydco and use #LiveinFaith.

HOME DAILY DEVOTIONAL READINGS
MARCH 25–31, 2024

MONDAY	TUESDAY	WEDNESDAY	THURSDAY	FRIDAY	SATURDAY	SUNDAY
Faith Revealed through Extravagant Love	Faith in God's Deliverance	Faith in God's Protection	Faith Challenged and Encouraged	An Unexpected Confession of Faith	Faith Despite Pain and Loss	Faith in the Risen Christ
Mark 14:1–9	Exodus 14:10–20	Exodus 14:21–31	Mark 14:17–26	Mark 15:25–39	Psalm 22:1–11, 28–31	Mark 16:1–8

THE RESURRECTION: KEY TO FAITH

ADULT TOPIC:	BACKGROUND SCRIPTURE: MARK 16
LIFE BEYOND DEATH	LESSON PASSAGE: MARK 16:1–8

MARK 16:1–8

King James Version

AND when the sabbath was past, Mary Magdalene, and Mary the mother of James, and Salome, had bought sweet spices, that they might come and anoint him.

2 And very early in the morning the first day of the week, they came unto the sepulchre at the rising of the sun.

3 And they said among themselves, Who shall roll us away the stone from the door of the sepulchre?

4 And when they looked, they saw that the stone was rolled away: for it was very great.

5 And entering into the sepulchre, they saw a young man sitting on the right side, clothed in a long white garment; and they were affrighted.

6 And he saith unto them, Be not affrighted: Ye seek Jesus of Nazareth, which was crucified: he is risen; he is not here: behold the place where they laid him.

7 But go your way, tell his disciples and Peter that he goeth before you into Galilee: there shall ye see him, as he said unto you.

8 And they went out quickly, and fled from the sepulchre; for they trembled and were amazed: neither said they any thing to any man; for they were afraid.

New Revised Standard Version

WHEN the Sabbath was over, Mary Magdalene and Mary the mother of James, and Salome bought spices, so that they might go and anoint him.

2 And very early on the first day of the week, when the sun had risen, they went to the tomb.

3 They had been saying to one another, "Who will roll away the stone for us from the entrance to the tomb?"

4 When they looked up, they saw that the stone, which was very large, had already been rolled back.

5 As they entered the tomb, they saw a young man dressed in a white robe sitting on the right side, and they were alarmed.

6 But he said to them, "Do not be alarmed; you are looking for Jesus of Nazareth, who was crucified. He has been raised; he is not here. Look, there is the place they laid him.

7 But go, tell his disciples and Peter that he is going ahead of you to Galilee; there you will see him, just as he told you."

8 So they went out and fled from the tomb, for terror and amazement had seized them; and they said nothing to anyone, for they were afraid.

[The Shorter Ending of Mark Concludes]

And all that had been commanded them they told briefly to those around Peter. And afterward Jesus himself sent out through them, from east to west, the sacred and imperishable proclamation of eternal salvation. Amen.

MAIN THOUGHT: "And he saith unto them, Be not affrighted: Ye seek Jesus of Nazareth, which was crucified: he is risen; he is not here: behold the place where they laid him. (Mark 16:6, KJV)

LESSON SETTING
    Time: Circa AD 30
    Place: Jerusalem

LESSON OUTLINE
  I. **A Visit to the Tomb**
     (Mark 16:1–4)
 II. **He Has Risen**
     (Mark 16:5–6)
III. **Deliver this Message:**
     Meet Me in Galilee
     (Mark 16:7–8)

UNIFYING PRINCIPLE

Feelings of dread and apprehension confront many people as they navigate life's uncertainties and tragedies. Where can we find a source of hope to calm our fears and alleviate our worries? The women who came to the tomb did not let their grief hinder them, and their faithfulness was rewarded with the good news of Christ's resurrection from the dead.

INTRODUCTION

During the hours before the Sabbath, Joseph of Arimathaea had begged Pilate to release the newly crucified body of Jesus of Nazareth. As the Roman governor contemplated his next move, several women at the scene were lovingly wiping away the mud, the blood, and the stains caused by this gruesome and disgraceful execution. Those who had followed Jesus to the cross were in shock and disbelief. Although the previous days proved that many were still with Him, there were now fewer. Nonetheless, the body of Jesus was cleaned, wrapped, and placed in Joseph's new tomb. However, the women felt their preparations were inadequate because the

Sabbath was rapidly closing in on the funeral party. They planned to return later when they could treat Jesus' body with the tender care it deserved.

EXPOSITION

I. A VISIT TO THE TOMB (MARK 16:1–4)

Mark begins his narrative by noting that the Sabbath had ended when the women came to the tomb. These women had been at the crucifixion, looking on from a distance (Mark 15:40). Many scholars believe that the women were Mary Magdalene, Mary, the mother of James, and Salome. However, Bratcher and Nida caution that the phrase "and Salome" may require a transposition to avoid the meaning of Mary being the mother of both James and Salome, e.g., "Mary from Magdala, Salome, and Mary, the mother of James." Richardson is probably closer to the truth, as he identifies Salome as a follower of Jesus who ministered to Him in Galilee and traveled with Him to Jerusalem (Mark 15:40; if Matthew 27:56 is a parallel, Mary may be the mother of James and John, the sons of Zebedee). Salome, with the two Marys (three women in total), brought spices for Jesus' burial (Mark 16:1). These women had been present at the crucifixion, looking on from a distance (Mark 15:40).

Jews of the period did not embalm bodies. The women came to anoint Jesus, as was customary in preserving the body until the flesh would decompose, after which the bones would be placed in an ossuary during a second burial. One of the spices the women may have used was myrrh, which could serve as a disinfectant. Ironically, myrrh was one of the gifts presented to the Holy Family following the birth of Jesus.

The women planned to go to the tomb once the Sabbath was over; however, there was a problem. A large, heavy stone had been rolled up to the entrance to seal the grave, and if the account of Matthew is considered, Pilate had the tomb sealed in Roman fashion, ordering a soldier to guard the tomb (Matthew 27:65–66). Although the women may not have been aware of the official sealing, it was at this point that they realized that anointing Jesus would be impossible unless they were to gain some masculine assistance to get inside the tomb. Asking themselves, "Who will roll away the stone?" could have signaled a defeat for these dedicated women. Though, as they approached the tomb, they realized that the heavy stone had been removed, and any guards that may have been present had disappeared.

Mark does not indicate whether the women had prayed for a miracle; nonetheless, their faith allowed them to continue to the tomb to fulfill their mission. The determination of these women reveals that they believed that God would be with them and meet their needs with His unrealized power. Here, the stone symbolizes an object that goes far beyond the sealing of the tomb. The stone represents an obstacle to any believer pursuing a walk and a closeness to the Lord. Their belief that Jesus' body needed their anointing did not diminish their faith in Jesus as Messiah. These women were not considering that the Jesus movement had ended, although they may not have expected Jesus to rise from the dead. Their mission was to bring peace to Jesus in a symbolic and loving act of devotion.

II. HE HAS RISEN (MARK 16:5–6)

The faith of this small group of women was rewarded, as they could enter the tomb without the large obstacle, which had already been removed. Tombs of the period were not the large mausoleums of our contemporary period but were much smaller. The party had to crawl into the opening to get to the slab where the body had been laid. Still, when the women entered the area, they found a man in the tomb. This young man was sitting on the slab where the body should have been, and the stone had been rolled away. Mark recalls that the women were amazed, the term here being *ekthambéō*, which indicates astonishment (and terror). It should not be a surprise that the women were afraid because they may not have previously experienced an angel's presence. The anointing party should not be viewed with disdain because the average person is known to be frightened by the appearance of an angel. Recall that an angel of the Lord appeared before the shepherds, and when they witnessed the glory of the Lord shining around them, they were frightened. Yet, the angel of the Lord reassured the women, saying, "Do not be afraid" (Luke 2:8–10).

Mark notes that the young man is dressed in a white robe which symbolizes purity. In the New Testament, the color white occurs in Christological images and also serves as a symbol of salvation. Moreover, in John's Revelation, "white" symbolizes a positive association with

God Almighty, Christ, or the righteousness of Christian believers who have conquered as Christ conquered. Furthermore, Mark observes that the angel is sitting on the right side of the burial slab. This position indicates power, as the belief is that the right hand is the more powerful of the two, epitomizing Jesus' standing at the right hand of God (Acts 7:55). If the women had believed that the young man was incapable of removing the stone, assuredly, by now, their thoughts changed.

At some point, the women realized the young man was an angel (*ángelos*), a messenger God sends to announce or proclaim. Reassuring the women, the angel told them not to be afraid. It was essential to alleviate their fears because, in their terror, they would not be able to understand or ingest the importance of the message they would receive. The unnamed angel stated that he knew they were looking for Jesus. The angel knew that Jesus had been crucified but had been raised, saying, "He is not here."

To further amplify the situation's beauty and demonstrate the power of God, the angel showed the women the slab where they had laid Jesus' body. Notice that the angel labeled Jesus as a Nazarene. Occasionally, Jesus is mistakenly called a "Nazirite," who declares a series of sacred vows, such as those that guided Samuel and Samson's (supposed) consecrated lifestyles. Jesus should not be considered a Nazirite because He consumed wine and touched the dead. In the New Testament, "Nazarene" is used most frequently to clarify the identity of Jesus by associating him with his hometown of Nazareth (Mark 10:47; John 18:7). In the early history of the Church, the term took on a different connotation and referred by extension to Jesus' followers, who were called "the sect of the Nazarenes" (Acts 24:5).

III. DELIVER THIS MESSAGE: MEET ME IN GALILEE (MARK 16:7–8)

As the women recovered from their initial shock and bout of fright, the angel commanded them to go and tell the remaining disciples about their experience with the angel and the tomb. Although the ultimate missive was to be given to the men, in this instance, the women became "angels" (messengers) of the Lord! The Lord was especially concerned about Peter's welfare and spiritual state; he was going through an inner battle because he had denied Jesus. However, God so loved Peter that he was not condemned for his actions; God's nature is to restore and redeem, and Peter was worth saving. Recall that after Jesus' arrest, Peter had inconspicuously followed Jesus and the arresting party as they led Him to several places where He would be condemned for His actions. While in the courtyard of possibly the home of the High Priest, which would have been Caiaphas, Peter was noticed by a servant girl. She immediately called out to Peter, "You were with the Nazarene." At this juncture, those closest to the High Priest and Sanhedrin were most likely aware of Jesus's situation. His followers were not in a favorable light but were subject to scorn and condemnation. Subsequentially (according to the familiar story), Peter responded that he did not know Jesus, which he repeated three times before the proverbial rooster crowed.

Recall that Jesus had predicted that Peter would deny Him, saying, "This very night, before the rooster crows twice, you will deny Me three times" (Mark 14:30). The focus of the women's message was that the disciples were to remember that Jesus had said that after He was raised, He would go ahead of them to Galilee (Mark 14:28). The key to this command was after [I have] been raised. This was a signal to leave their hiding places of (probably) the Upper Room and to return to the security of their homeland, Galilee, most likely, Capernaum. Remember that Jerusalem was a strange city to Jesus and the disciples. Outside of occasional visits for Passover and their ventures while visiting Bethany, Jerusalem was not Jesus' base of operations. The city was now revealing its hostility after initially showing the band some loving care.

Upon hearing the words of the angel, the women left the tomb. Mark describes that they fled from the tomb because they were afraid. Yet, if the angel had allayed their initial fears and calmed the women, their serenity would have all but disappeared. The fright that the women were experiencing now was not due to the angel's presence, for they had recovered from that. The new terror that gripped them was that they had to hurry to deliver the angel's message to the disciples and Peter. In their quest to reach the men, the women would have to pass various citizens of Jerusalem as the city began to awaken and start its usual morning rush. They might encounter inquiring people who were curious about why they had been in the tombs at such an early hour. However, Mark notes that they said nothing to anyone, their fear preventing them from saying anything as they hurried to the disciples with the message. Mark does not indicate how the disciples received the news of the Resurrection, but Matthew records that the women felt both fear and a sense of joy because they realized Jesus had risen! In their rush to reach Peter and company, they met Jesus, who greeted and reassured them, echoing the command of the angel to have the disciples meet Him in Galilee (Matthew 28:9–10). Luke notes that upon hearing the message, Peter got up and ran to the empty tomb (Luke 24:12). Moreover, John records Peter and an unnamed disciple running to the grave, during which the other disciple outran Peter (John 20:3)! Nonetheless, the women had experienced an empty tomb, signifying a risen Christ. They had delivered the message that the disciples must return to Galilee where they would see Jesus again!

The Gospel of Mark is the shortest of the four gospels because it was the first, and Mark served as a journalistic "legman" who reported the accounts as Peter had disclosed to him. Originally, Mark concludes at verse 8 in chapter 16. However, the next set of verses (9–20) serves as an appendix added later by someone who may have been Mark's scribe or disciple. The "longer ending of Mark" constitutes one of the most difficultly disputed textual problems in the New Testament. Were these verses included or omitted in Mark's original text? Most modern English translations call attention to the problem in some way, such as adding an explanatory footnote at verse 9 (NASB), setting this section apart from verse 8 with an explanatory note (NIV), or printing the entire section in the margin (RSV). Four possible reasons for this have been suggested: 1) Mark finished his Gospel, but the original ending either was lost or destroyed in an unknown way before it was copied; 2) Mark finished his Gospel, but the original ending was deliberately suppressed or removed for some reason now unknown; 3) Mark was unable to finish his Gospel for some reason now unknown—possibly sudden death; 4) Mark purposely intended to end his Gospel at verse 8.

THE LESSON APPLIED

The women at the tomb suppressed their initial fright to listen to the angel's message rather than run away in fear. As Christians, we must not run from any message God sends our way. We may not have the experience of a visible presence of an angel, but the Lord does send angels to "watch over" us daily. Jesus may not tangibly appear to us, but Christians should be able to profess and claim the moments that we have "had a little talk with Jesus."

If we can speak with Him in our prayer lives, we should realize that "there is no danger in God's waters" and that the will of the Lord will never take us to where the grace of the Lord will not protect us.

The Resurrection of Jesus is the basis of the Christian faith; no other faith can claim a resurrected Savior. Because Jesus got up, we can have resurrected spiritual lives, new marriages after turmoil, renewed relationships, and everlasting life. We can rest assured that we will see Jesus again, and that's Good News!

LET'S TALK ABOUT IT

A Christian believer may ask, "What is a living faith?"

Living faith is a definition of its state; it is foremost alive. A living faith exudes action to create and support an active walk with Jesus. Additionally, a living faith must be trusted, as it is a model of "in Whom" we place our trust, and that is Jesus. He is the living Lord of life, who sets the tone and life for our faith.

GET SOCIAL

Share your views and tag us @rhboydco and use #KeytoFaith.

Twitter
@rhboydco (#rhboydco)

Instagram
@rhboydco (#rhboydco)

Facebook
@rhboydco (#rhboydco)

www.rhboyd.com

HOME DAILY DEVOTIONAL READINGS
APRIL 1–7, 2024

MONDAY	TUESDAY	WEDNESDAY	THURSDAY	FRIDAY	SATURDAY	SUNDAY
Come and See	Heal Me, and I'll Be Healed	Jesus Provides Living Water	Worship God in Spirit and Truth	Tell What God Has Done	Here Am I; Send Me	Jesus Heals and Forgives
John 1:37–42	Jeremiah 17:12–17	John 4:4–18	John 4:19–29, 39–42	Psalm 66:1–5, 13–20	Isaiah 6:1–8	Luke 5:17–26

FAITH OF FOUR FRIENDS

ADULT TOPIC:	BACKGROUND SCRIPTURE: LUKE 5:17–26
HELPING A FRIEND IN NEED	LESSON PASSAGE: LUKE 5:17–26

LUKE 5:17–26

King James Version

AND it came to pass on a certain day, as he was teaching, that there were Pharisees and doctors of the law sitting by, which were come out of every town of Galilee, and Judaea, and Jerusalem: and the power of the Lord was present to heal them.

18 And, behold, men brought in a bed a man which was taken with a palsy: and they sought means to bring him in, and to lay him before him.

19 And when they could not find by what way they might bring him in because of the multitude, they went upon the housetop, and let him down through the tiling with his couch into the midst before Jesus.

20 And when he saw their faith, he said unto him, Man, thy sins are forgiven thee.

21 And the scribes and the Pharisees began to reason, saying, Who is this which speaketh blasphemies? Who can forgive sins, but God alone?

22 But when Jesus perceived their thoughts, he answering said unto them, What reason ye in your hearts?

23 Whether is easier, to say, Thy sins be forgiven thee; or to say, Rise up and walk?

24 But that ye may know that the Son of man hath power upon earth to forgive sins, (he said unto the sick of the palsy,) I say unto thee, Arise, and take up thy couch, and go into thine house.

New Revised Standard Version

ONE day while he was teaching, Pharisees and teachers of the law who had come from every village of Galilee and Judea and from Jerusalem were sitting nearby, and the power of the Lord was with him to heal

18 Just then some men came carrying a paralyzed man on a stretcher. They were trying to bring him in and lay him before Jesus,

19 but, finding no way to bring him in because of the crowd, they went up on the roof and let him down on the stretcher through the tiles into the middle of the crowd in front of Jesus.

20 When he saw their faith, he said, "Friend, your sins are forgiven you."

21 Then the scribes and the Pharisees began to question, "Who is this who is speaking blasphemies? Who can forgive sins but God alone?"

22 When Jesus perceived their questionings, he answered them, "Why do you raise such questions in your hearts?

23 Which is easier: to say, 'Your sins are forgiven you,' or to say, 'Stand up and walk'?

24 But so that you may know that the Son of Man has authority on earth to forgive sins"— he said to the one who was paralyzed—"I say to you, stand up and take your stretcher and go to your home."

The freedom of God's will

MAIN THOUGHT: And, behold, men brought in a bed a man which was taken with a palsy: and they sought means to bring him in, and to lay him before him. And when they could not find by what way they might bring him in because of the multitude, they went upon the housetop, and let him down through the tiling with his couch into the midst before Jesus. (Luke 5:18–19, KJV)

LUKE 5:17–26

King James Version	*New Revised Standard Version*
25 And immediately he rose up before them, and took up that whereon he lay, and departed to his own house, glorifying God.	25 Immediately he stood up before them, took what he had been lying on, and went to his home, glorifying God.
26 And they were all amazed, and they glorified God, and were filled with fear, saying, We have seen strange things to day.	26 Amazement seized all of them, and they glorified God and were filled with fear, saying, "We have seen incredible things today."

LESSON SETTING
Time: AD 27
Place: Galilee

LESSON OUTLINE
I. **The Freedom of God's Will (Luke 5:17–18)**
II. **God's Power Through Jesus Christ (Luke 5:20–21)**
III. **God's Perfection Through Jesus Christ (Luke 5:22–26)**

UNIFYING PRINCIPLE
People need a support system when trying to overcome life's obstacles. How can our friendships lend strength and support to others in crisis? Jesus celebrates the faith and tenacity of the four friends who helped a friend find healing and wholeness.

INTRODUCTION
"Life's most persistent and urgent question is 'What are you doing for others?'"
~ Rev. Dr. Martin Luther King, Jr.

If we look around close enough and ask the right questions, we will soon discover that we have friends who need our help. The Pandemic caused many who were previously financially stable now to have to rely on the compassion and benevolence of others. In America, some organize ice challenges for Amyotrophic Lateral Sclerosis (ALS), marathons for breast cancer awareness, and read-a-thons for Multiple Sclerosis. We see young people cutting off their hair to support friends with illnesses. Famous people are called upon to raise money for various causes, and we teach our children to be kind to others. Have you ever been in need? How did you receive help? Is it easier for you to give support or receive it? In today's lesson, we see a man in need and his friends who rescue him. They believed that if they could get their friend to Jesus, He would know what to do. They found an unconventional way to help him. Have you ever gone out of your way to assist someone desperate for your help? These friends did not worry about who would judge them, but they were able to bring this man to see Jesus "by any means necessary."

EXPOSITION
I. THE FREEDOM OF GOD'S WILL (LUKE 5:17–18)
Freedom is the attribute of God whereby He does whatever He pleases. Nothing in all creation can hinder God from doing His will. Therefore, this attribute of God is closely related to His will and power. Yet this aspect of freedom focuses on the fact that God is not constrained by anything

external to Himself and is free to do whatever He wishes. No person or force can ever dictate to God what He should do. He is under no authority or external restraint. God's freedom is mentioned in Psalm 115, where His great power contrasts with the weakness of idols: "Our God is in the heavens; he does whatever he pleases" (Psalm 115:3). Human rulers are not able to stand against God and effectively oppose his will, for "the king's heart is a stream of water in the hand of the LORD; he turns it wherever he will" (Proverbs 21:1).

Similarly, Nebuchadnezzar learns in his repentance that it is true to say of God, "He does according to His will in the host of heaven and among the inhabitants of the earth; and none can stay His hand or say to him, 'What are you doing?'" (Daniel 4:35). Because God is free, we should not try to seek any more ultimate answer for God's actions in creation than the fact that He willed to do something and that His will has perfect freedom. Sometimes people try to discover why God had to do one action or another (such as create the world or save us). It is better to say that God's free will (working in a way consistent with his character) was the final reason why he chose to create the world and save sinners.

Most of the roofs built during Jesus' time were flat and usually required a ladder on the side of the house. The rooftop was probably comprised of a mud and straw mixture, and the men needed to dig it out to lower the paralyzed man into the crowd. The houses during Jesus' time were not very big and were usually one story in nature. Jesus was impressed by their faith, and He responded to it. The paralyzed man demonstrated humility by trusting his friends to care for him and bring him to the Lord Jesus. They had to be physically strong as well. What do you think the reaction of the crowd was? These friends knew enough about Jesus to know He was the One to help their friend in his time of need.

II. GOD'S POWER THROUGH JESUS CHRIST (LUKE 5:20–21)

Another of God's many attributes is His power. God's omnipotence means He can do all things according to His holy will. The word omnipotence comes from two Latin words, *omni*, "all," and *potens*, "powerful," meaning "all-powerful." Whereas God's freedom refers to the fact that there are no external constraints on his decisions, God's omnipotence has reference to his power to do what he decides to do. This power is frequently mentioned in Scripture. God is "The Lord, strong and mighty, the Lord, mighty in battle!" (Psalm 24:8).

The rhetorical question, "Is anything too hard for the Lord?" (Genesis 18:14; Jeremiah 32:27) certainly implies (in the contexts in which it occurs) that nothing is too hard for the Lord. Jeremiah says to God, "Nothing is too hard for you" (Jeremiah 32:17). Paul says that God is "able to do far more abundantly than all that we ask or think" (Eph. 3:20), and God is called the "Almighty" (2 Corinthians 6:18; Rev. 1:8), a term (Gk. παντοκράτωρ; *Strong's Greek Lexicon*, G4120) that suggests the possession of all power and authority. Furthermore, the angel Gabriel says to Mary, "With God, nothing will be impossible" (Luke 1:37), and Jesus says, "With God, all things are possible"

(Matthew 19:26). These passages indicate that God's power is infinite and that He is, therefore, not limited to doing only what He has done. God can do more than He does. For example, John the Baptist says in Matthew 3:9, "God is able from these stones to raise up children to Abraham." God is one who "does whatever He wills." Reference the essay by John Piper, "Are There Two Wills in God? Divine Election and God's Desire for All to Be Saved," and *The Grace of God, the Bondage of the Will* Vol. 2, ed. by Tom Schreiner and Bruce Ware (Baker Books, 1995).

However, there are some things that God cannot do. God cannot will or do anything that would deny His character. For example, God cannot lie. Titus 1:2 speaks of "the unlying God" or the "God who never lies." The author of Hebrews says that in God's oath and promise, "it is impossible for God to lie" (Hebrews 6:18, author's translation). Second Timothy 2:13 says of Christ, "He cannot deny himself." Furthermore, James says, "God cannot be tempted with evil, and he himself tempts no one" (James 1:13). Thus, God cannot lie, sin, deny Himself, or be tempted with evil. He cannot cease to exist and be God or act in a way inconsistent with his attributes. God's exercise of power over His creation is also called God's sovereignty. God's sovereignty is His exercise of rule (as "sovereign" or "king") over His creation.

III. God's Perfection Through Jesus Christ
(Luke 5:22–26)

God's perfection means that God completely possesses all excellent qualities and lacks no part of any qualities that would be desirable for Him. It isn't easy to decide whether this should be listed as a separate attribute or simply included in the other attributes' description. Some passages say that God is "perfect" or "complete." Jesus tells us, "You, therefore, must be perfect, as your heavenly Father is perfect" (Matthew 5:48). And David says of God, "His way is perfect" (Psalm 18:30; cf. Deuteronomy 32:4). There is some scriptural precedent, therefore, for explicitly stating that God lacks nothing in His excellence; He fully possesses all of His attributes and lacks nothing from any one of those attributes. Furthermore, there is no quality of excellence that it would be desirable for God to have that which He does not have; He is "complete" or "perfect" in every way. This attribute is the first of those classified as a "summary" attribute because it does not fit well into the other categories that have been listed. Even though all the characteristics of God modify all the others in some sense, those that fit in this category seem more directly to apply to all the attributes or to describe some aspect of all the features that it is worthwhile to state explicitly.

To be "blessed" is to be happy in a very full and rich sense. Scripture often talks about the blessedness of those who walk in God's ways. Yet in 1 Timothy, Paul calls God "the blessed and only Sovereign" (1 Timothy 6:15) and speaks of "the glorious gospel of the blessed God" (1 Timothy 1:11). In both instances, the word is not *eulogetós;* (*Strong's,* G2329; often translated "blessed"), but *makários* (*Strong's,* G3421, which means "happy"). Thus, God's blessedness may be defined as follows: God's blessedness means that God delights thoroughly in Himself and in all that reflects His character. In this definition, the idea of God's happiness or blessedness is connected directly to His person as the focus of all that is worthy of joy or delight. This definition indicates that God is pleased and has the fullness of joy in Himself. The definition reflects that God takes pleasure in everything in creation that mirrors His excellence. When he finished his work of creation, He looked at everything He had made and saw that it was "very good" (Gen. 1:31). This indicates God's delight in and approval of His creation. Then in Isaiah, we read a promise of God's future rejoicing over His people: "As the bridegroom rejoices over the bride, so shall your God rejoice over you" (Isa. 62:5; cf. Prov. 8:30–31; Zeph. 3:17).

It may at first seem strange or even somewhat disappointing to us that when God rejoices in His creation, or even when He rejoices in us, it is the reflection of His excellent qualities in which He is rejoicing. But when we remember that the sum of everything desirable or excellent is found in infinite measure in God Himself, then we realize that it could not be otherwise; whatever excellence there is in the universe, whatever is desirable, must ultimately have come from Him, for He is the Creator of all and He is the source of all good. "Every good endowment and every perfect gift is from above, coming down from the Father of lights with whom there is no variation or shadow due to change" (James 1:17). We ought, therefore, to say to ourselves, as Paul says to the Corinthians, "What have you that you did not receive? If then you received it, why do you boast as if it were not a gift?" (1 Cor. 4:7). "For from him and through

him and to him are all things. To him be glory forever" (Romans 11:36).

We imitate God's blessedness when we find delight and happiness in all that is pleasing to God, both those aspects of our own lives that are pleasing to God and the deeds of others. When we are thankful for and delight in the specific abilities, preferences, and other characteristics with which God has created us as individuals, we imitate His attribute of blessedness. Furthermore, we imitate God's blessedness by rejoicing in the creation as it reflects various aspects of His excellent character. And we find our greatest blessedness, our greatest happiness, in delighting in the source of all good qualities, God himself. Spend some time thanking the Lord for your faithful friends who have helped you when you needed it. Write a letter or make a card to give to someone you value for being there for you throughout your life. What makes someone a great friend? Would others consider you a great friend? Jesus is described as a "friend who sticks closer than a brother." When has Jesus been a friend to you? He said in John 15 that He no longer calls us servants, but friends. Why is that? How can you show the world how Jesus is a friend to us?

THE LESSON APPLIED

Spend some time discussing with your class the character traits of the four friends and their determination to bring their friend to Jesus. What are some ways that you could get your friends to help others who are in need? What are some ways that you can physically, emotionally, and spiritually help your friends and those whom you do not know?

The friends showed persistence. We read that when the friends tried to press their way through the crowd to get their friend to Jesus, they were prevented from doing so. The compassion that they had for their friend made them press through a difficult situation.

Let's Talk About It

Do you know what it means to be available for a needy friend? What are the qualities of a good friend? (Take a few minutes to brainstorm ideas with your Christian circle.) Does risking your life or being inconvenienced to help others qualify as good friendship traits? Why or why not?

In today's lesson, the paralyzed man's friends showed persistence. We read that when the friends tried to press their way through the crowd to get the man to Jesus, they were prevented from doing so. Their compassion for their friend made them push through a difficult situation, and they ultimately got their friend to Jesus. Do you have family members, friends, or co-workers who need a healing touch from Jesus?

How must we show the same persistence and compassion in leading them to the healing hand of the Master? Persistence must be our way as well. Like the four friends, we must insist that there is a way for healing to take and bring one to Jesus. To be sure, all of us do not or may not have a physical need to be fulfilled or restored, but all of us do have a spiritual need of Him. Whatever the need we know Jesus can fix it. There was a song that many choirs sung a few years ago. It said, "I lay awake at night, but that's all right. Jesus will fix it, after while."

Deliberate expressions of benevolence, such as risking ourselves to benefit others, do qualify as good friendship traits because they are based off of love. Love is an event, it is an action. It is a deliberate expression of self-sacrificing good will toward another. Love was the way Jesus walked. It was the way in which He carried Himself. When we act lovingly, we are acting like our Lord and Savior. We are to always seek to emulate Him and to do His bidding. He told His disciples to love one another.

Get Social

Share your views and tag us
@rhboydco and use #Persistence.

Twitter
@rhboydco (#rhboydco)

Instagram
@rhboydco (#rhboydco)

Facebook
@rhboydco (#rhboydco)

www.rhboyd.com

Home Daily Devotional Readings
April 8–14, 2024

Monday	Tuesday	Wednesday	Thursday	Friday	Saturday	Sunday
Accept What God Has Made Clean	God's Servant Enlightens the Nations	God Is Praised among the Nations	Christ Is All and in All	Nations Shall Entreat God's Favor	All Flesh Shall See God's Salvation	Jesus Helps a Righteous Gentile
Acts 10:1–15	Isaiah 42:1–12	Malachi 1:10–14	Colossians 3:1–11	Zechariah 8:18–23	Luke 3:1–14	Luke 7:1–10

FAITH OF A CENTURION

| ADULT TOPIC: | BACKGROUND SCRIPTURE: LUKE 7:1–10 |
| HEALED FROM A DISTANCE | LESSON PASSAGE: LUKE 7:1–10 |

LUKE 7:1–10

King James Version

NOW when he had ended all his sayings in the audience of the people, he entered into Capernaum.

2 And a certain centurion's servant, who was dear unto him, was sick, and ready to die.

3 And when he heard of Jesus, he sent unto him the elders of the Jews, beseeching him that he would come and heal his servant.

4 And when they came to Jesus, they besought him instantly, saying, That he was worthy for whom he should do this:

5 For he loveth our nation, and he hath built us a synagogue.

6 Then Jesus went with them. And when he was now not far from the house, the centurion sent friends to him, saying unto him, Lord, trouble not thyself: for I am not worthy that thou shouldest enter under my roof:

7 Wherefore neither thought I myself worthy to come unto thee: but say in a word, and my servant shall be healed.

8 For I also am a man set under authority, having under me soldiers, and I say unto one, Go, and he goeth; and to another, Come, and he cometh; and to my servant, Do this, and he doeth it.

9 When Jesus heard these things, he marvelled at him, and turned him about, and said unto the people that followed him, I say unto you, I have not found so great faith, no, not in Israel.

10 And they that were sent, returning to the house, found the servant whole that had been sick.

New Revised Standard Version

AFTER Jesus had finished all his sayings in the hearing of the people, he entered Capernaum.

2 A centurion there had a slave whom he valued highly and who was ill and close to death.

3 When he heard about Jesus, he sent some Jewish elders to him, asking him to come and heal his slave.

4 When they came to Jesus, they appealed to him earnestly, saying, "He is worthy to have you do this for him,

5 for he loves our people, and it is he who built our synagogue for us."

6 And Jesus went with them, but when he was not far from the house, the centurion sent friends to say to him, "Lord, do not trouble yourself, for I am not worthy to have you come under my roof;

7 therefore I did not presume to come to you. But only speak the word, and let my servant be healed.

8 For I also am a man set under authority, with soldiers under me, and I say to one, 'Go,' and he goes, and to another, 'Come,' and he comes, and to my slave, 'Do this,' and the slave does it."

9 When Jesus heard this he was amazed at him, and, turning to the crowd following him, he said, "I tell you, not even in Israel have I found such faith."

10 When those who had been sent returned to the house, they found the slave in good health.

MAIN THOUGHT: Wherefore neither thought I myself worthy to come unto thee: but say in a word, and my servant shall be healed. (Luke 7:7, KJV)

LESSON SETTING
   Time: AD 26–28
   Place: Capernaum

LESSON OUTLINE
   I. **An Introduction to Luke**
   II. **The Desperation of
      a Centurion
      (Luke 7:1–3)**
   III. **The Faith of a Centurion
      (Luke 7:6–10)**

UNIFYING PRINCIPLE

Sometimes, the enormity of our problems diminishes our capacity to move forward. How should we respond to seemingly impossible situations? When a centurion whose servant was close to death replied in great faith, Jesus was amazed and miraculously restored the man to complete health.

INTRODUCTION

In a world of others vying for respect, whether or not they deserve it, authority comes in many forms. Someone may have told you to respect the authority of police officers, teachers, and parents. How has that practice helped you in your life? Do you think certain authority figures deserve to be respected, or are we all on the same level? Do you believe someone must earn the right to be respected? There are times that respect for authority is warranted in the case of emergencies; a firefighter would be the authority figure during a house fire. What makes someone respected? Some may say their level of education or reputation for doing certain things well makes them an authority figure. What are your thoughts about people

who claim to have supernatural healing powers? We know that the gift of healing exists. Do you believe that people today have the gift of healing? Is it of God? Most likely, these persons have to be in the presence of a sick individual to demonstrate healing, but today's story shows that Jesus only had to speak a word, and the servant was healed. The centurion had faith in the power of God. He respected Jesus' time and only wanted enough of His power to heal his servant. He was very humble and not greedy.

In Rome, during the days of Jesus, a centurion was an officer of the military forces who commanded one hundred men. To attain the level of centurion, the soldier had to prove himself worthy of the title. If you have served in the Armed Forces, you undoubtedly know the responsibility of commanding officers. Like military officers today, the centurion was responsible for training, disciplining, and assigning soldiers tasks. Despite being the disciplinarian and leader, the centurion in our story today demonstrated compassion toward his servant. His trust in Jesus' ability to heal his servant was one of great belief.

One could ask, why is faith important? Jesus announced to the crowd that the centurion's faith was remarkable. We understand how important faith is in the life of a believer as we read Hebrews 11:6, which says "and without faith it is impossible to please God because anyone who comes to him must believe that he exists and that he rewards those who earnestly seek him." We can infer that Jesus was pleased by the centurion's faith.

EXPOSITION

I. AN INTRODUCTION TO LUKE

Luke's writings are the most literary of the New Testament books, distinctive in the original for their fluid style and beauty. Luke is the only Gospel writer who wrote a sequel—Acts, which tells the story of the early Church and its spread. Unlike the other Gospels, whose content can be traced back to eyewitness accounts of Jesus' life shared by His disciples Matthew, John, and Peter, Luke's account is developed through what we call "investigative reporting." Luke tells us in his introduction that his work results from careful research, that he has written an "orderly account," and that his purpose was to enable the readers "to know the certainty of the things you have been taught." Luke most likely did the bulk of his research during the years that Paul was held in Caesarea awaiting trial (Acts 23–27).

Like the other Gospel writers, Luke has an audience in mind and shapes his material to stress themes of particular interest to him and his readers. Most agree that Luke is writing for the Hellenist—the person whose roots are in Greek culture. Always mindful of Jesus' deity, Luke still holds Him up as the ideal human being who redefines excellence. In Jesus, "excellence" is seen, not as a personal superiority that devalues others, but as a personal superiority expressed in concern for others. And the others whom Jesus values are those lightly dismissed by human societies: women, the poor, and the powerless. Jesus's reliance on prayer and the Holy Spirit reveals humankind in its true relationship with the universe, dependent on a God who exists beyond us and yet loves us so much that He chooses to be fully involved in our human lives. All this makes Luke perhaps the warmest and most sensitive of the four Gospels and provides the most attractive of their portraits of Jesus Christ. Unique themes in Luke's Gospel are salvation for all, women are important, and the poor have value.

II. THE DESPERATION OF A CENTURION (Luke 7:1–3)

Recall when you felt helpless and hopeless when someone you loved and respected was in great need. Draw or write about your feelings regarding such an occasion. What did you do about your helplessness? Name some people considered outside our responsibility (persons of other religions, different racial ancestry, greater or lesser economic status, etc.). In what ways can we respond to their needs? How can we broaden our sense of responsibility? How can we direct them to the help that Christ offers? The centurion was desperate for help; he knew he was not worthy, but Jesus was the only One who could heal his servant. He knew Jesus did not have to be in the room with his servant to heal him. He knew that Jesus stood for truth. We have that same assurance.

The essence of the authority of Scripture is its ability to compel us to believe and obey it and make such belief and obedience equivalent to believing and obeying God himself. Because this is so, it is needful to consider the truthfulness of Scripture since to believe all the words of Scripture implies confidence in the complete truthfulness of the Scripture that we believe. Since the biblical writers repeatedly affirm that the words of the Bible, though human, are God's own words, it is appropriate to look at biblical texts that talk about the character of God's words and to apply these to the character of the words of Scripture. Specifically, there are a number of biblical passages that talk about the truthfulness of God's speech. Titus 1:2 speaks of "God, who never lies," or (more literally translated) "the unlying God." Because God cannot speak anything untrue, His words can always be trusted. Since God speaks all of Scripture, all of Scripture must be "unlying," just as God Himself is: there can be no untruthfulness in Scripture.

Hebrews 6:18 mentions two unchangeable things (God's oath and His promise) "in which it is impossible for God to lie" (author's translation). Here the author says that God does not lie and that it is not possible for him to lie. Although the immediate reference is only to oaths and promises, if it is impossible for God to lie in these utterances, then certainly it is impossible for him ever to lie (for Jesus harshly rebukes those who tell the truth only when under oath: Matthew 5:33–37; 23:16–22). Similarly, David says to God, "You are God, and your words are true" (2 Samuel 7:28). Therefore, all the words in Scripture are completely true and without error in any part.

Since the words of the Bible are God's words, and since God cannot lie or speak falsely, it is correct to conclude that there is no untruthfulness or error in any part of the words of Scripture. We find this affirmed in several places in the Bible. "The words of the Lord are words that are pure silver refined in a furnace on the ground, purified seven times" (Psalm 12:6, author's translation). Here the psalmist uses vivid imagery to speak of the undiluted purity of God's words: there is no imperfection in them. Also, in Proverbs 30:5, we read, "Every word of God proves true; he is a shield to those who take refuge in him." It is not just some of the words of Scripture that are true, but every word. God's Word is fixed in heaven for all eternity: "Forever, O Lord, your word is firmly fixed in the heavens" (Psalm 119:89). Jesus can speak of the eternal nature of His own words: "Heaven and earth will pass away, but my words will not pass away" (Matthew 24:35).

The Bible is God's Word, and God's Word is the ultimate definition of what is true and what is not true; God's Word is itself truth. Thus, we are to consider the Bible the ultimate standard of truth, the reference point by which every other claim to truthfulness is to be measured. Those assertions that conform to Scripture are "true," while those that do not conform with Scripture are not true. What then is truth? Truth is what God says, and we have what God says (accurately but not exhaustively) in the Bible. Might some new fact ever contradict the Bible? Will any new scientific or historical fact ever be discovered contradicting the Bible? Here we can confidently say this will never happen—it is, in fact, impossible. If any supposed "fact" is ever discovered that is said to contradict Scripture, then (if we have understood Scripture rightly) that "fact" must be false because God, the author of Scripture, knows all facts (past, present, and future). No fact will ever turn up that God did not know about ages ago and consider when he ordained Scripture to be written. Every true fact is something God has known already from all eternity and, therefore, cannot contradict God's speech in Scripture.

III THE FAITH OF A CENTURION (LUKE 7:1–5)

Notice the humility of the centurion, an authority figure. He was undoubtedly accustomed to others regarding him as someone with great power and respect. However, in this instance, he humbled himself in the face of Christ's authority. Because of his love for his servant, he was willing to inconvenience himself to seek help for his friend. Servants were considered family members, although they were hired to help. Generally, someone of the centurion's caliber would not have bothered Jesus because he had the financial means to help anyone he wanted. But this centurion realized that neither his money nor his prestige could help him; he needed supernatural power.

Have you ever been in a situation where you had to do something out of the ordinary to help someone? This centurion knew he had to do something to help his servant and was willing to risk his reputation and status. Desperate, he cried out to the One who could meet his need. Jesus recognized this man's faith in front of everyone. Do you have faith that God would recognize? Investigate the relationship between Jesus and the village of Capernaum, suggesting that participants research Capernaum online or in a commentary. Consider the connection between our prayers for the sick and suffering and the centurion's plea to Jesus for help "from afar."

God's exercise of power over His creation is also called God's sovereignty. God's sovereignty is his exercise of rule (as "sovereign" or "king") over His creation. He has made us in such a way that we show in our lives some faint reflection of each of them. God has made us as creatures with a will. We exercise choice and make real decisions regarding the events of our lives. Although our will is not absolutely free in the way God's is, God has nonetheless given us relative freedom within our spheres of activity in the universe he has created.

In fact, we have an intuitive sense that it is our ability to exercise our wills and make choices, and to do so in a relatively free way, that is one of the most significant marks of God-likeness in our existence.

THE LESSON APPLIED

How is your faith exemplified in your actions? Do others know that you place your faith in Christ alone? Humility is the first step in being heard by the Lord. If we know that His place is above us, we will then be in right standing to receive help from Him. We must show Him that we need Him. The centurion understood his place in comparison to Jesus. He did not even want to trouble Jesus and said that he was not even worthy for Jesus to enter his home. He understood that Jesus' healing was not automatic and that his request had to be humble and sincere. How do you approach Jesus in prayer?

As we understand the practice of prayer in our lives, we will grow in maturity and we will learn more about what God's desires are so that we can align our desires with His. We will then be able to stand when hard situations arise in our lives and in the lives of our friends. We do not know if the servant was a believer, but the centurion had enough faith for him.

LET'S TALK ABOUT IT

1. Do you trust God to help your friends? Do your friends know that you are a believer?

The centurion trusted the Lord to heal his friend. We can trust that God hears our prayers offered for ourselves and for our friends. We need God because we are helpless on our own. Only Jesus has the power to heal and to rescue us from drowning.

God has called us to be concerned about the needs of others. The lost usually do not know they need Jesus; therefore, prayers for the lost are necessary. Our witness as prayer warriors is vital for the furthering of the Kingdom. Share with the group a time when you were desperate for God to move in your life.

Did you demonstrate faith that would have pleased Jesus, or did you experience a lack of belief? Where there is faith, there is hope. Faith is the cornerstone of our relationship with our Heavenly Father. We must have complete trust in His ability to care for us, whether that is healing, restoration, or provision.

2. Do you talk to your neighbors, co-workers, and friends about Jesus and the power that He has demonstrated in your life? Do you share your story of salvation with others?

Think about what led the centurion to Jesus. In verse 3 of our lesson text, the centurion sought out Jesus because he had heard of Him. Christians are often accused of telling nonbelievers how to live their lives and being critical of others. Discuss in your group how we can broadcast the Good News of Jesus Christ rather than being critical. What a joy it would be to know that someone has sought out a relationship with Jesus because of your testimony. Let today be the day that you begin to tell others about the joy of your salvation that you have found in Jesus Christ.

GET SOCIAL

Share your views and tag us @rhboydco and use #FaithinAction.

Twitter
@rhboydco (#rhboydco)

Instagram
@rhboydco (#rhboydco)

Facebook
@rhboydco (#rhboydco)

www.rhboyd.com

HOME DAILY DEVOTIONAL READINGS
APRIL 15–21, 2024

MONDAY	TUESDAY	WEDNESDAY	THURSDAY	FRIDAY	SATURDAY	SUNDAY
Jesus' Compassion for the Grieving	Sing Praises to God's Name	Confession, Prayer, and Healing	God Pardons Iniquity and Transgression	God Is Good and Forgiving	No Condemnation in Christ	Jesus Forgives a Sinner
Luke 7:11–18	Psalm 92	James 5:12–20	Micah 7:7–20	Psalm 86:1–7, 11–17	Romans 8:1–16	Luke 7:36–50

FAITH OF A WOMAN WHO LOVED JESUS

ADULT TOPIC:	BACKGROUND SCRIPTURE: LUKE 7:36–50
HOW MUCH DO YOU LOVE ME?	LESSON PASSAGE: LUKE 7:36–39, 44–50

LUKE 7:36–39, 44–50

King James Version

AND one of the Pharisees desired him that he would eat with him. And he went into the Pharisee's house, and sat down to meat.

37 And, behold, a woman in the city, which was a sinner, when she knew that Jesus sat at meat in the Pharisee's house, brought an alabaster box of ointment,

38 And stood at his feet behind him weeping, and began to wash his feet with tears, and did wipe them with the hairs of her head, and kissed his feet, and anointed them with the ointment.

39 Now when the Pharisee which had bidden him saw it, he spake within himself, saying, This man, if he were a prophet, would have known who and what manner of woman this is that toucheth him: for she is a sinner.

• • • • • •

44 And he turned to the woman, and said unto Simon, Seest thou this woman? I entered into thine house, thou gavest me no water for my feet: but she hath washed my feet with tears, and wiped them with the hairs of her head.

45 Thou gavest me no kiss: but this woman since the time I came in hath not ceased to kiss my feet.

46 My head with oil thou didst not anoint: but this woman hath anointed my feet with ointment.

47 Wherefore I say unto thee, Her sins, which are many, are forgiven; for she loved much: but to whom little is forgiven, the same loveth little.

New Revised Standard Version

ONE of the Pharisees asked Jesus to eat with him, and when he went into the Pharisee's house he reclined to dine.

37 And a woman in the city who was a sinner, having learned that he was eating in the Pharisee's house, brought an alabaster jar of ointment.

38 She stood behind him at his feet, weeping, and began to bathe his feet with her tears and to dry them with her hair, kissing his feet and anointing them with the ointment.

39 Now when the Pharisee who had invited him saw it, he said to himself, "If this man were a prophet, he would have known who and what kind of woman this is who is touching him, that she is a sinner."

• • • • • •

44 Then turning toward the woman, he said to Simon, "Do you see this woman? I entered your house; you gave me no water for my feet, but she has bathed my feet with her tears and dried them with her hair.

45 You gave me no kiss, but from the time I came in she has not stopped kissing my feet.

46 You did not anoint my head with oil, but she has anointed my feet with ointment.

47 Therefore, I tell you, her many sins have been forgiven; hence she has shown great love. But the one to whom little is forgiven loves little."

MAIN THOUGHT: [Jesus] said to the woman, "Your faith has saved you; go in peace." (Luke 7:50, KJV)

LUKE 7:36–39, 44–50

King James Version	*New Revised Standard Version*
48 And he said unto her, Thy sins are forgiven.	48 Then he said to her, "Your sins are forgiven."
49 And they that sat at meat with him began to say within themselves, Who is this that forgiveth sins also?	49 But those who were at the table with him began to say among themselves, "Who is this who even forgives sins?"
50 And he said to the woman, Thy faith hath saved thee; go in peace.	50 But he said to the woman, "Your faith has saved you; go in peace."

LESSON SETTING
> **Time: AD 65–70**
> **Place: Galilee**

LESSON OUTLINE
> I. **An Humble Act**
>   **(Luke 7:36–39)**
> II. **The Need for Forgiveness**
>   **(Luke 7:19–28)**
> III. **The Call to Answer**
>   **(Luke 7:29–50)**

UNIFYING PRINCIPLE

The humiliation of our public failures can make it difficult for a fresh start. How do we overcome the weight of judgment and scrutiny from those who refuse to see past our mistakes? Luke teaches about a woman whose great faith helped her rise above the rejection of others so that she might express her gratitude for Jesus' love and forgiveness.

INTRODUCTION

Have you ever been humiliated by those who regard themselves as superior? There are many stories of enslaved people and even Black Hollywood actors who were ridiculed and embarrassed by the laws of the land. In essence, it was lawful for them to be treated as less than human. They somehow had the dignity and self-worth to keep going in the face of prejudice and racial discrimination. They were affirmed by people who loved them and saw their value. In the famed movie, "Imitation of Life," the young lady is embarrassed by her mother, but her mother still desires her love and affection. Those who experience acceptance by others can rise above their rejection and shame. Jesus always has time for the rejected and shamed persons in society.

EXPOSITION

I. A HUMBLE ACT
(LUKE 7:36–39)

Faith in Jesus is for Gentiles as well as for Jews. Those Gentiles who believe will surely be blessed. Pharisees were the most respected in Jesus' time because they were the very religious "keepers of the Law." They publicly shamed those who did not follow the Law strictly. They acted no differently with Jesus, following Him around and making sure that He did not do anything to disrupt their strict adherence to the Law. They felt it was blasphemous not to take the Law seriously and to profess to be anything other than what they thought that person should be. Sinners did not follow the Law in their eyes. They were considered hopeless and not above the Law. In this passage, the Pharisee failed to fulfill the customary acts of a host when a guest was in the home. Simon disrespected Jesus. He mistreated the woman, as she gave her best. She knew Jesus was the Messiah and dared to honor Him with a year's wages.

It was common for Jesus and the people of the day to have dirty feet as they walked in sandals on dusty roads. Her heart was pure before Jesus, and He honored her despite her reputation and how she was normally treated. Notice the woman's humility; she knew she was not worthy. She understood that her place was below the mighty power of Jesus. He had heard her heart's prayer. James tells us that "God opposes the proud, but gives grace to the humble" (James 4:6; also 1 Peter 5:5). Therefore, he says, "Humble yourselves before the Lord, and he will exalt you" (James 4:10). Humility is thus the right attitude to have in praying to God, whereas pride is altogether inappropriate.

Jesus' parable about the Pharisee and the tax collector illustrates this. When the Pharisee stood to pray, he was boastful: "God, I thank you that I am not like other men, extortioners, unjust, adulterers, or even like this tax collector. I fast twice a week, I give tithes of all that I get" (Luke 18:11–12). By contrast, the humble tax collector "would not even lift up his eyes to heaven, but beat his breast, saying, 'God, be merciful to me a sinner!'" (Luke 18:13). Jesus said that he "went down to his house justified," rather than the Pharisee, "for every one who exalts himself will be humbled, but he who humbles himself will be exalted" (Luke 18:14). This is why

Jesus condemned those who "for a pretense make long prayers" (Luke 20:47) and those hypocrites who "love to stand and pray in the synagogues and at the street corners, that they may be seen by men" (Matthew 6:5). God is rightly jealous for His own honor. Therefore He is not pleased to answer the prayers of the proud who take honor to themselves rather than giving it to Him. True humility before God, which will also be reflected in genuine humility before others, is necessary for effective prayer. Just as Moses twice stayed on the mountain forty days before God for the people of Israel (Deuteronomy 9:25–26; 10:10–11), and just as Jacob said to God, "I will not let you go, unless you bless me" (Genesis 32:26), so we see in Jesus' life a pattern of much time given to prayer.

When great multitudes followed him, "he was often withdrawing into the wilderness regions and praying" (Luke 5:16, author's translation). At another time, "all night he continued in prayer to God" (Luke 6:12). Sometimes, as in the case of Moses and Jacob, prayer over a long period of time may be a prayer for one specific item (cf. Luke 18:1–8). When we earnestly seek God for an answer to a specific prayer, we may repeat the same request several times. Paul asked the Lord "three times" (2 Corinthians 12:8) that his thorn in the flesh would be taken from him. Jesus himself, when He was in the Garden of Gethsemane, asked the Father, "Remove this cup from me; yet not what I will, but what you will" (Mark 14:36). Then after He came and found the disciples sleeping, Jesus prayed again, making the same request in the same words: "And again he went away and prayed, saying the same words" (Mark 14:39).

These are instances of earnest repetition in prayer for a deeply felt need. They are not examples of what Jesus forbids—the heaping up of "empty phrases" in the mistaken belief that "many words" will earn a hearing (Matthew 6:7). There is also an element of a continual fellowship with God in praying over time. Paul calls on us to "pray constantly" (1 Thessalonians 5:17), and he encourages the Colossians to "continue steadfastly in prayer, being watchful in it with thanksgiving" (Colossians 4:2). Such continual devotion to prayer even while about daily duties should characterize the life of every believer. The apostles are a telling example. They freed themselves from other responsibilities to give more time to prayer: "But we will devote ourselves to prayer and to the ministry of the word" (Acts 6:4). Jesus himself, who is our model for prayer, prayed earnestly. "In the days of his flesh, Jesus offered up prayers and supplications, with loud cries and tears, to him who was able to save him from death, and he was heard for his godly fear" (Hebrews 5:7).

II. THE NEED FOR FORGIVENESS (LUKE 7:19–28)

John's question is comforting. If a man of such great commitment and faith can have doubts, we need not be overwhelmed by our uncertainties. But John's question is also a warning. John made the mistake of expecting Jesus to act as John supposed He must. Let's never suppose that God must limit Himself to act as we think He should. We must adjust to what God is doing. John announced the Kingdom. We participate in it. Our privilege is greater. And so is our responsibility. Consider what it cost the woman to approach Jesus. How did she gain entrance to the Pharisee's house? Why did she seem unconcerned about the value of the ointment she used or about the humiliation she risked by approaching a man in the company of others? Think about the most humiliating circumstances that you have experienced. What or who enabled or compelled you to see beyond your humiliation? The woman had already accepted the Gospel call, so she was not concerned about who was watching her; she needed her sins forgiven.

Anyone who comes to Christ for salvation must have a basic understanding of who Christ is and how He meets our needs for salvation. Therefore, explaining the facts concerning salvation must include at least the following: 1) All people have sinned (Romans 3:23). 2) Death is the penalty for our sins (Romans 6:23). 3) Jesus Christ died to pay the penalty for our sins (Romans 5:8). But understanding those facts and even agreeing that they are true is not enough for a person to be saved. There must also be an invitation for a personal response from the individual who will repent of their sins and trust in Christ.

When the New Testament talks about people coming to salvation, it speaks in terms of a personal response to an invitation from Christ Himself. That invitation is beautifully expressed in the words of Jesus: "Come to me all you who are weary and burdened, and I will give you rest. Take my yoke upon you and learn from me, for I am gentle and humble in heart, and you will find rest for your souls. For my yoke is easy, and my burden is light"

(Matthew 11:28–30 NIV). Jesus Christ is a Savior who is now alive in heaven, and each non-Christian should think of Jesus as saying, "Come to me...and I will give you rest" (Matthew 11:28). This is a genuine personal invitation that seeks a response from each one who hears it. John also talks about the need for a personal response when he says, "He came to his own, and his own people received him not. But to all who received him who believed in his name, he gave power to become children of God" (John 1:11–12). In emphasizing the need to "receive" Christ, John, too, points to the necessity of an individual response. To those who do not realize their spiritual blindness, the Lord Jesus again issues an invitation: "Behold, I stand at the door and knock; if any one hears my voice and opens the door, I will come in to him and eat with him, and he with me" (Rev. 3:20). Finally, just five verses from the end of the entire Bible, there is another invitation from the Holy Spirit and the church to come to Christ: "The Spirit and the Bride say, 'Come.' And let him who hears say, 'Come.' And let him who is thirsty come, let him who desires, take the water of life without price" (Revelation 22:17).

But what is involved in coming to Christ? Although this will be explained more fully in chapter 35, it is sufficient to note here that if we come to Christ and trust him to save us from our sin, we can no longer cling to sin but must willingly renounce it in genuine repentance. In some cases in Scripture, both repentance and faith are mentioned together when referring to someone's initial conversion (Paul said that he spent his time "testifying both to Jews and to Greeks of repentance to God and of faith in our Lord Jesus Christ," Acts 20:21). But at other times only repentance of sins is named and saving faith is assumed as an accompanying factor ("that repentance and forgiveness of sins should be preached in his name to all nations" [Luke 24:47; cf. Acts 2:37–38; 3:19; 5:31; 17:30; Romans 2:4; 2 Corinthians 7:10; et al.]). Therefore, any genuine Gospel proclamation must include an invitation to make a conscious decision to forsake one's sins and come to Christ in faith, asking Christ for forgiveness. If either the need to repent of sins or the need to trust in Christ for forgiveness is neglected, there is not a full and true proclamation of the Gospel.

But what is promised for those who come to Christ? This is the third element of the Gospel call—a Promise of Forgiveness and Eternal Life. Although the words of personal invitation spoken by Christ have promises of rest, and power to become children of God and partaking of the water of life, it is helpful to make explicit just what Christ promises to those who come to Him in repentance and faith. The primary promise of the Gospel message is the forgiveness of sins and eternal life with God. "For God so loved the world that he gave his only Son, that whoever believes in him should not perish but have eternal life" (John 3:16). And in Peter's preaching of the Gospel, he says, "Repent therefore, and turn again, that your sins may be blotted out" (Acts 3:19; cf. 2:38). Coupled with the promise of forgiveness and eternal life should be an assurance that Christ will accept all who come to Him in sincere repentance and faith seeking salvation: "[He] who comes to me I will not cast out" (John 6:37).

III. THE CALL TO ANSWER (LUKE 7:29–50)

This was not lip service but a change in the moral direction of one's life. It is stunning that the religious people of Jesus's time could not see that such a response was proof God was at work. Forgiveness received awakens love for God. In announcing the woman's sins were forgiven, Jesus stated what was already confirmed. The woman's love proved she had been forgiven. Love does not come first; it is a response to God working in our lives.

The incident summarizes themes developed in this chapter. Christ is compassionate and powerful. He heals bodies and souls. Those who have faith in Him experience His power in both the physical and spiritual realms. The Pharisees, representing the leaders of first-century Judaism, could not see or understand. Unlike John, whose questioning was rooted faith, their doubts were a blunt denial of the clear evidence of who Jesus was and is. The doctrine of the Gospel call is essential because we could not be saved without it. "How are they to believe in him of whom they have never heard?" (Romans 10:14). The Gospel call is vital because God addresses us in the fullness of our humanity through it.

THE LESSON APPLIED

Jesus is not like anyone else. He does not condemn and welcomes us when we are sorry for our sins. He is the only One who can give us hope. He is not concerned with the expectations of humans. He knows what it feels like to be mistreated; He empathizes with our pain from others. As a result, we are to show the same grace to others who are different from us and those who have not yet received the love of Jesus.

LET'S TALK ABOUT IT

Do the Pharisees get a bad rap in the New Testament?

There were some good Pharisees and some bad ones. The majority of them are seen as against Jesus because they believed in a system of legalism. They tried to live out what the Law required, rather than veer out according to faith, hope, and love. Therefore, they believed in only what they could see—good works, a perfect life, and ceremonial cleanliness.

GET SOCIAL

Share your views and tag us
@rhboydco and use #Forgiven.

Twitter
@rhboydco (#rhboydco)

Instagram
@rhboydco (#rhboydco)

Facebook
@rhboydco (#rhboydco)

www.rhboyd.com

HOME DAILY DEVOTIONAL READINGS
APRIL 22–28, 2024

MONDAY	TUESDAY	WEDNESDAY	THURSDAY	FRIDAY	SATURDAY	SUNDAY
God Provides for a Gentile Woman	God's Authority over Life and Death	God Blesses Whomever God Wills	Hear My Cry, O God	May God Grant Your Heart's Desire	God Gives Grace to the Humble	Jesus Hears a Desperate Mother's Plea
1 Kings 17:8–16	1 Kings 17:17–24	Luke 4:24–30	Psalm 61	Psalm 20	James 4:1–10	Matthew 15:21–28

THE FAITH OF A CANAANITE WOMAN

ADULT TOPIC: BACKGROUND SCRIPTURE: MATTHEW 15:21–28
HELP FOR AN OUTSIDER   LESSON PASSAGE: MATTHEW 15:21–28

MATTHEW 15:21–28

King James Version

THEN Jesus went thence, and departed into the coasts of Tyre and Sidon.

22 And, behold, a woman of Canaan came out of the same coasts, and cried unto him, saying, Have mercy on me, O Lord, thou son of David; my daughter is grievously vexed with a devil.

23 But he answered her not a word. And his disciples came and besought him, saying, Send her away; for she crieth after us.

24 But he answered and said, I am not sent but unto the lost sheep of the house of Israel.

25 Then came she and worshipped him, saying, Lord, help me.

26 But he answered and said, It is not meet to take the children's bread, and to cast it to dogs.

27 And she said, Truth, Lord: yet the dogs eat of the crumbs which fall from their masters' table.

28 Then Jesus answered and said unto her, O woman, great is thy faith: be it unto thee even as thou wilt. And her daughter was made whole from that very hour.

New Revised Standard Version

JESUS left that place and went away to the district of Tyre and Sidon.

22 Just then a Canaanite woman from that region came out and started shouting, "Have mercy on me, Lord, Son of David; my daughter is tormented by a demon."

23 But he did not answer her at all. And his disciples came and urged him, saying, "Send her away, for she keeps shouting after us."

24 He answered, "I was sent only to the lost sheep of the house of Israel."

25 But she came and knelt before him, saying, "Lord, help me."

26 He answered, "It is not fair to take the children's food and throw it to the dogs."

27 She said, "Yes, Lord, yet even the dogs eat the crumbs that fall from their masters' table."

28 Then Jesus answered her, "Woman, great is your faith! Let it be done for you as you wish." And her daughter was healed from that moment.

LESSON SETTING

Time: AD 60's
Place: Unknown

LESSON OUTLINE

I. The Law vs. Grace
   (Matthew 15:1–2)
II. Cleansed Heart
   (Matthew 15: 3–10
III. A Woman's Faith
   (Matthew 15:21–28)

UNIFYING PRINCIPLE

Systemic problems in society unfairly restrict access to resources for some while privileging others. How do we overcome the prejudice and hatred that denies some people equal access to resources that protect a decent standard of living? The Canaanite woman understood that Israel's Messiah would one day bring God's reign

MAIN THOUGHT: Then Jesus answered and said unto her, O woman, great is thy faith: be it unto thee even as thou wilt. And her daughter was made whole from that very hour. (Matthew 15:28, KJV)

to all people and, by faith, pressed Jesus to extend that blessing to her even before he'd completed his work among the people of Israel.

INTRODUCTION

In a world where many people of different races, creeds, and backgrounds are victims of society's long-standing prejudices and assumptions, we can be comforted knowing that Jesus empathizes with our pain. Even when we realize that we are both victims of societal norms and perpetrators of them, we do not always accept people who are different from us. However, we are capable of rising above social boundaries when we sense that we have the opportunity to do something honorable. If we seek to break down social barriers that limit our freedom and access, God will open doors for us to be healed on every level—spiritual, physical, emotional, etc.

EXPOSITION

I. THE LAW VS. GRACE (MATTHEW 15:1–2)

In the centuries before Christ, Jewish sages (rabbis, teachers of the Law) had concentrated on applying Old Testament Law to every aspect of Jewish life. Their goal was to "build a hedge" around the Law, explaining each command's implications so thoroughly that no one would break it being unaware. This intent, motivated by profound respect for the Scriptures, seems commendable. But it represented a dangerous approach to Scripture and created a legalistic attitude that distorted the Law's intent. Jesus draws attention to two flaws in the approach, which the Pharisee party

had enthusiastically endorsed. First, tradition had taken on the authority of Scripture itself so that, in fact, the "commandments of men" were often substituted for, and even contradicted, God's commands. Second, in focusing on what humankind must do to keep the Law rather than what God graciously does for humanity, the hearts of legalists became cold. Religion became a matter of externals rather than of a personal relationship. Jesus's focus on people and servanthood threatened the structure that tradition erected and aroused the active hostility of the religious elite.

The relationships between Jews and Canaanites (Gentiles) in the Roman world were not always pleasant. It was unlikely that a Canaanite woman would approach a Jewish man under any circumstances because she was considered beneath him. These were the days before what we know as women's rights. A woman could only address a man with her husband present. If a woman became a widow, she was penniless and depended on the mercy of those in charge. She was considered a second-class citizen. Consider the woman's knowledge of Jesus before he entered the Gentile region where she lived. How would she have heard of him? What did it mean for her to address him as "Son of David"? What did she know about the prophets who foretold the Messiah's advent?

How can we follow in her footsteps in acknowledging who Jesus is? Jesus' reputation followed Him into the lives of those considered less than, and He recognized them despite their status. This woman was already a believer in Christ before she met Him, which gave her the notion that she could ask for His help. She may have been hiding in the shadows when he was preaching, teaching, and performing miracles. Despite the Law of the land, Jesus' authority spoke to her; she was in the right place for her daughter to be healed.

II. Cleansed Heart (Matthew 15: 3–10)

Possessions might be devoted to God but used by the owner as long as they lived. The "gift" was thus a legal fiction that gave a person an excuse not to use his possessions to help a parent or other relative in need. This interpretation of the Old Testament's teaching on vows allowed a person to legally subvert God's intent when He called for His people to honor (respect, support, and care for) parents. The Old Testament calls for believers to be ritually clean to approach God. Later the prophets applied the imagery to one's moral and ritual condition. Here Jesus focuses on the moral but shifts the emphasis. It is not immoral acts that make a person unclean. It is an unclean heart that expresses itself in wicked and immoral acts. We do not need to clean up our lives. We need to let God cleanse our hearts. Then our lives will be clean.

Identify the prejudices that exist among various social groups in the world today. Who are the people most likely to be rejected by the ruling majority? What is most unfair about such rejection? Notice that it was rare for Jesus to be traveling in a Gentile region and unheard of for him to engage in a verbal exchange with a foreign woman. What led this woman to approach Jesus? Why did he respond to her with some hesitation? What seems to have convinced Jesus to help the child of the woman? Have you ever gone against the norm to receive help? Maybe you lost your job and are now in the lines to receive food and vouchers to pay your bills. Did your pride make you hesitant to ask for help, or did you go out of your way to receive support? This woman did not care about who saw her or what they may have said. She knew that Jesus was her only hope. Jesus saw her sincerity and desperation, and He acted on her behalf.

III. A Woman's Faith (Matthew 15:21–28)

In the Old Testament vision of the prophets, the Kingdom Messiah was to set up Israel's kingdom. Jesus, the King, was sent only to the lost sheep of Israel in that Israel must be given the first opportunity to respond to Jesus. This persistent Canaanite woman, a Gentile, appealed to Jesus for help and acknowledged Him as Lord. Her daughter's healing illustrated the great truth that Israel had missed.

Relationship with God is a matter of faith. But we may question why God chose faith to be the attitude of heart by which we would obtain justification. Why could God not have decided to give justification to all those who sincerely show love? Or who shows joy? Or contentment? Or humility? Or wisdom? Why did God choose faith as the means by which we receive justification? It is because faith is the one attitude of heart that is the exact opposite of depending on ourselves. When we come to Christ in faith, we say, "I give up! I will not depend on myself or my good works any longer. I know that I can never make myself righteous before God. Therefore, Jesus, I trust you and depend on you completely to give me a righteous standing before God." In this way, faith is the exact opposite of trusting in ourselves, and therefore it is the attitude that perfectly fits salvation that depends not at all on our merit but entirely on God's gift of grace. Paul explains this when he says, "That is why it depends on faith, in order that the promise may rest on grace and be guaranteed to all his descendants" (Romans 4:16).

This is why the Reformers from Martin Luther were so firm in their insistence that justification comes not through faith plus some merit or good work on our part, but only through faith alone. "For by grace you have been saved through faith, and this is not your own doing, it is the gift of God—not because of works, lest any man should boast" (Ephesians 2:8–9). Paul repeatedly says that "no human being will be justified in his sight by works of the law" (Romans 3:20); the same idea is repeated in Galatians 2:16; 3:11; 5:4. But is this consistent with the epistle of James? What can James mean when he says, "You see that a man is justified by works and not by faith alone" (James 2:24)?

Here, we must realize that James is using the word justified differently from the way Paul uses it. At the beginning of this chapter, we noted that the word justify has a range of meanings and that one significant sense was "declare to be righteous," but we should also notice that the Greek word *dikaióo* (*Strong's Greek Lexicon*, G1467) can also mean "demonstrate or show to be righteous." For instance, Jesus said to the Pharisees, "You are those who justify yourselves before men, but God knows your hearts" (Luke 16:15). The point here was not that the Pharisees went around

making legal declarations that they were "not guilty" before God, but rather that they were always attempting to show others that they were righteous by their outward deeds. Jesus knew that the truth was otherwise: "But God knows your hearts" (Luke 16:15). Similarly, the lawyer who put Jesus to the test by asking what he should do to inherit eternal life answered Jesus' first question well. But when Jesus told him, "Do this, and you will live," he was unsatisfied. Luke tells us, "But he, desiring to justify himself said to Jesus, 'And who is my neighbor?'" (Luke 10:28–29). Now he was not desiring to give a legal pronouncement about himself that he was not guilty in God's sight; rather, he was desiring to "show himself righteous" before others who were listening.

Other examples of the word justify meaning "show to be righteous" can be found in Matthew 11:19; Luke 7:35; and Romans 3:4. Our interpretation of James 2 depends not only on the fact that "show to be righteous" is an acceptable sense for the word justified but also on the consideration that this sense fits well in the context of James 2. When James says, "Was not Abraham our father justified by works when he offered his son Isaac upon the altar?" (James 2:21), he refers to something later in Abraham's life, the story of the sacrifice of Isaac, which occurred in Genesis 22. This is long after the time recorded in Genesis 15:6, where Abraham believed God "and he reckoned it to him as righteousness." Yet this earlier incident at the beginning of Abraham's covenantal relationship with God is what Paul quotes and repeatedly refers to in Romans 4. Paul is talking about the time

God justified Abraham once and for all, reckoning righteousness to him as a result of his faith in God. But James is talking about something far later, after Abraham had waited many years for the birth of Isaac and then after Isaac had grown old enough to carry wood up the mountain for a sacrifice. At that point, Abraham was "shown to be righteous" by his works, and in that sense, James says that Abraham was "justified by works when he offered his son Isaac upon the altar" (James 2:21).

The more considerable concern of James in this section also fits this understanding. James is concerned to show that mere intellectual agreement with the gospel is a "faith" that is no faith at all. He is concerned about those who say they have faith but show no change in their lives. He says, "Show me your faith apart from your works, and I by my works will show you my faith" (James 2:18). "For as the body apart from the spirit is dead, so faith apart from works is dead" (James 2:26).

What do you notice about the acts of courage shown by the woman in approaching and imploring Jesus and shown by Jesus in healing her daughter? Was Jesus concerned about the thoughts of others? How does one find the courage to surmount cultural norms and rejection to make one's voice heard and heeded? List some types of people who may not be entirely welcome in your community or church. Maybe someone on drugs or homeless. Perhaps a single mother who is unemployed, or a troublesome teenager. Consider the barriers to their acceptance that exist. Discuss ways that you and your classmates can extend a welcome to these people.

What are miracles? Can they happen today? A consideration of the subject of

miracles is closely connected with God's providence, which was considered in the previous chapter. We argued that God exercises extensive, ongoing, sovereign control over all aspects of his creation. For example, one definition of a miracle is "a direct intervention of God in the world." But this definition assumes a deistic view of God's relationship to the world, in which the world continues on its own, and God only intervenes occasionally. This is certainly not the biblical view, according to which God makes the rain fall (Matthew 5:45), causes the grass to grow (Psalm 104:14), and continually carries along all things by His word of power (Hebrews 1:3).

Another definition of a miracle is "a more direct activity of God in the world." But to talk about a "more direct" working of God suggests that his ordinary providential activity is somehow not "direct" and again hints at a sort of deistic removal of God from the world. Another definition is "God working in the world without using means to bring about the results he wishes." Yet to speak of God working "without means" leaves us with very few, if any, miracles in the Bible, for it is hard to think of a miracle that came about with no means at all; in the healing of people, for example, some of the physical properties of the sick person's body were doubtless involved as part of the healing. When Jesus multiplied the loaves and fishes, He at least used the original five loaves and two fishes that were there. When He changed water to wine, He used it and made it wine. This definition seems to be inadequate.

Yet another definition of a miracle is "an exception to a natural law" or "God acting contrary to the laws of nature." But the phrase "laws of nature" in popular understanding implies that there are certain qualities inherent in the things that exist, "laws of nature" that operate independently of God and that God must intervene or "break" these laws for a miracle to occur. Once again, this definition does not adequately account for the biblical teaching of providence. Another definition of a miracle is "an event impossible to explain by natural causes." This definition is inadequate because: 1) It does not include God as the one who brings about the miracle; 2) It assumes that God does not use some natural causes when he works in an unusual or amazing way, and thus it assumes again that God only occasionally intervenes in the world; and 3) It will result in a significant minimizing of actual miracles and an increase in skepticism, since many times when God works in answer to prayer the result is amazing to those who prayed, but it is not absolutely impossible to explain by natural causes, especially for a skeptic who refuses to see God's hand at work. Therefore, the original definition given above, where a miracle is simply a less common way of God's working in the world, seems preferable and more consistent with the biblical doctrine of God's providence.

THE LESSON APPLIED

How do you relate to people on the outskirts of society without prejudice? What about the neighborhood surrounding your church? God is calling us to meet the needs of the oppressed in our communities. We are to listen and not judge them. We will win more souls for Christ when we listen more than talk. Our humility is needed to help others. Our actions and verbal sharing of the Gospel are what Christ desires.

LET'S TALK ABOUT IT

How can we believe the messianic implications of addressing Jesus as "Son of David?"

If we believe in the messianic implications of addressing Jesus as the "Son of David," we understand the lineage of Christ. We can trust in God's unlimited power and love to help all people.

HOME DAILY DEVOTIONAL READINGS
APRIL 29–MAY 5, 2024

MONDAY	TUESDAY	WEDNESDAY	THURSDAY	FRIDAY	SATURDAY	SUNDAY
Vindicate Me, O Lord My God	Blessed Are They Who Fear God	Repent and Turn to God	God So Loved the World	Lord, Lead Me in Your Righteousness	Christ Our Atoning Sacrifice	Atonement by Christ's Blood
Psalm 35:1–7, 22–28	Psalm 112	Acts 3:12–26	John 3:1–8, 13–17	Psalm 5	1 John 1:1–2:2	Romans 3:21–30

Justified by Faith in Jesus

Adult Topic: Background Scripture: Romans 3:21–30
No Need to Boast   Lesson Passage: Romans 3:21–30

Romans 3:21–30

King James Version

BUT now the righteousness of God without the law is manifested, being witnessed by the law and the prophets;

22 Even the righteousness of God which is by faith of Jesus Christ unto all and upon all them that believe: for there is no difference:

23 For all have sinned, and come short of the glory of God;

24 Being justified freely by his grace through the redemption that is in Christ Jesus:

25 Whom God hath set forth to be a propitiation through faith in his blood, to declare his righteousness for the remission of sins that are past, through the forbearance of God;

26 To declare, I say, at this time his righteousness: that he might be just, and the justifier of him which believeth in Jesus.

27 Where is boasting then? It is excluded. By what law? of works? Nay: but by the law of faith.

28 Therefore we conclude that a man is justified by faith without the deeds of the law.

29 Is he the God of the Jews only? is he not also of the Gentiles? Yes, of the Gentiles also:

30 Seeing it is one God, which shall justify the circumcision by faith, and uncircumcision through faith.

New Revised Standard Version

BUT now, apart from the law, the righteousness of God has been disclosed and is attested by the Law and the Prophets,

22 the righteousness of God through the faith of Jesus Christ for all who believe. For there is no distinction,

23 since all have sinned and fall short of the glory of God;

24 they are now justified by his grace as a gift, through the redemption that is in Christ Jesus,

25 whom God put forward as a sacrifice of atonement by his blood, effective through faith. He did this to demonstrate his righteousness, because in his divine forbearance he had passed over the sins previously committed;

26 it was to demonstrate at the present time his own righteousness, so that he is righteous and he justifies the one who has the faith of Jesus.

27 Then what becomes of boasting? It is excluded. Through what kind of law? That of works? No, rather through the law of faith.

28 For we hold that a person is justified by faith apart from works prescribed by the law.

29 Or is God the God of Jews only? Is he not the God of gentiles also? Yes, of gentiles also,

30 since God is one, and he will justify the circumcised on the ground of faith and the uncircumcised through that same faith.

MAIN THOUGHT: Even the righteousness of God which is by faith of Jesus Christ unto all and upon all them that believe: for there is no difference: For all have sinned, and come short of the glory of God; Being justified freely by his grace through the redemption that is in Christ Jesus (Romans 3:22–24, KJV)

LESSON SETTING
Time: AD 58
Place: Written in Corinth

LESSON OUTLINE
I. Background of Romans 1–2
II. Righteousness
(Romans 3:21–24)
III. Atonement
(Romans 3:25–31)

UNIFYING PRINCIPLE

People want to secure their fate through hard work and a well-earned reputation. Do we all get what we deserve? Paul tells the Roman believers that their boasting will be excluded in God's economy and that a person is justified by faith apart from work.

INTRODUCTION

Who gets the credit for your success? In this age of being "self-made" and being a "boss," God rarely gets the glory for our successes. People are known to brag about their accomplishments to make others envious. Moral differences appear in our world when we notice those who rely upon God and those who do not. When we credit ourselves for the successes of our lives, we exclude the unique power that God gives us. We are willing to use methods that do not glorify the Lord and steal from Him when we only have ourselves to please. We are eager to seek advice from those who live by the world's standards when we leave out God's plan. God desires that we include Him in our plans.

EXPOSITION

I. BACKGROUND OF ROMANS 1–2

Paul sees himself as a servant of Jesus Christ on a mission. What a positive way

for us to see ourselves, too. These verses affirm both the humanity and the deity of Jesus. As a descendant of David, His human nature qualifies Him to be Israel's Messiah. The literal, physical resurrection of Jesus didn't make Him God's Son but demonstrated conclusively that He is the Son of God. Recognizing this reality, Paul gives Jesus His appropriate title as deity: Jesus (personal name) Christ (Old Testament identity as Israel's promised Messiah), our Lord (identification with Yahweh, the personal name of God in the Old Testament). Servants live among God's people as one of them. They do not use their position to lift themselves above others; this was the attitude of Paul. The word *Gospel*, means "Good News."

The Christian Gospel is about Jesus (its contents) and reveals God's gift of righteousness (its significance). It brings salvation (its outcome) to all who believe (its invitation). Salvation has past, present, and future aspects. Faith in Christ is the key to experiencing every aspect of salvation—from first to last. The sin and injustice that mar society and make life so painful is a divine judgment on humanity for rejecting Jesus and choosing immorality. Crime and injustice express humankind's sinful nature and constitute a present divine judgment on sin. It is not that people cannot know the truth about God; the problem is they stifle the truth they know.

Creation is God's "radio station," conveying that God exists to all. Paul implies more. Human beings are created with an internal radio receiver. People see and understand this truth but suppress rather than respond to God's self-revelation.

Humanity's sinfulness is seen in wicked acts and how people respond to God. A couple on a date holds hands because they feel close and want to become closer. But when men "knew God," rather than worship Him, they quickly jerked their hands away to worship creatures rather than the Creator. Paul lists as consequences the ultimate depravities: in morals, character, wickedness, relationships, envy, murder, deceit, and malice; in politics, and greed, publicly approving those things they know God condemns.

When you read Romans 2, imagine Paul dialoguing with a Jew who enthusiastically endorses his condemnation of the Gentiles. Paul's stunning charge is that the Jews are self-righteous, doing the same thing they condemn the Gentiles for doing, ignoring the fact that God will judge their sins. Paul will soon show that no one truly does good. Here his purpose is not to describe a way of salvation but the fruit of salvation. When God judges our works, those who possess eternal life will persist in doing good, not to win salvation, but because they care about "glory, honor, and immortality," not the things of this world. The Greek word conscience is a dread accuser, constantly to mind the faults and failures of the past. Here, Paul teaches that this faculty, shared by all men, shows that God has planted a moral sense in human nature which stands in judgment on those same issues of personal and social relationships with which God's Law deals. God will not judge the pagan who does not know the standards revealed in Scripture by biblical Law. God will judge human beings by their sense of right and wrong, and the Day of Judgment will reveal that every human has failed to live by personal own standards, much less by God's!

Paul ironically reviews the basis for Jewish claims of spiritual superiority. But Jews break the Law, just as Gentiles violate their conscience, so the claim of superiority is an expression of raw pride. And the effect of that pride is that the Gentiles ridicule not only the hypocrisy of the Jews but also God! Circumcision is an outward, physical sign of membership in the covenant community. But a relationship with God requires an inner, spiritual circumcision of the heart. Apart from an inner transformation, all the Jew relies on for salvation is an empty sham. Every sin has a consequence. As we know, there are no little or big sins in the eyes of God. The spiritual consequence is always disappointment from God and guilt and shame if we feel conviction from the Holy Spirit. Conviction from the Holy Spirit is for our protection. God is not up in heaven trying to take away our fun. Think of a fenced-in yard. Your dog may want to run away with the neighbor's cat, but the fence protects him from other dogs and fast cars. Boundaries are made from love. God wants to protect us from spiritual and physical dangers. We cannot look into the future and discover what pitfalls await us.

Because God is all-knowing, His love compels us to be protected if we desire. He will never force Himself upon us. We will sin because we are sinners. However, when we accept Jesus, our list of sins should be shorter. We are now concerned about God's heart and the things that break His heart. Humans cannot atone for their sins; only God can do away with sin. Jesus Christ, God in human form, has paid the price for atonement. In the Old Testament, people had to sacrifice animals for their sins to be forgiven; in the New Testament, John called Jesus the Lamb, who takes away the "sin of the world." Because His perfect, unblemished blood was shed once, we no longer have to sacrifice animals to receive forgiveness. Christ came down from glory to save this sinful world!

II. RIGHTEOUSNESS (ROMANS 3:21–24)

Any righteousness found in Law must come from human acts. Any righteousness God provides must come from His actions. Take a minute to reflect on the presence of sin in the world today. What evidence shows us the prominence of sin's effects on how we live and operate in society? How do we ignore or acknowledge the reality of sin and God's gift of grace to us and the world? Is God mentioned in corporate America in a way that shows His sovereignty? Does America reflect Christian values? In your opinion, what has happened to the reverence for God that we once had?

We have a responsibility as Christians to respond to the righteousness of God; after all, that is what we signed up for when we accepted Jesus as our Lord and Savior. We are to be His examples in this dying world. Can God count on you to reflect Him amid an anti-Christ nation? Sure, it is easier to keep quiet when our faith is questioned, or our jobs are on the line, but what daily sacrifices do you make for God? When we rely upon God daily, others will see our commitment to Christ. They will observe how you are calm in desperate situations and how you can stand in the face of grief or job loss. Then when we talk to them about their relationship with God,

they will be more open to hearing our testimony and the Word of God. They will have evidence that serving Jesus is worth it. They will know that they need a Savior and where they spend eternity matters. We have a responsibility to share Jesus with those around us. How terrible it would be if someone in our circle missed heaven because we did not share how to get there with them.

III. ATONEMENT (ROMANS 3:25–31)

The NIV use of the word "atonement" here is weak. The Greek word draws on Greek culture, in which "propitiation" implied averting terrible punishments and moving the gods to act favorably, and Hebrew culture, in which "atonement" implies the sacrificial death of a substitute who takes the punishment and offender deserves. Jesus surrendered Himself to His death, represented in the shedding of His blood. As a substitute, He took the awesome penalty our sins deserved and thus saved us from the punishment we deserve.

The Jews believed passionately that Paul's teachings of grace and salvation undermined Law and thus denied God's Old Testament revelation. Paul says that the Gospel upholds Law, but gives it the place God always intended. We may define the atonement as Christ's work in His life and death to earn our salvation. This definition indicates that we are using the word atonement more broadly than it is sometimes used. Sometimes it refers only to Jesus' dying and paying for our sins on the cross. But, as will be seen below, we have included that in our definition since saving benefits also come to us from Christ's life. What was the ultimate cause that led to Christ's coming to earth and dying for our sins?

To find this, we must trace the question back to something in the character of God Himself. And here, Scripture points to two things: the love and justice of God. The love of God as a cause of the atonement is seen in the most familiar passage in the Bible: "For God so loved the world that he gave his only Son, that whoever believes in him should not perish but have eternal life" (John 3:16). But the justice of God also required that He establish a way that the penalty due to us for our sins would be paid (for He could not accept us into fellowship with Himself unless the penalty was paid). Paul explains that this was why God sent Christ to be a "propitiation" (Romans 3:25 NASB) (that is, a sacrifice that bears God's wrath so that God becomes "propitious" or favorably disposed toward us): it was "to show God's righteousness because in his divine forbearance, he had passed over former sins" (Romans 3:25). Here Paul says that God had forgiven sins in the Old Testament, but no penalty had been paid—a fact that would make people wonder whether God was indeed just and ask how He could forgive sins without a penalty.

When God sent Christ to die and pay the penalty for our sins, "it was to prove at the present time that he himself is righteous and that he justifies him who has faith in Jesus" (Romans 3:26). Therefore, both the love and the justice of God were the ultimate cause of the atonement. Both the love and the justice of God were equally important. Was there any other way for God to save humankind than by sending his Son to die in our place? Before answering this question, it is important to realize that God did not need to save any people. When we appreciate that "God did not spare the angels when they sinned, but cast them into hell and committed them to pits of nether gloom to be kept until the judgment" (2 Peter 2:4), then we realize that God could also have chosen with perfect justice to have left us in our sins awaiting judgment. He could have chosen to save no one, just as He did with the sinful angels. But once God, in His love, decided to save some human beings, then several passages in Scripture indicate that there was no other way for God to do this than through the death of His Son.

In the Garden of Gethsemane, Jesus prays, "If it be possible, let this cup pass from me; nevertheless, not as I will, but as you will" (Matthew 26:39). We can be confident that Jesus always prayed according to the will of the Father, and that He always prayed with the fullness of faith. Thus, it seems that this prayer, which Matthew takes pains to record, shows Jesus couldn't avoid the death on the cross that was soon to come to Him (the "cup" of suffering that He had said would be his). If He was going to accomplish the work the Father sent Him to do, and if people were going to be redeemed for God, then it was necessary for Him to die on the cross. He said something similar after His resurrection while talking with two disciples on the road to Emmaus. They were sad that Jesus had died, but His response was, "O foolish men, and slow of heart to believe all that the prophets have spoken! Was it not necessary that the Christ should suffer these things and enter into his glory?" (Luke 24:25–26).

Jesus understood that God's plan of redemption (which he explained to the disciples from many Old Testament

Scriptures, Luke 24:27) made it necessary for the Messiah to die for the sins of His people. Is prayer a regular part of your church's worship service? Why do you think that is so? The next time you hear the same prayers by the deacons or prayer leaders, think about their words. Do you sense sincerity in the ways that they pray? Corporate prayer is a collective summoning of God's power and authority. Look at the church's prayer list, see what prayers have been answered, and celebrate with the congregation.

Corporate prayers have the strength that individual prayers may lack. Also, coming together for prayer strengthens the witness of the church at-large. This is how we live as people who are justified and redeemed by God. Our daily activities should reflect a dependence on God, regular witnessing to the lost, Bible Study, fellowship, and helping the poor. When the church has that reputation, we will not have to worry about low attendance and a weak witness in the world. Shame will not keep people from Jesus if we are welcoming and brag about our Heavenly Father and how He has mercifully given us grace and redemption.

THE LESSON APPLIED

When we acknowledge our sins with humility, God is willing and able to save us. His forgiveness allows us to operate guilt-free in Him. Then we are to share this same forgiveness and grace with the world. After we are saved, we are still sinners who must continually turn to Christ for grace and forgiveness. This process is to be a mainstay of our walk with Him. We are to share this process with others and point them to Him. Jesus did what we could not do for ourselves. Paul says that we are to boast in Him, not ourselves.

LET'S TALK ABOUT IT

What does God's forgiveness in your life mean? God's forgiveness should cause us to be better in our relationship with the Lord. Consequently, there is great joy in seeing others come to know Jesus through His loving forgiveness. We are to accept God's grace with humility, and we should not take the attributes of God for granted. We are to honor Him in all we do and share that same gratitude with others.

GET SOCIAL

Share your views and tag us @rhboydco and use #Justified.

Twitter
@rhboydco (#rhboydco)

Instagram
@rhboydco (#rhboydco)

Facebook
@rhboydco (#rhboydco)

www.rhboyd.com

HOME DAILY DEVOTIONAL READINGS
MAY 6–12, 2024

MONDAY	TUESDAY	WEDNESDAY	THURSDAY	FRIDAY	SATURDAY	SUNDAY
God Is Generous to the Unworthy	A Great and Blessed Nation	A Promise of Countless Heirs	Little Children, Your Sins Are Forgiven	God's Abundant Forgiveness	Trust God, Who Justified the Ungodly	Christ Was Raised for Our Justification
Matthew 20:1–16	Genesis 13:14–18	Genesis 15:1–6	1 John 2:12–17	Psalm 32	Romans 4:1–12	Romans 4:13–25

RECKONED AS RIGHTEOUS

ADULT TOPIC:	BACKGROUND SCRIPTURE: ROMANS 4
FOR OUR SAKE	LESSON PASSAGE: ROMANS 4:13–25

ROMANS 4:13–25

King James Version

FOR the promise, that he should be the heir of the world, was not to Abraham, or to his seed, through the law, but through the righteousness of faith.

14 For if they which are of the law be heirs, faith is made void, and the promise made of none effect:

15 Because the law worketh wrath: for where no law is, there is no transgression.

16 Therefore it is of faith, that it might be by grace; to the end the promise might be sure to all the seed; not to that only which is of the law, but to that also which is of the faith of Abraham; who is the father of us all,

17 (As it is written, I have made thee a father of many nations,) before him whom he believed, even God, who quickeneth the dead, and calleth those things which be not as though they were.

18 Who against hope believed in hope, that he might become the father of many nations, according to that which was spoken, So shall thy seed be.

19 And being not weak in faith, he considered not his own body now dead, when he was about an hundred years old, neither yet the deadness of Sarah's womb:

20 He staggered not at the promise of God through unbelief; but was strong in faith, giving glory to God;

New Revised Standard Version

FOR the promise that he would inherit the world did not come to Abraham or to his descendants through the law but through the righteousness of faith.

14 For if it is the adherents of the law who are to be the heirs, faith is null and the promise is void.

15 For the law brings wrath, but where there is no law, neither is there transgression.

16 For this reason the promise depends on faith, in order that it may rest on grace, so that it may be guaranteed to all his descendants, not only to the adherents of the law but also to those who share the faith of Abraham (who is the father of all of us,

17 as it is written, "I have made you the father of many nations"), in the presence of the God in whom he believed, who gives life to the dead and calls into existence the things that do not exist.

18 Hoping against hope, he believed that he would become "the father of many nations," according to what was said, "So shall your descendants be."

19 He did not weaken in faith when he considered his own body, which was already as good as dead (for he was about a hundred years old), and the barrenness of Sarah's womb.

20 No distrust made him waver concerning the promise of God, but he grew strong in his faith as he gave glory to God,

MAIN THOUGHT: He staggered not at the promise of God through unbelief; but was strong in faith, giving glory to God; And being fully persuaded that, what he had promised, he was able also to perform. (Romans 4:20–21, KJV)

ROMANS 4:13–25

King James Version	New Revised Standard Version
21 And being fully persuaded that, what he had promised, he was able also to perform.	21 being fully convinced that God was able to do what he had promised.
22 Therefore his faith "was reckoned for righteousness.	22 Therefore "it was reckoned to him as righteousness."
23 Now it was not written for his sake alone, that it was imputed to him;	23 Now the words, "it was reckoned to him," were written not for his sake alone
24 But for us also, to whom it shall be imputed, if we believe on him that raised up Jesus our Lord from the dead;	24 but for ours also. It will be reckoned to us who believe in him who raised Jesus our Lord from the dead,
25 Who was delivered for our offences, and was raised again for our justification.	25 who was handed over for our trespasses and was raised for our justification.

LESSON SETTING
Time: AD 58
Place: Written in Corinth

LESSON OUTLINE
I. **Abraham and the Abrahamic Covenant (Romans 4:1–8)**
II. **Guaranteed Salvation (Romans 4:13–15)**
III. **Jesus: The Object of Our Faith (Romans 4:24–25)**

UNIFYING PRINCIPLE
People want to be rewarded for their good efforts. What successes do we hope to earn from our hard work? Paul tells the Roman Christians that the blessing God gave Abraham was "reckoned to him as righteousness" and that God does the same for us on account of Christ.

INTRODUCTION
Are you known to be a promise keeper? Due to life issues, we may not always be able to meet the needs of others entirely, and that may cause tension in our relationships. This is why we must constantly point others to Jesus, who is all-sufficient. What is your reaction when you are not fairly compensated for your work? Do you confront your boss or trust the Lord to make a way for you? Today's lesson teaches us that God can supply our needs and fight our battles.

EXPOSITION

I. ABRAHAM AND THE ABRAHAMIC COVENANT (ROMANS 4:1–8)
In the Bible, God's covenant is His freely-given promise. When the Lord covenants with Abraham, it becomes clearer how promise, sacrifice, law, and sign are related to each other, though the fullness of the covenant idea awaits Moses, the Exodus, and Mt. Sinai. In the case of Abram, the Lord came to him when he needed reassurance and hope, calling on him not to fear, pledging protection, and a coming "great reward." It is not clear why Abram needed such a word from God, but Genesis 15 offers a clue by dating it "After

this" following on the events of Genesis 14: the defeat of the kings, the restoration of the king of Sodom, and the refusal of any share in the spoils.

Reading between the lines, perhaps Abram was afraid of a counter-attack by the four kings. Did he begin to wonder if possibly his victory had, after all, been the Lord's intended way of bringing him into possession of the land and that he had thrown away his opportunity? Great victories are often followed by significant depressions and misgivings! But for whatever reasons, Abram needed present and future reassurance, and the Lord gave it only to provoke a further reminder that life was not worth living without a son and heir. How patient the Lord is! As if His earlier promises were not enough, He returned to comforting His servant with two specific promises: the promise of a son and a family and the promise of the land of Canaan for them to live in. Since Abram was still not reassured, the Lord initiated covenant proceedings.

The sacrifice detailed in Genesis 15:9–17 is unexplained—though it is clear that Abram knew and understood what he was doing. But light is cast by Jeremiah 34:18, where people who wanted to undertake a solemn oath walked between the severed pieces of sacrificial animals, implying as they did so, "If I do not keep my oath, so be it done to me." In Abram's case, he was marginalized by a spiritual coma when he had arranged the sacrifice. He was not the oath-taker, but rather, merely a spectator to what the Lord would do—reiterating the promise of descendants and land, He took His whole dire oath upon himself: he would bear the full brunt of the broken covenant. The vision of the Lord as a "smoking brazier with a blazing torch" was not explained to Abram. Still, in hindsight, we know it to be a preview of the God of Sinai in fire and smoke, the pillar of cloud and fire, the holy God who by grace shrouds His holiness to come among His people. But all this is left unexplained.

Genesis 15:18, however, is quite specific that the Abrahamic covenant was inaugurated by sacrifice. Fifteen years after he arrived in Canaan and thirteen years after the Hagar compromise, the Lord came to Abram to complete the covenant arrangement. In Genesis 15:18, the technical word for inaugurating a covenant is used; in Genesis 6:17, the verb means "to implement," to put into action.; In Genesis 17:2, "confirm" is literally "put, place," and signifies that from now on the covenant will be the changeless mode of the relationship between the Lord and Abram. The passage amplifies the covenant action of Genesis 15 by spelling out the promise and adding the remaining two components of Law and sign.

Typically patriarchal, the Law is nonspecific but is a searching requirement of holiness within a divine fellowship. The promise, however, is detailed, covering four categories: personal, domestic, spiritual, and territorial. The covenant is sealed with the covenant sign of circumcision. Since circumcision is specifically called "the sign of the covenant," it must be interpreted in the same way as the identical words in Genesis 19. Circumcision signifies, not what Abraham is pledging to God, but what God is pledging to Abraham. For this reason, Romans 4:11 calls circumcision a seal of the righteousness he had by faith:

not a seal of faith, as if ratifying Abraham's response, but "of righteousness," ratifying what God had done for Abraham and what He had promised to him. As Abraham still waited for the promised son to be born, he could strengthen himself in days of impatience or doubt by recalling that he bore in his very flesh the confirmation of the divine promises—just as, for Noah, the bow in the clouds dispelled any fears that a gathering storm might arouse. The sign in each case proclaimed the promises of God, just as the covenant signs of baptism and the Lord's Supper do today.

Abraham is the towering figure to whom the Jews traced their origins and special place as God's chosen people. By quoting Genesis 15:6, Paul proves the roots of Old Testament faith are also anchored in an imputed rather than earned righteousness. The idea of wages is the same in all cultures. "Wage" implies a transaction involving exchanging services for money. Paul insists that God does not relate to us as an employer, "paying" us with salvation in exchange for some service we render by doing what is right and good. Since we have all sinned, the only wage we have "earned" is death! Instead, God relates to us through the promise and freely gives us righteousness (salvation) if we have faith in Him. Since "wages" and "gift" are contradictory concepts, "law" and "promise" can never be mixed in relating to God.

We must choose to relate to salvation either by faith or by works. We cannot have it both ways. David's psalms show that God forgives the sins of the person who believes. Faith solves humankind's relationship problems. The man who believes is credited with righteousness, and his sins are forgiven.

Before his name change, God selected Abraham because of his level of righteousness that others did not possess. God chooses those whom He can trust to fulfill His promises and plans. Because Abram was a willing vessel, God used him as the father of many nations. He is known to have radical faith that some would say was blind faith. His lineage would eventually lead to the birth of Christ—the One chosen to save His people from their sins. As a result of his obedience and faith in God, Abraham's faith grew even stronger as he watched the Lord do what He said He would do. He trusted God with everything, leaving behind all that was familiar to him. Could you leave your family to follow God in another country? Is your faith strong enough to follow God to unknown circumstances and situations? Abraham had strong faith, but doubt was always a possibility.

II. Guaranteed Salvation (Romans 4:13–15)

If salvation depended on us, we would be lost. But since our salvation depends on God keeping His promise to those who believe, we have the most certain of any possible guarantees. Abraham was not free of sin but trusted God to do what He had said. Scripture shows how God used flawed men to carry out His plans. If God had discounted Abram, perhaps his life would have turned out differently, and we would not consider him a man of great faith. Do you have any sin that would disqualify you from serving Him? How complete is our trust in God? What can we do to show that we believe in God's promise to us in Christ? Even Abraham's wife, Sarah, had a different perspective about God's power when He told them that they would have a child; in fact, Sarah laughed at God's plan. Isaac's name means "he laughs." Her trust in God was different as it relates to Abraham's faith. Her responses showed that her faith was immature. Do you have people in your life whose faith is weaker than yours? How do you combat that when they do not believe what God has told you? People who doubt God's promises can hinder your faith if you let the doubt of others minimize God's work in your life. God has nothing to prove to anyone; however, when unbelievers see His power and authority, they can not help but recognize that He is who He says He is.

How does God relate to humanity? Since the earth's creation, God's relationship to humanity has been defined by specific requirements and promises. God tells people how He wants them to act and promises how He will act toward them in various circumstances. The Bible contains several summaries of the provisions that define the different relationships between God and humanity that occur in Scripture, and it often calls these summaries "covenants."

With respect to covenants between God and humanity in Scripture, we may give the following definition: a covenant is an unchangeable, divinely imposed legal agreement between God and humankind that stipulates the conditions of their relationship. Although this definition includes the word agreement to show that there are two parties, God and humanity, who must enter into the provisions of the relationship, the phrase "divinely imposed" is also included to show that man can never negotiate with God or change the terms of the covenant; he can only accept the covenant obligations or reject them. Probably for this reason, the Greek translators of the Old Testament (known as the Septuagint) and, following them, the New Testament authors did not use the ordinary Greek word for contracts or agreements in which both parties were equal (*sunthéke*), but rather, chose the less common, *diathéke* (*Strong's* G1347), which emphasized that the provisions of the covenant were laid down by one of the parties only. (In fact, the word *diathéke* was often used to refer to a "testament" or "will" that a person would leave to assign the distribution of their estate after death.)

This definition also notes that covenants are unchangeable. They may be superseded or replaced by a different covenant, but they may not be changed once established. Although there have been many additional details specified in the covenants God has made with humankind throughout the history of Scripture, the essential element at the heart of all of them is the promise, "I will be their God, and they shall be my people" (Jeremiah 31:33; 2 Corinthians 6:16; et al.).

III JESUS: THE OBJECT OF OUR FAITH (ROMANS 4:24–25)

Paul makes two vital points in Romans 3 and 4. In Romans 3:24–26, the offering of Jesus as an atoning sacrifice is the basis upon which God forgives the sins of both Old Testament and New Testament saints. But, Jesus has not always been the object of saving faith; for instance, Abraham did not know or believe that Christ would appear and die for him. What Abraham believed was God's promise that he and Sarah would have a child, despite their advanced age. God's promise was the object of a believer's faith. Today, however, the basis of salvation and the object of faith are one: Jesus Christ. All of God's promises are in and through Him, and faith in Jesus and Him alone saves today.

THE LESSON APPLIED

Our world has little faith in what the Lord can do. We brag about being "self-made" bosses unbothered by the world around us. God is mentioned when it is convenient—at a mass shooting, or maybe Christmas. Watch the news after a tornado or hurricane. Very few will give God the credit for sparing their lives. Many will say that "they got lucky" or that "somebody was on their side." There are award shows that openly mock God, and it is not an issue. As Christians, our outlook should differ because we know how God saved us and how He continually provides for us.

On this Mother's Day, consider those women who struggle with infertility.

Mother's Day is not always easy for those who cannot conceive, have lost children, do not have good relationships with their children, or have lost their mother. Yes, it is a day to honor those who are great mothers, but please be mindful of those who are saddened the day and be an extension of God's grace, love and mercy.

LET'S TALK ABOUT IT

1. **Have you ever thought about what it would be like to witness to those who are lost?**

Look up stories from "The Voice of Martyrs" to encourage your journey. Are you recognized for your great faith? The next generation needs worthy role models of strong faith. They are facing a faithless generation with many false religions and ideals from which to choose.

2. **Has your desire for other people to experience God's faithfulness increased?**

Just as we have been impressed with our ancestors' and Abraham's faith, let us pray that they will look to our generation with the same awe and gratitude.

HOME DAILY DEVOTIONAL READINGS
MAY 13–19, 2024

MONDAY	TUESDAY	WEDNESDAY	THURSDAY	FRIDAY	SATURDAY	SUNDAY
Trusting in God Brings Perfect Peace	The Penalty Has Been Paid	God's Spirit Poured upon All Flesh	The Firstfruits of Reconciliation	Brothers at Long Last Reconciled	May God Bless Us with Peace	Peace with God through Jesus Christ
Isaiah 26:1–11	Isaiah 40:1–11	Acts 2:1–4, 14, 16–24, 36	Acts 2:37–47	Genesis 33:1–15	Psalm 29	Romans 5:1–11

RECONCILED TO GOD

ADULT TOPIC: REMAINING STRONG	BACKGROUND SCRIPTURE: ROMANS 5:1–11 LESSON PASSAGE: ROMANS 5:1–11

ROMANS 5:1–11

King James Version

THEREFORE being justified by faith, we have peace with God through our Lord Jesus Christ:

2 By whom also we have access by faith into this grace wherein we stand, and rejoice in hope of the glory of God.

3 And not only so, but we glory in tribulations also: knowing that tribulation worketh patience;

4 And patience, experience; and experience, hope:

5 And hope maketh not ashamed; because the love of God is shed abroad in our hearts by the Holy Ghost which is given unto us.

6 For when we were yet without strength, in due time Christ died for the ungodly.

7 For scarcely for a righteous man will one die: yet peradventure for a good man some would even dare to die.

8 But God commendeth his love toward us, in that, while we were yet sinners, Christ died for us.

9 Much more then, being now justified by his blood, we shall be saved from wrath through him.

10 For if, when we were enemies, we were reconciled to God by the death of his Son, much more, being reconciled, we shall be saved by his life.

11 And not only so, but we also joy in God through our Lord Jesus Christ, by whom we have now received the atonement.

New Revised Standard Version

THEREFORE, since we are justified by faith, we have peace with God through our Lord Jesus Christ,

2 through whom we have obtained access to this grace in which we stand, and we boast in our hope of sharing the glory of God.

3 And not only that, but we also boast in our afflictions, knowing that affliction produces endurance,

4 and endurance produces character, and character produces hope,

5 and hope does not put us to shame, because God's love has been poured into our hearts through the Holy Spirit that has been given to us.

6 For while we were still weak, at the right time Christ died for the ungodly.

7 Indeed, rarely will anyone die for a righteous person—though perhaps for a good person someone might actually dare to die.

8 But God proves his love for us in that while we still were sinners Christ died for us.

9 Much more surely, therefore, since we have now been justified by his blood, will we be saved through him from the wrath of God.

10 For if while we were enemies we were reconciled to God through the death of his Son, much more surely, having been reconciled, will we be saved by his life.

11 But more than that, we even boast in God through our Lord Jesus Christ, through whom we have now received reconciliation.

MAIN THOUGHT: Then Jesus answered and said unto her, O woman, great is thy faith: be it unto thee even as thou wilt. And her daughter was made whole from that very hour. (Romans 5:1, KJV)

LESSON OUTLINE
   I. True Christianity
      (Romans 5:1)
   II. Why Do We Suffer?
      (Romans 5:2–5)
   III. God's Love
      (Romans 5:6–11)

UNIFYING PRINCIPLE

People feel guilty if they are unable to overcome their weaknesses and failures. How can we remain strong and confident even when we encounter failure? In the letter to the Christians in Rome, Paul instills hope and assures us that we are justified, not by works, but by faith in Jesus Christ.

INTRODUCTION

As he neared the end of his earthly journey, the late US Representative John Lewis encouraged the citizens of this country to get into "good trouble," or engage in actions to bring forth justice. In today's lesson, we will learn how our Lord, Jesus Christ, got into the best "good trouble" of all. Jesus, determined to see His mission through, was despised and rejected by many. Nevertheless, His sacrifice of dying on the cross and shedding His blood was the redemption that humankind needed. His shed blood covers our "bad trouble" or sins and reconciles us to our Heavenly Father.

EXPOSITION

I. TRUE CHRISTIANITY
(ROMANS 5:1)

All we enjoy as Christians, and all that Paul is about to explain, depends on the sacrifice of Christ for us and our faith in Him. Note specifically: peace with God, access to God, grace, joy in our future, a new perspective on suffering, and a confident hope in God that pays current dividends in the continuing sense of His love for us. Never dismiss true Christianity as a "pie in the sky." Relationship with Jesus is a banquet table piled high with a feast we can enjoy here and now.

Harriet Tubman, known as the "Moses of her people," had strong Christian convictions that American slavery was wrong and against God's plan for His people. She made over nineteen trips to freedom, freeing several hundred enslave people. She was able to live out her final years in the fight for the abolition of slavery. She is remembered for her extraordinary bravery and courage. Her faith in God secured her fight for freedom, and she was willing to die for it.

II. WHY DO WE SUFFER?
(ROMANS 5:2–5)

The new perspective on suffering is that it is for a positive purpose. Suffering identifies us with Christ, shaping us for our spiritual good. God's inexhaustible supply of love is poured out generously by the Holy Spirit, who lives within us. Whatever happens to us, we are surrounded by love. Our experience of death completes our union with Christ. Another reason God allows us to experience death, rather than taking us immediately to heaven when we become Christians, is that through death, we imitate Christ in what He did and thereby experience closer union with Him. Paul can say that we are fellow heirs with Christ "provided we suffer with him in order that we may also be glorified with him" (Romans 8:17). And Peter tells his readers not to be surprised at the fiery testing that comes on them, but encourages them, "rejoice in so far as you share Christ's sufferings that you may also rejoice and be glad when his glory is revealed" (1 Peter 4:13).

As we noted above, such union with Christ in suffering includes connection with him in death as well (see Phil. 3:10). Jesus is the "pioneer and perfecter of our faith" (Hebrews 12:2). We follow after him as we run the race of life. Peter writes, "Christ also suffered for you, leaving you an example, that you should follow in his steps" (1 Peter 2:21). Our obedience to God is more important than preserving our lives.

Suppose God uses the experience of death to deepen our trust in Him and to strengthen our obedience to Him. In that case, we must remember that the world's goal of preserving one's physical life at all costs is not the highest goal for a Christian; obedience to God and faithfulness to Him in every circumstance is far more important. This is why Paul could say, "I am ready not only to be imprisoned but even to die at Jerusalem for the name of the Lord Jesus" (Acts 21:13; cf. 25:11). He told the Ephesian elders, "I do not account my life of any value nor as precious to myself if only I may accomplish my course and the ministry which I received from the Lord Jesus, to testify to the gospel of the grace of God" (Acts 20:24). It was this conviction—that obedience to God is far more important than the preservation of life—that gave Paul courage to go back into the city of Lystra after he had just been stoned and left for dead (Acts 14:20), and then return there again shortly after that (Acts 14:21–22). He endured many sufferings and dangers (2 Corinthians 11:23–27), often risking his life to obey Christ fully. Therefore, he could say at the end of his life, with a note of great triumph, "The time of my departure has come. I have fought the good fight, I have finished the race, I have kept the faith" (2 Timothy 4:6–7).

This same conviction empowered Old Testament saints to accept martyrdom rather than sin: "Some were tortured, refusing to accept release, that they might rise again to a better life" (literally, "that they might obtain a better resurrection," Hebrews 11:35). This conviction also gave Peter and the other apostles courage, when facing the threat of death, to say, "We must obey God rather than men" (Acts 5:29). Certainly this was the point of Jesus' command to the church at Smyrna, "Be faithful unto death and I will give you the crown of life" (Revelations 2:10).

We also read that there will be rejoicing in heaven when the faithful saints have conquered the devil "by the blood of the Lamb and by the word of their testimony, for they loved not their lives even unto death" (Revelations 12:11). The persuasion that we may honor the Lord even in our death, and that faithfulness to Him is far more important than preserving our lives, has given courage and motivation to martyrs throughout the history of the church. When faced with a choice of preserving their own lives and sinning, or giving up their own lives and being faithful, they chose to give up their own lives—"they loved not their lives even unto death" (Revelations 12:11). Even in times where there is little persecution and little likelihood of martyrdom, it would be good for us to fix this truth in our minds once for all, for if we are willing to give up even our lives for faithfulness to God, we shall find it much easier to give up everything else for the sake of Christ as well.

III. GOD'S LOVE
(ROMANS 5:6–11)

Christ's willingness to die for us when we were sinners is undeniable proof of God's amazing love. How foolish to suppose that God, who showed such love for us when we were enemies, would ever desert us now that we are His own. Theologians delight in this passage and debate how "death came to all men" through Adam's sin. But Paul's point is practical. Our racial heritage from Adam is one of sin, death, and alienation. But now we belong to Christ, the founder of a new race, and our heritage in Him is righteousness and life. Death is a complex term in both Testaments.

Here it is not so much biological as a description of humanity's spiritual condition, powerless in the grasp of an inner moral corruption that alienates human beings from God and makes final judgment dreaded certainty. Adam's sin insinuated biological and spiritual death into our race, making our present and future dark and grim. In contrast, Jesus interjects life, the opposite of death, making us alive to God and guaranteeing a bright, eternal future. God's love means that God eternally gives of Himself to others. This definition understands love as self-giving for the benefit of others. This attribute of God shows that it is part of His nature to give of Himself in order to bring about blessings or good for others. John tells us that "God is love" (1 John 4:8). We see evidence that this attribute of God was active even before creation among the members of the Trinity. Jesus speaks to His Father of "my glory which you have given me in your love for me before the foundation of the world" (John 17:24), thus indicating that there was love and a giving of honor from the Father to the Son from all eternity. It continues at present, for we read, "The Father loves the Son, and has given all things into his hand" (John 3:35). This love is also reciprocal, for Jesus says, "I do as the Father has commanded me, so that the world may know that I love the Father" (John 14:31).

The love between the Father and the Son also presumably characterizes their relationship with the Holy Spirit. This eternal love of the Father for the Son, the Son for the Father, and both for the Holy Spirit makes heaven a world of love and joy because each person of the Trinity seeks to bring joy and happiness to the other two. The self-giving that characterizes the Trinity clearly expresses God's relationship to humankind, especially to sinful men. "In this is love, not that we loved God but that he loved us and sent his Son to be the propitiation for our sins" (1 John 4:10, author's translation). Paul writes, "God shows his love for us in that while we were yet sinners Christ died for us" (Romans. 5:8). John also writes, "For God so loved the world that he gave his only Son, that whoever believes in him should not perish but have eternal life" (John 3:16). Paul also speaks of "the Son of God, who loved me and gave himself for me" (Galatians 2:20), thus showing an awareness of the direct personal application of Christ's love to individual sinners.

It should cause us great joy to know that it is the purpose of God the Father, Son, and Holy Spirit to give of themselves to us to bring us true joy and happiness. It is God's nature to act that way toward those upon whom He has set His love, and He will continue to act that way toward us for all eternity. We imitate this communicable attribute of God, first by loving God in return and second by loving others in imitation of the way God loves them. All our obligations to God are summarized: "You shall love the Lord your God with all your heart, and with all your soul, and with all your mind....You shall love your neighbor as yourself" (Matthew 22:37–38).

If we love God, we will obey His commandments (1 John 5:3) and thus do what is pleasing to Him. We will love God, not the world (1 John 2:15), and we will do all this because He first loved us (1 John 4:19). It is one of the most amazing facts in all Scripture, just as God's love involves His giving of Himself to make us happy, so we can in return give of ourselves and bring joy to God's heart. Isaiah promises God's people, "As the bridegroom rejoices over the bride, so shall your God rejoice over you" (Isaiah 62:5), and Zephaniah tells God's people, "The Lord, your God, is in your midst...he will rejoice over you with gladness, he will renew you in his love; he will exult over you with loud singing as on a day of festival" (Zephaniah 3:17–18). Our imitation of God's love is seen in our love for others. John makes this explicit: "Beloved, if God so loved us, we also ought to love one another" (1 John 4:11). In fact, our love for others within the fellowship of believers is so evidently an imitation of Christ that by it the world recognizes us as His: "By this all men will know that you are my disciples, if you have love for one another" (John 13:35; cf. 15:13; Romans 13:10; 1 Corinthians 13:4–7; Hebrews 10:24).

God Himself gives us His love to enable us to love each other (John 17:26; Romans 5:5). Moreover, our love for our enemies especially reflects God's love (Matthew 5:43–48). God's mercy, patience, and grace may be seen as three different attributes or aspects of God's goodness. The definitions given here show these attributes as notable examples of God's goodness when used to benefit specific classes of people. God's mercy means God's goodness toward those in misery and distress. God's grace means God's goodness toward those who deserve only punishment. God's patience means God's goodness in withholding punishment toward those who sin. God says, "I will be gracious to whom I will be gracious, and will show mercy on whom I will show mercy" (Exodus 33:19, quoted in Romans 9:15). Yet, God is regularly gracious toward His people: "Turn to me and be gracious to me, After Thy manner with those who love Thy name" (Psalm 119:132, NASB). In fact, Peter called Him "the God of all grace" (1 Peter 5:10).

Grace, as God's goodness especially shown to those who do not deserve it, is seen frequently in Paul's writings. He emphasizes that salvation by grace is the opposite of human effort, for grace is a freely given gift. "Since all have sinned and fall short of the glory of God, they are justified by his grace as a gift, through the redemption which is in Christ Jesus" (Romans 3:23–24). The distinction between grace and salvation earned by works that merit a reward is also seen in Romans 11:6: "But if it is by grace, it is no longer on the basis of works; otherwise grace would no longer be grace." Grace, then, is God's favor freely given to those who do not deserve this favor. Paul also sees that if grace is unmerited, then there is only one human attitude appropriate as an instrument for receiving such grace, namely, faith: "That is why it depends on faith, in order that the promise may rest on grace" (Romans 4:16).

Faith is the one human attitude that is the opposite of depending on oneself, for it involves trust in or dependence upon another. Thus, it is devoid of self-reliance or attempts to gain righteousness by human effort. If God's favor is to come to us apart from our own merit, then it must come when we have faith not in our works but on the merits of God's Son, Jesus Christ. Faith in Him and in what He has done are the key points that enable us to relate personally to Him. Through faith, Jesus Christ becomes our Lord and personal Savior.

THE LESSON APPLIED

Adults worldwide endure suffering for the sake of their faith in Christ. As we mature in Christ, we grow in our assurance that God will be with us in our every weakness. Then we can boast even more about the goodness of the Lord. Faith acts as the conduit that justifies us before God. It aligns us to His will and purpose. When we are justified or set right with God, it brings us into a closer relationship with Him. The closer we are to God means that His character is reflected in us and we become more like His Son, Jesus Christ.

LET'S TALK ABOUT IT

Where can we find peace with God?

We can have true peace as we rely on Jesus Christ for salvation from sin. Further, we can become more aware of being justified by faith in what God does, not in what we do. We know that God desires all people to be reconciled to Him. His peace then becomes ours. When we are reconciled to Him, John 16:33–34 becomes our motto. We experience tranquility through what He has done to satisfy our spiritual need of His divine presence.

GET SOCIAL

Share your views and tag us @rhboydco and use #Reconciled.

Twitter
@rhboydco (#rhboydco)

Instagram
@rhboydco (#rhboydco)

Facebook
@rhboydco (#rhboydco)

www.rhboyd.com

HOME DAILY DEVOTIONAL READINGS MAY 20–26, 2024						
MONDAY	**TUESDAY**	**WEDNESDAY**	**THURSDAY**	**FRIDAY**	**SATURDAY**	**SUNDAY**
Call On God and Be Saved	Striving on the Basis of Faith	All Israel Will Be Saved	God's Word Is Very Near	Do Not Fear, Only Believe	A Beautiful Announcement of Salvation	Confession and Belief Lead to Salvation
Joel 2:28–32	Romans 9:14–16, 25–33	Romans 11:1–4, 17–27	Deuteronomy 30:11–20	Mark 5:35–43	Isaiah 52	Romans 10:1–17

WHO HAS BELIEVED?

ADULT TOPIC:	BACKGROUND SCRIPTURE: ROMANS 10:1–21
HEARING AND BELIEVING	LESSON PASSAGE: ROMANS 10:1–17

ROMANS 10:1–17

King James Version

BRETHREN, my heart's desire and prayer to God for Israel is, that they might be saved.

2 For I bear them record that they have a zeal of God, but not according to knowledge.

3 For they being ignorant of God's righteousness, and going about to establish their own righteousness, have not submitted themselves unto the righteousness of God.

4 For Christ is the end of the law for righteousness to every one that believeth.

5 For Moses describeth the righteousness which is of the law, That the man which doeth those things shall live by them.

6 But the righteousness which is of faith speaketh on this wise, Say not in thine heart, Who shall ascend into heaven? (that is, to bring Christ down from above:)

7 Or, Who shall descend into the deep? (that is, to bring up Christ again from the dead.)

8 But what saith it? The word is nigh thee, even in thy mouth, and in thy heart: that is, the word of faith, which we preach;

9 That if thou shalt confess with thy mouth the Lord Jesus, and shalt believe in thine heart that God hath raised him from the dead, thou shalt be saved.

10 For with the heart man believeth unto righteousness; and with the mouth confession is made unto salvation.

11 For the scripture saith, Whosoever believeth on him shall not be ashamed.

New Revised Standard Version

BROTHERS and sisters, my heart's desire and prayer to God for them is that they may be saved.

2 For I can testify that they have a zeal for God, but it is not based on knowledge.

3 Not knowing the righteousness of God and seeking to establish their own, they have not submitted to God's righteousness.

4 For Christ is the culmination of the law so that there may be righteousness for everyone who believes.

5 Moses writes concerning the righteousness that comes from the law, that "the person who does these things will live by them."

6 But the righteousness that comes from faith says, "Do not say in your heart, 'Who will ascend into heaven?'" (that is, to bring Christ down)

7 "or 'Who will descend into the abyss?'" (that is, to bring Christ up from the dead).

8 But what does it say? "The word is near you, in your mouth and in your heart" (that is, the word of faith that we proclaim),

9 because if you confess with your mouth that Jesus is Lord and believe in your heart that God raised him from the dead, you will be saved.

10 For one believes with the heart, leading to righteousness, and one confesses with the mouth, leading to salvation.

11 The scripture says, "No one who believes in him will be put to shame."

MAIN THOUGHT: Even the righteousness of God which is by faith of Jesus Christ unto all and upon all them that believe: for there is no difference: For all have sinned, and come short of the glory of God; Being justified freely by his grace through the redemption that is in Christ Jesus (Romans 10:9, KJV)

ROMANS 10:1–17

King James Version	*New Revised Standard Version*
12 For there is no difference between the Jew and the Greek: for the same Lord over all is rich unto all that call upon him.	12 For there is no distinction between Jew and Greek; the same Lord is Lord of all and is generous to all who call on him.
13 For whosoever shall call upon the name of the Lord shall be saved.	13 For "everyone who calls on the name of the Lord shall be saved."
14 How then shall they call on him in whom they have not believed? and how shall they believe in him of whom they have not heard? and how shall they hear without a preacher?	14 But how are they to call on one in whom they have not believed? And how are they to believe in one of whom they have never heard? And how are they to hear without someone to proclaim him?
15 And how shall they preach, except they be sent? as it is written, How beautiful are the feet of them that preach the gospel of peace, and bring glad tidings of good things!	15 And how are they to proclaim him unless they are sent? As it is written, "How beautiful are the feet of those who bring good news!"
16 But they have not all obeyed the gospel. For Esaias saith, Lord, who hath believed our report?	16 But not all have obeyed the good news, for Isaiah says, "Lord, who has believed our message?"
17 So then faith cometh by hearing, and hearing by the word of God.	17 So faith comes from what is heard, and what is heard comes through the word of Christ.

LESSON SETTING
Time: AD 58
Place: Written in Corinth

LESSON OUTLINE
I. **Who Are My Brothers?**
   (Romans 10:1–5)
II. **Mouth and Heart**
   (Romans 10:6–12)
III. **Good News for All**
   (Romans 10:12–17)

UNIFYING PRINCIPLE
People want to follow prescribed steps that allow them to climb a guaranteed ladder to success. How do we react when others are offered a path to success that seemingly bypasses our carefully followed rules? In his letter to the Romans, Paul wrestles with the insufficiency of the zeal for God that comes through the Law versus the new path to God that comes through faith in Christ.

INTRODUCTION
Confession is defined as an admission of sins and a profession of belief in the doctrines of a particular faith. The Bible also uses the word *confession* to describe an open, bold, and courageous proclamation of one's faith. In the world, we have to earn the love of others. In Christ, we are born loved! God wants our hearts and our allegiance. We may not be recognized for our service in the world, but Christ rewards us eternally. Our lives and tongues should confess that Jesus is the only One who can save us. He is the only One qualified due to His willing death on the cross. Because of His sacrifice, we do not have to work for our salvation. Jesus already did the work! He asks us to live for Him, expecting a reward for our faithfulness. This reward far outweighs any human efforts to pay us for our work on

earth. In today's lesson, the Apostle Paul shares how the Law served its purpose, but faith in Jesus is the way to salvation.

EXPOSITION

I. WHO ARE MY BROTHERS? (ROMANS 10:1–5)

The Apostle Paul addresses his natural brothers, the Jews, not his brothers in Christ. While faith in Jesus creates a unique family relationship between believers, you and I, like Paul, retain close ties with the yet unconverted. Let's follow Paul's example and continue to identify with and care deeply for them. The Greek word *teleos* indicates the achievement of an intended goal and the completion of a process. It shows that Christ is the logical end of the Law, implying that the Law unveiled sin in such a way that human beings were forced to turn to Jesus to obtain righteousness. Verse 4 in this passage may mean that Law has ended because Christ has superseded it, or it may mean the Apostle Paul had an ongoing concern for Jews and Gentiles. Remember that the Roman church included Jews and Gentiles, as did other early churches. He desired that all persons be saved once they come into the knowledge of Jesus Christ.

Our hearts and mouths must be aligned to fully accept the Gospel and all that Jesus desires for us. Our mouth reflects what our heart believes. It is hard to separate the two. By having our hearts and mouth state who Jesus is and what He came to do, there is no mistaking what we believe. Confession shows God and those around us what we are willing to stand for regarding our faith. This practice shows up in other areas of our lives as well. If we believe God, it will show up in what we confess and exhibit. Paul outlines the plan of salvation very clearly in these verses; there is no other way in which human beings might be saved.

Are there degrees of sin? Are some sins worse than others? In terms of our legal standing before God, any one sin, even what may seem to be a very small one, makes us legally guilty before God and, therefore, worthy of eternal punishment. Adam and Eve learned this in the Garden of Eden, where God told them that one act of disobedience would result in the penalty of death. And Paul affirms that the judgment following one trespass brought condemnation. This one sin made Adam and Eve sinners before God, unable to stand in His holy presence. This truth remains valid throughout the history of the human race. Paul affirms it: "Cursed be everyone who does not abide by all things written in the book of the law, and do them." And James declares, "Whoever keeps the whole law but fails in one point has become guilty of breaking all of it. For he who said, 'Do not commit adultery,' also said, 'Do not kill.' If you do not commit adultery but do kill, you have become a transgressor of the law" (James 2:11–20).

Thank God for His plan for us to be saved through Jesus Christ! Jesus took on all the pain and suffering for our sins so that we would not have to endure spiritual death due to our iniquities. Jesus was obedient to His Father. If we live the rest of our days for Him, He is pleased to reward us for our faithfulness. Hell was not designed for His children, and our Heavenly Father does not want any of us to perish. He gives us chance after chance to be made right in His sight. Jesus gave His life so we could live with our Heavenly Father forever. Yes, we will still sin, but our "sin list" should be shorter and shorter as we mature in Christ; we no longer brag about our sins or make our sins small, but we use our old ways as an example of how not to live anymore. Our testimony should always point back to what Jesus did for us, not what we did as sinners who did not have Christ.

II. MOUTH AND HEART (ROMANS 10:6–12)

The word *heart* is used in its Old Testament broad sense to indicate the whole person, the conscious self, with every spiritual, intellectual, and rational sense. A heart belief, or a heart response to the Gospel, is a whole response. It is not just intellectual belief about who Jesus is, but a total commitment to Him. The heart represents man's inner nature, and the mouth expresses that inner nature in this world. There is no such term as a secret believer. If we genuinely commit to Jesus, our lives will express that commitment without wavering. Paul indeed distinguishes a person who is natural from one that is spiritual. Spiritual means influenced by the Holy Spirit. Our spirit makes us different from animals, and our spirit comes alive at regeneration. The essential nature of man is soul and spirit because our flesh will physically die. The Scriptures use soul and spirit interchangeably. Justification is a priceless gift from God because unclean human actions cannot enact the process. Justification happens by a holy God through Jesus Christ, the perfect Lamb. If you wash dishes with dirty water, the process is already tainted. You have wasted your time. Only a holy God can justify us through the sacrifice

that only He has chosen. Study verses 14–15. What is your understanding of the step-by-step progression outlined by Paul of hearing, believing, and sharing the good news of salvation? Where are you in faith and action? Paul outlines the justification process so clearly that it is difficult to dispute. Our salvation is whole and complete. Jesus will not take it back; it is sealed for eternity. We no longer have to sacrifice animals to make ourselves right with God. That is good news! God's invitation is still open, and He continues to offer salvation to the lost. The Bible is necessary for the knowledge of the Gospel. This statement follows this line of reasoning: 1) It first assumes that one must call upon the name of the Lord to be saved; 2) People can only call upon the name of Christ if they believe in Him as a Savior worthy of calling upon and will answer those who call; 3) People cannot believe in Christ unless they have heard of Him; 4) They cannot hear of Christ unless someone tells them about Christ, i.e., a preacher; 5) The conclusion is that saving faith comes by hearing (that is, by hearing the Gospel message), and this hearing of the Gospel message comes through the preaching of Christ. The implication seems to be that no one can be saved without hearing the preaching of the Gospel of Christ. This passage is one of several that teaches eternal salvation comes only through belief in Jesus Christ and not other ways. Jesus states clearly that He is "The Way, the Truth, and the Life" in John 14:6.

III. GOOD NEWS FOR ALL (ROMANS 10:12–17)

The practical implications of the doctrine of justification by faith alone are very significant. First, this doctrine enables us to offer genuine hope to unbelievers who know they could never make themselves righteous before God; if salvation is a free gift to be received through faith alone, then anyone who hears the Gospel may hope that eternal life is freely offered and may be obtained.

Second, this doctrine gives us confidence that God will never make us pay the penalty for sins that have been forgiven on Christ's merits. Of course, we may continue to suffer the ordinary consequences of sin (alcoholics and thieves may still go to jail or have family issues). Moreover, God may discipline us if we continue to act in ways that are disobedient to Him, doing this out of love and for our own good. But God can never or will ever take vengeance on us for past sins or make us pay the penalty that is due for them or punish us out of wrath and for the purpose of doing harm. "There is therefore no condemnation for those that are in Christ Jesus" (Romans 8:1). This fact should give us a great sense of joy and confidence before God that we are accepted by Him and that we stand before Him as "not guilty" and "righteous" forever.

The wonderful fact of justification is that it is permanent. We do not have a faith or a Savior who can be changed. The Bible talks about our salvation being sealed and as far as Paul was concerned, baptism in the Holy Spirit happens at conversion. He said that all the Corinthians were baptized in the Holy Spirit and the result was that they became members of the body of Christ. This baptism cleanses us and gives a clear break with the power and love of sin—the initial stage of sanctification. In this way, the baptism of the Holy Spirit refers to all that the Holy Spirit does at the beginning of our Christian lives. Everyone has equal standing with God. We are all sinners, but we are all invited to believe and be saved. The Gospel imperative is embedded deeply in these verses.

People need to hear if they are to believe. That means they need a messenger. The lone fact of that need, coupled with the fact that we have the Gospel, shows a divine Great Commission. We do not need a special call to challenge yourself to practice open confession of your faith in Christ. What next step is God calling you to take? Write down what Jesus' sacrifice means to you. Make a chart reflecting how the Christian faith is different from Muslims, Mormons, etc. Do some research on other religions and faith practices. Provide a prayer that the group can pray aloud together.

THE LESSON APPLIED

The Apostle Paul hoped for the salvation of Israel. He affirmed that the nation had a zeal for God, but that it had not been enlightened. Israel's refusal to accept Jesus as the Messiah was the real issue. However, without Jesus as Lord and Savior, her righteousness was not righteousness at all. Only Jesus lived a sinless life and embodied all of the qualities that satisfied the standard of righteousness required by God for human salvation (see 2 Corinthians 5:21; Hebrews 4:15; 1 Peter 2:22; 1 John 3:5). In other words, Jesus is essential to the salvation of Israel and to our salvation as well. He is the One through whom salvation is made possible. This text resoundingly states this fact.

Three things are important for us as we consider Jesus as the One-born, Son. First, faith in Him is essential. The call of the Fourth Evangelist is for readers to believe (John 3:16). Believe in Him is the objective for humanity. Faith is the conduit that plugs into His gracious acts of goodness and righteousness that give us the ability to communicate His presence in our lives to God Almighty It also provides us with the opportunity to be justified before God, that is to be made right with God. Second, closely akin to pistos (faith) is trust. Our salvation is predicated on trust, the deep abiding assurance that Jesus is the "Real McCoy," and that we can count on Him to do what He has promised. In John 14–16, Jesus spoke of protecting the disciples and them learning to trust Him completely. Trust is a viable part of what it means to be a true disciple.

Third, we must be obedient to His commandments. We are called to obedience. The Johannine writings inform us, "If you love Me keep My commandments (John 14–16). Love is an event that compels us to act on our faith. We must see it through. Love illustrates through our actions that we prefer Jesus' way of life over all other ways. Therefore, His righteousness is noted by both God and us as being supreme and it bridges the gap between human failure and God's standard of righteousness. Israel can be saved as can all other people. Christians must be willing to carry the message of divine salvation to a world that is lost in sin, but desires and needs to try a better way. Presenting the truth of Jesus is the way to do it. Proclaiming His truth with our voices and living His truth daily will allow us to paint a picture of God's abundant love that the world needs to see.

LET'S TALK ABOUT IT

What helps us to grow in our faith?

We should desire to grow in our faith. Our faith may not be as strong as the Apostle Paul's, but our faith should positively impact those around us. What is the legacy that you want to leave? Generations to come should be able to look at our faith and be inspired just as we are by the bold confidence of the Apostle Paul.

GET SOCIAL

Share your views and tag us @rhboydco and use #GoodNewsForAll.

Twitter
@rhboydco (#rhboydco)

Instagram
@rhboydco (#rhboydco)

Facebook
@rhboydco (#rhboydco)

www.rhboyd.com

HOME DAILY DEVOTIONAL READINGS
MAY 27–JUNE 2, 2024

MONDAY	TUESDAY	WEDNESDAY	THURSDAY	FRIDAY	SATURDAY	SUNDAY
God's Witnesses	Praise the Lord!	God's Children in Christ through Faith	The Lord's Blessing Makes Rich	Your Treasure Is with Your Heart	Seek First God's Kingdom	Christ, the Most Precious Gift
Isaiah 43:8–13	Psalm 113	Galatians 3:19–29	Proverbs 10:19–25	Matthew 6:19–24	Matthew 6:25–34	Colossians 1:24—2:3

Fourth Quarter

June

July

August

HOPE AMID SUFFERING

| ADULT TOPIC: | BACKGROUND SCRIPTURE: COLOSSIANS 1:19–2:5 |
| GLORIOUS RICHES | LESSON PASSAGE: COLOSSIANS 1:24–2:3 |

COLOSSIANS 1:24–2:3

King James Version

WHO now rejoice in my sufferings for you, and fill up that which is behind of the afflictions of Christ in my flesh for his body's sake, which is the church:

25 Whereof I am made a minister, according to the dispensation of God which is given to me for you, to fulfil the word of God;

26 Even the mystery which hath been hid from ages and from generations, but now is made manifest to his saints:

27 To whom God would make known what is the riches of the glory of this mystery among the Gentiles; which is Christ in you, the hope of glory:

28 Whom we preach, warning every man, and teaching every man in all wisdom; that we may present every man perfect in Christ Jesus:

29 Whereunto I also labour, striving according to his working, which worketh in me mightily.

• • • • • •

1 For I would that ye knew what great conflict I have for you, and for them at Laodicea, and for as many as have not seen my face in the flesh;

2 That their hearts might be comforted, being knit together in love, and unto all riches of the full assurance of understanding, to the acknowledgement of the mystery of God, and of the Father, and of Christ;

3 In whom are hid all the treasures of wisdom and knowledge.

New Revised Standard Version

I AM now rejoicing in my sufferings for your sake, and in my flesh I am completing what is lacking in Christ's afflictions for the sake of his body, that is, the church.

25 I became its minister according to God's commission that was given to me for you, to make the word of God fully known,

26 the mystery that has been hidden throughout the ages and generations but has now been revealed to his saints.

27 To them God chose to make known how great among the gentiles are the riches of the glory of this mystery, which is Christ in you, the hope of glory.

28 It is he whom we proclaim, warning everyone and teaching everyone in all wisdom, so that we may present everyone mature in Christ.

29 For this I toil and strive with all the energy that he powerfully inspires within me.

• • • • • •

1 For I want you to know how greatly I strive for you and for those in Laodicea and for all who have not seen me face to face.

2 I want their hearts to be encouraged and united in love, so that they may have all the riches of assured understanding and have the knowledge of God's mystery, that is, Christ,

3 in whom are hidden all the treasures of wisdom and knowledge.

MAIN THOUGHT: I want their hearts to be encouraged and united in love, so that they may have all the riches of assured understanding and have the knowledge of God's mystery, that is, Christ, in whom are hidden all the treasures of wisdom and knowledge. (Colossians 2:2–3, KJV)

LESSON OUTLINE

  I. **Paul's Motive and Purpose (Colossians 1:24–29)**
  II. **Concern for the Colossians (Colossians 2:1–3)**

UNIFYING PRINCIPLE

Physical or emotional suffering may cloud the heart and diminish hope for a brighter tomorrow. How might hope be restored? Paul rejoices in suffering for the faith as he shares the mystery of the Gospel with Gentiles, which affirms Christ in them, the hope of glory.

INTRODUCTION

To give some context for the culture and environment, Colossae was a city in Phrygia, in the Roman province of Asia (part of modern Turkey), about one hundred miles east of Ephesus (in the region of the seven churches of Revelation chapters 1–3). The city lay alongside the Lycus River, not far from where it flowed into the Meander River. Colossae was once a thriving city in the fifth century BC, when the Persian King Xerxes (Esther 1:1) marched through the region. Black wool and dyes (made from the nearby chalk deposits) were important products. In addition, the city was situated at the junction of the main north–south and east–west trade routes. By Paul's day, however, the main road had been rerouted through nearby Laodicea, thus bypassing Colossae and leading to its decline and the rise of the neighboring cities of Laodicea and Hierapolis.

Although Colossae's population was mainly Gentile, there was a large Jewish settlement present as well. Colossae's mixed population of Jews and Gentiles manifested itself both in the composition of the church and in the heresy that plagued it, which contained elements of both Jewish legalism and pagan mysticism. The church at Colossae began during Paul's three-year ministry at Ephesus (Acts 19). Its founder was not Paul, who had never been there (Colossians 2:1), but Epaphras (Colossians 1:5–7), who apparently was saved during a visit to Ephesus, then likely started the church in Colossae when he returned home.

Several years after the Colossian church was founded, a dangerous heresy arose to threaten it, one not identified with any particular historical system. It contained elements of what later became known as gnosticism: that God is good, but the matter is evil; that Jesus Christ was merely one of a series of emanations descending from God and, being less than God (a belief that led them to deny His humanity); and that a secret, higher knowledge about Scripture was necessary for enlightenment and salvation. Colossian heresy also embraced aspects of Jewish legalism— the necessity of circumcision for salvation, observance of the ceremonial rituals of the Old Testament law (dietary laws, festivals, Sabbaths), and rigid asceticism. It also called for the worship of angels and mystical experiences. Epaphras was so concerned about this heresy that he made the long journey from Colossae to Rome (Colossians 4:12–13), where Paul was a prisoner.

This letter was written from prison in Rome (Acts 28:16–31) and is, therefore, referred to as a Prison Epistle (along with

Ephesians, Philippians, and Philemon). It may have been composed almost contemporaneously with Ephesians and initially sent with that epistle and Philemon by Tychicus (Ephesians 6:21–22; Colossian 4:7–8). While in prison, Paul heard that the Colossian Christians, who had once been exemplary examples of faith and Christianity, had become vulnerable to false teachers and deception. False teachers were threatening to undermine what Epaphras had taught and their orthodoxy (Colossians 2:4, 8, 16, 21–23). Disturbingly, those erroneous implications threatened to remove the church of Colossae from its strong Christian foundation. Paul, an apostle, caretaker, and steward of the Lord's Church, knew that he was responsible for ensuring that the Church was healthy, strong, and mature. So, he wrote to refute the theological falsities and miseducation the Colossians were embracing.

Paul cared deeply that the church of Colossae understood God's love for them and their responsibilities as believers. To do that, he reestablishes that he, along with Epaphras, were true messengers of God and, therefore, the Colossians should listen to him. This was not the first time Paul had encountered false teachers. So like a thorough attorney, Paul pleads his case to the Colossian believers: his motive and purpose (Colossians 1:24–25; 28–29), the mystery of God (Colossians 1: 26–27), and its impact on believers (Colossians 2:1–4).

EXPOSITION

I. PAUL'S MOTIVE AND PURPOSE (COLOSSIANS 1:24–29)

Paul begins this passage by defending himself and cites his suffering for the Church (Colossians 1:24). Paul could have bragged about his many accomplishments, achievements, apostleship, or authority, but instead, he focused attention on his suffering. Even when writing this letter, it is believed that Paul was currently suffering as a prisoner of house arrest. This opening statement is counter-cultural because humans generally do not like to suffer, but Paul claims that he rejoices in his suffering. In fact, he believes that it is a privilege to suffer. The cause—his love for Christ and His mission—was so worthy, it didn't matter to him how much suffering he went through. From his point of view, his suffering is diminutive and still lacking compared to Christ's suffering for the Church. By beginning his defense by establishing his suffering, Paul challenges the validity of false teachers because they have not suffered for the Church as he and Christ did. He is literally saying, listen to me because my suffering for the Kingdom has given me the right to speak and be a true messenger of the Lord. It was almost as if to say, if you're not suffering for the cause of Christ, then you're not following Him closely enough. Jesus never promised an easy life for His believers; in fact, He promised the opposite (Matthew 5:10–12).

Stewards of the Lord's Church must be willing to suffer for the Church. Jesus demonstrated for the Church two ways of suffering. The first is redemptive suffering, which Christ did at Calvary for humanity. This is a once-and-for-all suffering that was fulfilled by Jesus exclusively. The second type of suffering is related to the Church and the ministry of Christ. This ongoing suffering invites followers and disciples of Christ to participate in it equally. Recall when Jesus told His disciples and followers, "If anyone would come after me, he must deny himself and take up his cross and follow me" (Mark 8:34). Now, Christ's work on the cross paid for all sin in perpetuity—Paul wasn't suffering to cover any remaining sin left behind. Instead, by sharing in the suffering of Jesus, we are more conformed to Him and become more Christlike. Rather than taking away the sins of the world, our suffering brings us closer to Jesus. Paul uses three phrases to describe his suffering. He used "for you," "for the sake of his body," and "which is the church" (Colossians 1:24). Those who are followers of Christ are not immune to suffering but are sure to suffer such difficulties like imprisonment, death, and other hardships. Paul suffered because he believed it to be one of the ministries God called him to undergo. His suffering in regard to the Colossians pertained to the difficulties he faced in attempting to persuade the Jewish believers to accept the Gentile converts.

Paul then moves to share his purpose. In Colossians 1:28, Paul proclaimed Christ, admonishing and teaching everyone with wisdom. Paul says he teaches Jesus over religious laws and rules, doctrine, and traditions. His focus is Christ; though he respects and studies the Scriptures of the Old Testament and his Jewish traditions, Paul points to and promotes Christ. At the time of Paul's writing, the canon we know as the Holy Bible was not in existence. There was no recording of the life of Jesus, just the oral tradition of proclaiming Christ from the apostles and other followers. When Adam and Eve first sinned and were cast out from the Garden of Eden, they became separated from God. The Lord could no longer dwell with them because He is perfect and is intolerant of sin. A veil was put up, so to speak, and it continued this way for generations. When Jesus came to earth and died for us, that veil was torn down and we were given full access to God. The Gospel was no longer a mystery because Christ revealed it to us through His words and actions, which were recorded into the Bible we have today.

Paul's purpose is to share the wisdom of Christ with everyone that it preaches and teaches, and his messages centers on Christ over human and interpreted laws. It is not surprising that Paul would want everyone to know or encounter Christ. It was a unique encounter with Christ on the road to Damascus that Paul (then Saul) met Christ, was converted, and his whole world was changed (Acts 9). The religious laws and rules of the day excluded the Gentiles, but the message of Christ was inclusive and focused on the love for all.

Paul stated that God had commissioned him as a servant (*diakonos*) of God to the church to present the Word of God in its fullness (Colossians 1:25). *Diakonos* is the origin of the word for deacon; this term is one of humility rather than authority or leadership. Paul viewed himself as a servant of Christ and the Church. Paul was selected by the Almighty, and his purpose and motive were to be a servant to present the Word of God in its fullness to both Jews and Gentiles. He took this mission very seriously and "held fast" to his faith, regardless of the challenges he faced. If we can demonstrate this same kind of faithfulness, throughout any trial, then we have the same reward waiting for us as Paul received: the crown of life and eternity with Christ in heaven.

II. Concern for the Colossians (Colossians 2:1–3)

Both the Colossians and Laodiceans were among those for whom Paul struggled so hard in order to bring them to maturity. We see in this verse that Paul had sent some of his people who actually founded the Church. It was at Paul's direction, so in a sense, Paul did start this church. Though we know Paul had not actually been with them in person, because we see that they had not seen Paul's face.

The people who worked with Paul had been trained by him, and they were now working under his supervision. Paul's concern for them was the same as for the churches he had personally started, because he felt responsible for what had been taught them at the first.

Colossians 2:2 could also be translated: "That their minds may be strengthened by being lovingly instructed, and so obtain all the wealth of assurance that comes from proper spiritual understanding." More precisely, "to obtain a mature knowledge of God's mystery about Christ." The Colossians' "minds" needed to be "instructed" in the truth to safeguard them against the circulating heresy

Paul was trying to do what he could to put them at ease by emphasizing the bond that should be between all believers in Christ. The heart of a man is what he really is; therefore, whatever we believe in our hearts determines what we really are. If we truly believe that Jesus is the Son of God, then this should change how we live and interact with one another. In the same vein, if a brother or sister in the Lord also has that same belief, then their background or upbringing or any other difference becomes irrelevant; all that matters is that we are both children of God. The following Scriptures have a great deal toward the explanation of the mystery of Christ: "At that time Jesus answered and said, I thank thee, O Father, Lord of heaven and earth, because thou hast hid these things from the wise and prudent, and hast revealed them unto babes. Even so, Father: for so it seemed good in thy sight. All things are delivered unto me of my Father: and no man knoweth the Son, but the Father; neither knoweth any man the Father, save the Son, and [he] to whomsoever the Son will reveal [him]" (Matthew 11:25–27). One of the most important parts of our salvation is found in Romans 10:9: "That if thou shalt confess with thy mouth the Lord Jesus, and shalt believe in thine heart that God hath raised him from the dead, thou shalt be saved."

We may not fully understand how salvation is accomplished, and that's okay. All we must believe is that Jesus paid the price for our salvation, and that He rose from the dead. This must not be a surface confession; we must truly believe in our hearts. "Hid" (verse 3) in this context does not mean unknown, for not all these "treasures of wisdom and knowledge" are unknown to humanity. Here, "hid" signifies "laid up," "stored away," or "reserved." Christ, then, is the source from which all wisdom and knowledge come. Wisdom that we have, therefore, is a gift from God. The treasure of knowledge can be ours by the study of the Bible as the Holy Spirit reveals to us exactly what it is saying. Proverbs 2:7 says that "the Lord has a hidden store house of wisdom made accessible to his godly ones," meaning that He won't withhold wisdom from those who seek Him.

THE LESSON APPLIED

In today's lesson, Paul states that the goal of his letter is for the Colossians to know the mystery of God, Christ. Knowing about Christ and knowing Christ are two very different things. Knowing about Christ is to know facts and information, which is not much different than standard search engines such as Google. Even demons knew about Christ (Acts 19:15). But to know Christ means having a relationship and experiences with Christ. It is when our knowledge and information impact how we relate to God and others. Knowing Christ is transformative; if your life isn't transformed, then you don't truly know Jesus.

When your life is changed through His saving grace, it doesn't stand to reason that you would keep living according to your prior lifestyle. If you are really appreciating Him for granting you this free salvation, it makes sense that you would respond by wanting to develop that relationship with Him further. This looks like spending time in His Word, prayer, attending services with fellow believers, experiencing community with your brothers and sisters in Christ, etc. By participating in these things (as well as others), you can really know Jesus and be changed from the inside out.

LET'S TALK ABOUT IT

How can we remain faithful to the cause of Christianity when the world increasingly hates Christians?

It's true that the world is becoming increasingly intolerant of Christians; indeed, the same social activists who are screaming for tolerance and equality are among the first to dismiss and condemn Christianity for being exclusive, outdated, etc. Sometimes it can feel like the only way to be accepted by our peers is to reject Christ and go along with the mainstream. However, this is not the life that Christ has called us to live. If we're being persecuted for our faith, we can take that as a sign that we're living closely to Jesus, and that is the best place to be.

GET SOCIAL
Share your views and tag us @rhboydco and use #KnowChrist.

Twitter
@rhboydco (#rhboydco)

Instagram
@rhboydco (#rhboydco)

Facebook
@rhboydco (#rhboydco)

www.rhboyd.com

HOME DAILY DEVOTIONAL READINGS
JUNE 3–9, 2024

MONDAY	TUESDAY	WEDNESDAY	THURSDAY	FRIDAY	SATURDAY	SUNDAY
Boldly Proclaiming the Kingdom	The Awesome Presence of God	The Consuming Fire	The Lord's Blessing Makes Rich	Your Treasure Is with Your Heart	Seek First God's Kingdom	Christ, the Most Precious Gift
Acts 28:23–31	Exodus 19:9–11, 16–25	Hebrews 12:18–29	Proverbs 10:19–25	Matthew 6:19–24	Matthew 6:25–34	Colossians 1:24—2:3

REFLECTING GOD'S SPIRIT

ADULT TOPIC:	BACKGROUND SCRIPTURE: 2 CORINTHIANS 3:1–18
BOLD MINISTERS	LESSON PASSAGE: 2 CORINTHIANS 3:5–18

2 CORINTHIANS 3:5–18

King James Version

NOT that we are sufficient of ourselves to think any thing as of ourselves; but our sufficiency is of God;

6 Who also hath made us able ministers of the new testament; not of the letter, but of the spirit: for the letter killeth, but the spirit giveth life.

7 But if the ministration of death, written and engraven in stones, was glorious, so that the children of Israel could not stedfastly behold the face of Moses for the glory of his countenance; which glory was to be done away:

8 How shall not the ministration of the spirit be rather glorious?

9 For if the ministration of condemnation be glory, much more doth the ministration of righteousness exceed in glory.

10 For even that which was made glorious had no glory in this respect, by reason of the glory that excelleth.

11 For if that which is done away was glorious, much more that which remaineth is glorious.

12 Seeing then that we have such hope, we use great plainness of speech:

13 And not as Moses, which put a veil over his face, that the children of Israel could not stedfastly look to the end of that which is abolished:

14 But their minds were blinded: for until this day remaineth the same vail untaken away in the reading of the old testament; which vail is done away in Christ.

15 But even unto this day, when Moses is read, the vail is upon their heart.

New Revised Standard Version

NOT that we are qualified of ourselves to claim anything as coming from us; our qualification is from God,

6 who has made us qualified to be ministers of a new covenant, not of letter but of spirit, for the letter kills, but the Spirit gives life.

7 Now if the ministry of death, chiseled in letters on stone tablets, came in glory so that the people of Israel could not gaze at Moses's face because of the glory of his face, a glory now set aside,

8 how much more will the ministry of the Spirit come in glory?

9 For if there was glory in the ministry of condemnation, much more does the ministry of justification abound in glory!

10 Indeed, what once had glory has in this respect lost its glory because of the greater glory,

11 for if what was set aside came through glory, much more has the permanent come in glory!

12 Since, then, we have such a hope, we act with complete frankness,

13 not like Moses, who put a veil over his face to keep the people of Israel from gazing at the end of the glory that was being set aside.

14 But their minds were hardened. Indeed, to this very day, when they hear the reading of the old covenant, the same veil is still there; it is not unveiled since in Christ it is set aside.

15 Indeed, to this very day whenever Moses is read, a veil lies over their minds,

MAIN THOUGHT: But we all, with open face beholding as in a glass the glory of the Lord, are changed into the same image from glory to glory, even as by the Spirit of the Lord. (2 Corinthians 3:18, KJV)

2 CORINTHIANS 3:5–18

King James Version	New Revised Standard Version
16 Nevertheless when it shall turn to the Lord, the vail shall be taken away.	16 but when one turns to the Lord, the veil is removed.
17 Now the Lord is that Spirit: and where the Spirit of the Lord is, there is liberty.	17 Now the Lord is the Spirit, and where the Spirit of the Lord is, there is freedom.
18 But we all, with open face beholding as in a glass the glory of the Lord, are changed into the same image from glory to glory, even as by the Spirit of the Lord.	18 And all of us, with unveiled faces, seeing the glory of the Lord as though reflected in a mirror, are being transformed into the same image from one degree of glory to another, for this comes from the Lord, the Spirit.

LESSON SETTING
Time: 55 CE
Place: Macedonia

LESSON OUTLINE
 I. Ministers of a New Covenant
    (2 Corinthians 3:5–6)
 II. Old vs. New Covenant
    (2 Corinthians 3:7–11)
 III. Boldness of the
     New Covenant
    (2 Corinthians 3:12–15)

UNIFYING PRINCIPLE
People become defensive and retreat when their credentials are challenged. How do we proclaim truth boldly in the face of such challenges? Paul declares that he is able to speak with greater boldness because of the evidence of believers' transformed lives.

INTRODUCTION
Second Corinthians was written in response to the Corinthians' reception of Paul's protege, Titus. Paul was attempting to reconcile his fragmented relationship with the Corinthian church as well as defending his apostolic legitimacy to the church. Paul's adversaries have arrived in Corinth, and Paul is attempting to win back the hearts and loyalty of the Corinthians through the power and author-ity given to him through Christ. Today's passage focuses on the new covenant that believers find with Jesus, as they are no longer bound to the covenant God made with Moses.

EXPOSITION
I. MINISTERS OF A NEW COVENANT (2 CORINTHIANS 3:5–6)
God appointed Paul as an apostle, that is, as "an emissary of a new covenant." Therefore, Paul does not act out of his own powers, as the Corinthians imagine. As an apostle, he is nothing other than a *diakonos*, an agent of another, a representative on a mission. In using the adverb "also" (*kai*) and the plural form "us," Paul implicitly places himself alongside other apostles. He here defines the nature of the apostolic calling in a manner reminiscent of his argument in 1 Corinthians 3:1–4:5, where he similarly sets himself alongside Apollos as an "agent on mission" (*diakonos*, 1 Corinthians 3:5). Now, however, he refers directly to the Scriptures, rather than merely borrowing its agricultural imagery. His unusual language should not be overlooked. One was not normally judged as "sufficient" or "competent" as an "emissary" or "agent" of another. Paul

here describes his role as an emissary of "a new covenant," which he defines as "not of the letter but of the Spirit." In introducing this expression, he clearly refers to the Lord's Supper tradition that he himself delivered to the Corinthians and, through the "cup-word" of that tradition, to the Jeremianic promise of a new covenant. Yet his anarthrous usage emphasizes the significance rather than the referent of his words. It is very likely that Paul's focus on his apostolic mission calls forth his usage of the term "covenant" here. Whether it is old or new, a covenant establishes a relationship between God and human beings. The nature of that relation is determined by the divine word that establishes the covenant, whether it is conditioned by demands or given by unconditional promise.

Paul's description of this covenant as "new" is already an indication that he does not conceive of God's dealings with the world in terms of a single, overarching covenant with Israel. The "new covenant" excludes that possibility; the new covenant is not of the letter but of the Spirit. The genitive relations "of the letter" and "of the Spirit" express the differing contents of the covenants (i.e., that which is delivered and dispensed by each of them). This distinction between demand and gift, which we shall consider in greater detail below, is already present in the "new covenant" of Jeremiah 31:31–34, to which Paul alludes. The old covenant provided the Law that the Israelites followed, but in a sense, it only focused on the outside. People were still separated from God since they were still sinners, therefore, the Law didn't transform their hearts. This could only happen through the presence of the Holy

Spirit, which was a gift that Jesus gave us after His resurrection.

Just as God gives comfort only to those in affliction (v. 7), the Spirit gives life only to that which the letter has put to death. This theological grammar of deliverance, found especially in the Psalms, is prominent in the Pauline letters as the definition of the saving power of the Creator that is displayed in the rebellious human creature. Paul does not speak of sin and transgression in salvation–historical categories, as if they were now behind us. Rather, he describes the intersection of the new creation with the fallen world. Insofar as unbelief and disobedience remain, the Corinthians need written instruction, including that of the Law. This instruction from the Law is no abstract expression of God's moral will but one of concrete demands that bring condemnation and death. The "letter" itself is an effective word that, in its own way, performs what God intends. Only where the Law has arrived is it possible to hear the Gospel rightly.

Paul's concluding affirmation, that "the Spirit makes alive," provides the basis for his following argument in verses 7–11 concerning the transcendent glory given to the apostolic mission. This argument culminates in a return to his affirmation in verses 6. The glory of Moses' mission has been done away with. The unseen glory of the gift of the Spirit and righteousness abides without end: the Spirit who makes alive, makes alive eternally.

II. OLD VS. NEW COVENANT (2 CORINTHIANS 3:7–11)

It is written: "'The days are coming,' declares the Lord, 'when I will make a new covenant with the people of Israel and with the people of Judah. It will not be like the covenant I made with their ancestors when I took them by the hand to lead them out of Egypt, because they broke my covenant, though I was a husband to them,' declares the Lord. 'This is the covenant I will make with the people of Israel after that time,' declares the Lord. 'I will put my law in their minds and write it on their hearts. I will be their God, and they will be my people'" (Jeremiah 31:31–34). No longer will there be any need for anyone to admonish and instruct another. The written Law, the very purpose of which is to provide the basis of instruction, no longer shall be necessary (cf. Exodus 24:12). All shall know the Lord and obey him with the spontaneity that marks true obedience (Jeremiah 31:34). All of these blessings are predicated and based on the forgiveness of sins; the new covenant arrives where the old covenant has been a temporary solution for transgression and condemnation. Indeed, the very naming of this covenant as "new" means that it is defined in contrast with the "old." The recipients of the "new covenant" know themselves to be nothing more than forgiven sinners. The covenant made at Sinai is constituted by the Law, which remains outside the human being as divine moral instruction, requirement, and demand. The new covenant is no longer a demand but an unqualified promise and gift. It is purely and simply the work of God the Creator, who through the Gospel enters into and lovingly recreates the human heart, thereby establishing a relationship with the rebellious human being. The former commandment thus is displaced by the fulfilled promise—which endures forever, as Paul emphasizes in context (v. 11). In all probability, it is the announcement of the "new covenant" in Jeremiah 31:31 that prompts Paul to speak of "the old covenant" in verse 14. The claim that the old and new covenants are somehow the same because the "content" of the Law is communicated or imparted by both of them is built upon a flawed and fatal abstraction. God's communication with fallen humanity cannot legitimately be abstracted from its form, so as to become a higher idea or concept. This would be equivalent to saying that, because two statements have to do with the amount of one thousand dollars, it makes no difference that one comes in the form of a bill of demand and the other in the form of a gift. Just as the form of the new covenant differs from the covenant made at Sinai, so does its content radically differ from the old covenant. They differ as much as a demand differs from a promise, condemnation differs from righteousness, and death from life.

Paul now appears temporarily to drop his personal defense for a complex discussion of an important Old Testament passage (Exodus 34:29–35; this recounts the giving of the Ten Commandments to Moses). Yet Paul's personal situation and what he now writes are probably related because those whom he was opposing were using arguments from the Old Testament to sustain their position. As we have seen, Paul was preparing in verses 1–6 for what he is now going to say. He is, therefore, not now drawn off into a side issue. His final words in verse 6 claimed that his ministry and that of his associates was a ministry of the new covenant. The old covenant had its glory, but it was one that faded. This does not mean that the Law had been slowly losing importance and influence from the time of its inauguration. Rather, the Law lacks permanent validity, a point that is seen with the coming of Christ. In its day, the Law had sufficient glory to dazzle the eyes of the Israelites; in Christ, there is an even brighter light. The bright light we find it hard to stare at fades steadily into nothingness when the sun shines behind it. So the ministry of the Spirit that comes through Christian ministers like Paul brings a greater splendor, greater than any splendor any minister of the old covenant, even Moses—its greatest minister—could provide. We do not have to wait for the end of all things for this ministry of the Spirit; it exists now, and it not only frees from condemnation but gives righteousness. It brings us into a new relation with the God who saves. Here Paul touches on the great themes he developed in Galatians and Romans. Paul and his associates, as ministers of the new covenant, grow with that growing glory. Thus when Paul returns in 2 Corinthians 4 to his own personal situation, he is in a position to make new claims for his ministry.

III. BOLDNESS OF THE NEW COVENANT (2 CORINTHIANS 3:12–15)

Whatever it was that sparked off this discussion, it resulted in Paul being turned aside from the direct defense of his ministry. What he has just been saying applies to all Christians. In fact, when he began in verse 12 with "we have such a hope" and not with "we have such a ministry," he was beginning to lose sight of the attacks on his own ministry. All Christians have a hope that frees them from the fear of death and condemnation and that enables them to share in the splendor that is permanent (vv. 7–11). Hope gives boldness (v. 12) and as Moses was bold enough to meet God within the tent of meeting with unveiled face, so "we all" see the glory of the Lord without veiled faces. Yet though Moses veiled his face when he came out of the tent, we should not attempt to veil the glory of God which is in our lives. We should be bold to confess Christ by allowing His glory to be seen in us.

In 2 Corinthians 3:13–18, the word "veil" occurs four times, in each of the verses (except verse 17). There is the veil that Moses wore over his face after his visage had been transformed by his encounter with God. After speaking to God in the tent of meeting, Moses would put on his veil to avoid making the Israelites uncomfortable; it seems that when they saw his face shining with the glory of his encounter with God, they were afraid (Exodus 34:29–35), and, as their own faces were still shining from the exertion of reveling before the Golden Calf (Exodus 32), they were probably ashamed by the comparison as well. Paul takes this story of Moses' veil and uses it as an allegory for reference to the old covenant (v. 14)—which is only set aside in Christ (i.e. the Gospel)–– and for the reading of "Moses" (v. 15, which is a euphemism for the Torah, or Pentateuch)—which is only comprehensible when one turns to God (v. 16). In both cases, Paul is making the claim that the old covenant, the old "good news," cannot be properly understood and accepted until the veil is removed. Then we ourselves with faces unveiled—which at this point is both a reference again to the Moses story, and a metaphor for hearts and minds that are set free by the Holy Spirit (v. 18)—will finally know the glory of God.

THE LESSON APPLIED

We determine competency in our culture by getting the job done. Ministry competency, however, does not come from self but Christ. He has made us competent ministers. Genuine ministry recruits the endorsement of God. We may be adequate for ministry but not because it originates in ourselves; it is because God initiates it in us. Therefore, He deserves the credit. We have nothing to boast about other than what God does through us. This is an important reminder for us, especially those of us with roles of leadership in ministry. It is a God-given gift to be able to share His wisdom, His love, and His compassion with everyone, and sharing that gift doesn't make anyone better than anyone else. It is only through the grace of God. Paul says repeatedly throughout his letters in the New Testament that he won't boast in himself because he knows that apart from God, he is a worthless sinner. May we all have that self-awareness and humility to recognize our true dependence on God alone.

LET'S TALK ABOUT IT

How does your perspective of Christ shift when you become a Christian?

As a Jew, Paul had no way of approaching God other than through the Law, and he believed it brought him life. As a follower of Christ, he began to see it all from a new angle. When we become Christians, or come to realize the importance of our Christian faith, we look back at what we were and obtain a new perspective on it. We may not have come to Christ or to a clear understanding of His importance from the Law; perhaps we came from another religion or we previously believed that good behavior is the way to please God. While these convictions previously may have seemed to have great value, now they appear poor in comparison to the splendor of Christ.

GET SOCIAL

Share your views and tag us @rhboydco and use #Boldness.

Twitter
@rhboydco (#rhboydco)

Instagram
@rhboydco (#rhboydco)

Facebook
@rhboydco (#rhboydco)

www.rhboyd.com

HOME DAILY DEVOTIONAL READINGS
JUNE 10–16, 2024

MONDAY	TUESDAY	WEDNESDAY	THURSDAY	FRIDAY	SATURDAY	SUNDAY
Servant Leadership	You Shall Receive Power	Anointed by God	How Pleasant to Live in Unity	Bear with One Another in Love	Embrace the Mind of Christ	Prayer for Hope, Joy, and Peace
Luke 22:25–30	Acts 1:1–11	Isaiah 61	Psalms 133–134	Ephesians 4:1–7	Philippians 2:1–13	Romans 15:1–13

EMPOWERED SERVANTS

ADULT TOPIC:	BACKGROUND SCRIPTURE: ROMANS 15:1–13
SHARING HOPE WITH OTHERS	LESSON PASSAGE: ROMANS 15:1–13

ROMANS 15:1–13

King James Version

WE then that are strong ought to bear the infirmities of the weak, and not to please ourselves.

2 Let every one of us please his neighbour for his good to edification.

3 For even Christ pleased not himself; but, as it is written, The reproaches of them that reproached thee fell on me.

4 For whatsoever things were written aforetime were written for our learning, that we through patience and comfort of the scriptures might have hope.

5 Now the God of patience and consolation grant you to be likeminded one toward another according to Christ Jesus:

6 That ye may with one mind and one mouth glorify God, even the Father of our Lord Jesus Christ.

7 Wherefore receive ye one another, as Christ also received us to the glory of God.

8 Now I say that Jesus Christ was a minister of the circumcision for the truth of God, to confirm the promises made unto the fathers:

9 And that the Gentiles might glorify God for his mercy; as it is written, For this cause I will confess to thee among the Gentiles, and sing unto thy name.

10 And again he saith, Rejoice, ye Gentiles, with his people.

11 And again, Praise the Lord, all ye Gentiles; and laud him, all ye people.

New Revised Standard Version

WE who are strong ought ought to put up with the failings of the weak and not to please ourselves.

2 Each of us must please our neighbor for the good purpose of building up the neighbor.

3 For Christ did not please himself, but, as it is written, "The insults of those who insult you have fallen on me."

4 For whatever was written in former days was written for our instruction, so that by steadfastness and by the encouragement of the scriptures we might have hope.

5 May the God of steadfastness and encouragement grant you to live in harmony with one another, in accordance with Christ Jesus,

6 so that together you may with one voice glorify the God and Father of our Lord Jesus Christ.

7 Welcome one another, therefore, just as Christ has welcomed you, for the glory of God.

8 For I tell you that Christ has become a servant of the circumcised on behalf of the truth of God in order that he might confirm the promises given to the ancestors

9 and that the gentiles might glorify God for his mercy. As it is written, "Therefore I will confess you among the gentiles and sing praises to your name";

10 and again he says, "Rejoice, O gentiles, with his people";

11 and again, "Praise the Lord, all you gentiles, and let all the peoples praise him";

MAIN THOUGHT: May the God of steadfastness and encouragement grant you to live in harmony with one another, in accordance with Christ Jesus, so that together you may with one voice glorify the God and Father of our Lord Jesus Christ. (Romans 15:5–6, KJV)

ROMANS 15:1–13

King James Version	New Revised Standard Version
12 And again, Esaias saith, There shall be a root of Jesse, and he that shall rise to reign over the Gentiles; in him shall the Gentiles trust.	12 and again Isaiah says, "The root of Jesse shall come, the one who rises to rule the gentiles; in him the gentiles shall hope."
13 Now the God of hope fill you with all joy and peace in believing, that ye may abound in hope, through the power of the Holy Ghost.	13 May the God of hope fill you with all joy and peace in believing, so that you may abound in hope by the power of the Holy Spirit.

LESSON SETTING
Time: 52–58 CE
Place: Corinth

LESSON OUTLINE
I. Help the Weak
(Romans 15:1–6)
II. Acceptance
(Romans 15:7–13)

UNIFYING PRINCIPLE
People enthusiastically serve a worthy cause, but hope falters when encountering obstacles. How do servants of such causes preserve or regain hope? Paul notes that the God of steadfastness and hope empowers harmonious and effective service for Christ.

INTRODUCTION
The book of Romans is named for the recipients to whom it is addressing, God's beloved in Rome (Romans 1:7). This passage is the climax of the broader argument of Romans about the division in the community between the "strong" and the "weak" that Paul is trying to overcome. Paul seeks to answer the question of what shapes and unifies the community that has trusted the promise fulfilled in Christ's first coming and eagerly awaits His second coming. Paul's answer, and his prayer for the community, is harmony and hope.

As Paul explains, the past—both Christ's work and Scripture—gives shape to and encouragement for the community's present harmony, which orients all in hope toward God's future.

EXPOSITION
I. HELP THE WEAK
(ROMANS 15:1–6)
Paul begins the chapter with a charge to the strong to bear the burdens of the weak (v. 1). As in the previous lesson, strength and weakness are in reference to faith, not physical prowess. Paul counts himself as the "strong," as evident in his use of first person plural. Paul says that the spiritually strong should lend assistance to the weak instead of criticizing them. Paul charges the strong not just to tolerate those who are weak or endure the weak but to bear the weak's burdens to help with what is oppressing them. This is similar to Galatians 6:2, where Paul again calls those who are strong in their faith to bear each other's burdens. For us today, this can be seen as counter-cultural because American society is very individualistic. We emphasize getting ahead by any means necessary, looking out for "number one," and admire those who are able to

"make it" on their own. But the ancient cultures were very community-oriented and focused on working together because they understood that they couldn't survive on their own. They depended on each other, and here Paul was encouraging the people to not forget about the weak members of the faith. Just because their faith was newer, it didn't mean that they didn't deserve support and uplifting.

Paul continues addressing the strong in verse 2, where he commissions them to live to please their neighbors. The word "pleasing" translates to *aresketo,* which can be substituted for love. Paul is not suggesting that Christians please others at the risk of their own witness. This is not a call to please others at all costs—including compromising the Gospel. Paul is suggesting, however, that Christians should attempt to please others so that they become stronger in faith. In verse 3, Paul uses Christ as an example of someone who did not please Himself and then cites Psalm 69. Intertwined with the life of Christ, Psalm 69 narrates the saga of a righteous sufferer who was attacked by His enemies and failed by His friends. Paul alludes that Christ was strong and bore suffering for the sake of humanity, with the weak as his prime example.

From the beginning of the letter to the Romans, Paul has argued that the Gospel is for both Jews and Greeks (Romans 1:14–17). This argument has been anchored throughout the letter in his reading of Scripture. Hope is mentioned in Romans 4:18 when highlighting Abraham as a model of faith; "hope against hope" that God is reliable and will keep His promise of giving Abraham a son despite

the circumstances. Paul also reminds the Romans that through Christ, they can "rejoice in the hope of sharing the glory of God" (Romans 5:2–5); present suffering will not dissipate hope, but instead, it should be used to discipline believers' endurance and to build good Christian character. So we have here a climax both to Paul's argument and to his way of arguing. Paul makes it clear in Romans 15:4 that the past ("whatever was written in former days") was meant for this very present time ("written for our instruction") in order to give hope. Hope is the present state of anticipating a particular future in which we can be confident because of what Scripture has said to us in the past. But more than that, we can be confident because what Scripture said in the past has already begun to come true. The Gospel of God's Son, the promised Messiah, has come (Romans 1:1–2).

Romans 15 draws to a close the lengthy argument of the letter that has unfolded since Romans 1:1. There, we heard that Scripture was the source of the promise about the coming Messiah. Here, we learn why it is that Paul makes such a big deal out of Scripture: "whatever was written in former days was written for our instruction so that by steadfastness and by the encouragement of the scriptures we might have hope" (v. 4). Scripture is reliable because God is reliable. That's why Paul shifts from applying "steadfastness and encouragement" to Scripture in Romans 15:4 to calling God the source of "steadfastness and encouragement" in Romans 15:5. How has God proven to be a source of steadfastness and encouragement in your life? Maybe He's provided a certain friend or family member that comes alongside you during a difficult time. Maybe He's provided a source of income in an unexpected way or a job opportunity that was completely out of the blue. When we take the time to look deeply at our lives and surroundings, it's impossible to not see God in the details. As the song says, even when we don't see it, He's working and He'll never stop. He loves us too much to not act on our behalf.

In verses 5–6, Paul begins to pray. He prays for unity between the above-mentioned groups, the strong and the weak. He also prays for endurance and consolation to be able to do the work of unification. Paul is quite clear about who is the source of endurance and consolation, and he knows if these qualities are evident in the community of Rome, then only the Almighty could provide them. Christians should always strive for unity in the church, but ultimately it is God who makes unification possible; it is a gift from God. It is only through the help of God that Christians are able to love and accept each other, celebrate differences, and be unified. Paul prays for sincere and genuine harmony among the Jews and Gentiles so that God may be glorified by the unified community. Let that be our prayer today as well: acceptance, unity, and harmony among the body of believers.

II. ACCEPTANCE (ROMANS 15:7–13)

This portion of chapter 15 has been recognized by many scholars as a summary of the entire letter. Paul pleads with the church of Rome to have mutual acceptance for one another. He pleads with them to be accommodating and non-judgmental in their care for each other. He writes that whether Jew or Gentile, a person should find the followers of Christ welcoming and impartial. Paul knew that everyone should feel liberated by the hospitality of Christians. Knowing this, he describes the Kingdom of God with terms like joy and peace. In verse 7, Paul urges believers to accept one another not as Jew or Gentile, but just as Christ has accepted you. Believers should accept one another regardless of differences because God, through Christ Jesus, has united believers with each other. Imagine if there was a rigid standard that every Christian must meet before we could be accepted into the family of Christ; many of us would never be accepted. Thank God He accepts us just as we are!

When Christians accept one another regardless of differences, then God gets the glory. When Christians love and accept one another, despite our differences, it's a powerful witness and testimony to God's love. When we show love and respect to others, even if we don't agree on everything, it reflects the character of God and His love for all of us. When we come together in unity, despite our differences, we can bring glory to God in a powerful way. Paul highlights the mutual acceptance that Christ has extended to all of humanity. He urges his readers to welcome one another as Christ has welcomed them.

This is the Gospel in a nutshell. Christ has welcomed Christians, all Christians, and promised to bring them home to God and each other. Do not become sentimental about this welcome because with this welcome comes a responsibility. To open our arms to those who otherwise are strangers and even enemies is nothing short of a miracle of grace. The experience of that welcome is the way we learn that "hope does not disappoint us because God's love has been poured into our hearts through the Holy Spirit who has been given to us" (Romans 5:5).

Verses 8–9 continue to unpack and explain how Christ accepted both Jews and Gentiles for the glory of God. Verses 8–9 emphasize the importance of God's gracious acceptance of both Jews and Gentiles. Paul writes that God "has been merciful to you, but has shown his power in the case of others." He goes on to explain that God has used this to bring "the full number of the Gentiles into the obedience that comes from faith" while still honoring the Jews as His chosen people. This is a powerful reminder that God welcomes all people into His family, regardless of their background or identity. It is also a reminder of the importance of unity within the body of Christ, as "all Israel will be saved" when the fullness of the Gentiles comes in. By welcoming both Jews and Gentiles alike, God is ultimately glorified as His plan for salvation is fulfilled. Christ came as a minister for the Jews on behalf of the truth of God. The truth of God to His covenant faithfulness by which God remains "true" to His covenantal promises of salvation.

Verses 9–12 are scriptural citations that substantiate the thesis that Gentiles and Jews together were to be recipients of covenantal blessing. Paul goes to great lengths in these verses to support his claim that Gentiles, as well as Jews, were to be the beneficiaries of God's covenantal mercy. Because of the mercies freely given to them, their response should be twofold: to extend that mercy to others and to show thankfulness to God through praise. In verse 13, Paul prays that the God who gives hope will fill both Jews and Gentiles with "all joy and peace in believing." Joy and peace both stem from faith and are by-products of believing in God's great promises. It also follows that the worship described in verses 9–12 is joyful and full of peace. Paul is informing the Romans that God gives hope by increasing faith, which results in joy and peace. Thus hope is not produced by human beings, but by the power of the Holy Spirit. It is a gift that He gives us, one that we could not create on our own.

THE LESSON APPLIED

Paul's plea to the church of Rome is one that should be taken to heart by all of us. We should strive to be accepting and respectful of one another, no matter our differences. We can learn a lot from each other, and the more we can be open and understanding, the better our relationships will be. Let us all take a moment to consider how we can build bridges instead of walls and create a supportive, loving community.

LET'S TALK ABOUT IT

How can we welcome others into the church?

Paul encourages us to accept others as they are and to celebrate our differences. It's important to take a look at our churches to make sure that we are living up to that standard. Are we being truly welcoming to Boomers, Millennials, Generation Zs, and younger generations?

Are we inclusive of those in recovery from substance abuse and those recently released from incarceration? What about single parents, widows, members of the LGTBQIA+ community, and people who prefer different fashion styles, for example? It's important that we create a church environment that is welcoming to everyone and one that celebrates the wide range of diversity in our community.

It is essential that our churches create a warm, welcoming atmosphere for all people, regardless of their age, gender, sexual orientation, background, or style of dress. We must recognize that God created us all uniquely and celebrate that diversity. To do this, we must strive to create an environment that is inclusive and understanding of the needs of all our church members. This can include providing support groups and activities that are tailored to the different groups we serve, promoting education and awareness, partnering with local organizations to provide resources, and encouraging open dialogue around difficult topics.

Additionally, we should ensure that our church language and messaging is inclusive and welcoming to all members of our church family. Ultimately, we want to ensure that everyone in our church feels that they are valued, respected, and accepted.

One way to make your church more welcoming is to ensure that everyone is made to feel included. Try to create an environment that is open and inviting to all, regardless of background or beliefs. Invite members of the community to come to visit and learn more about your church. Hold events that are fun and engaging, and provide opportunities for members of the congregation to get to know each other. Make sure that everyone feels comfortable and respected. Lastly, don't forget to reach out to those who are outside of the church community and let them know that they are welcome. Take some time to reflect and discuss ways to help make your church a more welcoming, accepting, and inclusive family of faith.

GET SOCIAL

Share your views and tag us
@rhboydco and use #Empowered.

Twitter
@rhboydco (#rhboydco)

Instagram
@rhboydco (#rhboydco)

Facebook
@rhboydco (#rhboydco)

www.rhboyd.com

HOME DAILY DEVOTIONAL READINGS
JUNE 17–23, 2024

MONDAY	TUESDAY	WEDNESDAY	THURSDAY	FRIDAY	SATURDAY	SUNDAY
Hope in God Our Help	Whoever Has the Son Has Life	Boldness in Christ for Prayer	The Lord Is My Shepherd	Trust in God Our Salvation	Maturing in Christ	Trust God's Promises
Psalm 42	1 John 5:1–13	1 John 5:14–21	Psalm 23	Isaiah 12	Hebrews 6:1–8	Hebrews 6:9–20

FULL ASSURANCE

ADULT TOPIC: GOD IS TRUSTWORTHY	BACKGROUND SCRIPTURE: HEBREWS 6:9–20 LESSON PASSAGE: HEBREWS 6:9–20

HEBREWS 6:9–20

King James Version

BUT, beloved, we are persuaded better things of you, and things that accompany salvation, though we thus speak.

10 For God is not unrighteous to forget your work and labour of love, which ye have shewed toward his name, in that ye have ministered to the saints, and do minister.

11 And we desire that every one of you do shew the same diligence to the full assurance of hope unto the end:

12 That ye be not slothful, but followers of them who through faith and patience inherit the promises.

13 For when God made promise to Abraham, because he could swear by no greater, he sware by himself,

14 Saying, Surely blessing I will bless thee, and multiplying I will multiply thee.

15 And so, after he had patiently endured, he obtained the promise.

16 For men verily swear by the greater: and an oath for confirmation is to them an end of all strife.

17 Wherein God, willing more abundantly to shew unto the heirs of promise the immutability of his counsel, confirmed it by an oath:

18 That by two immutable things, in which it was impossible for God to lie, we might have a strong consolation, who have fled for refuge to lay hold upon the hope set before us:

New Revised Standard Version

EVEN though we speak in this way, beloved, we are confident of better things in your case, things that belong to salvation.

10 For God is not unjust; he will not overlook your work and the love that you showed for his sake in serving the saints, as you still do.

11 And we want each one of you to show the same diligence so as to realize the full assurance of hope to the very end,

12 so that you may not become sluggish but imitators of those who through faith and patience inherit the promises.

13 When God made a promise to Abraham, because he had no one greater by whom to swear, he swore by himself,

14 saying, "I will surely bless you and multiply you."

15 And thus Abraham, having patiently endured, obtained the promise.

16 Humans, of course, swear by someone greater than themselves, and an oath given as confirmation puts an end to all dispute among them.

17 In the same way, when God desired to show even more clearly to the heirs of the promise the unchangeable character of his purpose, he guaranteed it by an oath,

18 so that through two unchangeable things, in which it is impossible that God would prove false, we who have taken refuge might be strongly encouraged to seize the hope set before us.

MAIN THOUGHT: Which hope we have as an anchor of the soul, both sure and stedfast, and which entereth into that within the veil; Whither the forerunner is for us entered, even Jesus, made an high priest for ever after the order of Melchisedec. (Hebrews 6:19–20, KJV)

HEBREWS 6:9–20

King James Version	New Revised Standard Version
19 Which hope we have as an anchor of the soul, both sure and stedfast, and which entereth into that within the veil; 20 Whither the forerunner is for us entered, even Jesus, made an high priest for ever after the order of Melchisedec.	19 We have this hope, a sure and steadfast anchor of the soul, a hope that enters the inner shrine behind the curtain, 20 where Jesus, a forerunner on our behalf, has entered, having become a high priest forever according to the order of Melchizedek.

LESSON SETTING
  Time: 63–64 CE
  Place: Rome
LESSON OUTLINE
  I. **Follow God Diligently** (Hebrews 6:9–12)
  II. **God's Promises Are Certain** (Hebrews 6:13–18)
  III. **We Have this Hope** (Hebrews 6:19–20)

UNIFYING PRINCIPLE

People become distrustful when they experience broken promises. Where can one obtain trustworthy promises in an imperfect world? The writer of Hebrews assures believers that God's promises are guaranteed because it is impossible that God would prove false.

INTRODUCTION

From the earliest days of Christian history, the epistle to the Hebrews has been shrouded in obscurity. It is the only truly anonymous letter in the New Testament. Complicating the problem of authorship is the uncertainty regarding other background issues such as date, recipients, and place of writing. There is no clear and unequivocal internal evidence for any of these issues. Consequently, Hebrews is probably the most enigmatic book in the New Testament in terms of provenance.

Though we may not know the exact author, time or place, we know that this letter was written as an encouragement to believers who were struggling and faced persecution for their beliefs.

EXPOSITION

I. FOLLOW GOD DILIGENTLY (HEBREWS 6:9–12)

In the first half of chapter 6 (and the end of chapter 5), the author is rebuking readers and warning them quite severely for their lack of growth in Christ. Correction requires first showing the error of someone's ways, and that's just what the writer does. But, after correction, it requires showing them what they should be doing. Throughout the Bible, we can see this dual teaching: what you should do and what you should not do—for example, the Ten Commandments and the Beatitudes. The writer, much like a parent, gives their child negative feedback, rebukes, and disciplines, and later seeks to compliment and build the child up. In the previous eight verses of this chapter, the author encouraged new believers to leave Judaism and press on toward maturity in Christ. Failure to do so, he warned, would disastrously affect their spiritual lives. However, he was confident that such would not be the case for a true child of God; thus, his warning is offset by an encouraging, positive message.

After having rebuked the pupils into attention and warned them of the perils of drifting away, the author is now ready and able to praise them. Having impressed upon them the dangers and the demands of Christian maturity, the author wants to supply encouragement. They have what it takes to endure when all is said and done. Others may fall away, but the author is confident that the readers will not be among them. After all, they have worked diligently and served lovingly in the past and the present alike. He calls his audience "dear friends" in verse 9, the only place in the epistle where this term occurs. This word underscores the author's deep love and concern for his readers and his attempt to reassure them. The author does not identify any specifics concerning the "better things" he is persuaded of concerning his readers. The author has a genuine and caring attitude toward his readers. He is trying to assure them that things will be better, without providing specifics because he wants them to have faith that things will work out. He wants to give them hope and support in a difficult time. The only explanation of "better things" is the following statement connected by explanatory *kai*: "things that accompany salvation." The author does not say the "better things" refer to entrance into salvation but to that which "accompanies" salvation. The author assumes, and thus implies by his language, that the readers are believers. This is also brought out by the final statement in the Greek text of verse 9, which is placed first in the NIV: "Even though we speak like this." In spite of the author's previous warning, he affirms the condition of his hearers as that of genuine converts. Semantically, this is a concessive idea: "although" or "notwithstanding." But the author is "confident" of the "better things" concerning them, where the perfect tense verb translated "as we are confident" is emphatic by its position in the sentence.

Verse 10 is introduced with *gar*, "for," giving a twofold reason for the author's confidence expressed in verse 9: God's righteous character and the reader's previous love and good works. The use of "unjust" followed by the infinitive translated "to forget" could be taken in the sense of degree: "God is not so unjust as to forget," or in the sense of result, "God is not unjust resulting in his forgetting." Still, it is probably better taken in an explanatory sense: "he is not unjust so that he would forget." The author does not specify exactly what he means by the "work and love" of the readers. Many commentators think this refers to what is stated in Hebrews 10:32–34, where the readers at one point sympathized with those in prison and suffered for it. The NIV translates "the love you have shown him," that is, God, where the Greek reads "for his name." This can be taken in two ways: it could mean the object of love is God's name in the sense of "for his sake" or in the sense of God Himself. It could also be taken as indicating reference: "with reference to his name," but in the sense of meaning "to him," or simply as the equivalent of "him," as in the NIV.

The final two participles in verse 10 translated "as you have helped his people and continue to help" express the means by which the love and good works are shown, with the use of the aorist followed by the present tense referring to past service and present service respectively. It is indeed interesting to consider the juxtaposition of these two verses in the context of sanctification. The author is encouraging us to show love and kindness to the people of God, as this is the same love and kindness that is shown to God. As we walk the path of sanctification, it's important to remember that our good works are seen, recognized, and rewarded by God, and that through our loving actions toward others, we are expressing our love for God.

Verse 11 is a reminder to keep our faith in God and to be diligent in our efforts to remain faithful to Him. It emphasizes the importance of having assurance in our hope in Him and continuing to keep our faith until the end. It is a warning to not drift away or fall away from God, but to hold firm in our faith.

This verse is showing us that even though God is sovereign and has saved us, we still have a responsibility to respond to His message, and to confess our sins and obey Him. We are responsible for our own faith and our relationship with God, and that we have a duty to strive to remain faithful to Him. The assurance of hope until the end is our assurance that if we remain dedicated to Him, He will continue to be faithful to us. One of the great benefits of the Bible is that it records the real lives of many believers. It shows us both their successes and their failures. These people (Noah, Abraham, Joseph, David, Ruth, Daniel, etc.) are examples for us. We can imitate their great faith and learn from them how to deal with a variety of trials and temptations.

II. GOD'S PROMISES ARE CERTAIN (HEBREWS 6:13–18)

In verse 13, the writer introduced the idea of having faith in God's promises. He reminds the readers of the faith of Abraham. God made several promises to Abraham, including promises for descendants and giving him the land (Genesis 22). The key promise to Abraham, as listed here in verse 14, is that God would give him many descendants. This was not an easy promise to believe.

Abraham is a great example of faith and obedience. Despite the fact that his promise seemed far-fetched and his doubts led him to fall into sin, he still held onto God's word and trusted in His promise. Abraham was willing to take his family and move to an unknown place to fulfill what God had asked of him. He waited patiently and trusted that God's promise would come true, and in the end, it did. Isaac was the first step in fulfilling the promise, and while Abraham may not have seen the entire fulfillment of the promise during his lifetime, he could be confident that it would eventually come true.

The writer reminds readers that when God made Abraham a promise, God used Himself as collateral. God swore by God's own name as a guarantee that the promise would become true. That's a powerful reminder that God is true to His word and will always keep His promises! We can trust in God's faithfulness, knowing that He will always fulfill the promises He makes. We can take comfort in the knowledge that no matter what challenges we face, God will always come through for us as there is no one greater than God for Him to swear by.

The interesting thing about this is that God's promise is inviolable. He did not need to take an oath on top of His promise. But in the case with Abraham, He did so to bolster Abraham's faith and, as the author stated in verse 17, God did so to show to all the heirs of the promise His own fidelity in keeping those promises.

The author is attempting to illustrate the inviolability of both men and God's oaths by using a comparison. The emphasis of the words "end" and "all" is used to strengthen the point that a vow confirms the argument. The use of the article "*orkos*" (oath) is a generic use of the article, indicating what is generally true about oaths. There is some debate over what the Greek nominal phrase "for confirmation" is connected with. It can be connected with "end" with a purposeful meaning, with "the oath" in the sense of "given for confirmation," or with the entire clause. The Greek noun translated "confirmation" is thought to be a legal guarantee. The use of the Greek emphatic *neuter* adjective as an adverb in this passage is significant in how it conveys God's unchanging will and the confirmation of His promise. This is further reinforced by the reference to God's "oath" in Hebrews 8–9 and the connection to Psalm 110:4, which affirms Jesus' role as High Priest. The author's use of this language is a powerful way of expressing God's unchangeable commitment to His promise and the importance of Jesus in the new covenant.

III. We Have this Hope (Hebrews 6:19–20)

Christian hope is often described as an anchor, a symbol that was popular among early Christians. This metaphor of an anchor reflects the security, stability, and strength of our hope. The anchor represents the hope we have that will not bend, twist, or break when under strain and will not slip or drag in a storm. This metaphor of an anchor is also seen in Hebrews 2:1, where a nautical metaphor of a drifting ship is used. This anchor is firmly and securely placed in the lives of Christians, providing a reliable source of hope and strength. The use of the present participle to describe hope as "entering the inner sanctuary behind the curtain" implies continuous, ongoing action.

This is a powerful metaphor that draws on the symbolism of the tabernacle and temple, which contained a physical veil that separated the holy place from the Holy of Holies. This inner sanctuary was the dwelling place of the glory of God, and only the high priest could enter once a year on the Day of Atonement. This powerful imagery of hope entering the inner sanctuary is taken up by the author of Hebrews in reference to Jesus' atoning work and His entrance into the heavenly sanctuary following His resurrection and ascension.

The author of Hebrews is making a very clear point in the repetition of the phrase "in the order of Melchizedek" in Hebrews 5:10 and 6:20. By using the inclusion of this phrase, the author is bracketing the semantic unit of Hebrews 5:11–6:20 to emphasize the role of Jesus in the order of Melchizedek. Furthermore, the addition of "forever" at the end of the clause in verse 20 is used to emphasize Jesus' high priesthood and draw attention to the fact that it will last eternally. This is evidenced by the literal translation of the Greek, which states, "according to the order of Melchizedek a high priest having become unto the ages." This has been interpreted in the NIV to mean "He has become a high priest forever, in the order of Melchizedek," indicating the reason for Jesus entering on our behalf. The aorist participle "having become" summarizes the work of Jesus throughout His life, from His incarnation to His resurrection, ascension, and exaltation. It is a powerful reminder of the authority and power of Jesus as a high priest for eternity. This section is formally ended by repeating the phrase "in the order of Melchizedek" at the beginning and end, thus providing closure to the discourse.

THE LESSON APPLIED

In the lesson, the writer writes about the hope Christians have in God. Let this hope be the anchor of your soul. Let it keep you focused on eternity. Set your affections on things above, not on things of this earth. When the storms of life threaten to cause you to doubt, meditate on your eternal hope.

LET'S TALK ABOUT IT
What kind of hope is promised to us in the Bible?

The hope described throughout the Bible is a firm confidence in God's promises. God promises every Christian hope: of resurrection (Acts 24:15); of the glory of God (Romans 5:2); of righteousness (Galatians 5:5); of our calling to salvation (Ephesians 1:18); of heaven (Colossians 1:5); of the Gospel (Colossians 1:23); of glory (Colossians 1:27); of Christ's return to take us to heaven (1 Thessalonians 4:1); of eternal life (Titus 1:2); a hope that is alive, not dead (1 Peter 1:3). Praise the Lord we have so many examples to look to in the Bible of our blessed hope! These can be so comforting on the days that feel truly hopeless, because we know that God's Word is true and it's impossible for Him to promise us something that isn't real.

GET SOCIAL
Share your views and tag us @rhboydco and use #Assurance.

Twitter
@rhboydco (#rhboydco)

Instagram
@rhboydco (#rhboydco)

Facebook
@rhboydco (#rhboydco)

www.rhboyd.com

HOME DAILY DEVOTIONAL READINGS
JUNE 24–30, 2024

MONDAY	TUESDAY	WEDNESDAY	THURSDAY	FRIDAY	SATURDAY	SUNDAY
My Heart Shall Not Fear	The Treasure of Knowing Christ	Jesus Makes a Difference	God Will Help the Fearful	The Wise Shall Shine Brightly	Encounter with Christ	A New Creature
Psalm 27	Philippians 3:1–14	Galatians 1:13–24	Isaiah 41:1–15	Daniel 12	Acts 9:1–9	Acts 26:1–11

FEARLESS WITNESS

ADULT TOPIC:	BACKGROUND SCRIPTURE: ACTS 26:1–11
HOPE IN GOD TRANSFORMS US	LESSON PASSAGE: ACTS 26:1–11

ACTS 26:1–11

King James Version

THEN Agrippa said unto Paul, Thou art permitted to speak for thyself. Then Paul stretched forth the hand, and answered for himself:

2 I think myself happy, king Agrippa, because I shall answer for myself this day before thee touching all the things whereof I am accused of the Jews:

3 Especially because I know thee to be expert in all customs and questions which are among the Jews: wherefore I beseech thee to hear me patiently.

4 My manner of life from my youth, which was at the first among mine own nation at Jerusalem, know all the Jews;

5 Which knew me from the beginning, if they would testify, that after the most straitest sect of our religion I lived a Pharisee.

6 And now I stand and am judged for the hope of the promise made of God, unto our fathers:

7 Unto which promise our twelve tribes, instantly serving God day and night, hope to come. For which hope's sake, king Agrippa, I am accused of the Jews.

8 Why should it be thought a thing incredible with you, that God should raise the dead?

9 I verily thought with myself, that I ought to do many things contrary to the name of Jesus of Nazareth.

10 Which thing I also did in Jerusalem: and many of the saints did I shut up in prison, hav-

New Revised Standard Version

AGRIPPA said to Paul, "You have permission to speak for yourself." Then Paul stretched out his hand and began to defend himself:

2 "I consider myself fortunate that it is before you, King Agrippa, I am to make my defense today against all the accusations of the Jews,

3 because you are especially familiar with all the customs and controversies of the Jews; therefore I beg of you to listen to me patiently.

4 "All the Jews know my way of life from my youth, a life spent from the beginning among my own people and in Jerusalem.

5 They have known for a long time, if they are willing to testify, that I have belonged to the strictest sect of our religion and lived as a Pharisee.

6 And now I stand here on trial on account of my hope in the promise made by God to our ancestors,

7 a promise that our twelve tribes hope to attain, as they earnestly worship day and night. It is for this hope, your Excellency, that I am accused by Jews!

8 Why is it thought incredible by any of you that God raises the dead?

9 "Indeed, I myself was convinced that I ought to do many things against the name of Jesus of Nazareth.

10 And that is what I did in Jerusalem; with authority received from the chief priests, I not

MAIN THOUGHT: And now I stand and am judged for the hope of the promise made of God, unto our fathers. (Acts 26:6, KJV)

ACTS 26:1–11

King James Version	*New Revised Standard Version*
ing received authority from the chief priests; and when they were put to death, I gave my voice against them.	only locked up many of the saints in prison, but I also cast my vote against them when they were being condemned to death.
11 And I punished them oft in every synagogue, and compelled them to blaspheme; and being exceedingly mad against them, I persecuted them even unto strange cities.	11 By punishing them often in all the synagogues I tried to force them to blaspheme, and since I was so furiously enraged at them, I pursued them even to foreign cities.

LESSON SETTING
Time: 70–90 CE
Place: Rome

LESSON OUTLINE
I. Paul's Defense Introduction (Acts 26:1–3)
II. Paul's Jewish Credentials (Acts 26:4–8)
III. Paul's Persecution Past (Acts 26:9–11)

UNIFYING PRINCIPLE

Our actions and life choices may seem strange and even unacceptable to others who observe us from a distance. What are we to do when those in authority question our actions and motives? Paul boldly bears witness to King Agrippa of his hope in God's promise to his ancestors.

INTRODUCTION

Paul's speech before King Agrippa is the culmination and climax of Paul's defense in chapters 21–26. It brings together and presents in final form all the themes of the previous five chapters. The charges against Paul that began with the temple mob in Acts 21:28 were given their final verdict by the Jewish king himself: Paul was innocent on all counts—he could have been set free (v. 31ff). Paul's own account of his conversion and commission from Christ, which

constituted the main subject of his speech before the crowd in the temple square (Acts 22:3–21), was repeated in the speech before Agrippa and indeed in its fullest form, as Paul shared his fulfillment of the commission—his witness for Christ (vv. 19–23). The theme of the Resurrection, which began with the divided Sanhedrin (Acts 23:6–10) and continued to remain a major issue in Paul's defense (Acts 24:15, 21; 25:19) was now given its most complete exposition (vv. 6–8, 23). Paul wanted all to know that his commitment to the risen Christ was the real reason for his bonds. The parallels to the passion of Christ, which began with Paul's journey to Jerusalem in chapter 21, likewise reach their high point in chapter 26.

EXPOSITION

I. PAUL'S DEFENSE INTRODUCTION (ACTS 26:1–3)

Paul's defense before King Agrippa was truly remarkable. Not only did he bring together all the themes from the previous chapters, but he also presented them in their fullest form. Paul passionately declared his innocence and also touched on his personal conversion and commission from Christ. He detailed his mission to preach the Gospel and his unwavering commitment to the risen Christ, which was the cause of his imprisonment. Paul's defense also echoed the passion of Christ, beginning with his own journey to Jerusalem in Acts 21. It was an emotional and powerful defense; nevertheless, Paul was sent to Rome as a prisoner because, as a citizen of Rome, he appealed to Caesar.

Paul was a courageous figure, standing before two of the most powerful authorities of his time—the Roman procurator and the Jewish king—yet refusing to back down from his beliefs. His faith and strength of character were remarkable; just as Jesus had been, he was found innocent of any wrongdoing. It is inspiring to think that, despite the power of these authorities and the danger of the situation, Paul was able to remain true to himself.

Paul paused for a moment to allow the revenant atmosphere to envelop the room fully. His presence was met with a wave of anticipation as he stood ready to address the audience. After making a few brief acknowledgments to the distinguished members of the audience, such as Festus (Acts 25:23–27), Paul began his speech with a humble and respectful demeanor, further adding to the solemnity of the occasion. Paul then motioned to the audience to indicate the beginning of his address. It was not the gesture for the silence that he had used to quiet the temple mob (Acts 21:40), but rather, the outstretched hand of a Greek orator.

Paul's address to King Agrippa and his distinguished hearers was presented in an eloquent and sophisticated manner. He was not pleading his case in a formal trial but rather providing Festus with the necessary information to present to Caesar. Paul used his persuasive rhetoric to emphasize the importance of his message, which was to be a witness to the truth of the Gospel. Through his words, Paul sought to make a lasting impression on his audience and to present a convincing argument in defense of the Gospel message. Of all the speeches in Acts, this one is cast in the most elevated, cultured language. Luke described Paul as beginning his defense (*apologeomai*). It was not a defense in the sense of a formal trial, since it was only a hearing to assist Festus in drawing up his report to Caesar (Acts 25:27). Paul was not defending himself before charges but instead offering his apologia, his personal testimony for his life as a Christian. Paul was actually pleased to be sharing his testimony with such high and esteemed rulers; he considered it an honor to be able to bear witness to what Jesus had done for him to these powerful men.

Addressing the king directly, Paul begins with a brief salutation and gratitude. Paul's appeal was directed to the king, asking him to listen patiently because of his knowledge of Judaism and his acquaintance with all the Jewish customs and controversies (vv. 2–3). As far as the "accusations of the Jews" were concerned, there was really only one left at this point. Tertullus' two charges had long been dismissed (Acts 24:5–7). Festus had already found Paul innocent of the charges of sedition and political agitation (Acts 25:18). The charge that Paul had defiled the temple had died out for want of any witnesses (Acts 24:18). There was really only one left—that Paul was teaching against the Jewish law (Acts 21:28). Festus knew himself to be incompetent in such matters; Agrippa was in a better position to judge.

II. Paul's Jewish Credentials (Acts 26:4–8)

As in the temple square speech, Paul began his testimony by referring to his upbringing in strict Judaism. He was reared among his own people, even in Jerusalem. He had been a Pharisee and had lived according to the strictest observances of the Jewish religion. Before the Sanhedrin, Paul stressed that his Pharisaic background closely linked up with his faith in the Resurrection and that this was the real issue behind his trial (Acts 23:6). Here, in the speech before Agrippa, he made the same connection. The references to his being a Pharisee (v. 5) and to his being on trial because of his hope in God's promises to the fathers (v. 6) are closely linked. The "hope" was realized in the Resurrection (cf. Acts 24:15). Paul had been born a true Jew, reared a true Jew, trained in the strictest Pharisaic viewpoint of Judaism, and still remained a true Jew. It was precisely his faith in the Resurrection of Jesus that most pointed to his fidelity to Judaism because in the Resurrection, Israel's hope in God's promises had been fulfilled. Paul's faith in the Resurrection of Jesus was a testament to his unwavering loyalty to Judaism. He was an advocate of the Pharisaic viewpoint of Judaism, and his faith in the Resurrection of Jesus was a confirmation of his faith in God's promises to Israel.

The Jews believed fervently in this hope. In their worship, they prayed for its fulfillment day and night. The hope was shared by all "twelve tribes"—all of Israel. It was truly unbelievable to Paul that the Jews, who had been hoping and praying for so long for the promises of God to be fulfilled, would turn against him because of his belief that Jesus had brought about those promises. Paul reiterates to Agrippa that "it is because of this hope that the Jews are accusing me." Even though it was heartbreaking, Paul never wavered in his faith and continued to spread the Gospel of Christ. At first, addressing the king (v. 7), he turned to the audience chamber's whole crowd and raised the question of why any of them would find it unbelievable that God should raise the dead. Was he putting this question to Jews or to the mainly Gentile gathering in the chamber or to all? Perhaps it was to all. Gentiles like Festus could not comprehend the idea of resurrection at all. Except for the Sadducees, the Jews believed in resurrection and fervently hoped for it but rejected Paul's conviction that it had begun in Christ. Paul's preaching of the Resurrection of Christ was remarkable and inspiring, as it demonstrated the fulfillment of God's promise that everyone could be saved, regardless of their background. He wanted all people to understand the power of Christ's resurrection and how it could bring them hope and peace. Through Christ, Jews and Gentiles could come together in unity and live their lives with joy and love.

Paul then asks a rhetorical question at this point "Why should any of you consider it incredible that God raises the dead?" It comes across as a general challenge to skeptical Jews on the basis of scriptural teaching. There were plenty of examples of miracles from the Old Testament that the Jews would've known inside and out, yet the idea of the promised Messiah rising from the dead was somehow beyond the limits of their beliefs. Paul is probably also appealing to Gentiles in the audience, saying in effect, "Once one admits there is an all-powerful God, why should anyone find the idea of resurrection incredible?" As such, it is a preliminary challenge to Festus, Agrippa, and others personally about Jesus and the Resurrection.

III. PAUL'S PERSECUTION PAST (ACTS 26:9–11)

Paul continues his testimony by saying that he too was once convinced to oppose Jesus Christ. Paul's conviction as a Pharisee was clear: he believed it was his duty to oppose the name of Jesus of Nazareth. He was driven by a sense of necessity to act as he did, which likely included challenging Jesus' teachings and attacking (and killing) those who believed in him. It must have been a difficult decision for Paul to make, but one that he felt compelled to do nonetheless. We can only imagine the internal struggle Paul must have experienced as he navigated his way through this dilemma. He then describes the cruelty and extents he went to in opposition of Christians. Not only had he been a Pharisee and a strict observant Jew, but he also had been a persecutor of the Christians. Like those Jews who were now accusing him, he too once felt that it was God's will for him to do everything possible to oppose the name of Christ.

Paul's transformation from a persecutor of Christians to a leader of the early Christian church is indeed a remarkable story. It is mentioned in many places throughout Acts, including his own description of his former zeal in pursuing the church (Acts 8:1; 9:1; 22:4). This transformation is a powerful testimony to the power of the Gospel and a reminder of how God can use even our worst mistakes for His glory.

Paul begins to share more details about his persecution of Christians in Jerusalem. He admits to having acted on the authority of the chief priests, though in Acts 9:1–2, Luke refers only to such authorization for the persecution of Christians in Damascus. Paul's involvement in the process of persecution across the region was comprehensive: he put many of the Lord's people in prison, and to have them sentenced to death, he also cast his vote against them. The last statement implies that Paul had a role in the process by which the Sanhedrin imposed the death penalty on Christians. However, there is no evidence to support that Paul was a member of the Sanhedrin, but rather, is simply pictured as approving of the death of Stephen (Acts 7:58; 8:1; 22:20). Paul's testimony also implies that there were many believers other than Stephen and James executed because of their faith in Jesus Christ.

Paul traveled from synagogue to synagogue harassing and imprisoning Christians. Paul confesses in his speech that he tried to force Christians to blaspheme. The text is not clear if Paul attempted to force them into blasphemy by making the Christians deny Christ in some way or whether Paul tried to get Christians to say things about Jesus that were considered blasphemous from a Jewish perspective and thereby worthy of punishment.

Paul was so zealous in his efforts that he even tracked Christians outside of Jerusalem to a place called Damascus (v. 11). This was the height of his persecution and, oddly, also the place where it concluded. Paul even admits that his cruel and zealous pursuit of the early disciples sprang not from earnest concerns for justice but from floods of rage. This rage demonstrates that despite his devout religious upbringing, he still didn't have a personal, loving relationship with God. We see from this text that Paul felt regret about his earlier actions and beliefs, and maybe this address to Agrippa was a way of purging those feelings and coming to peace with his past mistakes.

THE LESSON APPLIED

Rev. Dr. Martin Luther King Jr. once said, "We must accept finite disappointment, but we must never lose infinite hope." Based on the fact that hope is confidence in God's promises and that God's promises are fulfilled in Jesus, hope is not just "I wish it will happen," or "I dream it will happen," or "if my circumstances go this way, I can hold on." Hope is: I'm grounded in the person and work of Jesus. He IS sufficient. He IS enough. He IS good. He IS present—right now. In that sense, hope is not some far-off belief of a "someday" but it's clear and present in this very moment; it has already arrived because Jesus has already arrived. Praise the Lord!

GET SOCIAL

Share your views and tag us @rhboydco and use #WeHaveHope.

LET'S TALK ABOUT IT

Discuss how you feel when you are hopeful. What does hope feel like?

Hope gets inside of you; there's anticipation, and there's excitement, and you want to share it with others. It bubbles over from within and cannot be contained. It is internal, which means we can draw from it on days when we feel like giving up and we have nothing left. This is essentially what Paul says: "Hope got inside me in such a way that it sent me." Can you relate to that feeling? The life-shaping hope built on the promises of God is always a *sending* hope. Emily Dickinson once wrote, "'Hope' is the thing with feathers *[as if to say it causes you to fly]*, That perches in the soul, And sings the tune without the words, And never stops—at all."

If you find people who are invested, driven, and long to see God move and work, you will always find people of deep and abiding hope. Without the hope of change and a better tomorrow, people would never be motivated to look beyond their present circumstances.

Twitter
@rhboydco (#rhboydco)

Instagram
@rhboydco (#rhboydco)

Facebook
@rhboydco (#rhboydco)

www.rhboyd.com

HOME DAILY DEVOTIONAL READINGS
JULY 1–7, 2024

MONDAY	TUESDAY	WEDNESDAY	THURSDAY	FRIDAY	SATURDAY	SUNDAY
Forgive Us Our Trespasses	An Evil King Seals Judah's Fate	God's People Are Cast into Exile	Boldly Approach the Throne of Grace	God Will Remember Sins No More	Joy Comes with the Morning	Hope in God's Steadfast Love
Matthew 6:9–15	Jeremiah 52:1–15	Jeremiah 52:16–30	Hebrews 4:12–16	Hebrews 8:6–13	Psalm 30	Lamentations 3:16–24

CEASELESS LOVE

ADULT TOPIC: BACKGROUND SCRIPTURE: LAM. 3:16–24; PS. 30; JER. 52:1–30
HOPE COMES IN THE MORNING   LESSON PASSAGE: LAMENTATIONS 3:16–24

LAMENTATIONS 3:16—24

King James Version	*New Revised Standard Version*
HE hath also broken my teeth with gravel stones, he hath covered me with ashes.	HE has made my teeth grind on gravel, he has made me cower in ashes;
17 And thou hast removed my soul far off from peace: I forgat prosperity.	17 my soul is bereft of peace; I have forgotten what happiness is;
18 And I said, My strength and my hope is perished from the LORD:	18 so I say, "Gone is my glory and all that I had hoped for from the Lord."
19 Remembering mine affliction and my misery, the wormwood and the gall.	19 The thought of my affliction and my homelessness is wormwood and gall!
20 My soul hath them still in remembrance, and is humbled in me.	20 My soul continually thinks of it and is bowed down within me.
21 This I recall to my mind, therefore have I hope.	21 But this I call to mind, and therefore I have hope:
22 It is of the LORD's mercies that we are not consumed, because his compassions fail not.	22 The steadfast love of the Lord never ceases, his mercies never come to an end;
23 They are new every morning: great is thy faithfulness.	23 they are new every morning; great is your faithfulness.
24 The LORD is my portion, saith my soul; therefore will I hope in him.	24 "The Lord is my portion," says my soul, "therefore I will hope in him."

LESSON SETTING

Time: 586–575 BCE
Place: Unknown

LESSON OUTLINE

I. **God As an Adversary**
   (Lamentations 3:16–18)
II. **Sinking Soul**
   (Lamentations 3:19–20)
III. **God As Faithful**
   (Lamentations 3:21–24)

UNIFYING PRINCIPLE

We experience pain in life. In the midst of profound pain and disappointment, how do we overcome despair? The writer of Lamentations reminds us that God's steadfast love and faithfulness triumphs over despair.

INTRODUCTION

The book of Lamentations describes the fall of Jerusalem in 587–586 BC and is

MAIN THOUGHT: This I call to mind, and therefore I have hope: The steadfast love of the Lord never ceases, his mercies never come to an end. (Lamentations 3:21–22, KJV)

traditionally associated with the prophet Jeremiah, who was a witness to the fall (see 2 Chronicles 35:25). The destruction of Jerusalem, and particularly of the temple, was crushing to the Jewish people, for much of their theology was founded on the belief that God had given them this land, that God's glory dwelt in the temple, and that God would protect them from their enemies. The components of the book indicate that the poems were written not long after the destruction of Jerusalem in 586 BCE. Despite all the destruction and despair that the author had witnessed, he still calls on the people to praise God for His mercy in the midst of trials and hardship.

EXPOSITION

I. GOD AS AN ADVERSARY (LAMENTATIONS 3:16–18)

Lamentations is certainly an appropriate name for this book of the Bible, but why that is true requires some understanding of the situation of the time. For about thirty months, King Nebuchadnezzar of Babylon laid siege to Jerusalem. The city's encirclement was complete, and no one inside could get out, and no provisions from outside could get in. The people trapped in Jerusalem endured appalling conditions, and the majority either died then or when the siege was finally broken as the city walls were breached and the Babylonian soldiers broke through and massacred the people. The book of Lamentations spares nothing with its gruesome and graphic descriptions of suffering, death, slavery, and humiliation.

This lament has been interpreted either as a reflection of the personal experiences of the writer or as a personification of Jerusalem speaking for all the suffering people of the city. Were it not in the book of Lamentations, it is unlikely that the suffering described would be associated with the travail of Jerusalem, except for verses 40–51. The other verses could describe any individual's painfully distressing situation. The lament includes many phrases taken from lament psalms with which the author was familiar. The suffering is so great that the author compares God to being like an adversary in this scenario, leaving the Israelites to their fates.

Verse 16 describes the violence and brutality the writer has been privy to. The writer's description was as though God had broken the victim's teeth by forcing him to eat rocks and then trampled him in the dust. He had been deprived of peace, happiness, well-being, and prosperity. He had been stripped of his former strength and is a shell of himself. His future is bleak. The speaker reached the lowest point of despair in verse 18, declaring that all his hope in the Lord had been destroyed. Suffering and the Lord's seeming indifference had driven him to this conclusion. Hope has dissipated because it seems as if the Lord has turned a blind eye to his suffering. Have you ever felt like you were suffering and the Lord had abandoned you? Like there was no hope left, and you had nothing left to give? That is the feeling of the writer in this section. It's a desperate, agonizing place to be.

II. Sinking Soul (LAMENTATIONS 3:19–20)

It is a heartbreaking situation when someone feels abandoned by the Lord and can no longer find hope. We may not be able to understand all the reasons why a person goes through such suffering, but we can still offer comfort and be a source of strength. It is important to recognize that these feelings of despair do not last forever and that, even in our darkest moments, we can still reach out to God and trust in His divine plan. In times of hardship, it is important to remember that the Lord is always with us and that He is always working to bring us peace and prosperity.

In verse 20, the writer states that the suffering is so traumatic that it constantly reverberates in his mind and soul. He thinks about it continuously. The suffering is retrospectively impressed upon his heart and memory, and now it has left him depressed and full of despair. His soul is bowed down within himself. The remembrance creates inner despondency, intimately felt oppression, and even sorrow.

Indeed, the writer is not the first or only person in the Bible to accuse God of cruelty. Many of our ancestors endured harsh and inhumane treatment throughout history, but despite their injustice, they continued to have faith that God would eventually free them and bless their descendants. The stories of their resilience and determination in the face of difficult circumstances are an inspiration to us all.

All this horror lies in the background of the book of Lamentations. No wonder it is filled with so much regret, sadness, and despair as the scarred minds of survivors reflect on those dreadful months of terror, death, and humiliation. It was all because the people and their leaders had turned away from God. So easily, therefore, they could now reach the ultimate conclusion that God had given up on them, that there would be no rescue and, therefore, no future for them. Instead of being known as the chosen people, they would be the abandoned people. In the midst of that darkness—and right in the middle of the book of Lamentations—shines a light that offers a future worth living for.

III. GOD AS FAITHFUL (LAMENTATIONS 3:21–24)

At the writer's deepest despair, and as he recalled his pain and affliction, a remarkable transition in his attitude took place. His hopelessness, expressed in verses 18–20, turned to hope as he remembered the Lord. His mourning was turned into dancing. The unbroken mood of despair was displaced by a beautiful affirmation of hope in spite of suffering. This is not a smug or naively optimistic hope, but a serious and profound act of expectation that is only too aware of the painful reality from which it demands deliverance. Hope is something of great value. Thankfully, what the writer of Lamentations found was good hope and not empty hope.

This first part of the hinge, then, looks backward to all that has come before in the poem, grounding its inflection of hope in the writer's expressions of hurt and complaint. But what causes the writer to go from hopeless to full of hope? The basis for renewed hope is God's "great love." The Hebrew word *hesed*, translated as "covenant love" or "loyal love," is a word that has the basic meaning of loyalty or faithfulness, especially as related to the covenant initiated by God; the word involves obligations to family, friends, and the community. Another basis of hope is God's unfailing "compassion." It is similar to the tender, caring love of a mother for her child. The writer says these compassions are experienced in a fresh and new way every day. God's care and love never run stale or trite every day. They are fresh and fulfilling. This *ḥeseḏ* love has its source in God's character. He is the God who is love through and through, whose love is not dependent on deserving but is poured out even on the weakest and worst in society. And *ḥeseḏ* love is shown to His people because of God's commitment. The Lord brought Israel into existence, made them His own, and though they have failed and though that failure has caused dire consequences, He will not give up on them. It's a love that's unflinching and unending, a firm love that never gives up on His people.

Earlier, the writer accused God of cruelty and faithlessness. Now, he exalted God's love and "faithfulness." From such committed love comes the certainty that good times are ahead because there will be no less love tomorrow than today, as the writer says of God's compassions in verse 23. Verse 23 is the best-known and often quoted verse in Lamentations and quoted in the great hymn of the Christian Church, "Great Is Thy Faithfulness." The writer is particular about God's consistency; He will not love us today but forget us tomorrow. The writer of Hebrews described the Lord Jesus as "the same yesterday and today and forever" (Hebrews 13:8). That is God's consistent character: His faithfulness.

In the midst of chaos and depression, the poet revealed a deep faith (vv. 22–24) in the trustworthiness of God: "Great is your faithfulness" (*ĕmûnâ*). This word is from *'mn* in the verb and is connected to the word *'amen*, which means "so be it,"

the word that closes prayers. Its meaning in English is connected to truth, faith, and trustworthiness. Concerning God, this word occurs only during and after the exile (Jeremiah 52). The semantic field of the word is that of constancy and reliability. It was a unique characteristic of the Lord. Contrary to the way neighboring peoples viewed their gods, the Jews now understood their God to be faithful to them, and there is no greater hope than knowing that God is totally reliable. God had always been faithful (Exodus 34:6–7), but the point here is that the people finally realized it. Often in life, people do not realize the faithfulness of God until the "bottom has fallen out" of their lives. In Lamentations 3, God's "faithfulness" is interpreted in light of His promise to destroy, which He had done, and His promise to restore, which he would do. The poet realized that restoration was on its way, both nationally and individually. This was both an individual and communal restoration. In a metaphor made bold by such a context of judgment, he claimed God as his "portion" (*ḥeleq*). This is a word that describes something that belongs to someone: "Yahweh is all I have." The writer realized that God was all he had but was also all he needed.

The other reason we can trust God is His goodness. Because His love for us will be the same tomorrow as today, the blessings we have known in the past will be matched with the blessings He gives us in the future. Some people seem to imagine God has a limited store of good things for their lives, and perhaps His stock has been exhausted, and therefore the future for them will be inevitably bad. But their ideas are wrong. God's store is not limited, and the goodness of God we have known before we will know again.

The writer knows the one true God is good, and His love is still there for him now and will be there every day. Therefore, he will have this one true God as his portion. This God will be his choice. This God will be his investment. This God will have his loyalty, his love, and his service. It's a choice made without conditions. "I will wait for him," he writes. He won't try to control God by demanding that He acts by "this date" or in "this way." You may have known people who gave up on God because He didn't do what they asked when they asked. God did not meet their timetable: the terms they'd decided were reasonable if God was to merit their loyalty. But this is not the attitude that the writer of Lamentations has here, and we can follow his example.

THE LESSON APPLIED

The hope and faith that the writer comes to can be illustrated as a small child running straight to their parent and jumping into their parent's arms. Not for a moment does the child think their parent will keep their arms by their side and let them fall to the ground. The child knows for sure that their parent will open up those arms, wrap them close to them, and hold them safe. It's what a loving parent would do, and the child has no doubts about their parent's love for them. This same security that a child feels is the same security Christians can have in God's faithfulness and love.

LET'S TALK ABOUT IT

Have you ever felt as if your hope was dissipating?

Maybe you can relate to the feeling of despair that the author is describing in this passage (and whole book). No human is immune to the struggles of this world, whether that's financial burdens, relationship woes, trauma, abuse, a chronic illness, etc. All of these situations can make someone feel hopeless. What caused you to regain your hope? How has your hope in God helped you in difficult times?

GET SOCIAL
Share your views and tag us @rhboydco and use #CeaselessLove.

Twitter
@rhboydco (#rhboydco)

Instagram
@rhboydco (#rhboydco)

Facebook
@rhboydco (#rhboydco)

www.rhboyd.com

HOME DAILY DEVOTIONAL READINGS
JULY 8–14, 2024

MONDAY	TUESDAY	WEDNESDAY	THURSDAY	FRIDAY	SATURDAY	SUNDAY
The Fragrance of Knowing God	The Testimony of the Redeemed	Sing of God's Deeds with Joy	Hope Laid Up in Heaven	Proclaim Christ's Boundless Riches	Refuge in the Lord	I Will Hope and Praise Continually
2 Corinthians 2:12–17	Psalm 107:1–9	Psalm 107:10–22	Colossians 1:3–12	Ephesians 3:1–13	Psalm 71:1–11	Psalm 71:12–21

CONTINUAL PROCLAMATION

ADULT TOPIC:	BACKGROUND SCRIPTURE: PSALM 71:12–21
GOD IS FAITHFUL	LESSON PASSAGE: PSALM 71:12–21

PSALM 71:12–21

King James Version

O GOD, be not far from me: O my God, make haste for my help.

13 Let them be confounded and consumed that are adversaries to my soul; let them be covered with reproach and dishonour that seek my hurt.

14 But I will hope continually, and will yet praise thee more and more.

15 My mouth shall shew forth thy righteousness and thy salvation all the day; for I know not the numbers thereof.

16 I will go in the strength of the Lord God: I will make mention of thy righteousness, even of thine only.

17 O God, thou hast taught me from my youth: and hitherto have I declared thy wondrous works.

18 Now also when I am old and greyheaded, O God, forsake me not; until I have shewed thy strength unto this generation, and thy power to every one that is to come.

19 Thy righteousness also, O God, is very high, who hast done great things: O God, who is like unto thee!

20 Thou, which hast shewed me great and sore troubles, shalt quicken me again, and shalt bring me up again from the depths of the earth.

21 Thou shalt increase my greatness, and comfort me on every side.

New Revised Standard Version

O GOD, do not be far from me; O my God, make haste to help me!

13 Let my accusers be put to shame and consumed; let those who seek to hurt me be covered with scorn and disgrace.

14 But I will hope continually, and will praise you yet more and more.

15 My mouth will tell of your righteous acts, of your deeds of salvation all day long, though their number is past my knowledge.

16 I will come praising the mighty deeds of the Lord God, I will praise your righteousness, yours alone.

17 O God, from my youth you have taught me, and I still proclaim your wondrous deeds.

18 So even to old age and gray hairs, O God, do not forsake me, until I proclaim your might to all the generations to come. Your power

19 and your righteousness, O God, reach the high heavens. You who have done great things, O God, who is like you?

20 You who have made me see many troubles and calamities will revive me again; from the depths of the earth you will bring me up again.

21 You will increase my honour, and comfort me once again.

MAIN THOUGHT: I will hope continually, and will praise you yet more and more. (Psalm 71:14, KJV)

UNIFYING PRINCIPLE

Our interpretation of past events profoundly influences our experience of the present. What helps us interpret past and present situations in ways that are beneficial to us and others? In Psalm 71, the poet's hope is maintained by continual praise for God's past acts of faithfulness and love.

INTRODUCTION

No author is named for this psalm. There are Davidic expressions—for example, "my rock and my fortress," "my enemies," and "make haste!" But as the writer is drawing freely on earlier psalms, this tells us little. All that we know, or need to know, is that he is old or aging and has seen exceptional trouble (v. 7), which shows no sign of abating. Against his failing strength, he now sets a long memory of God's faithfulness and a growing hope in his life-renewing power. This psalm has been dubbed the "Psalm for the Aging." Even if we're not near the end of our life, everyone is aging each day and could benefit from reflecting on the goodness of God in their lives. This psalm also reminds readers of the dual existence of tragedy and joy, heartbreak and thankfulness. These things aren't mutually exclusive, which is the reason why we're able to praise God in any circumstance.

EXPOSITION

I. HELP ME AGAINST MY ENEMIES (PSALM 71:12–13)

The psalmist knew the sweetness of his salvation, and he knew the glory of the days he had walked with the Lord; but he did not know how many days remained for him to do so (vv. 12–15). In verse 12, the writer pleads with God to be near to him. The poet clearly felt like the walls were closing in around him and he didn't know what to do other than cry out to the Lord. Can you relate to this feeling? In many situations, there is nothing that anyone can do to help, so we cry out to God for supernatural intervention. The help the psalmist requested was for his enemies to be confused and consumed. He wanted God to strike his adversaries with confusion—perhaps so that his location would remain hidden. Perhaps so they would forget their mission to find him.

We're not sure exactly what confusion he wanted God to bring about, but this was the only solution that the psalmist could come up with. He also wanted others not to trust his enemies' opinions, beliefs, and prophecies, which is why he requested that they be discredited. Maybe if his enemies were going around seeking information and support from local towns and cities, if they were discredited, no one would provide the reinforcements they were seeking. However it happened, the writer just wanted his enemies stopped in their tracks and he didn't care how that was accomplished.

The prayer became more prophetic than supplication. A prophetic rant and admonishment. The prayer was full of conviction and passion. It was a passionate call to action, urging God to take action and make a difference in the circumstance. The writer is begging God to defend and avenge him against his adversaries to the point that the enemies will be embarrassed and silenced. Perhaps you can relate to this feeling. Have you ever wished that something bad would happen to someone who was "out to get you?" Nothing terrible, but maybe that they'd spill coffee on their new shirt or they would look foolish in front of their boss in a staff meeting. It's human nature to seek retaliation when we have deemed that someone has wronged us, no matter how small or petty the grievance is. The psalmist here felt very strongly about his enemies because they were seeking to kill him, probably. Therefore, he wanted God to take them out before they could take him out, however God wanted to accomplish that. He understood that his only chance for survival was if God interfered with their evil plans. One way to interpret these statements is as they are prophetic—not, "will you please do this for me" but "let this be done as I say." There was more of a demand than a polite question, which seems to be on par with the writer's desperation.

II. RISING HOPE
   (PSALM 71:14–16)

Despite the writer's panicked pleas and demands, Psalm 71 is a beautiful testament to the power of faith and the strength of resilience. It's a reminder that even in the darkest of times, it's possible to still cling to hope and trust in God's goodness. The psalmist acknowledges his distress and calls out to God for help, yet he also expresses his faith in God's protection and love. This psalm is a powerful reminder that even when life is difficult, we can still believe in the hope and faith that God provides. In our world, we struggle to put things into boxes and make them black and white. If things are black and white, then they're easier to understand, categorize and deal with. But human emotions are not so easily compartmentalized, and often things coexist in the most unexpected ways. Consider how a mother in labor is feeling intense pain yet ecstatic joy simultaneously. On a day when a parent's child graduates high school or college, the parent is overwhelmed with pride but also sadness that their child is one step farther into adulthood and not their little baby anymore. All around us, we experience these conflicting emotions, and this psalm is representative of that.

The psalmist makes a bold declaration to have hope continuously. Though the psalmist has aged and he has witnessed devastation and trauma, he still has hope despite all the pain. The psalmist maintained hope that God would deliver him. Not only will the psalmist remain hopeful, but also full of praise. Even if God didn't choose to save him in that moment, he had an entire lifetime to look back on and see the times where God did provide and make a way, and for that, God still deserved praise. Hope was immortal and eternal, burning intensely bright for the psalmist bringing forth a song of praise which, as it shall always continue to arise, so shall it always gather new force. Hope based on God brings forth a new possibility of praise. The psalmist expresses hope and praise (v. 14), which is the proper response to God's righteous acts and deeds of salvation (v. 15). The psalmist then says that he will continue on in the strength that comes from God alone, and he will continue telling others of God's righteousness.

Even when he's feeling defeated, the psalmist is committed to exalting God's name, no matter what circumstances he may be facing. If in that moment he doesn't have anything to give thanks or praise for, he can look ahead to the future when his circumstances will be different and thank God in advance for the work that is yet to be done. What a powerful challenge for us today! Yet again, this is a reminder that God is always worthy of praise, no matter what situation we're in. If your circumstances are dire, look back at how God has redeemed a situation before, or look ahead and imagine how God will redeem this one in the future. This is how we can give thanks in all circumstances, as it says in 1 Thessalonians 5:16–18.

How good are you at this? It's often easy to praise God in the good times, when things are going our way, but as soon as the scales tip, we go from praising to pleading for help. Rather than one over the other, it should be both simultaneously: recognizing that our help comes from God alone and praising Him if He chooses to intercede or not, according to His perfect will. Sometimes He will and sometimes He won't; He sees the bigger picture that's impossible for our human minds to understand. But we know and trust that He is good and has our best interests at heart. So let everything that has breath praise the Lord, as it says in Psalm 150:6.

God had been faithful to the psalmist in his youth (v. 17); God's faithfulness will continue unto his old age. That is, God had guided and instructed him from his earliest years. He had made known to him his own being and perfections. He had made his duty plain and he had led him along the dangerous path of life.

"And hitherto have I declared," meaning, "I have made known." That is, the psalmist had done this by public praise; he had done it by his writings; he had done it by maintaining and defending the truth. In all situations of life, up to that time, he had been willing to stand up for God and His cause. With a reason annexed to it, suggested in the following words: "Until I have showed thy strength unto this generation" or "thine arm" (v. 18)—which sometimes refers to the Messiah (Isaiah 53:1)—by whose power the worlds were made, in whom all things consist, who has wrought out the salvation of people, and is the arm on which they lean and are upheld. The psalmist may have desired to continue a while longer and be favored with the presence of God and the influences of His Spirit and grace, that he might show forth in prophecy—both by word and writing to those of his present age—more things concerning the person, office, and grace of Christ.

Sometimes the arm of the Lord denotes His power and strength (Psalm 44:3), and so it may be taken here. And the next clause seems to be an explanation of it: "To everyone that is to come." That is, to come into the world or to be born into it—namely, the power of God, not only in creating all things out of nothing, and supporting what is made, but in the redemption of men, in the conversion of sinners, in the preservation of the saints, and in enabling them to hold on and out unto the end. This is shown forth by the psalmist in what he has committed to writing, and which continue, and will continue, to the end of the world, for the instruction of those that come into it (see Psalm 22:31).

The writer is saying that he is older and wiser in his old age, but his strength of youth is gone. He is saying, in essence, I was young and now I am old, but I know You will be with me and I shall win. He knew he was not fighting them in his strength, but in God's strength. He wanted to show the next generation just how powerful God is. The power and character of God is so far above anything that we know, that it is impossible to imagine it in its entirety. The goodness of God is above all. There is no one on the earth or in heaven, or anywhere else, that is a match for God.

This is not asking God to do it, but is spoken in holy confidence knowing that God will do this. "Your righteousness, O God," is very high; the psalmist considered the greatness of God, first in that His righteousness was of a different order than that of men, very high above that of men, and then that God is the one who has done great things, beyond what men can do. The surpassing righteousness and power of God made him ask, "O God, who is like You?" The psalmist felt like he could go on all day with praise for God, that is how indescribable and all-encompassing it was. There are truly no limits to God's glory and salvation, therefore, there can be no limits to our praise for Him! We should follow the writer's example in our everyday lives. Truly, there is no excuse to not praise the Lord when you consider how this psalmist was praising God despite fearing for his life and being surrounded by enemies. If he can do that, so can we!

When the psalmist is emphasizing God's righteousness over all others, he was making a point to recognize God's superiority over the pagan gods of the time. Whether the writer was speaking to future readers who might come across this poem or just reminding himself, he understood that no false idols had the righteousness and faithfulness of the Lord, the one true God. Idols may look different today but the point is still true. God is still greater than any political hero, any celebrity, any hobby or pastime, or even a significant other or family member. While those things may be nice, they in no way compare to God's righteousness nor can they accomplish what He can in your life. Anyone who promises otherwise is attempting to deceive you, and we must be on our guard always!

Remember that "your enemy the devil prowls around like a roaring lion looking for someone to devour" (1 Peter 5:8). Just as he sought to destroy the Israelites of old, so does he want to destroy you now; his methods have simply changed. Instead of a neighboring country going to war, he sneaks in through social media, status, and promises of power and influence. But praise the Lord that no matter what method he utilizes, God is still greater! As long as we have our faith in Him, we know we will be on the winning side of history. God doesn't owe us this—or anything—as we are wretched sinners without Him, but He offers His protection and power freely to His children.

THE LESSON APPLIED

Regardless of who wrote this psalm, we know that it was written by an aging believer who was looking back on his life and recognizing God's faithfulness. As he was able to look back and see what God had done for him, he had confidence and faith in the Lord to remain faithful to him for the rest of his days on earth.

In essence, this is why the Bible is so important for believers today. It allows us to look back on years and generations of stories, examples, and instances when God was faithful to His people. If it was true then, it is true still today. Therefore, we can have the same faith and confidence in God that this psalmist did.

When you face challenges throughout life, you can fall back on these words of the psalmist to remind yourself that God is faithful and no one can match His righteousness. Moreover, you can look back on your own life and recall how God has been active in your life. Whatever the circumstance, no matter how dire things appear, there is nothing too big for God to handle. There is nothing beyond His reach of saving, or outside His scope of expertise or jurisdiction. That in and of itself is worthy of praise!

LET'S TALK ABOUT IT
How has the Lord been faithful to you?

This will look differently for each student, because God has an individual relationship with His children. How He interacts and provides for one child may be drastically different than another, and that doesn't mean He loves one more or less. Instead, it reveals how personal His relationship is with each of us because He knows that we all have different needs and desires. Aren't you glad that you aren't just a number to Him, but a real person with a specific personality, likes and dislikes? He knows you intimately because He created you! When you consider your own siblings, did your parents treat you all exactly the same—or did they recognize that your brother preferred X while you preferred Y? That's what a loving parent does. When you look back on your walk with the Lord, what examples can you see of Him being faithful? How can you use these examples of righteousness as a testimony to others, or as a testimony and reminder to yourself on the difficult days?

GET SOCIAL
Share your views and tag us @rhboydco and use #GodIsGood.

Twitter
@rhboydco (#rhboydco)

Instagram
@rhboydco (#rhboydco)

Facebook
@rhboydco (#rhboydco)

www.rhboyd.com

HOME DAILY DEVOTIONAL READINGS
JULY 15–21, 2024

MONDAY	TUESDAY	WEDNESDAY	THURSDAY	FRIDAY	SATURDAY	SUNDAY
Equipped for Every Good Work	Resist Temptation	Every Word of God Proves True	Let Christ's Word Abound in You	Doers of the Word	Lord, Teach Me Your Statutes	Hope in God's Word
2 Timothy 3:10–17	Matthew 4:1–11	Proverbs 30:1–9	Colossians 3:12–17	James 1:19–27	Psalm 119:57–72	Psalm 119:73–80

DELIGHTFUL PRECEPTS

ADULT TOPIC:	BACKGROUND SCRIPTURE: PSALM 119:73–80
GOD'S WORD BRINGS HOPE	LESSON PASSAGE: PSALM 119:73–80

PSALM 119:73–80

King James Version

THY hands have made me and fashioned me: give me understanding, that I may learn thy commandments.

74 They that fear thee will be glad when they see me; because I have hoped in thy word.

75 I know, O Lord, that thy judgments are right, and that thou in faithfulness hast afflicted me.

76 Let, I pray thee, thy merciful kindness be for my comfort, according to thy word unto thy servant.

77 Let thy tender mercies come unto me, that I may live: for thy law is my delight.

78 Let the proud be ashamed; for they dealt perversely with me without a cause: but I will meditate in thy precepts.

79 Let those that fear thee turn unto me, and those that have known thy testimonies.

80 Let my heart be sound in thy statutes; that I be not ashamed.

New Revised Standard Version

YOUR hands have made and fashioned me; give me understanding that I may learn your commandments.

74 Those who fear you shall see me and rejoice, because I have hoped in your word.

75 I know, O LORD, that your judgments are right, and that in faithfulness you have humbled me.

76 Let your steadfast love become my comfort according to your promise to your servant.

77 Let your mercy come to me, that I may live; for your law is my delight.

78 Let the arrogant be put to shame, because they have subverted me with guile; as for me, I will meditate on your precepts.

79 Let those who fear you turn to me, so that they may know your decrees.

80 May my heart be blameless in your statutes, so that I may not be put to shame.

LESSON SETTING

Time: 450 BC

Place: Unknown

LESSON OUTLINE

I. **The Provision of God's Hands (Psalm 119:73–74)**

II. **When God Afflicts (Psalm 119:75–77)**

III. **The Proud vs. the Humble (Psalm 119:78–80)**

UNIFYING PRINCIPLE

People are unsure where to seek help and comfort. Where do we find hope, and how do we encourage others in times of need? In Psalm 119, the psalmist finds delight and assurance in God's Word.

INTRODUCTION

Psalm 119 is twice as long as any of the other psalms included in the collection

MAIN THOUGHT: Your hands have made and fashioned me; give me understanding that I may learn your commandments. (Psalm 119: 73, KJV)

of Psalms. Throughout the psalm, it includes proverbial literature. There are also numerous hints about what the author was like. The author of Psalm 119 trusts in the Lord. The author is teachable, desiring to learn the Lord's way (v. 73), and aspires to obey the Lord's Word. The author expresses a deep commitment to God's way but also realizes how prone he is to wander from it (v. 80). Similarly, it is difficult to determine the exact events or occasions surrounding and prompting the creation of this psalm. It is, however, evident that the psalmist was facing affliction (v. 71; 83) and a desperate crisis (v. 84; 87). It is clear that the psalmist faced wickedness and took his refuge in God as the Giver of all, including his strength to face the evils of the world. When we take refuge in the Lord, He promises to protect us. In a previous psalm, the writer said, "I will take refuge in the shadow of your wings until the disaster has passed" (Psalm 57:1). It's a common theme in this book for the writer to go running to God when times are tough, and that's what our immediate reaction should be today as well! There is no safer place to go. The world may tempt us that we should put our hope in a political candidate, a world leader, or a new bill being passed into law, but in the end, all of those things will end in disappointment. God is the only One who will never fail you.

EXPOSITION

I. THE PROVISION OF GOD'S HANDS (PSALM 119:73–74)

This section of the psalm begins with a quotation from Job 10:8: "Your hands have made me and fashioned me," but Job added, "An intricate unity." Every human is complex in working, but it works as a unit. The only thing missing from a person is the "understanding" to connect with and use God's "commandments" (words showing what should and shouldn't be done). "Thy hands" figuratively refers to God's involvement in human life (Psalm 139:13–16). It is a recognition by the psalmist of the fact that he was created by God. The statement "fashioned me" reminds readers of the fact that God reached into the dust of the earth and formed and fashioned a clay doll that He called man. He breathed the breath of life into that clay doll, and he became a living soul. He is saying, "God, You made me, so it is in Your power to give me understanding." This is very much like Jesus opening the understanding of the disciples. The psalmist does not just want to read the commandments, but he wants to understand what they are saying. He wants to learn from the One who fashioned him and who knows him thoroughly, so he calls on the Lord to give him understanding that will enable him to learn what He has commanded. He needs understanding from God if he is to learn God's Word.

"They that fear Thee" is possibly speaking of those who reverence God. All who "fear God" are "glad" to know there's another who has "hoped" in God's "word." When God opens our understanding to His teachings, we should share it with others so that they might understand too. Christians should be overjoyed when God has revealed something to someone. There is no place for jealousy among believers. It seems here that the Lord revealed the truth to the psalmist, because he placed his hope in the Word. If you diligently study the Bible, you will be amazed at what God will reveal to you. The psalmist realizes that the Lord is both working in him and through him. His individual life is a small but vital part in the Lord's larger plan, and he wants his life with its hope in God's Word to encourage others who revere the Lord. He is confident that how he responds to the Lord will prompt others to praise the Lord as well. This goes to show the responsibility that believers have to one another; the faith of one can uplift another.

II. WHEN GOD AFFLICTS (PSALM 119:75–77)

The psalmist expresses his confidence in God's sovereignty over human affliction referred to in this passage (vv. 119:67, 71; compare Deuteronomy 32:39; Isaiah 45:7; Lamentations 3:37–38). He trusts the fact that God would not allow anything to come upon him that was not for his own good. Many times, afflictions make us closer to God. We pray more when there is a problem in our lives. Even Paul had a thorn in his flesh. We will see what Paul has to say the reason for his affliction was: "And lest I should be exalted above measure through the abundance of the revelations, there was given to me a thorn in the flesh, the messenger of Satan to buffet me, lest I should be exalted above measure" (2 Corinthians 12:7). Afflictions are sometimes for our good. Neither the psalmist here, nor Paul, questioned the judgment of God in their afflictions. Picking up his thought from verse 67, the psalmist affirms that the Lord did what was right when He afflicted him. He had gone astray before he was afflicted, so the Lord had

responded to his sin in a manner that was righteous and faithful. What the Lord says and does flows out of who He is. When "affliction" occurs, we know God wants us to emerge with a yield of "the peaceable fruit of righteousness to those who have been trained by it" (Hebrews 12:11).

Afflictions are times to see God's "merciful kindness" (attempts to help) as "comfort," according to His "word" (what He actually has said). He is the "God of all comfort, who comforts us in all our tribulation, that we may be able to comfort those who are in any trouble, with the comfort with which we ourselves are comforted by God" (2 Corinthians 1:3–4). God's merciful kindness is shown in the provision and promise of a Savior. In the forgiveness of sins through Him, discovery and application of which yields comfort under afflictions.

"According to thy word unto thy servant" is a message of promise wherein God had assured the psalmist of His love, grace, mercy, and kindness. It was also a promise that He would continue it to him and comfort him with it. The psalmist here is not asking God to remove the affliction; he is just asking Him to make it possible for him to go through it. He is even saying, "help me to find comfort in the affliction." God does not mind us reminding Him of His Word. In fact, He likes to know that we know what His Word says.

The untranslatable particle *nā'* indicates that in verse 76, the psalmist strongly entreats the Lord to comfort him. He does not make demands of the Lord; instead, he beseeches Him as a servant to his master. Instead of trying to comfort himself or to turn to others for comfort, he seeks the faithful love of the Lord to comfort him. He calls on the Lord to be true to His promised commitment to him.

Again the psalmist appeals to the Lord's character, only this time to his *raḥămîm* ("compassion"). This rich term "signifies a warm compassion, a compassion which goes the second mile, which is ready to forgive sin, to replace judgment with grace" (*New American Commentary: Psalms 73–150*, Estes, Daniel J. B&H Publishing Group, 2019) His life, which delights in the Lord's instruction (cf. v. 97), is dependent on divine grace and mercy. Affliction can help us see God's "tender mercies" (reminders of His love for us) "that I may live" (still have a purpose, knowing God cares for me). Through it all, we see God's "law" (words guiding the straight path) is the only thing that brings "delight" (satisfaction at progress).

"That I may live" is evidence that this was uttered in view of some great calamity by which his life was threatened. He was dependent for life, for recovery from sickness, or for deliverance from danger, wholly on the compassion of God. "For thy law is my delight" is urged here as a reason for the divine interposition. The meaning is that he was a friend of God; that he had pleasure in His service and in His commandments; and that he might, therefore, appeal to God to interpose on his behalf. This is a proper ground of appeal to God in our prayers, not on the ground of merit or claim, but because we may reasonably suppose that God will be disposed to protect His friends and to deliver them in the day of trouble. Notice that he has added the word "tender" to the mercies of God. This type of mercy would be the kind a loving Father would show to His young child. Well, is that not what the believers are?

III. THE PROUD VS. THE HUMBLE (PSALM 119:78–80)

Referring here to his enemies, the psalmist asks that they might be confounded or put to shame. That is, that they might fail to accomplish their purposes in regard to him. They were not honest, and they were not true to their professions of friendship to the psalmist. This means that they deceived him in their dealings with him. We remember who "the proud" are: they are too proud to humble themselves and receive the Lord. They are lost. This would be a common practice of someone who was lost; they would have no conscience, and they would do whatever it took to benefit them. He is saying, that even though they dealt with him in a crooked manner, he will not do the same to them, because he remembers the teachings of God's Law. "The proud" have not triumphed by their wrongful mistreatment "with falsehood;" for the believer has survived their false attacks, seeing truth in God's Word and ways. After the affliction and false attacks, experience gives even more reason to "meditate" (give slow, thoughtful consideration of) God's "precepts" (what God has emphasized or pointed out).

Because the psalmist feels alone in adversity, he longs for others who, like him, revere the Lord to come alongside him in his time of affliction (cf. v. 63, where the psalmist states that he is a friend of all who fear the Lord). This is fellowship built on shared commitment to the Lord and His Word. The believer who endures with faith becomes an encouragement to all others who "fear

God." Everyone who "knows God" has combined "testimonies" (words pointing beyond to God) with experiences. "Those who can see and appreciate the beauty of thy commandments" is the ground of true friendship in religion, the common love of God, of His Law, and of His service. All friendship that is founded on earthly distinctions—all derived from titled birth, from rank, from affluence, from civil, military, or naval renown, from beauty, strength, or nobleness of form—must be temporary. But that which is founded on attachment to God, to His Law, and to the Savior, will abide forever.

"Those that fear thee" is possibly speaking of those who hold God in high esteem. The psalmist here is saying for God to cause those who believe in God to come and line up with him. He understood the comfort that comes from people walking alongside you when you're going through a tough time. Even if there's nothing they can physically do to help you, it can be so uplifting to recognize the emotional support of a friend or loved one. Just to have someone check in and say they've been praying for you can make a huge difference in your general mood and outlook on the situation.

As he appeals to the Lord to sustain him in his time of need, the psalmist is not blind to his own weaknesses. Realizing that for humans, the heart is the root of the problem (cf. Jer 17:9), he longs to have a blameless or united heart (cf. Ps. 86:11) before God, not a divided heart that will lead to disobedience and disgrace. Godly living throughout the Bible begins in the heart and works out into transformed behavior; it is not a cosmetic makeover that tries to produce the appearance of godliness through actions that are not prompted by a heart devoted to the Lord. The psalmist desires that he might have a sincere regard for the ways and worship, ordinances and commands of God. Not in show and appearance only, but heartily as to the Lord, and in reality and truth, like an Israelite indeed, in whom there is no guile.

"That I be not ashamed" before God at the throne of grace—where a believer sometimes is ashamed to come, having not regarded God's statutes as he should have—that he might not be ashamed before him at the last day. Instead, he wants to have confidence, having the righteousness of Christ imputed to him, and the true grace of God implanted in him, which engaged him to regard all his commandments. There is a different kind of confidence to approach the throne of God when we know that we've been saved and redeemed.

It's been said over and over that we are what our hearts are. The most important thing is to be right with God in our own hearts. This is even more important than having others come and stand with you. You could have five hundred people praying for you, but if you don't personally accept Jesus, you won't be saved. To be sound of heart would mean that the heart was not sick with sin. Only those who have a conscience are ashamed when things are wrong, which is why nonbelievers don't have shame in their sin. Our prayer should be to survive, knowing "the purpose of the commandment is love from a pure heart, from a good conscience, and from sincere faith" (1 Timothy 1:5). We must never be "ashamed" of God's "statutes" (words outlining proper actions), for we need them to remain in "the way," for Jesus said: "where I go you know, and the way you know" (John 14:4). Instead, we can rejoice in them because by following His laws, we are living a life that is pleasing to Him and one that will bear no shame when we stand before Him. Isn't that a comforting thought? Praise the Lord!

THE LESSON APPLIED

Throughout life, we know we are promised trials and struggles—this is just the nature of a fallen world. But we are also promised that God will be with us throughout every step and won't ever abandon us. That's why we can still have faith in God during the hard times, like the psalmist did in today's passage. We can take comfort in God's Word because we know that He is good and faithful; He will bring us out to the other side of our affliction according to His perfect will and timing. And in the midst of the affliction, we can lean on God's Word and the promises therein, and continue to fear the Lord. In this way, we are being faithful to Him in response to His eternal faithfulness to us.

LET'S TALK ABOUT IT

How has God comforted you through a time of affliction?

No one will make it through this life unscathed. Whether that means you personally have struggled or suffered a tragedy, or you have to watch someone you love go through it, we will all face afflictions. Yet hope is not lost because we know that we can turn to God, no matter the circumstance. There is no instance of Him being too far away or too distant to care. He loves you and is waiting for you to reach out so that He can comfort you during the dark days. Jesus offers a life of abundance (John 10:10) and we know that God's Word is true. Therefore, we can take Him at His word and have full confidence that He will do what He has promised. That in itself is comforting, but we also have the examples in the Bible to fall back on as well. For example, look at Daniel in the lions' den. Look how God was faithful to Daniel in his time of need!

HOME DAILY DEVOTIONAL READINGS
JULY 22–28, 2024

MONDAY	TUESDAY	WEDNESDAY	THURSDAY	FRIDAY	SATURDAY	SUNDAY
Await the Dawning Day	Await and Hasten God's New Creation	Watch for God My Fortress	Watch and Be Ready	Watch and Work Faithfully	Wait for God's Salvation	Wait and Hope in the Lord
2 Peter 1:16–21	2 Peter 3:1–15	Psalm 59:1–9, 17	Matthew 25:1–13	Matthew 25:14–21, 24–30	Lamentations 3:25–36	Psalm 130

EXPECTANT WATCHFULNESS

PSALM 130

King James Version	*New Revised Standard Version*
OUT of the depths have I cried unto thee, O LORD.	OUT of the depths I cry to you, O LORD.
2 Lord, hear my voice: let thine ears be attentive to the voice of my supplications.	2 Lord, hear my voice! Let your ears be attentive to the voice of my supplications!
3 If thou, LORD, shouldest mark iniquities, O Lord, who shall stand?	3 If you, O LORD, should mark iniquities, Lord, who could stand?
4 But there is forgiveness with thee, that thou mayest be feared.	4 But there is forgiveness with you, so that you may be revered.
5 I wait for the LORD, my soul doth wait, and in his word do I hope.	5 I wait for the LORD, my soul waits, and in his word I hope;
6 My soul waiteth for the Lord more than they that watch for the morning: I say, more than they that watch for the morning.	6 my soul waits for the Lord more than those who watch for the morning, more than those who watch for the morning.
7 Let Israel hope in the LORD: for with the LORD there is mercy, and with him is plenteous redemption.	7 O Israel, hope in the Lord! For with the Lord there is steadfast love, and with him is great power to redeem.
8 And he shall redeem Israel from all his iniquities.	8 It is he who will redeem Israel from all its iniquities.

LESSON SETTING
Time: 539 BC
Place: Unknown

LESSON OUTLINE
I. **Urgent Prayer and Confession (Psalm 130:1–4)**
II. **Patience (Psalm 130:5–6)**
III. **Hope of Israel (Psalm 130:7–8)**

UNIFYING PRINCIPLE
People are often their own worst enemies. What are ways to address the enemy that is "us"? Psalm 130 reminds us that our sins may drag us down, but the Lord's power to redeem us will set us on our feet again.

INTRODUCTION
Psalm 130 has been linked to the lament genre of psalms. It is unclear who the author is of this psalm or what the occasion or cause was for writing the psalm. Because Psalm 130 is marked by an awareness of sin and a powerful assurance of forgiveness, many scholars identify it among the

MAIN THOUGHT: O Israel, hope in the Lord! For with the Lord there is steadfast love, and with him is great power to redeem. (Psalm 130:7, KJV)

seven penitential psalms (Psalm 6, 32, 38, 51, 102, 130, 143). It begins with a personal testimony of God rescuing the writer from sin, and then leads to encouraging the Israelites to hope in the Lord because He is their ultimate redemption. The psalmist is able to share from personal experience how lost he was and how grateful he was to the Lord for saving him. He then shares this news with his community because he realizes it's too good to not share. We can follow the example of the psalmist still today. Sharing our testimonies is a powerful way to spread the Gospel because we're drawing on personal experience, which is something that others can connect with. If you're a Christian, you have a testimony of being saved by grace; it's as simple and beautiful as that!

EXPOSITION

I. URGENT PRAYER AND CONFESSION (PSALM 130:1–4)

Previously in the psalms there have been cries from the depths of the earth (Psalm 71:20) or the depths of the grave (Psalm 86:13). Once again, from a place of deep and overwhelming danger, the psalmist cries out to Yahweh, the covenant God of Israel. It is not clear if the "I" (v. 1) refers to a priest speaking on behalf of the community or if it is a personal appeal to the Lord. Either way by crying out to the Lord, he implicitly admits his need and distress as he appeals for divine help. The plea to God is emphasized using repetition as a poetic tool. The depths is an image of dangerous waters (cf. Psalm 69:2[3]) that pictures chaos or overwhelming disaster. In Isaiah 51:10, this metaphor is applied to the waters from which Yahweh delivered

Israel at the time of the exodus from Egypt. In this context in Psalm 130, the depths represent the great distance between the psalmist and the Lord due to the incompatibility of human sin with God's holiness (v. 3). As Jonah indicated in a similar situation (Jonah 2:3–7), the psalmist in his sin feels as though he is going down for the third time because of his sin and his resultant guilt before the Lord. People experience depths of poverty, sorrow, confusion, and pain. Yet the depth that the psalmist cried from here was the depth of the awareness and guilt of sin (v. 3). Many have been spiritually drowned in these depths. At the same time, his act of crying out to the Lord is in itself an act of faith in God. If he didn't have some microscopic hope that God was out there, then why bother to pray at all? But Jesus tells us that even the faith the size of a mustard seed is enough to move a mountain (Matthew 17:20). It's not about the amount of faith that you have, but rather, that you have any at all—God can work with any size! All it took was the psalmist crying out to God for the Lord to act, and the same is true for us believers now.

Just as God heard the psalmist's prayer, God also hears our prayers, even when it feels like God does not. His prayers are put up in a humble, suppliant manner for grace and mercy, not by pleading merit and righteousness. The psalmist desires God would hearken to and hear, listen unto, bow, and incline his ears, as God does. The good news is God is always attentive to our cries. The Bible says He knows our needs even before we even ask (Matthew 6:8). Even though He already knows what we'll ask, the act of asking is how we develop our relationship with Him. He wants it to go both ways, just as any healthy human relationship would function as well. The more we commune with Him, the stronger our bond of trust becomes and the deeper our faith will grow. It's the same as taking care of a plant—how can anything grow without proper nourishment and nurturing?

In asking for God to help, the psalmist also understood that he had no confident reason to ask or to be heard by God apart from His great forgiveness. Without this graciousness, no one could stand before Yahweh. "To stand" is a judicial phrase and notes a person being absolved or justified upon an equal trial, where it is opposed to falling. In his petition, the psalmist poses a rhetorical question asking who could "stand" before the just Lord. Years of a previous relationship with God had taught the psalmist that there is, in fact, forgiveness with God. It can be hard to believe when we are struck with our awareness of sin, but it is true: there is forgiveness with God. If God were to keep a complete record of human sins, of all the ways in which they distort His desires, then who could maintain his stand in His presence (cf. Psalm 1:5; Ezra 9:15)? The short answer is: none of us!

This question, then, is the psalmist's indirect admission of guilt, his implied hope that he will not get from the just God what he deserves for his sins. If the Lord in His character were only just, then no human would have any hope before Him. We've all committed the crime and there's no getting around that. There would be nothing to excuse our behavior or hide behind that God couldn't see the mistakes we've made. We would all be sent straight to hell in punishment for our corruption. Thankfully that is not where God leaves us. The good news that will come in verse 4 is that the Lord is indeed perfectly just, but at the same time, He is gracious beyond measure. People who do not live up to the Lord's justice can still cast themselves on His mercy because God's grace is more significant than human guilt. Aren't you grateful that is true? Glory to God!

Coming after verse 3, in which the justice of the Lord is stated, the conjunction *kî* beginning in verse 4 likely is adversative, with the antithetical nuance, "but." As the Lord indicated in His self-description to Moses in Exodus 34:6, in His essential nature, He is forgiving. The psalmist acknowledges that what humans cannot earn by merit (vv. 1–3), the Lord offers by His grace. By his forgiveness, the Lord proves Himself more powerful than sin. His grace, however, should not cause us to think less of him, but it is intended to cause us to respect Him. As Paul argues in Romans 6:1, God's grace should prompt us to praise Him, not presume upon Him. This forgiveness is not just a covering of sin, but sins have been removed completely. One of the great purposes of God's forgiveness is to build a sense of gratitude and reverence in those He forgives. His pardon should lead to purity and His forgiveness to an appropriate fear of displeasing the One who has been so gracious. If a believer truly recognizes how depraved and sinful they were before God entered their lives, and they can see how much better their lives are now with Him in it, this should cause endless praise for the believer! We should relate to the blind man who shares his testimony in

John 9:25: I once was blind but now I see! Being overwhelmed by God's goodness and mercy should inspire us to live lives that are wholly pleasing to Him. Instead of viewing salvation as a "get out of jail free" card where you can do whatever you want because God loves you anyway, we should have the view that we've been redeemed at a price and our lives should reflect a humble, grateful attitude.

II. PATIENCE
(PSALM 130:5–6)

The psalmist emphasizes that the Lord's faithfulness inspires hope in Him. This is not a tepid, half-hearted trust, but the psalmist is all in for the Lord as he completely places himself and his need into the Lord's hands. The psalmist expresses a certain hope since God's Word cannot fail. His waiting necessarily involves listening; the psalmist has cried out of the depths to the Lord, and now he is silent before the Lord as he anticipates the divine reply. This is not a passive hope that maybe God might be listening and might decide to answer him. Instead, this is a confident expectation that the Lord will hear his prayer and will send an answer. Though the Lord doesn't always answer our prayers in the way we'd like them to be, we know that He always hears them. There is not a single thought or tear that escapes His notice; isn't that incredible? So when we don't feel heard in the moment, we can trust that the answer is on its way.

"They that watch for the morning" probably refers to shepherds with a night watch, which ends with the sun's rising. The poet used a vivid image to express his patient anticipation in waiting on God. We see a watchman in the darkness of the early morning, scanning the horizon for the first sign of the dawn. In the Old Testament, the morning was the time for legal judgment to be given (Psalm 101:8). The morning is often depicted as the time of God's intervention on behalf of His people in need. The watchman doesn't doubt that morning will come, but only wonders when, and watches for it diligently. So it was for the psalmist who watched for God and the help God promised to bring. This comparison combines intense yearning with confident hope, thus providing a window into the heart of the psalmist as he waits for the Lord to respond to his cry so that he can emerge from the darkness of guilt into the light of forgiveness. While some prayer requests may take longer than others to be answered, we can be thankful that the prayer of salvation and deliverance from sin is always answered immediately! There is no time delay for that one.

III. HOPE OF ISRAEL
(PSALM 130:7–8)

With the seventh verse, the phrasing turns from the personal to the public. What the psalmist learned in waiting upon God and trusting Him from the depths is now put to use as he calls upon Israel to put their hope in Yahweh. The psalmist put his faith and hope in the Lord Himself, not in the mercy or redemption God would bring. He looked to the Giver before the gift. The Israel referenced here is that spiritual Israel (believers in Christ), who hope in the Lord. We received redemption by the mercy of God. Redemption is offered to all. Only those who do what it says in Romans 10:9–10 receive this redemption. The psalmist's renewed hope spills over to affect others, as in verse 7 he calls on others in Israel to join him in hoping in the Lord as he seeks to set into motion concentric circles of confidence in the Lord. His personal experience prompts his public exhortation in (vv. 7–8). He has come to know that the Lord is faithful and forgiving (1 John 1:9). How have you come to know that God is faithful? Some of us grew up in the church and it seems like we've never known a day without the Lord—praise God for that! But others had to learn a more difficult way. Maybe they went through a hardship and turned to other things for comfort and hope, and those things disappointed them. Maybe they started out in a walk of faith but became sidetracked by worldly temptations and fell off. Whatever your story, it isn't beyond God's redemption. He is still faithful to you even when you aren't faithful to Him. Just look at the countless stories of the Israelites turning their backs on Him, yet He still saved them every time they called on His name. This is because God's faithfulness and goodness has nothing to do with our ability to match it, and everything to do with His character.

What the psalmist learned in his personal life, he can put to application for the whole nation. When God's people humbly look to Him, there is mercy and abundant redemption for both the individual and the community. Even when our sins are great and of large quantity, with God there is matchless mercy. The redemption that He provides is ample for all who hope in Him because with the Lord is faithful love, an essential component of the divine self-description in Exodus 34:6. Redemption may echo the exodus experience, but it is clear in Isaiah 50:2 that the Lord's redemptive power must never be underestimated. As Paul's testimony in 1 Timothy 1:13–16 indicates, not even a blasphemer, a persecutor, and a violent man like Saul of Tarsus was beyond the range of God's mercy. If God could still offer salvation and redemption for a man like that, He can offer it to anyone. That is how great and wide His love is! There is no limit on His mercy for us, praise the Lord, so we can always cry out to Him no matter what we've done or where we've been. Truly, the understanding for the depths of God's love and mercy are beyond comprehension.

In the final verse, the psalmist continues his expression of redemption for himself and Israel. Not only does the psalmist face the reality of his sins, but also the nation of Israel. The psalmist knows that what the Lord has done in forgiving him, God can also do for Israel. Just as the psalmist has hope in God, so can Israel because of the Lord's redeeming ability. This is the confident conclusion to the psalm, demonstrating trust that God will indeed bring redemption and rescue to both the individual and the nation overwhelmed in the depths of their sin. What God has demonstrated in the private life, He will also perform for the community that cries out to Him. Our world today is a world that needs to cry out to God. We're desperately lost without Him. The biggest leaders worldwide think that science is the answer—specifically, that we should leave planet Earth and just start fresh somewhere else. Humanity knows it needs a fresh start, but it is unwilling to accept the easy truth: the answer we're seeking is God. With Him, we find renewal and rebirth. With Him, our slates are washed clean and we can start over. We can enjoy an eternity of praising the Lamb instead of shoveling coals in hell. All we have to do is cry out to the Lord and He hears us, offers His grace freely, and forgives us immediately.

THE LESSON APPLIED

The psalmist in Psalm 130 offers a powerful reminder of the grace and mercy of God. It suggests that instead of attempting to address the symptoms of guilt through activities, possessions, achievements, positive thoughts, and denial, we can turn to God on the night of our guilt and find His unmerited mercy. Attempts to relieve guilt by activity, possessions, achievements, positive thoughts, and denial are as ineffective as taking aspirin to heal a tumor. While they may address the symptoms, they cannot cure the disease. The good news of Psalm 130 is that when sinners cry out to God in the night of their guilt, he is gracious in forgiving them. Their hope is not in their merit before the Lord but in the Lord's unmerited mercy to

them. We can take solace and strength in the knowledge that God is always there to forgive us and restore us. This is a wonderful reminder of the power and comfort of God's grace and forgiveness. If you have already experienced this forgiveness and new life, then it becomes your responsibility to share it with others. When the news is this good, you shouldn't be able to keep it to yourself!

LET'S TALK ABOUT IT

Have you ever felt as though you committed a sin that was too great for God to forgive?

This psalm portrays the Lord as just (v. 3) but also forgiving (v. 4). God's faithful love prompts the Lord to redeem sinful people. Psalm 130, then, presents the Lord as the God whose grace is more significant than human sin, and that truth provides hope even for those who are in the depths of their guilt. Have you ever felt the guilt of disappointing God? How did you attempt to minimize or eliminate your guilt?

GET SOCIAL

Share your views and tag us
@rhboydco and use #WatchAndPray.

Twitter
@rhboydco (#rhboydco)

Instagram
@rhboydco (#rhboydco)

Facebook
@rhboydco (#rhboydco)

www.rhboyd.com

HOME DAILY DEVOTIONAL READINGS
JULY 29– AUGUST 4, 2024

MONDAY	TUESDAY	WEDNESDAY	THURSDAY	FRIDAY	SATURDAY	SUNDAY
Words of Hope	Encourage One Another	Encouraging Words	Two Are Better Than One	Bear One Another's Burdens	My Help Comes from the Lord	Encouraged in Faith
1 Thessalonians 4:13–18	Hebrews 10:19–25	2 Chronicles 30:21–27	Ecclesiastes 4:7–12	Galatians 6:1–10	Psalm 121	1 Thessalonians 2:13–3:5

THE FELLOWSHIP OF ENCOURAGEMENT

ADULT TOPIC: BACKGROUND SCRIPTURE: 1 THESSALONIANS 2:13–3:5
HOPE IN CHRISTIAN FELLOWSHIP   LESSON PASSAGE: 1 THESSALONIANS 2:13–3:5

1 THESSALONIANS 2:13–3:5

King James Version

FOR this cause also thank we God without ceasing, because, when ye received the word of God which ye heard of us, ye received it not as the word of men, but as it is in truth, the word of God, which effectually worketh also in you that believe.

14 For ye, brethren, became followers of the churches of God which in Judaea are in Christ Jesus: for ye also have suffered like things of your own countrymen, even as they have of the Jews:

15 Who both killed the Lord Jesus, and their own prophets, and have persecuted us; and they please not God, and are contrary to all men:

16 Forbidding us to speak to the Gentiles that they might be saved, to fill up their sins alway: for the wrath is come upon them to the uttermost.

17 But we, brethren, being taken from you for a short time in presence, not in heart, endeavoured the more abundantly to see your face with great desire.

18 Wherefore we would have come unto you, even I Paul, once and again; but Satan hindered us.

19 For what is our hope, or joy, or crown of rejoicing? Are not even ye in the presence of our Lord Jesus Christ at his coming?

20 For ye are our glory and joy.

New Revised Standard Version

WE also constantly give thanks to God for this, that when you received the word of God that you heard from us, you accepted it not as a human word but as what it really is, God's word, which is also at work in you believers.

14 For you, brothers and sisters, became imitators of the churches of God in Christ Jesus that are in Judea, for you suffered the same things from your own compatriots as they did from the Jews,

15 who killed both the Lord Jesus and the prophets, and drove us out; they displease God and oppose everyone

16 by hindering us from speaking to the Gentiles so that they may be saved. Thus they have constantly been filling up the measure of their sins; but God's wrath has overtaken them at last.

17 As for us, brothers and sisters, when, for a short time, we were made orphans by being separated from you—in person, not in heart—we longed with great eagerness to see you face to face.

18 For we wanted to come to you—certainly I, Paul, wanted to again and again—but Satan blocked our way.

19 For what is our hope or joy or crown of boasting before our Lord Jesus at his coming? Is it not you?

20 Yes, you are our glory and joy!

MAIN THOUGHT: We also constantly give thanks to God for this, that when you received the word of God that you heard from us, you accepted it not as a human word but as what it really is, God's word, which is also at work in you believers. (1 Thessalonians 2:13, KJV)

1 THESSALONIANS 2:13–3:5

King James Version	New Revised Standard Version
• • • • • •	• • • • • •
1 Wherefore when we could no longer forbear, we thought it good to be left at Athens alone;	1 Therefore when we could bear it no longer, we decided to be left alone in Athens;
2 And sent Timotheus, our brother, and minister of God, and our fellowlabourer in the gospel of Christ, to establish you, and to comfort you concerning your faith:	2 and sent Timothy, our brother and co-worker for God in proclaiming the gospel of Christ, to strengthen and encourage you for the sake of your faith,
3 That no man should be moved by these afflictions: for yourselves know that we are appointed thereunto.	3 so that no one would be shaken by these persecutions. Indeed, you yourselves know that this is what we are destined for.
4 For verily, when we were with you, we told you before that we should suffer tribulation; even as it came to pass, and ye know.	4 In fact, when we were with you, we told you beforehand that we were to suffer persecution; so it turned out, as you know.
5 For this cause, when I could no longer forbear, I sent to know your faith, lest by some means the tempter have tempted you, and our labour be in vain.	5 For this reason, when I could bear it no longer, I sent to find out about your faith; I was afraid that somehow the tempter had tempted you and that our labor had been in vain.

LESSON SETTING

Time: AD 51

Place: Corinth

LESSON OUTLINE

I. Thanksgiving
(1 Thessalonians 2:13–16)

II. Life After Leaving Thessalonica
(1 Thessalonians 2:17–20)

III. Timothy Is Sent
(1 Thessalonians 3:1–5)

UNIFYING PRINCIPLE

People may become discouraged when long distances separate them from friends or family. What can relieve loneliness during long seasons of separation? When Paul cannot visit the Thessalonians, he sends Timothy to visit them and to encourage their steadfastness as they await Christ's return.

INTRODUCTION

The letter opens by identifying the writers as Paul, Silvanus, and Timothy, although later in the letter Paul speaks alone (1 Thessalonians 2:18; 3:5), suggesting that his voice dominates. Paul, Silas, Timothy, and others brought the message of Christ to the city of Thessalonica. As a result, many people became followers of Christ, but there was a riot when Paul and Silas were accused of defying Caesar by declaring that Jesus was the authentic king and Caesar was an imposter (Acts 17:1–9). Sometime after their escape, Paul became concerned that the believers in Thessalonica might become weak in their faith and turn from Christ. However, he receives news that Thessalonian Christians had remained faithful. In response, this letter is penned that recounts Paul's first trip to Thessalonica, and offers important teachings and encouragement to continue in community through Christian love and the challenge to work hard.

EXPOSITION

I. THANKSGIVING
(1 THESSALONIANS 2:13–16)

The lesson begins with Paul giving thanks for the Thessalonians. Paul is commending and celebrating the Thessalonian reception to the teachings of Christ and their faithfulness despite Jewish opposition. Paul is grateful that the Gospel that he and the others handed to the Thessalonians had been received (v. 13). The Gospel had been received, heard, and acted upon in active reception. In addition, God's Word is now "at work in you believers." Whatever the importance of the apostles and their labor, God is now active among the Thessalonians themselves. The apostles have been and will continue to be significant for them, but it is also the case that God works among them directly, just as God chose them in the beginning (1 Thessalonians 1:4).

Now comes the explanation about how the Thessalonians had become imitators by drawing a parallel. The Thessalonians had imitated the churches in Judea (v. 14). The explanation in verses 15–16 of what "the Jews" did left scholars with serious questions and concerns regarding the text. Some scholars argue that these verses are an interpolation and are written by someone else other than Paul, for the following reasons.

First, it seems out of place here. Reference to the Jews interrupts Paul's recollection about his relationship with the Thessalonians. In fact, one could skip from the end of verse 13 to the beginning of verse 17 and not sense that something had been omitted. The reference also seems out of place in that this letter addresses a predominantly Gentile congregation, one with little knowledge of Jewish tradition or history.

Second, Paul does not elsewhere claim that the Jews killed Jesus. This statement would be more at home in the Acts of the Apostles, where Jesus' death is attributed to the ignorance and malice of Jerusalem Jews (Acts 2:23; 3:14–15; 13:27–28) or in Matthew's Gospel, where Jews explicitly take upon themselves responsibility for Jesus' death (Matthew 27:25). Only in 1 Corinthians 2:6 might Paul be understood as assigning human responsibility for Jesus' death, when he recalls that "powers of this age" put Jesus to death, although these are probably cosmic rather than human rulers. Elsewhere, Paul ascribes Jesus' death to His own self-giving (see, for example, Galatians 1:4; 2:19; Philippians 2:8) or to God's will (see Galatians 1:4; Romans 3:25).

Third, the assertion that Jews "displease God and oppose everyone" sounds suspiciously like well-known Gentile slurs against Jews, but that does not explain what such comments are doing here, on the lips of a Jew. Even if we classify them as prophetic outrage—the strident language we would expect from an Amos or an Isaiah—it is hard to hear Paul address such stinging words about Jews to a Gentile audience. These are the sorts of things one says to siblings at home, not in public beyond the confines of the family.

Finally, however it is translated, the announcement about God's wrath is difficult to reconcile with the extended discussion of Israel Paul produces in Romans 9–11. There, as he struggles to articulate the apparent contradiction between God's election of Israel and the refusal of most

Jews to confess Jesus as the Christ of Israel, Paul says none of the ugly things affirmed here. By striking contrast, he concludes that reflection with the claim that "all Israel will be saved," a claim that stands in tension with 1 Thessalonians 2:16.

II. LIFE AFTER LEAVING THESSALONICA (1 THESSALONIANS 2:17–20)

Paul used emotionally-charged language to describe his absence from Thessalonica. The missionaries were forced to leave the city under duress; they were run out of town. The strong bond between Paul and the church, comparable to the bond between loving parent and beloved child, made separation a distress to the apostle, although he had only been away from them "for a short time." And although a physical separation had been forced upon him, they were never apart from him in thought or heart. Paul's description of his separation from the church was designed to express clearly that his absence did not result from indifference on his part. This had to affirm and be a relief to the Thessalonians.

In verse 18, Paul expresses his desire to travel to Thessalonica. The author has made frequent and sincere efforts to see the Thessalonian Christians, but unfortunately the adversary prevented those attempts to visit. How Satan stopped the missionaries is unknown but some possibilities are illness or the Thessalonian authorities. By coming to the text with a sense of curiosity, we use what we do know to infer what we do not. We know that Satan is known to use deception, lies, and any other means to distract and deter Christians.

There was a familial bond between Paul and the Thessalonian Christians. Paul feels as if the Thessalonians are his spiritual children and brags about them as his pride and joy. It is no wonder why Paul desired to see these Christians because they brought so much joy, hope, and pride to the apostle and other missionaries—not out of obligation but out of hope. The hope indicated here is the hope Paul harbored for the Thessalonians, a "hope that the divine work so well begun in them will increase to maturity." Paul's hope then was the hope that he would not have run in vain (1 Thessalonians 3:5) but that the Thessalonians would persevere and his labors in the service of the Gospel would be validated by their persistent faith.

III. TIMOTHY IS SENT (1 THESSALONIANS 3:1–5)

Time and again in this narration, Paul expressed his great concern for the Thessalonians. At the beginning and at the end of this passage, he wrote that his concern reached a level that he could no longer bear. A clear demonstration of the genuineness of his concern for the church was his decision to send Timothy to Thessalonica. Timothy's credentials were mentioned here to remind the readers that Timothy is not a flunky or just an assistant, but one who has a ministry in his own right. The work in which they both were engaged was that of "spreading the gospel of Christ." If Timothy at a later date was not received with respect in some churches because of his youth or some other cause, it might have been necessary for the apostle to make clear his high regard for Timothy as his associate. Timothy is a —valued apostolic emissary, not an underling lacking authority or messenger for Paul.

By stressing the status of Timothy, Paul also stressed that the Thessalonians were important to him.

The purpose for which Timothy was sent is described in 1 Thessalonians 3:2–3. Three infinitival clauses explain Timothy's mission. Timothy was sent to strengthen and encourage the faith of the Thessalonians. Similarly, Paul prayed in a later letter that God would "strengthen" the church (1 Thess. 3:13; 2 Thess. 2:17). He also used the term as the goal of his own visit to the Roman church (Romans 1:11).

So strengthened and encouraged, Paul hoped none of the church would be unsettled by the afflictions they were experiencing. "Unsettled" is translated to *sainesthai,* which indicates a literal meaning of "to shake, to upset, or to agitate." The potential seriousness of such agitation is reflected by Paul's fear that his efforts among the Thessalonians might have been in vain. Paul then reminds the church that they were destined or appointed for afflictions. Christians are set on the path of following a Savior who suffered at the hands of evil men; therefore, they should expect the same treatment that Christ received.

THE LESSON APPLIED

Texts like the one in today's lesson should cause modern-day Christians to ponder how to address the passage because of its anti-Judaism tone. Many have rejected the idea of Jewish communal guilt for the crucifixion of Jesus. Christians have a responsibility not to harm or cause harm but to express love. Be mindful of this when discussing this passage.

LET'S TALK ABOUT IT

How do you continue to bring value to your relationships in times of separation?

There is an adage that says "absence makes the heart grow fonder." At the height of the COVID-19 pandemic, many believers were (and some still are) separated from each other. What are/were ways used to value the bonds of care, love, and togetherness to create community among believers despite physical absences?

GET SOCIAL
Share your views and tag us
@rhboydco and use #ChristianFellowship.

Twitter
@rhboydco (#rhboydco)

Instagram
@rhboydco (#rhboydco)

Facebook
@rhboydco (#rhboydco)

www.rhboyd.com

HOME DAILY DEVOTIONAL READINGS
AUGUST 5–11, 2024

MONDAY	TUESDAY	WEDNESDAY	THURSDAY	FRIDAY	SATURDAY	SUNDAY
The Love of Christ Compels Us	Love the Lord Your God	Fulfill the Royal Law of Love	Love One Another	Renewed in Love	An Everlasting Love	God's Beloved Children
2 Corinthians 5:16–21	Deuteronomy 6:4–13	James 2:8–13	John 13:31–35	Zephaniah 3:14–20	Jeremiah 31:1–9	1 John 3:1–10

CHRIST'S LOVE AS THE RULE

ADULT TOPIC: CHILDREN OF GOD	BACKGROUND SCRIPTURE: 1 JOHN 3:1–10 LESSON PASSAGE: 1 JOHN 3:1–10

1 JOHN 3:1–10

King James Version

BEHOLD, what manner of love the Father hath bestowed upon us, that we should be called the sons of God: therefore the world knoweth us not, because it knew him not.

2 Beloved, now are we the sons of God, and it doth not yet appear what we shall be: but we know that, when he shall appear, we shall be like him; for we shall see him as he is.

3 And every man that hath this hope in him purifieth himself, even as he is pure.

4 Whosoever committeth sin transgresseth also the law: for sin is the transgression of the law.

5 And ye know that he was manifested to take away our sins; and in him is no sin.

6 Whosoever abideth in him sinneth not: whosoever sinneth hath not seen him, neither known him.

7 Little children, let no man deceive you: he that doeth righteousness is righteous, even as he is righteous.

8 He that committeth sin is of the devil; for the devil sinneth from the beginning. For this purpose the Son of God was manifested, that he might destroy the works of the devil.

9 Whosoever is born of God doth not commit sin; for his seed remaineth in him: and he cannot sin, because he is born of God.

10 In this the children of God are manifest, and the children of the devil: whosoever doeth not righteousness is not of God, neither he that loveth not his brother.

New Revised Standard Version

SEE what love the Father has given us, that we should be called children of God; and that is what we are. The reason the world does not know us is that it did not know him.

2 Beloved, we are God's children now; what we will be has not yet been revealed. What we do know is this: when he is revealed, we will be like him, for we will see him as he is.

3 And all who have this hope in him purify themselves, just as he is pure.

4 Everyone who commits sin is guilty of lawlessness; sin is lawlessness.

5 You know that he was revealed to take away sins, and in him there is no sin.

6 No one who abides in him sins; no one who sins has either seen him or known him.

7 Little children, let no one deceive you. Everyone who does what is right is righteous, just as he is righteous.

8 Everyone who commits sin is a child of the devil, for the devil has been sinning from the beginning. The Son of God was revealed for this purpose, to destroy the works of the devil.

9 Those who have been born of God do not sin, because God's seed abides in them; they cannot sin because they have been born of God.

10 The children of God and the children of the devil are revealed in this way: all who do not do what is right are not from God, nor are those who do not love a brother or sister.

MAIN THOUGHT: See what love the Father has given us, that we should be called children of God; and that is what we are. The reason the world does not know us is that it did not know him. (1 John 3:1, KJV)

LESSON OUTLINE
   I. The Father's Love
      (1 John 3:1–3)
   II. Lawlessness
      (1 John 3:4–10)

UNIFYING PRINCIPLE

People can behave cruelly without regard for right and wrong. How does love become the rule for our thoughts and behaviors? First John says all who look forward to Christ's coming have Christ's love and purity as a model for their own lives.

INTRODUCTION

Scholars have traditionally credited 1 John to the apostle John, son of Arbedee and the brother of James. He is credited by many to have penned five books of the New Testament (also the Gospel of John and book of Revelation), though some doubts were raised in the early church concerning John's authorship of 2 and 3 John and Revelation. Strong similarities between 1 John and the Gospel of John argue for common authorship of these books. The author, probably John, focuses in this chapter on the love God has for us, and how we should respond to that love by joining God's family.

EXPOSITION

I. THE FATHER'S LOVE
   (1 JOHN 3:1–3)

John starts this chapter by informing his readers that it is both a privilege and responsibility to be one of God's children. John has already named the readers as children of God, but now John is explaining what it really means to be children of God. God's love for His children is so great that it's beyond measure. This description of God's love is exactly what we read later on in 1 John 4 about the priority of God's love. While the readers were previously aware that God's love is the basis of the saving work of Christ already described, now the reader encounters an explicit statement of this fact. The status of being children of God is then a gift or the effect of the gift of God's love. Therefore, no one should boast that she or he is a child of God, for then the new status is viewed as an accomplishment or work rather than a gift. The Johannine conviction of God's priority and God's election (1 John 4:10), shared by Paul (Romans 8:31–39), is the logical correlative of the assurance of God's love and grace. The doctrine of God's election speaks to the question of how I, a sinner, come to stand within God's grace rather than to the question of whether or not I have free will. I experience free will, but that freedom only becomes a possibility within the realm of God's grace when I am no longer enslaved to sin.

As soon as this love and acceptance are affirmed, however, their opposite comes into view. The world's failure to acknowledge believers as children of God is grounded in its ignorance of God Himself. Thus the theme of the world is taken up again, and after the denunciation of the opponents, it is clear enough that they also continue in view.

No sooner is the world mentioned, however, than it is left behind as John returns to the theme of the appearance of Christ (vv. 2–3). In fact, verse 2 refers to the appearance of God, for "God" is the nearest possible antecedent of the pronoun "him." Yet since Jesus seems to be the one who appears, or comes, in 1 John 2:28. Also, the promise that we shall be like Him takes up the admonition to walk as Jesus walked (1 John 2:6). The eschatological teaching of this passage is stated unmistakably but subtly (v. 2). It is characteristic of Christian eschatology to speak with reserve or in a veiled way about the eschatological future, that is, life beyond death or in the Kingdom of God. The most famous example is Paul's statement in 1 Corinthians 13:12: "For now we see in a mirror dimly, but then face to face. Now I know in part; then I shall understand fully, even as I have been fully understood." John's affirmation here is of a piece with Paul's, marked by confidence but also by modesty and reserve. Unfortunately, Christians have sometimes been misled by taking the book of Revelation to be a series of predictions about future worldly events rather than apocalyptic imagery or symbolism, and consequently have abandoned this necessary and appropriate modesty and reserve. For our time and our knowledge, the most important fact about the eschatological future is its Christocentricity. That is, what we shall be will be modeled after who Christ is, and even that can only be fully known when the time comes.

The uncertainty implied by our not knowing what we shall be (v. 2) is more than offset by the assurance that we are already God's children. There is an uncertainty in the verse; the uncertainty leaves the believer in a state of hopeful expectation: "We shall see him as he is." The disciples at least saw the earthly Jesus, but even they were not able to see Him as He was (or is). After His death, their post-resurrection knowledge of Him perfected the inadequacy of their earlier sightings. Most believers have not seen Jesus at all (John 20:29). The promise to "see him as he is" is relevant and hopeful, especially when accompanied by the reassurance that "we shall be like him." It is, in fact, a reiteration of the prayer and promise of Jesus that His disciples would be with Him in heaven to behold the glory that He had before creation (John 17:24).

The final note (v. 3) seems a bit strange because the idea of purification, especially ritual purification, is quite foreign to modern, secular people. It is, of course, an idea common to most ancient religions and particularly prominent in Judaism. Basically, the process of purification rids people and their immediate environment of pollution. In ancient Judaism and early Christianity, this pollution was already understood in ethical terms as the pollution of sin, but the religious and social basis of the concept is much broader.

II. LAWLESSNESS (1 JOHN 3:4–10)

John proceeds to provide evidence how being a child of God is incompatible with practicing sin. When John writes of lawlessness, he is referring to more than just the absence of God's Law. It is a willful rejection of, and deliberate and active disobedience against, God. John's emphasis here is vital to his argument against the false teachers. From all indications, the apostle is dealing with individuals who are indifferent to sin. They believed that they could engage in any and all kinds of sinful activities and still be in fellowship with God. In their line of reasoning, their acts were merely amoral. It was such licentious beliefs that John confronts. Sin is not amoral. On the contrary, sin is a willful disregard for God. No one is excluded from the obligation to obey God; therefore, the seccessionists were placing themselves, by their sinful acts, in direct opposition to God.

John then writes that Christ came to take away or remove sin. His tone is much like when John the Baptist said, "Behold the Lamb of God who takes away the sin of the world" (John 1:29). Christ's sacrificial act was one of finality. Christ removed the record of sin committed by God's children. In Christ, there is no sin (v. 5). Not only did Christ not sin, but He was not capable of committing sin; it was not His nature. Therefore, Christ could not, did not, and will not sin. Jesus is the model and sovereign example of what His children should be. Since Christ came to take away sin, since there is no sin in Him, and since the believer is to pattern his life after Christ, it is obviously true that the one who remains in Him will not live a life of sin. John asserts that if a person is abiding in Christ, it is an absolute impossibility, to "keep on sinning."

John's affirmation that "no one who lives in him keeps on sinning" has been the center of much debate. What is John proposing here? Is the apostle suggesting that a believer does not commit acts of sin? What about his earlier statements that Christians do sin (1 John 1:8, 10; 2:1–2)? How can this statement be balanced with these earlier assertions? Is John contradicting himself? These are all legitimate questions the serious biblical exegete must wrestle with. Perhaps John is suggesting that those who abide in Christ will absolutely fall prey to committing sinful acts from time to time, but they will not have a sinful heart leading them to live a life of continuously sinning. The apostle asserts with absolute clarity that those who live in habitual sin have not seen Christ and do not know Christ (v. 7). This is the same as saying they do not have a saving relationship with Christ. On the other hand, those who abide in Him live a life marked by habitual righteousness and purity instead of lawlessness (rebellion) and disobedience. While the unbeliever lives in sin and has not seen or known Christ, the believer has terminated a life of sin for a life of abiding in Him. The child of God has experienced a decisive break with sin; sin no longer controls his life.

Then John writes that those who live full of habitual sinfulness is in relationship with the devil. John says Satan is the father of those who live lawlessly or those who willfully live life full of sin because he is a slanderer and accuser of the believers. He instigates sin, and those who live in sin are his children. He stands as the direct opponent of God and righteousness.

John makes another universal declaration that "no one who is born of God will continue in sin" (v. 9). The believer does not surrender to a sinful life because God's seed remains in him. This implanted seed motivates and enables Christians to live a life that avoids sin. Some scholars believe that the seed is a reference to the Holy Spirit. While there is no definitive proof, it is clear that the believer cannot continue in sin because the righteousness that has been implanted through the new life and new nature that all receive upon belief in Christ Jesus. Two of John's major themes—righteousness and love—are combined as evidence of the new birth. Those who fail to practice righteousness and/or neglect to love other Christians are not of the same spiritual heritage as the child of God. The family of God is marked by the practice of righteousness and love.

In summarizing this section of the epistle, the child of God is reminded of his unique calling and heritage. The believer's life is one marked by righteousness. Sin does not characterize the child of God. Our pattern is the Righteous One, Jesus Christ, who came to destroy the works of the devil and the power of sin. Those who have been born of God live a life that resembles the righteous life of Christ.

THE LESSON APPLIED

Christian life in this world can be viewed as a response to God's love, as obedience to Christ's commands, or as purification or preparation in hope. Although not put in exactly those terms, we have here a kind of test case of those who truly hope in Christ: they purify themselves as Jesus Christ is pure. That is, they live in response to God's love and in obedience to Christ's commands.

LET'S TALK ABOUT IT

How is the Church already manifesting God's love in its identity? In its actions? In the ways it is known to the community around it?

The Church needs not gaze wistfully for a "someday" to come in order to possess the fullness of its identity. There is no need to wait until there are more members, or more resources, or more of whatever we might believe is necessary to be a good, or faithful, or missional church. Like the readers of 1 John, perhaps the people gathered for worship in today's churches could benefit from an occasional reminder that God has already bestowed upon them the thing that is most important for being the people they are called to be. They are children of God. Already. Today. Now.

GET SOCIAL

Share your views and tag us @rhboydco and use #LoveRules.

Twitter
@rhboydco (#rhboydco)

Instagram
@rhboydco (#rhboydco)

Facebook
@rhboydco (#rhboydco)

www.rhboyd.com

HOME DAILY DEVOTIONAL READINGS
AUGUST 12–18, 2024

MONDAY	TUESDAY	WEDNESDAY	THURSDAY	FRIDAY	SATURDAY	SUNDAY
The Lord Is Just and Upright	Bought with a Price	A Godly Life Overcomes Evil	Walking a Straight Path	God Helps and Rescues the Righteous	Deliverance Is the Lord's	God Redeems and Purifies
Deuteronomy 32:1–6	1 Corinthians 6:9–20	Romans 12:9–21	Proverbs 15:20–25	Psalm 37:27–40	Jonah 2:1–9	Titus 1:1–3; 2:11–15

UPRIGHT AND GODLY

ADULT TOPIC:	BACKGROUND SCRIPTURE: TITUS 1:1–13; 2:11–15
ZEALOUS FOR GOOD DEEDS	LESSON PASSAGE: TITUS 1:1–13; 2:11–15

TITUS 1:1–13; 2:11–15

King James Version

PAUL, a servant of God, and an apostle of Jesus Christ, according to the faith of God's elect, and the acknowledging of the truth which is after godliness;

2 In hope of eternal life, which God, that cannot lie, promised before the world began;

3 But hath in due times manifested his word through preaching, which is committed unto me according to the commandment of God our Saviour;

4 To Titus, mine own son after the common faith: Grace, mercy, and peace, from God the Father and the Lord Jesus Christ our Saviour.

5 For this cause left I thee in Crete, that thou shouldest set in order the things that are wanting, and ordain elders in every city, as I had appointed thee:

6 If any be blameless, the husband of one wife, having faithful children not accused of riot or unruly.

7 For a bishop must be blameless, as the steward of God; not selfwilled, not soon angry, not given to wine, no striker, not given to filthy lucre;

8 But a lover of hospitality, a lover of good men, sober, just, holy, temperate;

9 Holding fast the faithful word as he hath been taught, that he may be able by sound doctrine both to exhort and to convince the gainsayers.

New Revised Standard Version

PAUL, a servant of God and an apostle of Jesus Christ, for the sake of the faith of God's elect and the knowledge of the truth that is in accordance with godliness,

2 in the hope of eternal life that God, who never lies, promised before the ages began—

3 in due time he revealed his word through the proclamation with which I have been entrusted by the command of God our Savior,

4 To Titus, my true child in the faith we share: Grace and peace from God the Father and Christ Jesus our Savior.

5 I left you behind in Crete for this reason, that you should put in order what remained to be done, and should appoint elders in every town, as I directed you:

6 someone who is blameless, married only once, whose children are believers, not accused of debauchery and not rebellious.

7 For a bishop, as God's steward, must be blameless; he must not be arrogant or quick-tempered or addicted to wine or violent or greedy for gain;

8 but he must be hospitable, a lover of goodness, prudent upright, devout, and self-controlled,

9 He must have a firm grasp of the word that is trustworthy in accordance with the teaching, so that he many be able both to preach with sound doctrine and to refute those who contradict it.

MAIN THOUGHT: The grace of God has appeared, bringing salvation to all, training us to renounce impiety and worldly passions, and in the present age to live lives that are self-controlled, upright, and godly, while we wait for the blessed hope and the manifestation of the glory of our great God and Saviour, Jesus Christ. (Titus 1:11–13, KJV)

TITUS 1:1–13; 2:11–15

King James Version	*New Revised Standard Version*
10 For there are many unruly and vain talkers and deceivers, specially they of the circumcision:	10 There are also many rebellious people, idle talkers and deceivers, especially those of the circumcision;
11 Whose mouths must be stopped, who subvert whole houses, teaching things which they ought not, for filthy lucre's sake.	11 they must be silenced, since they are upsetting whole families by teaching for sordid gain what it is not right to teach.
12 One of themselves, even a prophet of their own, said, the Cretians are alway liars, evil beasts, slow bellies.	12 It was one of them, their very own prophet, who said, "Cretans are always liars, vicious brutes, lazy gluttons."
13 This witness is true. Wherefore rebuke them sharply, that they may be sound in the faith;	13 That testimony is true. For this reason rebuke them sharply, so that they may become sound in the faith,
. . . . . .	. . . . . .
11 For the grace of God that bringeth salvation hath appeared to all men,	11 For the grace of God has appeared, bringing salvation to all,
12 Teaching us that, denying ungodliness and worldly lusts, we should live soberly, righteously, and godly, in this present world;	12 training us to renounce impiety and worldly passions, and in the present age to live lives that are self-controlled, upright, and godly,
13 Looking for that blessed hope, and the glorious appearing of the great God and our Saviour Jesus Christ;	13 while we wait for the blessed hope and the manifestation of the glory of our great God and Saviour, Jesus Christ.
14 Who gave himself for us, that he might redeem us from all iniquity, and purify unto himself a peculiar people, zealous of good works.	14 He it is who gave himself for us that he might redeem us from all iniquity and purify for himself a people of his own who are zealous for good deeds.
15 These things speak, and exhort, and rebuke with all authority. Let no man despise thee.	15 Declare these things; exhort and reprove with all authority. Let no one look down on you.

LESSON SETTING
Time: AD **64–65**
Place: Nicopolis

LESSON OUTLINE
I. **Paul's Greeting**
   (Titus 1:1–3)
II. **Motivation for Ministry**
   (Titus 2:11–15)

UNIFYING PRINCIPLE

Some people enjoy living recklessly, without regard for consequences. How does a thoughtful consideration of the future inform our actions in the present?

Paul instructs Titus to lead others toward lives that are self-controlled, upright, and godly with a view toward the blessed hope of Christ's return.

INTRODUCTION

Scholars note that there are great similarities between Paul's letter to Titus and his first letter to Timothy. Both letters are concerned for the leadership of the local church and their qualifications. Both letters give direction in how to deal with opponents to the Gospel. And both Titus and Timothy are seen in similar light as they stand out from the local leadership to function as Paul's representatives. In fact, in noticing these similarities, many think no more of Titus so as to consider it a light version of 1 Timothy. But for all these similarities, there are several differences as well. While both 1 Timothy and Titus are foundational books when understanding biblical ecclesiology, 1 Timothy focuses primarily upon the leadership while Titus opens the discussion to the church's entire congregation. This book reveals where faith meets holiness and thus produces good deeds.

EXPOSITION

I. PAUL'S GREETING
(TITUS 1:1–3)

In his letters to churches or to individuals, Paul used the form of introductory greeting customary in first-century letter writing. In the epistle to Titus, Paul identified himself as the source of the letter and Titus as the recipient, followed by his stated desire for God's blessing upon Titus. With the exception of the Thessalonian correspondence, Paul typically added some words or phrases that described himself (e.g., "an apostle of Christ Jesus," "a prisoner of Christ Jesus," "a bond-servant of Christ Jesus"). These self-descriptions at the beginning of his letters served to establish his authority and right to speak. In Titus, Paul also used these self-descriptive phrases to introduce theological statements that indicate the scope and nature of God's plan for redemption of humanity. Romans

and Galatians are the only other epistles in which Paul expanded his greeting.

Paul identifies himself as apostle of Jesus Christ (v. 1): a messenger, especially commissioned by Christ, equal in authority to the disciples. Under unique divine revelation and appointment, his authority was widely recognized in the churches. Paul neither sought nor rejected the imperative of preaching, but was called to it, as though a necessity had been laid upon him (1 Corinthians 9:16). Paul's identity is pungently expressed in two seemingly conflicting metaphors: God's slave and Christ's messenger. The slave role is the opposite of narcissistic, self-willed actions. Paul writes by the authority of Christ's own commissioning, to which he exists under the obligation of bondservant.

The concept of faith takes on various nuances in Scripture and in our understanding. But there is another sense in which the term "faith" refers to our dependence upon God. It is this subjective faith that Paul is writing in the interest of in Titus. Sometimes we get these two concepts confused. We think that our personal faith is "the" faith. When we do this, we may impose our faith on others, condemning them for unfaithfulness because their faith is different than our faith. Such is, at best, unfair and, at worst, arrogant, disrespectful and divisive.

A second goal of Paul's servanthood and apostleship pertains to their knowledge of the truth that leads to godliness—the "their" is referring to God's elect. This knowledge can also be understood as in accordance with godliness. Such "godliness" is a prominent theme in 1 Timothy. Godliness is more than just knowing the facts and principles of the Bible. It's about living out those truths and putting them into practice in our everyday lives. We must strive to be doers of the Word, not just hearers. When we make a conscious effort to live our lives in a way that honors God, we are showing the world what it looks like to have a relationship with God.

Paul's purpose upon this earth is in service to God's elect, those whom God has chosen and selected to be His own from before the foundations of the earth. Paul preaches for their faith or so that they might believe. Paul preaches for the knowledge of the truth or so that they might know the truth. This truth leads to true godliness. Paul preaches for the hope of eternal life, or so that God's elect might have hope of eternal life. Hope (*elpis*) (ἐλπίς) carries a much stronger idea than our modern English conveys. This word indicates a confident assurance or expectation of things to come. This is not just wishful thinking. Eternal life is something that can be counted on. It is assured because the God who is not able to lie promised it from before the foundations of the earth. The same word used to describe this life eternal also describes the time where God promised this life.

II. Motivation for Ministry (Titus 2:11–15)

The New Testament concept of the grace of God is His beneficial activity on behalf of humanity. God's grace toward us is based solely on God's love and humanity's inability to meet God's standards. God's grace is a gift that no one deserves and cannot earn. Without God's grace, there can be no salvation since grace is foundational to salvation (Ephesians 2:4–9). Salvation is universally offered to all without exception.

God's grace "has appeared" (*epephanē*). This verb occurs in Luke 1:79 (metaphorically) with regard to Jesus' birth and in Acts 27:20 (literally) with regard to the appearance of the sun and stars. The only other occurrences of this verb are in Titus 2:11 and 3:4, where it clearly refers to the manifestation of God's salvation. Paul may have intended this highly suggestive term to illustrate the dawning of the light of God's Gospel upon a dark and lost world, or he may have chosen this term as a contrast to its common usage with reference to the appearances of the Roman emperors. In either case, Paul stated that God's salvation characterized by His grace appeared at a given time in history for everyone, Jew and Gentile, slave and free, indiscriminately. The grace of God was revealed and personified in Jesus Christ.

Paul did not limit the operation of God's grace toward Christians to justification in the restricted, legal sense of the conversion experience. Rather, throughout his letters, Paul indicated that God's grace continues to operate in the sanctification process of the Christian's life. God's grace is active and powerful. Grace simply refers to God's unmerited favor on wretched sinners. The Gospel teaches that all people are under God's wrath because of sin (John 3:36, Romans 6:23). People sin against God by rejecting Him and His righteous laws and living as though He doesn't exist. Because God is a just God, He will judge all people eternally for their sins in a place of fire called hell. However, since God is also loving, merciful, and gracious, He offers a way for people to be saved from His wrath and have eternal life through His Son, Jesus Christ (John 3:16). God's Son came to this earth as a man and died for our sins and in that death, He was separated from God for us. God accepted His death for our sins and raised Him from the dead. As followers of Christ, we have all experienced God's grace in salvation.

God's saving grace not only makes Christians evangelistic, righteous, and holy, but it also teaches us to "wait for the happy fulfillment of our hope" which is the "glorious appearing of our great God and Savior, Jesus." "Our great God and Savior" is one of the clearest declarations of Christ's deity in Scripture. Christ is innately glorious as fully God, yet at His first coming, his glory was veiled in his human body and low position on the earth. Certainly, there were aspects of His glory that were revealed as He turned water into wine, multiplied bread, healed the sick, and preached the Good News. However, the full display of Christ's glory to everyone will be at His second coming where all will humble themselves before Him as our "great God and Savior." Unbelievers will do so in their judgment, while believers will do so as Christ completes their salvation.

In 1 John 3:2–3, John said those who have this hope purify themselves, in the sense of continually striving to grow in holiness so that we may be pleasing to Him at His coming. This implies that the practice and enjoyment of sin will dull our desire for Christ's coming. Also, a love for the temporary things of this world will also dull it. In 1 John 2:15, John taught that if we love this world, and all that is in it, the love of the Father is not in us. We must always

guard and stoke our passion for Christ and His coming Kingdom. Longing and praying for Christ to make all things right on this earth and in our lives is a proof that we have experienced saving grace, and it is also an indicator of our spiritual health.

Christ died to set us free from every kind of lawlessness. "Set us free" can also be translated as redeem: to set free by paying a price. It was a word used as paying the ransom for a slave, so he could now be a free man. Mark 10:45 says this about Christ: "For even the Son of Man did not come to be served but to serve, and to give his life as a ransom for many." Therefore, by teaching that Christ died to "redeem us" or "set us free," Paul teaches that every believer before they were saved was a slave of sin. Therefore, what Christ did by dying on the cross was twofold.

First, He paid the ransom by paying the penalty for our sins. The word "death" in Romans 6:23 just means separation. We were separated from God before salvation because of sin. Those who do not accept Christ's payment for our sins will be eternally separated from God under His wrath in a real place of judgment called hell. Though we were caught in the slave market of sin under God's just judgment, Christ paid our ransom by bearing our sins on the cross and receiving God's wrath for those sins, so we could be set free. In Titus 2:14, when Paul says Christ "gave" himself for us, that means He did this freely. Sure, His sacrifice was in obedience to God as John 3:16 teaches, but He also voluntarily did it. When Paul says Christ gave "himself," that means He gave everything. When Paul says for "us," it means He was our substitute; He took what we deserved. However, if Christ had only paid the penalty for our sins, it would only be a partial salvation.

Second, He delivered us from the power of sin. One day, He will deliver us from the presence of sin, either at our death or the rapture, whichever happens first. Because Christ delivered us from the power of sin, Paul says we must "consider" ourselves differently. This means that even though we may have fallen yesterday to anger, lust, or dishonesty, we can start over right now because sin is no longer our master. We should never quit, give up, or lose hope in our struggle with sin, because the battle has already been won.

When Paul tells Titus to communicate these things (v. 15), in the immediate context, he is referring to the need for Christians to reflect on the saving grace they profess, that they would practice good works that align with sound doctrine (Titus 2:1). Salvation is not just fire insurance that we take and then live the way we want; it changes us. It requires us to continually repent of sins as we follow God and seek to be holy.

THE LESSON APPLIED

What are the marks of saving grace in a believer's life? What are proofs that we have been born again—made into new creations in Christ (2 Corinthians 5:17)? It seems clear the Cretan believers were professing Christ but continuing in sin (Titus 1:10–16). Therefore, Paul commanded Titus to teach them to produce works that accorded with sound doctrine (Titus 2:1) and to live out the marks of the saving grace they professed to have experienced (Titus 2:11–15). Let us do the same!

LET'S TALK ABOUT IT

Why is accountability important for believers, particularly those in leadership?

Accountability is especially important for those in leadership, but it is also important for all believers. Since we are the Church, a family of believers, we must hold one another accountable in our obedience to God and His words. What are some ways that you practice accountability with fellow believers?

HOME DAILY DEVOTIONAL READINGS
AUGUST 19–25, 2024

MONDAY	TUESDAY	WEDNESDAY	THURSDAY	FRIDAY	SATURDAY	SUNDAY
Do Good Wherever You Can	Defend the Rights of the Poor	Saved by God's Rich Mercy	Faith without Works Is Dead	Walk in God's Way	Shine Your Light Before Others	Saved by God's Mercy
Proverbs 3:27–35	Proverbs 31:1–9	Ephesians 2:1–10	James 2:14–26	Isaiah 30:18–26	Matthew 5:13–20	Titus 3:3–11

DEVOTED TO GOOD WORKS

ADULT TOPIC: BACKGROUND SCRIPTURE: TITUS 3:3–11
GRACE AND GOOD WORKS   LESSON PASSAGE: TITUS 3:3–11

TITUS 3:3–11

King James Version

FOR we ourselves also were sometimes foolish, disobedient, deceived, serving divers lusts and pleasures, living in malice and envy, hateful, and hating one another.

4 But after that the kindness and love of God our Saviour toward man appeared,

5 Not by works of righteousness which we have done, but according to his mercy he saved us, by the washing of regeneration, and renewing of the Holy Ghost;

6 Which he shed on us abundantly through Jesus Christ our Saviour;

7 That being justified by his grace, we should be made heirs according to the hope of eternal life.

8 This is a faithful saying, and these things I will that thou affirm constantly, that they which have believed in God might be careful to maintain good works. These things are good and profitable unto men.

9 But avoid foolish questions, and genealogies, and contentions, and strivings about the law; for they are unprofitable and vain.

10 A man that is an heretick after the first and second admonition reject;

11 Knowing that he that is such is subverted, and sinneth, being condemned of himself.

New Revised Standard Version

FOR we ourselves were once foolish, disobedient, led astray, slaves to various passions and pleasures, passing our days in malice and envy, despicable, hating one another.

4 But when the goodness and loving-kindness of God our Saviour appeared,

5 he saved us, not because of any works of righteousness that we had done, but according to his mercy, through the water of rebirth and renewal by the Holy Spirit.

6 This Spirit he poured out on us richly through Jesus Christ our Saviour,

7 so that, having been justified by his grace, we might become heirs according to the hope of eternal life.

8 The saying is sure. I desire that you insist on these things, so that those who have come to believe in God may be careful to devote themselves to good works; these things are excellent and profitable to everyone.

9 But avoid stupid controversies, genealogies, dissensions, and quarrels about the law, for they are unprofitable and worthless.

10 After a first and second admonition, have nothing more to do with anyone who causes divisions,

11 since you know that such a person is perverted and sinful, being self-condemned.

MAIN THOUGHT: When the goodness and loving kindness of God our Savior appeared, he saved us, not because of any works of righteousness that we had done, but according to his mercy, through the water of rebirth and renewal by the Holy Spirit. (Titus 3:4–5, KJV)

LESSON SETTING
   Time: AD **64–65**
   Place: Nicopolis

LESSON OUTLINE
  I. Before Christ
    (Titus 3:3–8)

  II. Paul's Warning
    (Titus 3:9–11)

UNIFYING PRINCIPLE

Some people insist on picking fights and creating controversy. What is the best way to avoid a quarrel with a contentious person? Paul advises Titus to lead people away from pointless controversies by directing their attention to the saving work of God in Christ and the hope of eternal life.

INTRODUCTION

In this letter, Paul is calling on believers to remember some things. First, he wants them to remember to live good and kind lives with one another. It is our Christian duty to take care of one another—building one another up, encouraging each other, spending time in community by breaking bread. All of these things are how we strengthen the body of Christ. Second, they should remember what kind of life God has rescued them from—a sinful one destined for death. On a related note, the third thing to remember is the great salvation that comes from God alone. No matter what glittery things the world promises, and how desperate you may feel, true salvation can only come from the Lord. Finally, they must remember to keep on the steady course of a Christian life, without being swayed by the temptations around them. Many things may be thrown their way in an effort to discourage them and hinder the cause, but these difficult moments are when we need to cling to God and keep the faith the most

EXPOSITION

I. BEFORE CHRIST (TITUS 3:3–8)

Paul begins this passage by describing the societal conditions without Christ. Identifying himself and all Christians with sinful and degenerate humanity, Paul emphatically asserted, "At one time we too were foolish, disobedient, deceived and enslaved by all kinds of passions and pleasures." The use of "for" in the Greek text establishes the logical connection between the statements in verses 1–2 and 3–8. Christians, though at one time degenerate and lost, were recipients of God's kindness and love, which resulted in their salvation. Christians are to demonstrate this same kindness and love to lost individuals and society, making Christianity attractive and resulting in the salvation of others (cf. Titus 2:10).

The verb "were," placed at the beginning of this sentence, emphatically contrasts the Christian's former degenerate condition, which is described in verse 3, with the present regenerate condition ("but when"), which is described in verses 4–7. Paul set forth the unregenerate human condition with eight descriptive characteristics. He stated that we too were foolish and senseless. Our minds did not grasp self-evident truths about God. We were "disobedient" to God and His will for our lives. We were "deceived," misled, perhaps by Satan. We were "enslaved by all kinds of passions and pleasures." In Romans 6:6–23,

Paul expressly characterized sin in terms of bondage. "Malice" refers to wickedness, perhaps characterized by "ill-will" to others. "Envy" denotes a continual dissatisfaction with one's own position, possessions, or power as compared to that of another. And finally, Paul concluded that we were "being hated" and "hating one another." These terms, both passive and active, represent the logical results of self-centered, sinful humanity. There is nothing contained in this description of the depraved human condition that could be characterized as un-Pauline (Romans 1:18–32).

On the contrary, in comparison to other biblical portrayals of the human condition, it is a rather mild expression. Speaking of man's sinful condition, Jeremiah 17:9 succinctly sums up the matter: "The heart is deceitful above all things and desperately corrupt; who can understand it?" Why is Titus reminding readers about where they came from? It demonstrates that their past is not so far behind them, and by reminding themselves of that, they can be motivated to stay close to the Lord. If you've been a Christian for a long time, it can be easy to fall into this trap of pride and arrogance as well; you're a good person who does good deeds, not like unbelievers who wallow in their sin. But the truth is, apart from Jesus, you would be just as depraved as a non-believer—and that has everything to do with God's goodness and mercy and nothing to do with your good works. Therefore, we can look back on our past and give thanks to God that He loved us too much to leave us in that state.

The term for kindness, *chrēstotēs*, is unique to Paul in the New Testament. This term's "divine orientation" is noted in its usual application to God, its designation as a fruit of the Spirit (Galatians 5:22), and the fact that Paul expressly stated that man does not naturally possess this attribute. God's "kindness" includes His generosity and goodness, especially toward humanity and for humanity's benefit (Romans 2:4). The term rendered "love" is *philanthrōpia*, from which the English word "philanthropy" is derived. It specifically denotes God's "love for mankind." The combination of such infinite "kindness" and "love for mankind" facilitates our understanding of "the grace of God … that brings salvation to all men" (Titus 2:11). The purpose of the manifestation of God's kindness and love was to bring salvation; therefore, God is referred to as "our Savior." The fact that people cannot earn salvation strikes at the very heart of human pride and thus denies people the opportunity of exalting themselves. It is a reflection of this pride that popular conceptions of attaining salvation revolve around keeping the Law, doing more good deeds, or living up to a moral standard.

Theologically, the purpose of the Old Testament law is not to show how humans could save themselves. Rather, the purpose of the Law is to show humans that they *cannot* save themselves and that their only hope for salvation is in the gracious promise of God (Galatians 3:10–27). Humanity's sinful acts are the result of a sinful nature. Salvation cannot be attained by suppressing sinful acts, by doing more righteous acts than sinful acts, or by living a better life in comparison to others. Salvation can only be attained by effectively dealing with humanity's sinful nature. This requires a new birth (John 3:3–8), a transference from being in Adam to being in Christ (Romans 5:12–19), and a new creation (2 Corinthians 5:17). These metaphors for salvation indicate the radical change in heart that can be accomplished by God alone. This strong, clear, and precise statement in Titus 3:5 concerning the basis of salvation reflects a determined effort by Paul to eliminate any confusion in the minds of the Cretan Christians regarding the role of good works in the Christian life. Thus far in this letter, Paul had emphasized the necessity for good works among Christians and toward the pagan world as a demonstration of the true Gospel. Good works are the result, not the cause, of the saving, transforming power of God's grace in one's life. Theologically, they have no saving, transforming power.

Concerning the Holy Spirit, Paul continued, "Whom he poured out on us generously through Jesus Christ our Savior." It is noteworthy that each Person of the Trinity is referred to in this passage and particularly in this text: God poured out the Holy Spirit through Jesus Christ. The verb "poured out" echoes the description of the coming of the Holy Spirit at Pentecost. The additional words "on us" (*eph hemas*) indicate that the pouring out of the Holy Spirit is not limited to the historic event at Pentecost but is shared by all believers. The descriptive term "generously" suggests that God's pouring out of the Holy Spirit is totally sufficient for the needs of every believer. This contrasts with the limited personal role of the Holy Spirit demonstrated in the Old Testament (2 Corinthians 3:2–6). This generous outpouring of the Holy Spirit

is the direct result of the work of "Jesus Christ, our Savior."

Paul restated the basis of our salvation with a clause introduced by "so that". The phrase "having been justified by his grace" recalls the main verb of the entire sentence, "he saved us" (v. 5). The use of the term "justified" expresses a favorite Pauline expression for salvation (Romans 3:24; 5:1, 9; 1 Corinthians 6:11; Galatians 2:16–17; 3:24). The expression "by his grace" refers to "God's grace," which is the basis of Christian salvation (cf. Titus 2:11; 3:4). The force of the term rendered "so that" is applied to the final phrase, which truly expresses the goal, purpose, or result of our salvation: so "that … we might become heirs having the hope of eternal life." New Testament salvation is often expressed in the familial terms of "children" (Romans 8:16). The logical extension from "son" to "heir" can be seen throughout the New Testament. The soteriological and eschatological aspects of Christians' being "heirs" is readily apparent in this final phrase. Paul asserted that "he saved us" (v. 5) "so that…we might become heirs" (v. 7).

II. PAUL'S WARNING (TITUS 3:9–11)

Paul now warns Titus about false teachers (v. 9). Paul's warning is to avoid foolish controversies, genealogies, arguments, and quarrels about the Law because they are unprofitable and useless. Paul tells Titus not to argue with false teachers because there is nothing to gain except divisiveness, confusion, and frustration. Also, engaging false teachers would not be a good steward of time and energy and it may give validation to the false teacher. Paul concluded, "You may be sure that such a man is warped and sinful; he is self-condemned." Because the factious man refused to change, Titus could "be sure" of three things concerning this person: he was sinful, continues to sin, and, because he willfully continued his sin, he is self-condemned. Paul's use of the rare term "self-condemned" suggests that, having refused correction, the factious person actually participates in his condemnation since he is without excuse.

The significance of refuting false teaching in this letter is indicated by Paul's direct attack on factious men at the beginning of the letter (Titus 1:10) and now at its conclusion (vv. 9–11). The false teachers, with their erroneous teaching, motivate their followers to works that deny true knowledge of God (Titus 1:16) and destroy the doctrinal unity of the Church. When the Church cannot agree on the essentials of Christianity and is characterized by conflict and divisions, it is displeasing to God and ineffective to a lost world.

THE LESSON APPLIED

Paul wanted to encourage the people by reminding them where they had been and where they were now. They had been sinners trapped in death, but glory to God, they were now rescued and set free! Accordingly, they should be giving thanks to God and living a life that pleases Him. Since they were no longer sinners, they should be avoiding the lifestyle of the sinner and instead focus on God, His salvation, and preaching this Good News to others.

LET'S TALK ABOUT IT

How often do you preach the Gospel to yourself? To others?

If you've been in the faith for an extended period of time, it's easy to forget how good you have it now. It's easy to take salvation for granted. However, it is still a precious gift that was bought at an incredible price, one that no "good" person would ever be able to pay. As Paul says, we must remind ourselves of where we've been so we can appreciate the goodness of God and what He did for us.

*PARTIAL BIBLIOGRAPHY

First Quarter Lessons

Andrews, Evan. 2018. "6 Child Monarchs Who Changed History." HISTORY. August 22, 2018. https://www.history.com/news/6-child-monarchs-who-changed-history.

Arichea, D. C., and E. A. Nida. 1976. A Handbook on Paul's Letter to the Galatians. United Bible Societies.

Berquist, J. L. 2000. "Marriage." In Eerdmans Dictionary of the Bible, edited by A. C. Myers and A. B. Beck. W. B. Eerdmans.

Blum, E. A. 1985a. "Galatians." In The Bible Knowledge Commentary: An Exposition of the Scriptures, edited by J. F. Walvoord and R. B. Zuck. Vol. 2. Wheaton, IL: Victor Books.

———. 1985b. "John." In The Bible Knowledge Commentary: An Exposition of the Scriptures, edited by J. F. Walvoord and R. B. Zuck. Vol. 2. Wheaton, IL: Victor Books.

Bosman, H. L. 2000. "Adultery." In Eerdmans Dictionary of the Bible, edited by A. C. Myers and A. B. Beck. W. B. Eerdmans.

Coble, A. 2000. "Sabbath." In Eerdmans Dictionary of the Bible, edited by A. C. Myers and A. B. Beck. W. B. Eerdmans.

Davids, P. H. 1988. "Fullness of Time." In Baker Encyclopedia of the Bible. Vol. 1. Baker Book House.

Deere, J. S. 1985. "Deuteronomy." In The Bible Knowledge Commentary: An Exposition of the Scriptures, edited by J. F. Walvoord and R. B. Zuck. Vol. 1. Wheaton, IL: Victor Books.

Dictionary of Paul and His Letters. 1993. Downers Grove, IL: InterVarsity Press.

Ellingworth, P., H. Hatton, and P. Ellingworth. 1995. A Handbook on Paul's First Letter to the Corinthians. United Bible Societies.

Geisler, N. L. 1985. "Colossians." In The Bible Knowledge Commentary: An Exposition of the Scriptures, edited by J. F. Walvoord and R. B. Zuck. Vol. 2. Wheaton, IL: Victor Books.

Hoehner, H. W. 1985. "Ephesians." In The Bible Knowledge Commentary: An Exposition of the Scriptures, edited by J. F. Walvoord and R. B. Zuck. Vol. 2. Wheaton, IL: Victor Books.

Hughes, R. K. 1989. Colossians and Philemon: The Supremacy of Christ. Crossway Books.

———. 1991. Romans: Righteousness from Heaven. Crossway Books.

———. 1996. Acts: The Church Afire. Crossway Books.

Jusu, John et. al. 2016. Africa Study Bible. Carol Stream, Ill: Tyndale, Oasis International.

Lowery, D. K. 1985. "1 Corinthians." In The Bible Knowledge Commentary: An Exposition of the Scriptures, edited by J. F. Walvoord and R. B. Zuck. Vol. 2. Wheaton, IL: Victor Books.

Lumby, J. R. 1891. The Acts of the Apostles with Maps, Notes and Introduction. Cambridge University Press.

Martin, J. A. 1985. "Luke." In The Bible Knowledge Commentary: An Exposition of the Scriptures, edited by J. F. Walvoord and R. B. Zuck. Vol. 2. Wheaton, IL: Victor Books.

Mirecki, P. 2000. "Gnosticism, Gnosis." In Eerdmans Dictionary of the Bible, edited by A. C. Myers, A. B. Beck, and D. N. Freedman. W.B. Eerdmans.

Moser, P. K. 2000. "Apostle." In Eerdmans Dictionary of the Bible, edited by A. C. Myers, A. B. Beck, and D. N. Freedman. W. B. Eerdmans.

Newman, B. M., and E. A. Nida. 1972. A Handbook on the Acts of the Apostles. United Bible Societies.

———. 1973. A Handbook on Paul's Letter to the Romans. United Bible Societies.

———. 1993. A Handbook on the Gospel of John. United Bible Societies.

Ryken, Leland, James C. Wilhoit, and Tremper Longman III. 1998. Dictionary of Biblical Imagery. Downers Grove, IL: InterVarsity Press.

Ryrie, C. 1995. New American Standard Study Bible. Chicago: Moody Press.

Schreiner, Thomas R. 1998. Romans. Grand Rapids: Baker Academic.

Team, Doctors Health Press Editorial. 2017. "What Is Dropsy? | Edema | Symptoms, Causes & Home Remedies." Doctors Health Press - Daily Free Health Articles and Natural Health Advice (blog). July 23, 2017. https://www.doctorshealthpress.com/what-is-dropsy-edema-symptoms-causes-home-remedies/.

Thompson, F. C. 1997. Thompson Chain Reference Bible: Topical Index. Kirkbride Bible Company.

Toussaint, S. D. 1985. "Acts." In The Bible Knowledge Commentary: An Exposition of the Scriptures, edited by J. F. Walvoord and R. B. Zuck. Vol. 2. Wheaton, IL: Victor Books.

Witmer, J. A. 1985. "Romans." In The Bible Knowledge Commentary: An Exposition of the Scriptures, edited by J. F. Walvoord and R. B. Zuck. Vol. 2. Wheaton, IL: Victor Books.

Zodhiates, S. 2000. "New Testament." In The Complete Word Study Dictionary (Electronic Ed.). AMG Publishers.

*PARTIAL BIBLIOGRAPHY

Second Quarter Lessons

"Asa of Judah." 2023. In Wikipedia. https://en.wikipedia.org/w/index.php?title=Asa_of_Judah&oldid=1133469209.

"Baal God Origin & Biblical Significance | Who Is Baal?" n.d. Study.Com. Accessed April 30, 2023. https://study.com/academy/lesson/baal-god-origin-biblical-significance.html.

Baker, Warren. 2013. Hebrew-Greek Key Word Study Bible: ESV. Chattanooga: AMG Publishers.

Berlin, Adele, and Marc Zvi Brettler, eds. 2014. The Jewish Study Bible. Second edition. Oxford: Oxford University Press.

"Definition of FEAR." 2023. April 28, 2023. https://www.merriam-webster.com/dictionary/fear.

Easton, M. G. 1893. In Illustrated Bible Dictionary and Treasury of Biblical History, Biography, Geography, Doctrine, and Literature. Harper & Brothers.

Elwell, W. A., and B. J. Beitzel. 1988. "Maon (Place)." In Baker Encyclopedia of the Bible. Vol. 2. Baker Book House.

Green, J. B. 1997. The Gospel of Luke. W. B. Eerdmans.

Henry, Matthew. 1997. Matthew Henry's Concise Commentary on the Whole Bible: Nelson's Concise Series. Nashville: Thomas Nelson.

Jackson, G. S. 2000. "Ruth, Book Of." In Eerdmans Dictionary of the Bible, edited by A. C. Myers and A. B. Beck. W. B. Eerdmans.

McKeown, J. 2015. Ruth. Edited by J. G. McConville and C. Bartholomew. W. B. Eerdmans.

NIV Life Application Study Bible. 2020. 3rd edition. Grand Rapids: Zondervan.

Pelikan, Jaroslav Jan. 1996. Mary Through the Centuries: Her Place in the History of Culture. New Haven: Yale University Press.

Pfeiffer, Charles F., and Everett Falconer Harrison. 1990. The Wycliffe Bible Commentary. Chicago: Moody Press.

Ryrie, C. 1995. New American Standard Study Bible. Chicago: Moody Press.

Stanley, Charles F., ed. 1995. NASB, Charles F. Stanley Life Principles Bible. Nashville: Thomas Nelson Bibles.

Strong, J. 1995. Enhanced Strong's Lexicon. Woodside Bible Fellowship.

The Pulpit Commentary on the Whole Bible. 1978. Vol. 21. Grand Rapids: Thomas Nelson.

Tsumura, D. 2007. The First Book of Samuel. W. B. Eerdmans.

Van Reken, D. E. 1988. "Barrenness." In Baker Encyclopedia of the Bible. Vol. 1. Baker Book House.

Zodhiates, S. 2000. "New Testament." In The Complete Word Study Dictionary (Electronic Ed.). AMG Publishers.

Third and Fourth Quarter Lessons

Barclay, William. 1976. The Daily Study Bible: The Letters of James and Peter (Revised Edition). Philadelphia: Westminster Press.

Barrett, C.K. 1968. "The First Epistles to the Corinthians." In Harper's New Testament Commentaries. San Francisco: Harper & Row.

Berlin, Adele, and Marc Zvi Brettler, eds. 2014. The Jewish Study Bible. Second edition. Oxford: Oxford University Press.

Cedar, Paul A. 1984. The Communicator's Commentary: James, 1, 2 Peter, Jude. The Communicator's Commentary Series 11. Waco, Tex: Word Books.

Demarest, G. W. 1982. "1,2 Thessalonians, 1,2 Timothy, Titus." In Communicator's Commentary. Waco: Word Books Publishers.

Grosheide, F. W. 1980. "Commentary on the First Epistle to the Corinthians." In The English Text with Introduction, Exposition and Notes. Grand Rapids: W. B. Eerdmans.

Guest, John. 1982. "Jeremiah–Lamentation." In The Communicator's Commentary. Waco: Word Books Publishers.

Hughes, P. 1980. "Paul's Second Epistle to the Corinthians." In The English Text with Introduction, Exposition and Notes. Grand Rapids: W. B. Eerdmans.

Jackson, G. S. 2000. "Ruth, Book Of." In Eerdmans Dictionary of the Bible, edited by A. C. Myers and A. B. Beck. W. B. Eerdmans.

Lennox, S. J. 1999. Psalm: A Commentary in the Wesleyan Tradition. Indianapolis: Wesleyan Publishing House.

McKeown, J. 2015. Ruth. Edited by J. G. McConville and C. Bartholomew. W. B. Eerdmans.

Mounce, Robert. 1995. "Romans." In The New American Commentary. Vol. 27. Nashville: Broadman & Holman.

Robertson, A. T. 1931a. "The Epistles of Paul." In Word Pictures in the New Testament. Vol. 4. Nashville: Broadman Press.

———. 1931b. "The General Epistles and the Revelation of John." In Word Pictures in the New Testament. Vol. 6. Nashville: Broadman Press.

Ryrie, C. 1995. New American Standard Study Bible. Chicago: Moody Press.

Saunders, S. n.d. "Philippians and Galatians." In Interpretation Bible Studies. Louisville: John Knox Press.

* See Full Bibliography online at rhboyd.com.

Printed in the USA
CPSIA information can be obtained
at www.ICGtesting.com
JSHW061541080823
46072JS00014B/25

9 798886 350739